THE COMPLETE BOOK OF
CROCHET

THE COMPLETE BOOK OF
CROCHET

Revised Edition

ELIZABETH L. MATHIESON

THOMAS Y. CROWELL COMPANY
Established 1834/NEW YORK

Special acknowledgment is made to C. J. Bates & Son, Chester, Connecticut and S. Semler & Son, Inc., New York, N.Y. for supplying information used in preparing the revised edition of *The Complete Book of Crochet*.

Manufactured in the United States of America

Library of Congress Cataloging in Publication Data

Mathieson, Elizabeth Laird, 1898–
  The complete book of crochet.

  Includes index.
  1. Crocheting.   I. Title.
TT820.M36   1977   746.4'34   76-28737
ISBN 0-690-01156-3

10 9 8 7 6 5 4

ACKNOWLEDGMENTS

In preparing *The Complete Book of Crochet* I wish to acknowledge my indebtedness to the wholehearted cooperation and vast experience of my two colleagues—Mrs. Marie M. Muth and Mrs. George Frasher.

Sincerest thanks are also due to the following people for their invaluable help in compiling this volume: Mrs. Anne Darragh, Miss Margaret Hanley and Miss Marilyn August.

Elizabeth L. Mathieson

Contents

HISTORY OF
CROCHET

TODAY, when crochet is enjoying such unprecedented vogue, it is doubly interesting to delve into its past and discover that what once helped save a nation from starvation became the accomplishment of queens. By curious irony, though its history dates back to the sixteenth century, crochet only came into its own with the birth of the machine age and has been growing in popularity ever since.

The word itself is derived from the French *croche*, meaning hook. Originally the crochet hook was one of a number of tools used in the intricate process of lace making. As time went on, a repertoire of stitches and designs evolved, and crocheting graduated into a separate and pleasurable art. In the beginning it was almost entirely a convent art, classified with other types of handiwork under the general heading of nuns' work. It took a famine—the great Irish Famine of 1846—to give crochet its greatest impetus. At that time nuns taught it to their pupils and the proceeds derived from the sales of crocheted articles helped alleviate existing miseries. It was then that it became, along with playing the harpsichord, one of the graceful accomplishments of the well-born young lady.

Fascinating and versatile, crochet has become one of our best-loved handcrafts. With hook and thread, agile fingers are capable of producing an endless variety of beautiful modern and traditional designs, each with its own special charm. Probably one of the loveliest is that known as Irish Crochet, famous as far back as 1743 when the Royal Dublin Society awarded prizes for outstanding examples of the art. During the famine it became more generally popular when rare patterns of old lace were so skillfully copied by the Irish girls.

Crochet owes its widespread appeal to the fact that it is easy to do and lends itself to so many delightful interpretations. The simplicity and adaptability of the basic stitches tempt the novice to try her hand and challenge the expert to outdo herself. This art offers a wide latitude of choice: Laces, delicate as cobwebs for tablecloths and doilies, others more suitable for curtains and bedspreads . . . rugs and afghans in glowing colors in which texture and design are artfully blended . . . all of which spell beauty and utility for every home. Crochet knows the fashionable graces too, how a crocheted hat and bag can "dress up" a costume, how a lacy cocktail sweater can "make" an evening. Fashion and crochet have united to design some of the most sought-after accessories, as well as every sort of warm and beguiling beauty for the carriage trade.

The machine has brought us many comforts and luxuries, but when it comes to the touch of beauty which is every woman's birthright, nothing, it appears, will ever supplant the charm and inimitable loveliness of the "handmade." This is especially true of crochet. There is a joy in wearing it, a subtle magic that goes into it, that the machine cannot copy or equal. That is the secret of the charm of crochet—whether it is done for profit, or as a hobby, a means of brightening a wardrobe or beautifying a home. It is an art that grows on you.

Threads and Hooks

CROCHET THREADS AND YARNS . . . It is important to remember that texture plays an interesting part in the beauty of crochet and this, in turn, depends largely on the materials used. Rug Yarn is used with best results for rugs, hot plate mats, pot holders and bags. Speed- or Knit-Cro-Sheen or Bedspread Cotton is suitable for bedspreads, luncheon sets, chair sets, hats, bags and various other fashion articles. The finer mercerized threads are more effective for the delicate designs used for tablecloths, doilies, edgings and accessories, while yarn is best for afghans, blankets, baby garments, sweaters, ponchos, and other fashion items. Fortunately, the popular prices of these materials, as well as the simplicity of crochet, make this an art accessible to all.

CROCHET HOOKS . . . Crochet hooks are made of aluminum, plastic, wood, or steel, aluminum and plastic being the most popular. Aluminum crochet hooks are available in sizes B-1 (the smallest), C-2, D-3, E-4, F-5, G-6, 7, H-8, I-9, J-10, K-10½ and N-11 (the largest). Plastic crochet hooks correspond to the aluminum sizes but start at D-3 and run up to K-10½. Extra large plastic hooks are available in sizes P, Q and S. Wooden crochet hooks are available in sizes 13 and 15. Just to confuse the issue, steel crochet hooks are numbered in the reverse order of the other hooks—00 (2/0) is the largest, 0 (1/0) follows, then decreasing in size from 1 to 14. The afghan hook, a combination of crochet hook and knitting needle, is used when making the afghan stitch. It is available in three lengths: a 9-inch aluminum hook, sizes F, G, H, I and J; a 14-inch aluminum or plastic hook, sizes F, G, H, I, J and K; and a 20-inch flexible aluminum hook in sizes F, G, H, I, J and K (used for afghans worked in one piece).

Each hook is especially adapted for use with a certain size of thread or yarn. To insure the correct results, it is important that you use the number hook specified in the directions. Equally important is the given gauge, especially for wearing apparel. (See discussion of gauge, page 18.) Hooks are now also available in new millimeter sizes. The following chart shows how to convert from millimeter to standard letter sizes.

MM Size	2.00	2.50	3.00	3.50	4.00	4.50	5.00	5.50	6.00	6.50	7.00	8.00/9.00	10.00
Letter Size		B	C	D	E	F	G	H	I		J	K	N	P

CROCHET ABBREVIATIONS

Ch .... Chain	D tr .... Double Treble	St .... Stitch
Sl st .... Slip Stitch	Tr tr .... Triple Treble	Sts .... Stitches
Sc .... Single Crochet	Pc st .... Popcorn Stitch	Rnd .... Round
H dc .. Half Double Crochet	Bl .... Block	Incl .... Inclusive
Dc .... Double Crochet	Sp .... Space	Inc .... Increase
Tr .... Treble	P .... Picot	Dec .... Decrease

* (asterisk) Sometimes in the directions these phrases appear:
1. Repeat from * across.
2. Repeat from * around.
3. Repeat from * 3 (or any number) more times. In Nos. 1 and 2, follow the directions from the first to the last * (asterisk) completely across row or around. In No. 3, follow the directions from the first * (asterisk) as many times as specified.

"Work even" means to work without increasing or decreasing, maintaining the pattern as established.

4

CHAPTER ONE

"Learn How" Steps for Basic Stitches

P<small>RACTICE PIECES</small> . . . Directions are given for a small practice piece or swatch for each stitch that you learn. When you have learned these stitches, attractive articles can be made by following the directions given at the end of the "Learn How" steps.

HOW TO BEGIN — MAKE A LOOP

1. Grasp thread near end between thumb and forefinger of left hand.

2. With right hand make a loop by lapping long thread over short thread.

3. Hold loop in place between thumb and forefinger of left hand (Fig. 1).

4. Take hold of broad bar of hook as you would a pencil.

5. Insert your hook through loop, with right hand catch long end of thread, draw it through (Fig. 2).

6. Do not remove hook from thread.

7. Pull short end and ball thread in opposite directions to bring loop close around the end of the hook, but not too tight (Fig. 3).

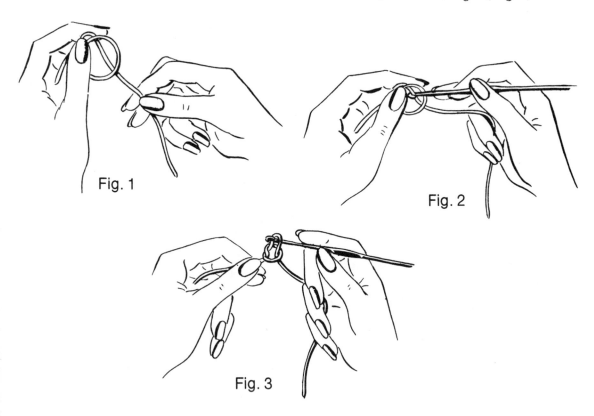

Fig. 1

Fig. 2

Fig. 3

WHAT TO DO WITH THE LEFT HAND

1. Measure with your eye about 4 inches down ball thread from loop on hook.

2. At about this point insert thread between your ring and little fingers, having palm of hand facing up (Fig. 4).

3. Bring thread toward back, under little and ring fingers, over the middle finger, and under the forefinger toward the thumb (Fig. 5).

4. Grasp hook and loop between thumb and forefinger of left hand.

5. Gently pull ball thread so that it lies around the fingers firmly but not tightly (Fig. 6).

6. Catch knot of loop between thumb and forefinger.

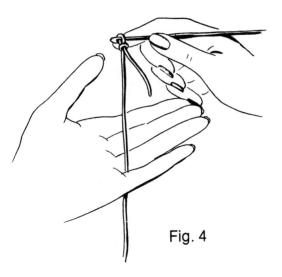

Fig. 4

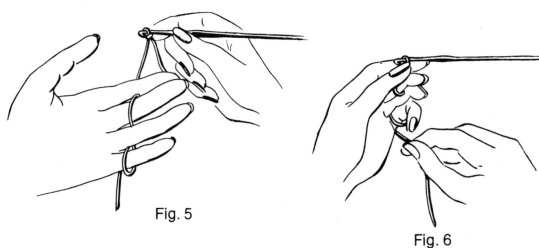

Fig. 5

Fig. 6

WHAT TO DO WITH THE RIGHT HAND

1. Take hold of broad bar of hook as you would a pencil.

2. Bring middle finger forward to rest near tip of hook (Fig. 7).

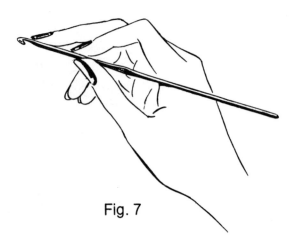

Fig. 7

CHAIN STITCH
Abbreviation — ch

1. Adjust fingers of left hand as in Fig. 8. The middle finger of left hand is bent in such a way as to regulate the tension, while the ring and little fingers prevent the thread from moving too freely. As you practice, you will become more familiar with the correct position. Keep in mind that the motion of the hook in the right hand and the thread in the left hand should be easy and smooth. One of the most common faults of beginners is either to crochet too tightly or too loosely. Ease will come with practice.

2. Pass your hook under thread and catch thread with hook. This is called "thread over" (Fig. 9).

3. Draw thread through loop on hook. This makes one chain (ch).

4. Repeat steps 2 and 3 until you have as many chain stitches (ch sts) as you need— 1 loop always remains on the hook (Fig. 10).

5. Always keep thumb and forefinger of your left hand near stitch on which you are working.

6. Practice making chain stitches until they are even in size.

Note: In all crochet it is customary to pick up the 2 top loops (or threads) of each stitch as you work, unless otherwise specified. When only the back loop (or thread) is picked up, a different effect is produced.

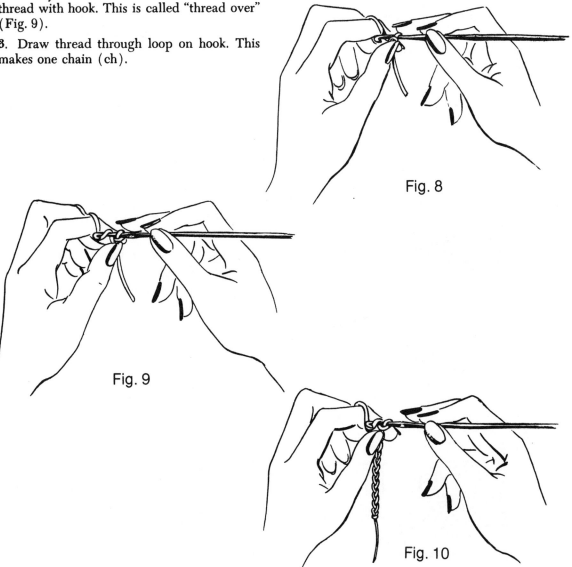

Fig. 8

Fig. 9

Fig. 10

ROWS OF SINGLE CROCHET
Abbreviation — sc

Make a starting chain of 20 stitches for practice piece.

FIRST ROW

1. Insert hook from the front under the 2 top threads of second chain from hook (Fig. 11).

2. Catch thread with hook—this is known as "thread over" (Fig. 12)—and draw through chain. There are 2 loops on hook (Fig. 13).

3. Thread over (Fig. 14) and draw through 2 loops—1 loop remains on hook. You have now completed 1 single crochet (sc) (Fig. 15).

4. For next single crochet (sc), insert hook under 2 top threads of next ch and repeat steps 2 and 3.

5. Repeat step 4 until you have made a single crochet (sc) in each ch.

6. At end of row of single crochets, ch 1 (Fig. 16). The ch-1 enables you to turn your work more easily.

7. Turn your work so that the reverse side is facing you (Fig. 17).

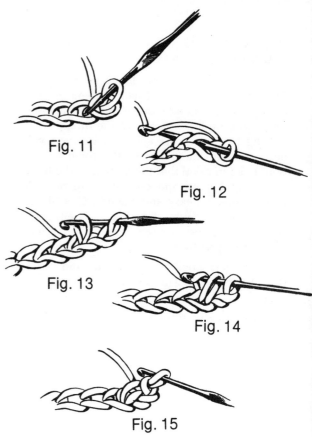

Fig. 11

Fig. 12

Fig. 13

Fig. 14

Fig. 15

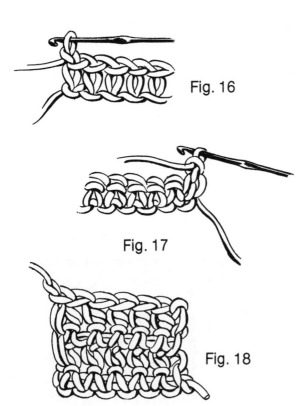

Fig. 16

Fig. 17

Fig. 18

SECOND ROW

1. Insert hook from the front under the 2 top loops of first stitch (st)—the last stitch made on previous row.

2. Catch thread with hook ("thread over") and draw through st —2 loops remain on hook.

3. Thread over and draw through 2 loops —1 loop remains on hook.

4. For next single crochet (sc), insert hook from the front under the 2 top loops of next st and repeat steps 2 and 3.

5. Repeat steps 4, 2 and 3 until you have made a single crochet (sc) in each st. Ch 1 and turn.

Repeat Second Row until you are familiar with this st. Break off (Fig. 18).

HOW TO "BREAK OFF"

1. Do not make a turning chain at end of last row.

2. Clip thread about 3 inches from work, bring loose end through the one remaining loop on hook, and pull tightly (Fig. 18).

HOW TO TURN YOUR WORK

In crochet, a certain number of chain stitches is added at the end of each row to bring work in position for the next row. The number of turning chains required depends on the stitch with which you intend to begin the next row. Listed below are the **turning chains** for each of the basic stitches shown in this book.

Single Crochet (sc) . . . . Ch 1 to turn.
Half Double Crochet (half dc) Ch 2 to turn.
Double Crochet (dc) . . . . Ch 3 to turn.
Treble (tr) . . . . Ch 4 to turn.
Double Treble (d tr) . . . . Ch 5 to turn.
Triple Treble (tr tr) . . . . Ch 6 to turn.

SLIP STITCH
Abbreviation — sl st

It is not necessary to make a practice piece for slip stitch (sl st), because it is only used when an invisible stitch is required. When the directions say **join,** you always use a slip stitch.

1. Insert hook from the front through the 2 top threads of chain (Fig. 19).

2. Thread over and with one motion draw through chain and loop on hook —1 loop remains on hook (Fig. 20). This completes a slip stitch (sl st).

HOW TO FOLLOW THE ASTERISK (*)

Sometimes in the directions these phrases appear:

1. Repeat from * across.

2. Repeat from * around.

3. Repeat from * 3 (or any number) more times. In Nos. 1 and 2, follow the directions from the first to the last * (asterisk) completely across row or around. In No. 3, follow the directions from the first * (asterisk) as many times as specified.

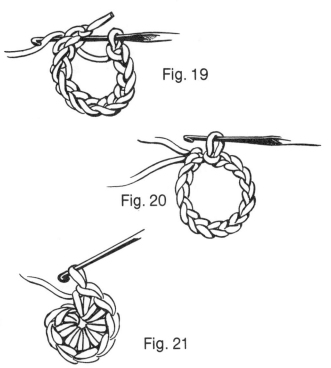

Fig. 19

Fig. 20

Fig. 21

ROUNDS OF SINGLE CROCHET— INCREASING TO MAKE A CIRCLE

Make a chain of 4 stitches (sts). Join with slip stitch (sl st) in 1st ch to form a ring (Figs. 19 and 20).

First Round (1st rnd): Make 8 single crochet (sc) in ring (Fig. 21).

Place a safety pin in the last sc of 1st rnd to mark end of rnd. Move the safety pin to the last sc of the following rnds.

Second Round (2nd rnd): 2 single crochet (sc) in each sc of previous round (rnd). There are 16 sc on rnd.

Third Round (3rd rnd): * 2 single crochet (sc) in next sc—an increase (inc) made in last sc (Fig. 22), sc in next sc. Repeat from * around (24 sc on rnd).

Fourth Round (4th rnd): * Single crochet (sc) in next 2 sc, 2 sc in next sc (inc made in last sc). Repeat from * around (32 sc on rnd).

Fifth Round (5th rnd): * Single crochet (sc) in next 3 sc, 2 sc in next sc. Repeat from * around (40 sc on rnd).

Sixth Round (6th rnd): Single crochet (sc) in each sc around. Slip stitch (sl st) in next 2 sc (Figs. 19 and 20). Break off (Fig. 18).

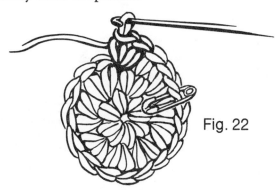

Fig. 22

9

INCREASING TO MAKE A SQUARE

Make a chain of 4 stitches (sts). Join with slip stitch (sl st) in first ch to form a ring (Figs. 19 and 20).

First Round (1st rnd): 8 single crochet (sc) in ring (Fig. 21).

Place a safety pin in the last sc of 1st rnd to mark end of rnd. Move the safety pin to the last sc of the following rnds.

Second Round (2nd rnd): * 3 single crochet (sc) in next sc (1 sc has been increased on each side of corner sc; corner sc is the center sc of the 3-sc group); sc in next sc. Repeat from * around (Fig. 23).

Third Round (3rd rnd): * Single crochet (sc) in next sc, 3 sc in next sc (corner or center st of 3-sc group—Fig. 24), sc in next 2 sc. Repeat from * around.

Fourth Round (4th rnd): * Single crochet (sc) in next 2 sc, 3 sc in next sc (corner or center st of 3-sc group), sc in next 3 sc. Repeat from * around.

Fifth Round (5th rnd): * Single crochet (sc) in next 3 sc, 3 sc in next sc (corner or center st of 3-sc group), sc in next 4 sc. Repeat from * around. Slip stitch (sl st) in next 2 sc (Figs. 19 and 20). Break off (Fig. 18).

HOW TO DECREASE SINGLE CROCHET ON ROWS OR ROUNDS

To decrease (dec) 1 single crochet (sc), work off 2 sc as 1 sc. To work off 2 sc as 1 sc—insert hook from front under the 2 top loops of next sc and pull loop through; insert hook from front under the 2 top loops of the following sc and pull loop through (3 loops on hook—Fig. 25); thread over and draw through all loops on hook (Fig. 26).

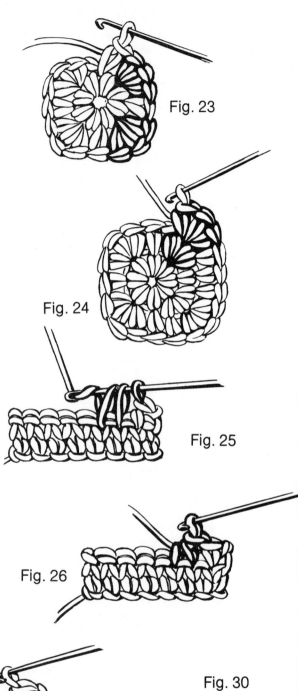

Fig. 23

Fig. 24

Fig. 25

Fig. 26

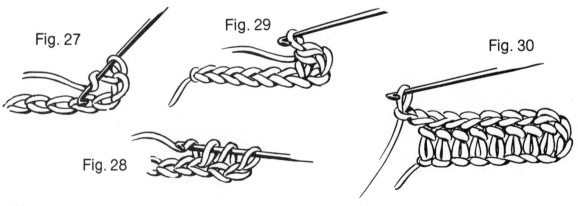

Fig. 27

Fig. 29

Fig. 30

Fig. 28

SINGLE CROCHET BELT

Materials: PEARL COTTON, *Size 5, 2 balls each of Yellow, Green, and Red . . . Steel Crochet Hook No. 1.*

Use 2 threads throughout
(1 thread from each of 2 balls).

Starting at short end with Yellow, ch 13. **1st row:** Sc in 2nd ch from hook, sc in each ch across (12 sc on row). Ch 1, turn. **2nd row:** Sc in each sc across (12 sc on row). Ch 1, turn. Repeat 2nd row until piece measures 2 inches longer than desired waist measurement. Break off (Fig. 18).

Circle Trim: With Red make 4 Circles same as Circle on page 17.

Square Trim: With Green make 4 Squares same as Square on page 18.

Finishing: Leaving 2 inches free at one end for underlap, alternate circle and square trim (setting squares in diamond shape) on belt and sew in place. Fasten belt with snap fasteners.

ROWS OF HALF DOUBLE CROCHET
Abbreviation — half dc or h dc

Make a starting chain of 20 stitches for practice piece.

First Row (1st row): 1. Pass hook under the thread of left hand (this is called "thread over"—Fig. 27).

2. Insert hook from the front under the 2 top loops (or threads) of 3rd ch from hook (Fig. 27).

3. Thread over hook and pull loop through chain (3 loops on hook), thread over (Fig. 28), and draw through all loops on hook—1 loop remains on hook (Fig. 29). A half double crochet (half dc) is now completed.

4. For next half double crochet (half dc), thread over, insert hook from front under the 2 top threads of next ch.

5. Repeat steps 3 and 4 until you have made a half dc in each ch.

6. At end of row, ch 2 (Fig. 30) and turn.

Note: You will notice there is an extra loop directly below the 2 top loops of each half dc. **Work only in the 2 top loops.**

Second Row (2nd row): 1. Thread over hook, insert hook from front under the 2 top loops of first stitch (st)—the last st on previous row.

2. Thread over hook and pull through stitch —there are 3 loops on hook; thread over and draw through all loops on hook.

3. For next half double crochet (half dc), thread over hook, insert hook from the front under the 2 top loops of next stitch (st) and repeat step 2.

4. Repeat steps 3 and 2 until you have made a half double crochet (half dc) in each stitch (st). Ch 2 and turn.

Note: The turning ch 2 of each row does not count as a stitch on the following row.

Repeat Second Row until you are familiar with this stitch. Break off at end of last row (Fig. 18).

11

HALF DOUBLE CROCHET VANITY CASE

Materials: PEARL COTTON, *Size 5, 3 balls . . . Steel Crochet Hook No. 6.*

Starting at side edge, ch 82 to measure 10 inches. **1st row:** Half double crochet (half dc) in 3rd ch from hook, half dc in each ch across (80 half dc on row). Ch 2, turn. **2nd row:** Half double crochet (half dc) in each half dc across (80 half dc on row). Ch 2, turn. Repeat 2nd row until piece measures 6½ inches. Break off (Fig. 18).

Finishing: Line crocheted piece. Fold piece to measure 4 x 6½ inches, having a 2-inch flap. Sew up side seams.

Button loop: Ch 10. Join with slip stitch (sl st) to form ring (Figs. 19 and 20). Slip stitch (sl st) in each st of ring. Break off (Fig. 18). Sew ring to center of flap. Sew on button to correspond with button loop.

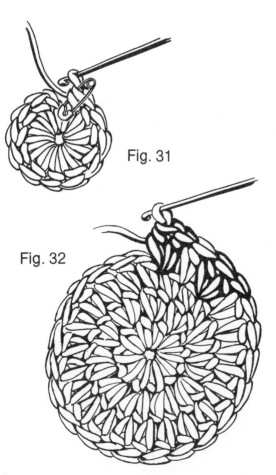

Fig. 31

Fig. 32

ROUNDS OF HALF DOUBLE CROCHET

Notice when working rounds of half dc that there is an extra loop on the wrong side directly below the 2 top loops of each half dc.

Work only in the 2 top loops of each stitch.

Make a chain of 4 stitches (sts). Join with slip stitch (sl st) in 1st ch to form a ring (Figs. 19 and 20).

INCREASING TO MAKE A CIRCLE

First Round (1st rnd): Ch 2, 11 half double crochet (half dc) in ring (Fig. 31).

Place a safety pin in the last half dc of 1st rnd to mark end of round. Move the safety pin to the last half dc of the following rounds.

Second Round (2nd rnd): 2 half double crochet (half dc) in each half dc around (22 half dc on round).

Third Round (3rd rnd): Half double crochet (half dc) in each half dc around (22 half dc on rnd).

Fourth Round (4th rnd): * Half double crochet (half dc) in next half dc, 2 half dc in next half dc. Repeat from * around (Fig. 32)—33 half dc on rnd.

Fifth Round (5th rnd): Half double crochet (half dc) in each half dc around.

Sixth Round (6th rnd): 2 half double crochet (half dc) in each half dc around (66 half dc on rnd).

Seventh Round (7th rnd): Half double crochet (half dc) in each half dc around. Sl st in next 2 half dc (Figs. 19 and 20). Break off (Fig. 18).

Note: If a larger circle is desired, **do not break off** but increase 9 half dc evenly on each round to keep work flat. Do not have increases fall over those of previous rnd.

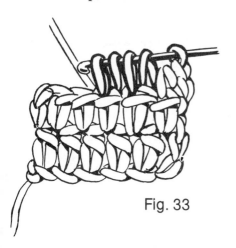

Fig. 33

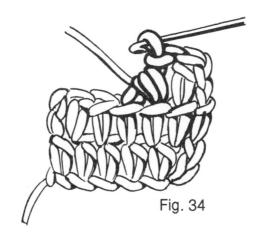

Fig. 34

HOW TO DECREASE HALF DOUBLE CROCHET ON ROWS OR ROUNDS

To decrease (dec) 1 half double crochet (half dc), work off 2 half dc as 1 half dc. To work off 2 half dc as 1 half dc, * thread over, draw a loop through next half dc. Repeat from * once more (5 loops on hook) (Fig. 33), thread over and draw through all loops on hook (Fig. 34).

A-588 . . . Materials: COATS & CLARK'S O.N.T. SPEED-CRO-SHEEN MERCERIZED COTTON, *3 balls of No. 76-A Aqua . . . Steel Crochet Hook No. 2/0 (double zero).*

GAUGE: 11 h dc make 2 inches; 7 h dc rnds make 2 inches.

CROWN . . . Starting at center top of crown, ch 21 to measure 4 inches. **1st rnd:** 2 h dc in 2nd ch from hook, h dc in each ch across to within last ch, 4 h dc in last ch; working along opposite side of starting chain, h dc in each ch across to within last ch, 2 h dc in same ch as first 2 h dc were made—44 h dc. Do not join rnds, but carry a contrasting colored thread up between last and first st of each rnd to indicate beg of rnd.

Note: Hereafter work in back loop only of each h dc unless otherwise stated.

2nd rnd: *(2 h dc in next h dc—1 h dc increased)* 4 times; h dc in next 14 h dc, inc 1 h dc in each of next 8 h dc, h dc in next 14 h dc, inc 1 h dc in each of last 4 h dc—60 h dc. **3rd rnd:** H dc in each h dc around. **4th rnd:** In-

creasing 6 h dc evenly spaced across each end, h dc in each h dc around—72 h dc. **Next 4 rnds:** Repeat 3rd and 4th rnds alternately. There are 96 h dc on last rnd. **9th rnd:** Repeat 3rd rnd. **10th rnd:** Increasing 3 h dc evenly spaced across each end, h dc in each h dc around—102 h dc. **Next 2 rnds:** Repeat 3rd and 10th rnds. There are 108 h dc on last rnd. Now work even until length from starting chain is 7 inches; then sc in next st, sl st in following st. Break off and fasten. Remove marker.

Lay work flat, having the same number of sts on each side of starting chain. Place a colored thread for marker on each side of last rnd. There should be 54 sts between each marker. Carry markers up as before.

BRIM . . . With wrong side facing, attach thread to the 27th st following any marker— *this is center back.* Work is now done in rows. **1st row:** Sc in back loop of each st across. Ch 1, turn. **2nd row:** Working through **both** loops, sc in each sc across to first marker; increasing 4 sc evenly spaced, sc in each sc across to next marker for front; sc in each remaining sc. Ch 1, turn. Being careful that increases do not fall over each other, repeat 2nd row until Brim measures 1½ inches. Work even for ½ inch. Break off and fasten. Remove markers. Sew back seam. Turn up back.

CORD . . . Cut 18 stands of thread, each 38 inches long. Tie all strands together at one end. Divide strands evenly into 3 sections and braid. Make a knot 1½ inches from each end and trim. Place around base of crown, adjusting to desired head size; overlap ends at center front of brim and tack in place. Drape crown as shown.

ROWS OF DOUBLE CROCHET

Abbreviation – dc

Make a starting chain of 20 stitches for practice piece.

FIRST ROW

1. Thread over and insert hook from the front under the 2 top threads of 4th ch from hook (Fig. 35).

2. Thread over and draw through stitch (st). There are now 3 loops on hook.

3. Thread over (Fig. 36) and draw through 2 loops—2 loops remain on hook (Fig. 37).

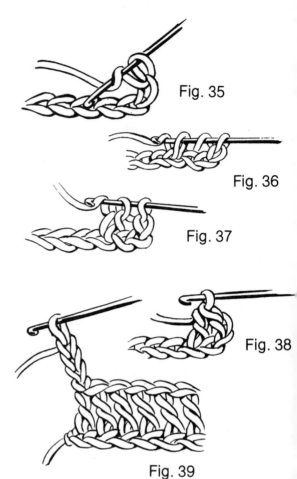

Fig. 35

Fig. 36

Fig. 37

Fig. 38

Fig. 39

4. Thread over again and draw through the 2 remaining loops—1 loop remains on hook. One double crochet (dc) is now completed (Fig. 38).

5. For next double crochet (dc), thread over, insert hook from the front under the 2 top loops of next stitch (st), and repeat steps 2, 3, and 4 until you have made a double crochet (dc) in each chain.

6. At end of row, ch 3 (Fig. 39) and turn.

The turning ch-3 counts as the first double crochet (dc) on next row. Therefore the first dc of each row is always skipped.

SECOND ROW

1. Thread over, insert the hook from the front under the 2 top loops of the 5th stitch from the hook (second stitch on previous row).

2. Repeat steps 2 to 6 of First Row. Repeat the Second Row until you are familiar with this stitch. Break off.

A-604 . . . Materials: J. & P. Coats Knit-Cro-Sheen, *1 ball of No. 42 Cream, 2 balls of No. 108 Steel Blue . . . Steel Crochet Hook No. 7.*

Cozy measures 10 inches in diameter and will hold 12 rolls.

GAUGE: 9 sts make 1 inch; 3 dc rnds and 3 sc rnds make 1¼ inches.

FIRST AND SECOND CIRCLES . . . Starting at center with Steel Blue, ch 4. **1st rnd:** Make 11 dc in 4th ch from hook. Join with sl st to top of starting chain.

Note: Hereafter work in back loop only of each st throughout.

2nd rnd: Ch 1, *2 sc in joining*—1 sc increased; make 2 sc in each dc around—24 sc. Join to first sc. **3rd rnd:** Ch 3, skip joining, *2 dc in next sc*—1 dc increased; * dc in next sc, 2 dc in next sc. Repeat from * around—36 dc, counting the ch-3 as 1 dc. Join to top of ch-3. **4th rnd:** Ch 1, increasing 12 sc evenly spaced, sc in each dc around. Join. **5th rnd:** Ch 3, skip joining, increasing 12 dc evenly spaced, dc in each sc around. Join. **Next 2 rnds:** Repeat 4th and 5th rnds, omitting the joining on last rnd. Drop Steel Blue, attach Cream. With Cream join to top of ch-3. **8th rnd:** Ch 1, sc in joining, * *dc around bar of next dc*—**raised dc made** (see figure below); skip the dc directly behind raised dc, sc in next 6 dc, 3 sc in next dc, sc in next 6 dc. Repeat from * around, ending with sc in last 5 dc. Drop Cream, pick up Steel Blue. Join. **9th rnd:** Ch 3, skip joining, * *3 dc in next raised dc*—**3-dc group made;** dc in each sc across to within next raised dc. Repeat from * around, ending with dc in each remaining sc. Drop Steel Blue, pick up Cream. Join. **10th rnd:** Ch 1, sc in joining, sc in next dc, * raised dc around bar of next dc, skip the dc directly behind raised dc; making 3 sc in the center dc between last 3-dc group used and next 3-dc group, sc in each dc across to within center dc of next 3-dc group. Repeat from * around, ending with 3 sc in center dc between last 3-dc group used and next 3-dc group; sc in each remaining sc. Drop Cream, pick up Steel Blue. Join. **11th rnd:** Ch 3, skip joining, * dc in each

sc across to within next raised dc, 3 dc in next raised dc. Repeat from * around, ending with dc in each remaining sc. Drop Steel Blue, pick up Cream. Join. **12th rnd:** Ch 1, sc in joining and in each sc to within center dc of next 3-dc group, * raised dc around bar of next dc, skip the dc directly behind raised dc; making 3 sc in center dc between last 3-dc group used and next 3-dc group, sc in each dc across to within center dc of next 3-dc group. Repeat from * around. End, change color, and join as on 10th rnd. **Next 10 rnds:** Repeat 11th and 12th rnds alternately. **Following rnd:** Repeat 11th rnd. **Last rnd:** Ch 5, skip joining and following 2 dc, * working through **both** loops, sl st in next dc, ch 5, skip next 2 dc. Repeat from * around, ending with ch 5. Join. Break off both colors and fasten.

THIRD CIRCLE . . . Work as for previous circles, reversing the colors.

Black, press. Place circle with Cream center over circle with Steel Blue center, matching sections. Leaving the 3-inch center of solid color free, sew sections together, leaving outer edges free to form 6 pockets. Place remaining circle under the two sewed circles, matching sections. Sew seams between the seams of the first 2 circles to form alternating pockets.

Fig. 40

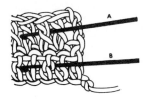

ROUNDS OF DOUBLE CROCHET

Make a chain of 6 stitches (sts). Join with slip stitch (sl st) in 1st ch to form a ring.

First Round (1st rnd): Ch 3 to count as 1 double crochet (dc)—11 dc in ring. Join in top of starting ch-3 (Fig. 41)—there are 12 dc on rnd.

Second Round (2nd rnd): Ch 3, double crochet (dc) in joining, 2 dc in each dc around. Join (24 dc on rnd).

Third Round (3rd rnd): Ch 3, * 2 double crochet (dc) in next dc, dc in next dc. Repeat from * around (Fig. 42). Join (Fig. 41)—36 dc on rnd.

Fourth Round (4th rnd): Ch 3, double crochet (dc) in joining, * dc in next 2 dc, 2 dc in next dc. Repeat from * around. Join—there are 48 dc on rnd.

Continue in this manner, increasing 12 dc evenly around —**do not have increases fall over each other**—on each round to keep work flat and joining each round to top of starting chain (Fig. 41). Break off.

HOW TO DECREASE DOUBLE CROCHET ON ROWS OR ROUNDS

*To decrease (dec) 1 double crochet (dc), work off 2 dc as 1 dc. To work off 2 dc as 1 dc, * thread over, draw a loop through next dc (3 loops on hook), thread over (Fig. 43) and draw through 2 loops (2 loops on hook—Fig. 44). Repeat from * once more (3 loops on hook—Fig. 45); thread over and draw through all loops on hook (Fig. 46). You have now worked 2 dc as 1 dc and there is 1 dc less on row.*

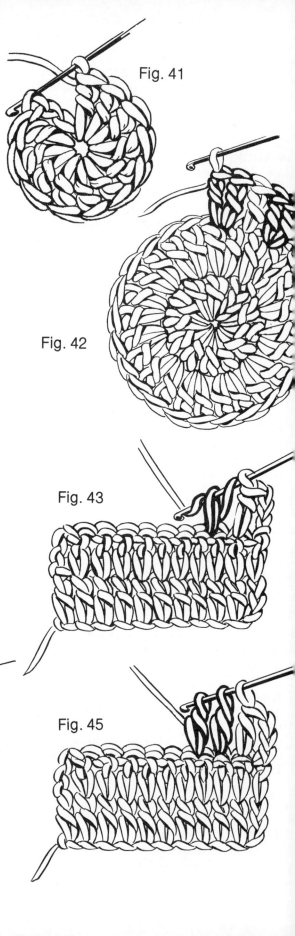

Fig. 41

Fig. 42

Fig. 43

Fig. 44

Fig. 45

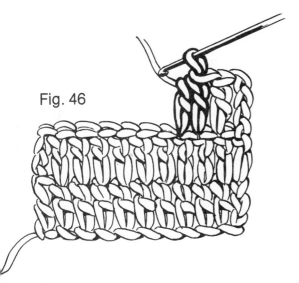

Fig. 46

Fig. 47

Fig. 48

Fig. 49

Fig. 50

Fig. 51

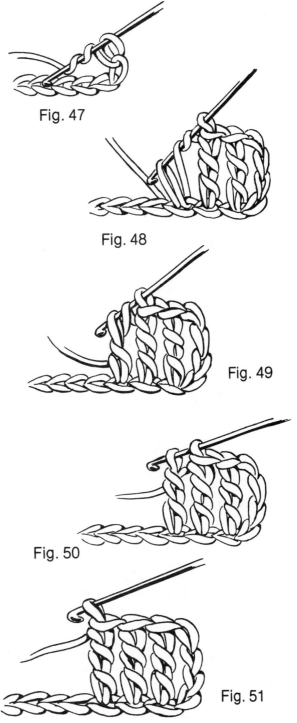

PRACTICE PIECES

Practice pieces may be worked for the following three basic stitches in order to make you familiar with them. However, the treble (tr), double treble (d tr), and the triple treble (tr tr) are rarely used by themselves. They are more often combined with other basic stitches to make attractive designs and to lend variation of height wherever it is required.

ROWS OF TREBLE CROCHET
Abbreviation — tr

Make a starting chain of 20 stitches for practice piece.

FIRST ROW

1. Thread over twice and insert hook from the front under the 2 top threads of 5th ch from hook (Fig. 47).

2. Thread over and draw through the ch. There are now 4 loops on hook (Fig. 48).

3. Thread over again and draw through 2 loops (3 loops remain on hook—Fig. 49).

4. Thread over again and draw through 2 more loops (2 loops remain on hook—Fig. 50).

5. Thread over again and draw through the 2 remaining loops (1 loop remains on hook—Fig. 51). One treble is now completed.

6. For next treble (tr), thread over twice and insert hook under the 2 top threads of next st and repeat steps 2 to 6 until you have made a treble in each chain (Fig. 51).

7. At end of row, ch 4 and turn. **The turning ch-4 counts as the first treble (tr) on next row, therefore the first tr of each row is always skipped.**

17

SECOND ROW

1. Insert hook from the front under the 2 top loops of 6th st from hook (2nd st on previous row).

2. Repeat steps 2 to 7 of First Row.

Repeat the Second Row until you are familiar with the stitch. Break off (Fig. 18).

ROWS OF DOUBLE TREBLE CROCHET

Abbreviation — d tr

Make a chain of 20 stitches.

1. Thread over hook 3 times, insert hook in 6th ch from hook and draw a loop through (5 loops on hook); thread over (Fig. 52) and draw thread through 2 loops at a time 4 times. This completes a double treble (d tr). Make a d tr in each ch across. Ch 5 to turn. **The turning ch-5 counts as the first d tr on next row, therefore the first d tr of each row is always skipped.**

2. Continue as for other practice pieces.

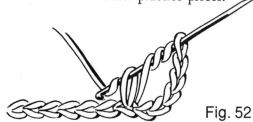

Fig. 52

ROWS OF TRIPLE TREBLE CROCHET

Abbreviation — tr tr

Make a chain of 20 stitches.

1. Thread over hook 4 times, insert hook in 7th ch from hook, and draw a loop through (6 loops on hook); thread over (Fig. 53) and draw through 2 loops at a time 5 times—this completes a triple treble (tr tr). Make a tr tr in each ch across. Ch 6 to turn. **The turning ch-6 counts as the first tr tr on next row, therefore the first tr tr of each row is always skipped.**

2. Continue as for other practice pieces.

Fig. 53

THE IMPORTANCE OF GAUGE

1. What does gauge mean?

2. It means the number of stitches per inch and the number of rows per inch.

3. Using the thread and hook specified, make a practice piece 3 inches square and follow the directions for the stitch to be used.

4. Place the swatch on a flat surface and do not stretch it.

5. With a ruler measure horizontally the number of stitches there are to 1 inch (Fig. 54).

6. If the **gauge** calls for 5 sts per inch and you have only 4 sts, use a hook one size smaller.

7. If you have 6 sts instead of 5 sts per inch, use a hook one size larger.

8. Measure the rows vertically instead of horizontally and be sure you have the correct number of rows to the inch.

9. Do not begin your garment until your **gauge** corresponds with the gauge indicated in the directions.

Fig. 54

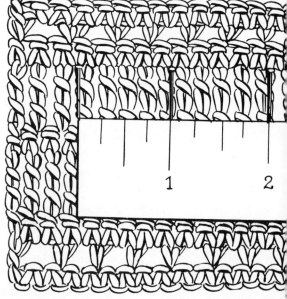

HOW TO BLOCK GARMENTS

When you have finished your garment, it must be pressed carefully in order to have a professional look.

1. Examine the measurements at the beginning of the directions.

2. Use only rust-proof blocking pins.

3. Pin Back out exactly to the measurements given, having pins one half inch apart (Fig. 55).

4. **For wool:** Steam with a steam iron or through a damp cloth, allowing steam to go through piece, **but never letting full weight of iron rest on crochet.**

For synthetics (acrylic, orlon, etc.): **Do not use iron.** Cover with a damp cloth and allow to dry.

5. Pin both Fronts **at one time** exactly to measurements given (Fig. 56) and repeat step 4.

6. Pin both Sleeves **at one time** exactly to measurements given (Fig. 57) and repeat step 4.

7. When thoroughly dry, remove pins and proceed according to the directions.

Fig. 55

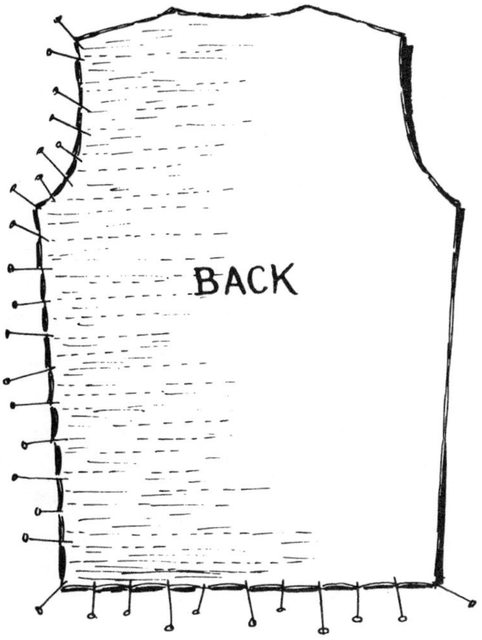

CROCHETED BEDJACKET AND BEDSOCKS

Medium Size

Materials: BABY WOOL (*1-ounce balls*), *10 balls for Bedjacket, 3 balls for Bedsocks . . . Aluminum or Plastic Crochet Hook E-4.*

BEDJACKET

GAUGE: 5 sts make 1 inch; 1 tr row and 3 sc rows make 1 inch.

BLOCKING MEASUREMENTS:

Bust—37 inches; width across back at underarm—18 inches; width across each front at underarm—10 inches; width across back between armholes—14 inches; length from shoulder to lower edge—20½ inches; length of side seam—13 inches; width of sleeve at upper arm—13 inches; length of sleeve seam—16 inches (including edging).

BACK . . . Starting at lower edge, ch 92. **1st row:** Sc in 2nd ch from hook, sc in **each** ch across (91 sc). Ch 1, turn. **2nd row:** * Sc in next sc, ch 1, skip 1 sc. Repeat from * across, ending with skip 1 sc, sc in last sc. Ch 1, turn. **3rd row:** * Sc in next sc, sc in next ch-1 sp. Repeat from * across, ending with sc in last sc (91 sc). Ch 4, turn. **4th row:** Skip 1st sc, tr in each sc across (91 tr, counting

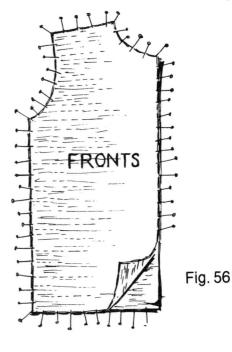

Fig. 56

turning chain as 1 tr). Ch 1, turn. **5th row:** Sc in each tr across, sc in top of turning ch-4. Ch 1, turn. The last 4 rows (2nd to 5th rows incl) constitute the pattern. Work in pattern until piece measures 13 inches in all, ending with the 4th row.

To Shape Armholes: 1st row: Sl st across the first 5 tr. Ch 1, work in pattern across to last 4 tr (4 sts decreased at each end). Ch 1, turn. **2nd row:** Work across in pattern, decreasing 1 st at both ends of row—*to dec 1 st, work off 2 sts as 1 st.* Repeat the 2nd row until 71 sts remain. Work straight (without decreasing) until piece measures 7½ inches from 1st row of armhole shaping, ending with the 2nd row. Break off.

RIGHT FRONT . . . Starting at lower edge, ch 52. Work as for Back until piece measures 13 inches in all, ending with the 4th row—row ends at side edge.

To Shape Armhole: Sl st across the first 5 tr (4 sts decreased), ch 1, work in pattern across. Now decrease 1 st at armhole edge each row until 41 sts remain on row. Work straight until piece measures 5 inches from 1st row of armhole shaping, ending at armhole edge.

To Shape Neck: Work in pattern across to last 18 sts (18 sts decreased). Turn and work over the remaining sts until piece measures 7½

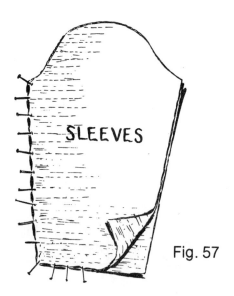

Fig. 57

inches from 1st row of armhole shaping, ending with the 2nd row. Break off.

LEFT FRONT . . . Same as Right Front, reversing all shapings.

SLEEVES . . . Starting at lower edge, ch 66. Work in pattern as for Back until piece measures 15½ inches, ending with a tr row.

To Shape Top: Dec 4 sts at both ends of the next row. Dec 1 st at both ends of each row until 45 sts remain. Work straight (without decreasing) until piece measures 4½ inches from 1st row of top shaping. Dec 2 sts at both ends of each row 4 times. Break off.

Sew up side and shoulder seams. Sew up sleeve seams and sew in sleeves.

EDGING . . . **1st rnd:** Make a rnd of sc all around edges, holding neck edge in to fit and making 3 sc in each corner. Join. **2nd rnd:** * In next sc make sc, dc, 5 tr, dc and sc, ch 1, skip 1 sc. Repeat from * around. Sl st in 1st sc. Break off. Finish sleeves in the same way.

Sew in shoulder pads. Fold top fronts back to form lapels. Cut a 45-inch length of ribbon in half and sew to bottom of each lapel.

BEDSOCKS

GAUGE: 5 sc make 1 inch; 6 rows make 1 inch.

Sizes	Small	Medium	Large
SOLE . . . Starting at center of sole, chain	24 sts	29 sts	34 sts

1st rnd: 3 sc in 2nd ch from hook, sc in each ch across, 3 sc in last ch. Working along opposite side of starting chain, make sc in each ch across. Sl st in 1st sc. Mark center sc of first 3-sc group as center front of Sole and center sc of second 3-sc group as center back. There are on rnd

	48 sc	58 sc	68 sc

2nd rnd: Ch 1, 2 sc in next 3 sc, sc in each sc to next 3-sc group, 2 sc in next 3 sc, sc in each sc to end of rnd. Join. **3rd rnd:** Ch 3, dc in joining, 2 dc in next 5 sc, sc in each sc to next 2-sc group, 2 sc in next 6 sc, sc in each sc to end of rnd. Join in top of ch-3. **4th rnd:** Ch 1, sc in each st around, increasing 4 sc evenly

around front of sole. Join. **5th, 6th, and 7th rnds:** Ch 1, sc in each sc around, increasing 4 sc evenly around both front and back of Sole. Join. There are on 7th rnd

94 sc	104 sc	114 sc

8th rnd: Sl st in each sc around. Break off.

TOP . . . Starting at top, chain (very loosely)

46 sts	48 sts	50 sts

Join.

1st rnd: Ch 4, tr in each ch around. Join in top of ch-4. **2nd rnd:** Ch 4, tr in each tr around. Join in top of ch-4. Repeat the 2nd rnd until piece measures 5 inches in all.

Shape instep as follows: **1st row:** Ch 1, sc in **back loop** of next

16 tr	17 tr	18 tr

Ch 1, turn. **2nd row:** Sc in back loop of each sc across. Repeat the 2nd row until piece measures from 1st row of instep shaping

4″	4½″	5″

Next row: Make sc in back loop of each sc across, decreasing 1 sc at both ends of row— *to dec 1 sc, work off 2 sc as 1 sc* (Figs. 25 and 26). Ch 1, turn. Repeat this row 2 more times.

SIDE OF INSTEP . . . 1st rnd: Sc in the

10 sc	11 sc	12 sc

across instep; make

27 sc	31 sc	35 sc

along side edge of instep, sc in next

30 tr	31 tr	32 tr

across back; make

27 sc	31 sc	35 sc

across opposite side of instep. Join in 1st sc. There are on rnd

94 sc	104 sc	114 sc

2nd rnd: Ch 4, tr in each st around. Join in top of ch-4. Repeat the 2nd rnd 2 more times. Break off.

Sew Top to Sole. Make Edging as for Bedjacket around top. Draw a piece of ribbon through each sock at ankle and tie ends.

CHAPTER TWO

Accessories

THIS CHAPTER reminds us of the rhyme about Jack Horner who, no matter where he stuck in his thumb, always came out with a plum. We've crammed it full of "little" accessories, all the pretty, witty tidbits that add a special flavor to the fashions of the moment. You'll find something for everybody here.

We've included a treasure trove of natty watchbands and belts to spice up any outfit; a dainty pair of gloves for special occasions; a feminine halter top; and a cozy pair of bedroom slippers.

If younger sister feels left out, the matching scarf, hat, and mitten set is sure to please. You'll find this collection as bright a set of accessories as ever you'll get your hooks into!

5424 . . . **Materials:** COATS & CLARK'S RED HEART KNITTING WORSTED, 4 Ply ("Tangle-Proof" Pull-Out Skeins), 7 ounces of No. 282 Rust, and 4 ounces of No. 1 White for Scarf and Hat . . . 3 ounces of No. 282 Rust, 2 ounces of No. 1 White for Mittens . . . Wooden Crochet Hook No. 15.

GAUGE: With double yarn: 4 sc makes 3 inches; 2 rows make 1 inch.

Use 2 strands of yarn held together throughout. Scarf measures 8 x 55 inches excluding pompoms.

SCARF

Starting at a point, using 2 strands of Rust held together, ch 3. **1st row:** Sc in 2nd ch from hook, sc in next ch—2 sc. Ch 1, turn. **2nd row:** 2 sc in each of 2 sc—4 sc. Ch 1, turn. **3rd row:** Sc in each sc across. Ch 1, turn. **4th row:** 2 sc in first sc, sc in 2 sc, 2 sc in last sc. Ch 1, turn. **5th row:** Repeat 3rd row—6 sc. Ch 1, turn. **6th row:** 2 sc in first sc, sc in 4 sc, 2 sc in last sc—8 sc. Ch 1, turn. Repeat 3rd row until total length is 52 inches. Ch 1, turn. **Next row:** Skip first sc, sc in each sc to within last 2 sc, skip next sc, sc in last sc. **Following row:** Sc in each sc. Ch 1, turn. **Next 2 rows:** Repeat last 2 rows —4 sc. Ch 1, turn. **Following row:** (Skip next sc, sc in next sc) twice—2 sc. Break off and fasten.

EDGING . . . **1st rnd:** Using 2 strands of Rust held together, attach yarn to 2nd ch of starting chain, 3 sc in same ch where yarn was attached; working loosely along ends of rows, make sc in end st of first row, * skip next row, sc in end st of next row. Repeat from * across to last row, sc in end st of last row, 3 sc in next sc on last row; work along other long edge to correspond with opposite edge. Join with sl st to first sc of rnd. Break off and fasten. **2nd rnd:** Using 2 strands of White held together, attach yarn to same sc used for joining, sc in same sc where yarn was attached, 3 sc in next sc; working loosely, sc in each sc to within center sc of 3-sc group at next point, 3 sc in center sc, sc in each remaining sc. Join to first sc. Ch 1, turn. **3rd rnd:** * Sc in each sc to within center sc of next 3-sc group, 3 sc in center sc. Repeat from * once; sc in remaining 2 sc. Join. Break off and fasten.

Steam through a damp cloth.

POMPON (Make 6) . . . Wind White 44 times around 2 fingers, slip loops off fingers and with a separate double strand 4 inches long, tie loops tightly together at center; cut loops at both ends. Using the tying strands, hold 3 pompons together, holding 2 pompons ½ inch shorter than center pompon and tie strands together into a knot. Tack knot to one point of scarf. Attach other 3 pompons to other point in same way.

HAT

Starting at center back, using 2 strands of Rust held together, ch 6. **1st row:** Sc in 2nd ch from hook and in each remaining ch—5 sc. Ch 1, turn. **2nd row:** Sc in each sc across. Ch 1, turn. Repeat 2nd row until piece measures 19 inches or until piece fits, without stretching, around head. At end of last row, break off and fasten. Sew top edge of last row to starting chain.

TOP EDGING . . . Using 2 strands of Rust held together, attach yarn to top end of seam. **1st rnd:** Working along end of rows, * make sc in end st of next row, skip next row. Repeat from * around. Join with sl st to first sc. Break off

and fasten. **2nd rnd:** Attach double strand of White in same sc used for joining, sc in same sc where yarn was attached, sc in each sc around. Join to first sc. **3rd rnd:** Ch 1, sc in same sc used for joining, sc in each sc around. Join. Break off and fasten. Working loosely, work 3 rnds of Top Edging along lower edge of hat.

Steam through a damp cloth.

Make 3 Pompons same as for Scarf. Tie Pompons together as for Scarf and tack to one side of hat below top edging.

MITTENS

Starting at edge of cuff, using 2 strands of Rust held together, ch 12. **1st row:** Sc in 2nd ch from hook, sc in each remaining ch—11 sc. Ch 1, turn. **2nd row:** Sc in each sc across. Repeat last row until piece measures 10 inches. Ch 1, turn. **Next row:** Sc in first 5 sc, *2 sc in next sc* —inc made for thumb shaping; sc in next 5 sc. Ch 1, turn. **Following row:** Sc in 5 sc, 2 sc in each of next 2 sc, sc in 5 sc. Ch 1, turn. **Next row:** Sc in 5 sc, ch 2, skip next 4 sc for Thumb opening, sc in next 5 sc. Ch 1, turn.

HAND . . . 1st row: Sc in 5 sc, *draw up a loop in each of next 2 ch sts, yarn over hook and draw through all 3 loops on hook—joint sc made; sc in next 5 sc—11 sc. Ch 1, turn. 2nd through 5th rows: Sc in each sc across. Ch 1, turn. 6th through 10th rows: Make joint sc over first 2 sc, sc in each remaining sc. Ch 1, turn—6 sc on last row. Ch 1, turn. 11th row: (Joint sc over 2 sc) 3 times. Break off, leaving a 24-inch length of yarn. Thread a darning needle with this end of yarn, gather remaining sts tightly together and with same strand sew ends of rows together to within 5 inches from starting chain; fasten securely—remaining 5 inches form cuff.

THUMB . . . Attach double strand of Rust to first of 4 skipped sc on Thumb opening. 1st row: Sc in same sc where yarn was attached, sc in next 3 sc, draw up a loop in bar of next sc on previous row, draw up a loop in next ch, complete a joint sc, make another joint sc over next ch and bar of following sc—6 sc. Ch 1, turn. 2nd through 5th rows: Sc in each sc across. Ch 1, turn. 6th row: Work same as for 11th row of Hand. Break off, leaving a 6-inch length of yarn. Thread darning needle with end of yarn, gather remaining sts together and sew ends of Thumb rows together. Fasten securely.

Cuff Edging . . . With wrong side of mitten facing, attach double strand of Rust to end of side seam at cuff edge. 1st row: Working along ends of cuff rows, sc evenly along side edge of cuff to next corner, 3 sc in corner st; working along opposite side of starting chain, sc in each ch to next corner, 3 sc in corner st, sc evenly along ends of rows on next side edge to seam. Break off and fasten. Do not turn. 2nd row: Attach double strand of White to first sc at beg of last row, sc in same sc where yarn was attached, * sc in each sc to within center sc of next 3-sc group at corner, 3 sc in center sc. Repeat from * once; sc in each remaining sc. Ch 1, turn. 3rd row: Starting at * work same as last row. Break off and fasten. Turn cuff back to right side. Sew first 3 or 4 sts of last row of edging to last 3 or 4 sts on same row.

Steam through a damp cloth.

Working Pompons same as for Scarf, make and tie together a group of 3 pompons; tack group of pompons to end of cuff seam.

Make other mitten in same way.

5169 . . . Materials: J. & P. Coats Knit-Cro-Sheen: *1 ball each of 2 colors will make all 6 straps.*

For Striped Strap: *About 12 yards of first color; 6 yards of second color.*

For Cross-Stitch Strap: *About 13 yards of first color; 3 yards of second color.*

For Braid Strap: *About 10 yards each of 2 colors.*

For Floral Motif Strap: *About 20 yards of one color.*

For Wheel Motif Strap: *About 12 yards of first color; 14 yards of second color.*

For Ruffled Strap: *About 14 yards of first color; 12 yards of second color . . .* **Steel Crochet Hook No. 8** . . . *Buckles or suitable fastenings.*

GAUGE: 10 sc make 1 inch.
The Floral Motif measures ⅞ inch in diameter.
The Wheel Motif measures 1 inch in diameter.
All other Straps measure ⅝ inch in width.

To Attach Watch: Either weave strap through side loops of watch as shown or tack sides of watch securely to center of strap.

STRIPED STRAP

With first color, ch 92 to measure 9½ inches. 1st row (wrong side): Sc in 2nd ch from hook, sc in each ch across—91 sc. Ch 1, turn. 2nd row: 2 sc in first sc, sc in each sc across to within last sc, draw up a loop in last sc, drop first color, draw a loop of 2nd color through 2 loops on hook. With 2nd color, ch 1, turn. 3rd row: Sc in each sc across to within last sc, 2 sc in last sc. Ch 2, turn. 4th row: *Draw up a loop in each of first 2 sc, thread over hook and draw through all 3 loops on hook—joint sc made; sc in each sc across to within last sc, draw up a loop in last sc, drop 2nd color, pick up first color and draw a loop of first color through 2 loops on hook. Ch 1, turn. 5th row:* With first color, sc in each sc across to within last 2 sc, make a joint sc over last 2 sc. Ch 1, turn. 6th row (right side): Sc in joint sc, sc in each sc across, then work sc in the end sc of each of the next 5 rows. Break off and fasten.

Work across shaped end of strap as follows: With right side facing, attach first color in ch st at end of starting chain. Ch 1, sc in end sc of each of next 2 rows, 2 sc in end sc of each of next 2 rows, sc in end sc of each of next 2

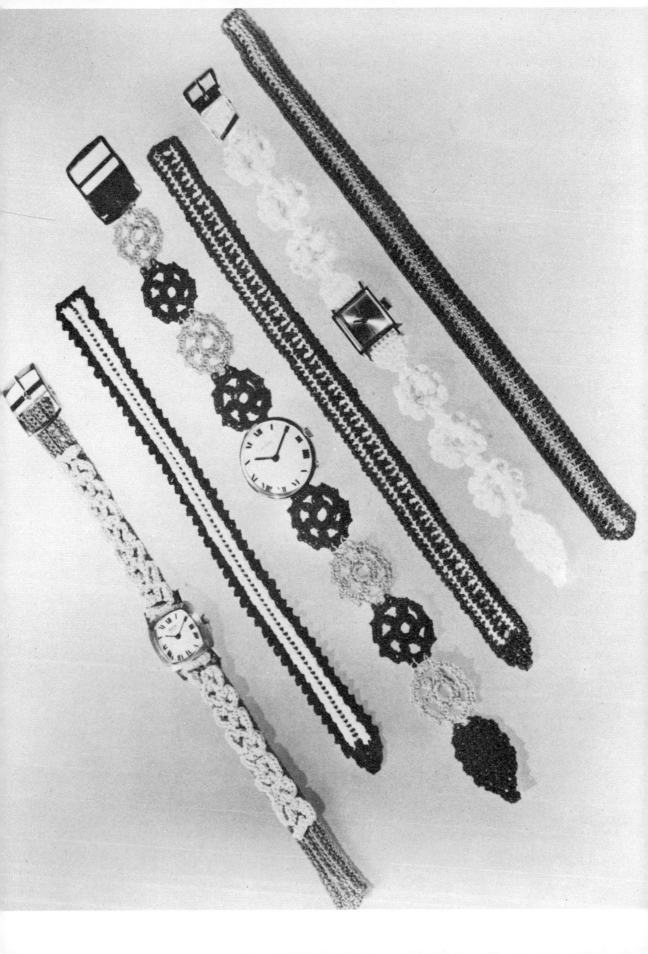

rows. Break off and fasten. Press through damp cloth. Attach buckle or suitable fastening as desired.

CROSS-STITCH STRAP

With first color, ch 91 to measure 9½ inches. Break off and fasten. Attach 2nd color to last ch st made. **1st row (right side):** Ch 1, sc where thread was attached, sc in each ch across— 91 sc. Break off and fasten. Do not turn. Attach first color to first sc made. **2nd row:** Ch 3, * *skip next sc, dc in next sc, hold last dc made to front of work and working behind it make dc in skipped sc*—**cross st made;** dc in next sc. Repeat from * across. Break off and fasten. Attach 2nd color to top of ch-3 at beg of last row. **3rd row:** Ch 1, sc where thread was attached, sc in each dc across—91 sc. Break off and fasten.

EDGING . . . With right side facing, attach first color to first ch st on opposite side of starting chain, ch 1, sc where thread was attached, * ch 1, sc in next ch. Repeat from * across, ending with ch 1, in last ch make (sc, ch 1) twice; sc in the end sc of first row, ch 1, in the end of cross st row make sc, ch 1 and sc; ch 1, sc in end of next row, ch 1, in next sc make (sc, ch 1) twice; working across last sc row (instead of chain), work along long edge same as for opposite edge, ending with ch 1, sc in last sc. Work along ends of rows as follows:

TAB . . . **1st row:** Sc in end sc of next row, 3 sc in end of cross st row, sc in end sc of next row, sl st in next sc. Ch 1, turn. **2nd row:** Sc in 5 sc. Ch 1, turn. **3rd row:** *Draw up a loop in each of first 2 sc, thread over hook and draw through all 3 loops on hook*—**joint sc made;** sc in next sc, joint sc over next 2 sc. Ch 1, turn. **4th row:** Joint sc over next 2 sc, draw up a loop in last sc used and in next sc, complete a joint sc as before. Ch 1, turn. **5th row:** Joint sc over 2 sc. Break off and fasten.

Press through damp cloth. Attach buckle or suitable fastening as desired.

BRAID STRAP

BRAID . . . With first color, ch 2. Sc in 2nd ch from hook (Fig. 58); turn. Sc in 2nd ch made (Fig. 59); turn. * Insert hook in 2 loops at side of previous st (Fig. 60) and draw loop through, thread over hook and draw through 2 loops on hook; turn. Repeat from * until total length is about 9½ inches, having an uneven number of loops on each side (Fig. 60). Break off and

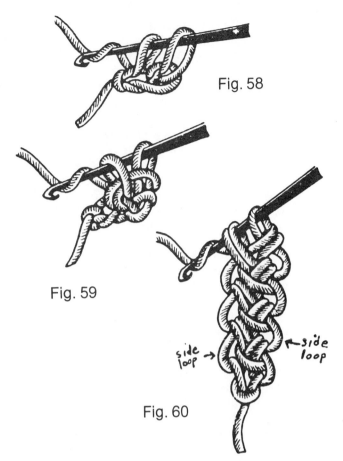

Fig. 58

Fig. 59

side loop →   ← side loop

Fig. 60

fasten. Make another piece exactly the same as first piece.

BRAID JOINING . . . Attach 2nd color to first side loop on first Braid. Insert hook in same loop where thread was attached and in first side loop of 2nd Braid, thread over hook and draw through all 3 loops on hook, * insert hook in next side loop on first Braid and also in next loop on 2nd Braid, thread over, and draw through all 3 loops on hook. Repeat from * across. Break off and fasten. This is wrong side.

EDGING . . . With right side facing, attach 2nd color to first side loop on outer edge, ch 1, in same loop make sc, ch 2 and sc; * skip next loop, in next loop make sc, ch 2 and sc. Repeat from * across. Break off and fasten. Work edging along opposite edge in same way but do not break off. Work 5 sc evenly along narrow edge. Sl st in first sc of edging. Break off and fasten.

TAB . . . With right side facing, attach 2nd color to last sc of edging at other narrow end.

1st row: Work 5 sc evenly along narrow edge. Sl st in first sc of edging. Ch 1, turn. **2nd through 5th rows:** Work same as 2nd through 5th rows of Tab of Cross Stitch Strap.

Press through damp cloth. Attach buckle or suitable fastening as desired.

FLORAL MOTIF STRAP

FIRST HALF—FIRST MOTIF . . . Starting at center, ch 6. Join with sl st to form ring. **1st rnd:** Ch 1, 8 sc in ring. Join with sl st to back loop of first sc. **2nd rnd:** * Ch 3, *holding back on hook the last loop of each dc make 3 dc in same back loop where last sl st was made, thread over and draw through all 4 loops on hook—cluster made;* ch 3, sl st in same back loop, sl st in back loop of next sc. Repeat from * around, ending with sl st in same back loop where last cluster was made—8 petals made. **3rd rnd:** Working in front loops of sc's on first rnd, sl st in front loop of first sc, ch 5, *sl st in 3rd ch from hook—picot made;* * h dc in front loop of next sc, ch 3, complete a picot. Repeat from * around—8 picots. Join with sl st to 2nd ch of ch-5 at beg of rnd. Break off and fasten.

SECOND MOTIF . . . Work same as First Motif until first rnd has been completed. **2nd rnd:** Working in back loops of sc's, ch 3, make a cluster in same place, then holding First Motif with wrong side facing, sl st in top of any cluster on First Motif, ch 3, sl st in same back loop on Second Motif to complete a petal; sl st in back loop of next sc and complete 2nd rnd, then 3rd rnd same as for First Motif. Make another Motif, joining it to last motif made as Second Motif was joined to First Motif, having 3 petals free between joinings.

TAB . . . With right side facing, attach thread to top of 4th free cluster on last motif made. **1st row:** Ch 1, 2 sc where thread was attached. Ch 1, turn. **2nd row:** 2 sc in each of 2 sc. Ch 1, turn. **3rd row:** 2 sc in first sc, sc in next 2 sc, 2 sc in last sc. Ch 1, turn. **4th through 9th rows:** Sc in each sc across. Ch 1, turn. At end of 9th row, break off and fasten. Work a Tab on the 4th free cluster on motif at other end in same way. Make Second Half of Strap same as First Half, but do not break off at end of 9th row of 2nd Tab. Ch 1, turn. **10th row:** *Draw up a loop in each of 2 sc, thread over hook and draw through all 3 loops on hook—joint sc made;* sc in next 2 sc, joint sc over last 2 sc. Ch 1, turn. **11th row:** (Joint sc over next

2 sts) twice. Ch 1, turn. **12th row:** Sc in 2 sc. Ch 1, turn. **13th row:** Joint sc over next 2 sts. Break off and fasten.

Press through damp cloth. Attach watch between halves. Attach buckle or suitable fastening to straight end of first half.

WHEEL MOTIF STRAP

FIRST MOTIF . . . Starting at center with first color, ch 6. Join with sl st to form ring. **1st rnd:** Ch 1, 12 sc in ring. Join with sl st to first sc. **2nd rnd:** Ch 3, dc in same sc used for joining, * ch 3, skip next sc, *holding back on hook last loop of each dc, make 2 dc in next sc, thread over hook and draw through all 3 loops on hook—cluster made.* Repeat from * 4 times more; ch 3. Join with sl st to top of first dc. **3rd rnd:** Ch 1, in each ch-3 sp make (sc, ch 2 and sc) twice. Join with sl st to first sc. Break off and fasten.

SECOND MOTIF . . . With 2nd color, work same as First Motif until 2nd rnd has been completed. **3rd rnd:** Ch 1, in first ch-3 sp make (sc, ch 1, sl st in corresponding ch-2 loop on First Motif, ch 1 and sc) twice; complete same as 3rd rnd of First Motif. Alternating colors, make and join 7 more motifs, joining each motif to last motif made same as Second Motif was joined to First Motif, having 4 ch-2 loops free between joinings.

STRAIGHT TAB . . . With right side facing, attach 2nd color to 5th ch-2 loop on last motif made. **1st row:** Ch 1, sc where thread was attached, ch 2, sc in next loop. Ch 1, turn. **2nd row:** 2 sc in first sc, 2 sc in ch-2 space, 2 sc in last sc. Ch 1, turn. **3rd row:** 2 sc in first sc, sc in next 4 sc, 2 sc in last sc—8 sc. Ch 1, turn. **4th through 9th rows:** Sc in each sc across. Ch 1, turn. At end of 9th row, break off and fasten.

POINTED TAB . . . With right side facing, attach 2nd color to 5th ch-2 loop on motif at other end of strap, work same as Straight Tab until 9th row has been completed, but do not break off. Ch 1, turn. **10th row:** *Draw up a loop in each of 2 sc, thread over hook and draw through all 3 loops on hook—joint sc made;* (sc in next sc, joint sc over next 2 sc) twice. Ch 1, turn. **11th row:** Joint sc over first 2 sc, sc in next sc, joint sc over last 2 sc. Ch 1, turn. **12th row:** Joint sc over first 2 sc, draw up a loop in last sc used and in last sc, complete a joint sc as before. Ch 1, turn. **13th row:** Joint sc over 2 sc. Break off and fasten.

Press through damp cloth. Attach buckle or suitable fastening as desired.

RUFFLED STRAP

FIRST HALF . . . With first color, ch 46 to measure 4¾ inches. **1st row (right side):** Sc in 2nd ch from hook, sc in each ch across—45 sc. Ch 1, turn. **2nd row:** Sc in each sc across. Ch 1, turn. **3rd row:** Sc in back loop of each sc across. Ch 1, turn. **4th row:** Sc in front loop of each sc across. Ch 1, turn. **5th row:** Repeat 3rd row. Ch 1, turn. **6th row:** Sc in each sc across. Break off and fasten.

SECOND HALF . . . With first color, ch 46. **1st row (right side):** Sc in 2nd ch from hook, sc in each ch across—45 sc. Ch 1, turn. **2nd row:** 2 sc in first sc, sc in each remaining sc— 46 sc. Ch 1, turn. **3rd row:** Sc in back loop of each sc across to within last sc, 2 sc in back loop of last sc—47 sc. Ch 2, turn. **4th row:** *Draw up a loop in front loop of each of 2 sc, thread over hook and draw through all 3 loops on hook—joint sc made;* sc in front loop of each remaining sc—46 sc. Ch 1, turn. **5th row:** Sc in back loop of each sc across to within last 2 sc, make a joint sc in back loops of last 2 sc—45 sc. Ch 1, turn. **6th row:** Sc in each sc across. Break off and fasten.

Work across shaped end of strap as follows: With right side facing, attach first color to end sc on last row, ch 1, sc where thread was attached, sc in end sc of each of next 2 rows, 2 sc in end sc of next row, sc in end sc of next 2 rows. Break off and fasten.

RUFFLE . . . With right side facing, attach 2nd color to free front loop of 4th sc on 2nd row of First Half of Strap. Working in free loops of the 2nd, 3rd and 4th rows, ch 2, 2 h dc in same loop where thread was attached, (3 h dc in 4th free loop on next row) twice; * 3 h dc in front loop of each of next 2 sc on same row, (skip next free loop on row below, 3 h dc in next free loop) twice; 3 h dc in each of next 2 loops on same row, (skip next free loop on row above, 3 h dc in next loop) twice. Repeat from * across to within 1 inch from end. Break off and fasten. Work Ruffle on Second Half of Strap in same way.

Attach buckle or suitable fastening as desired.

2061 . . . Materials: KNIT-CRO-SHEEN, *4 balls of any color* . . . SIX STRAND EMBROIDERY FLOSS, *1 skein of a contrasting color* . . . *Plastic Crochet Hook No. 5.*

Use 5 threads throughout			
Sizes	Small	Medium	Large
BOTTOM SOLE . . . Chain loosely (3½ ch sts to 1 inch)	22 sts	26 sts	30 sts

1st rnd: 3 sc in 2nd ch from hook, sc in each of next 11 ch / 13 ch / 15 ch, dc in each of next 8 ch / 10 ch / 12 ch, make 7 dc in last ch (toe end). Then, working along opposite side of starting chain, make dc in each of 8 ch / 10 ch / 12 ch, sc in each of next 11 ch / 13 ch / 15 ch, 2 sc in same place where first 3 sc were made.

2nd rnd: Sc in each st around, increasing 3 sc evenly across heel and 5 sc evenly across toe— *to inc, work 2 sc in 1 sc.* Repeat last rnd 2 more times. Work sc to center back of heel. **Next rnd:** Sl st in each st around, sl st in the 1st sl st. Break off.

TOP SOLE . . . Work exactly the same as Bottom Sole.

BOTTOM HEEL PIECE . . . Ch 14. **1st row:** Sc in 2nd ch from hook, sc in each ch across, 5 sc in last ch. Working along opposite side of starting chain, make sc in each ch across. Ch 1, turn. **2nd, 3rd and 4th rows:** Sc in each sc, increasing 3 sc evenly across curved end. Ch 1, turn. **5th row:** Sl st in each st across. Break off.

TOP HEEL PIECE . . . Ch 9. Work same as Bottom Heel Piece.

Trace the outline of a sole piece onto cardboard. Cut just inside outline. Sew the 2 heel pieces together, catching only 1 loop on the outside of each piece. Place cardboard sole on top of Bottom Sole and sew joined heel pieces in place on Bottom Sole. Sew Top Sole in place on joined pieces.

VAMP . . . Starting at toe, chain loosely 8 sts / 10 sts / 12 sts

1st row: Sc in 2nd ch from hook, sc in next 2 ch / 3 ch / 4 ch, 3 sc in next ch, sc in each remaining 3 ch / 4 ch / 5 ch. Ch 1, turn.

2nd row: Sc in each sc across. Ch 1, turn. **3rd row:** Sc in each sc across to center sc, 3 sc in

2061

center sc, sc in each remaining sc. Repeat 2nd and 3rd rows alternately 6 more times; then repeat 2nd row once more. There are on row

| 23 sc | 25 sc | 27 sc |

Break off.

With Six Strand embroider cross stitches evenly across every other row of Vamp. Sew Vamp in place on Top Sole, leaving toe end open and catching only one loop of each sl st on Top Sole. Make other scuff same as this.

2804 . . . Materials: KNITTING WORSTED (3½-ounce skeins), 2 skeins for Small, Medium and Large Sizes . . . Aluminum or Plastic Crochet Hook I-9.

2804

Use 2 strands throughout			
Sizes (Length of Sole):	Small (8½″)	Medium (9½″)	Large (10½″)

SOLE . . . Starting at center, chain

	20 sts	24 sts	28 sts
1st rnd: Make 5 sc in 2nd ch from hook, sc in next	10 ch	12 ch	14 ch
dc in next	7 ch	9 ch	11 ch
make 7 dc in last ch (toe). Then, working along opposite side of starting chain, make dc in next	7 ch	9 ch	11 ch
sc in next	10 ch	12 ch	14 ch

2nd, 3rd, and 4th rnds: Sc in each st around, increasing 3 sc evenly across heel and 5 sc evenly across toe. 5th rnd: Turn and, with wrong side facing, work sl st in each st around, sl st in 1st sl st. Break off.

UPPER . . . **1st rnd:** With right side facing, attach yarn in a **sl st** at center back, ch 3, dc in each **sl st** around. Join with sl st in top st of ch-3. **2nd rnd:** Ch 1, sc in each st around, decreasing 2 sts evenly across heel and 5 sts evenly across toe—*to dec, work off 2 sts as 1 st.* Join with sl st in 1st sc. **3rd rnd:** Ch 3, dc in each st around, decreasing 7 sts as on last rnd. Join. **4th rnd:** Repeat 2nd rnd. **5th rnd:** Ch 1, sc in each st around. Join and break off.

CORD . . . Make a chain about 24 inches long. Lace through front of Upper. Make a knot at each end of chain. Tie in a bow. Make other slipper same as this.

B-708 . . . **Materials:** COATS & CLARK'S RED HEART KNITTING WORSTED, 4 Ply ("Tangle-Proof" Pull-Out Skeins), 2 ounces of No. 253 *Tangerine for 25-inch length, 3 ounces for longer belts. 1 ounce of No. 230 Yellow for All Sizes* . . . Crochet Hook Size G . . . Kilt Pin.

GAUGE: 9 sc makes 2 inches.

Starting at narrow straight edge with Tangerine, ch 2. **1st row:** 5 sc in 2nd ch from hook. Ch 1, turn. **Note:** Hereafter work in the **back** loop only of each sc throughout. **2nd row— wrong side:** *2 sc in first sc—1 sc increased;* sc in next sc, *3 sc in next sc—3-sc group made;* sc in next sc, inc 1 sc in last sc—9 sc. Ch 1, turn. **3rd row:** Inc 1 sc in first sc, sc in each sc to within center sc of the 3-sc group, 3 sc in center sc of the 3-sc group, sc in each sc to within last sc, inc 1 sc in last sc—4 sc increased. Ch 1, turn. **4th, 5th, and 6th rows:** Repeat 3rd row. Ch 1, turn. There are 25 sc on last row.

Ch 1, turn. **7th row:** *Draw up a loop in each of first 2 sc, yarn over, and draw through all loops on hook—1 sc decreased;* sc in each sc to within center sc of the 3-sc group, 3 sc in center sc of the 3-sc group, sc in each sc to within last 2 sc, dec 1 sc over last 2 sc—25 sc. Ch 1, turn. **8th and 9th rows:** Repeat 7th row. Ch 1, turn. **10th row:** Work as for 7th row to within last 2 sc, draw up a loop in each of last 2 sc, drop Tangerine; with Yellow, yarn over and draw through all loops on hook. Ch 1, turn. **Always change color in same way. Carry yarn not in use loosely along side edge. 11th row:** Repeat 7th row. **12th row:** Work as for 7th row, changing color at end of row. **13th, 14th, and 15th rows:** Repeat 7th, 12th, and 7th rows. **16th row:** Work as for 7th row, changing color at end of row, then break off Yellow and fasten. **17th through 25th rows:** Repeat 7th row. **26th row:** Repeat 7th row, attaching and changing to Yellow at end of row. Repeat last 16 rows (11th through 26th rows) for pattern. Work in pattern until total length, including point, is about 26 inches or length desired, ending with Tangerine on wrong side. Ch 1, turn. With Tangerine, sl st through **both** loops of each of the 25 sts on last row; making 3 sc in one st at each corner, sc evenly around belt to within first sl st. Join with sl st to first sl st. Ch 1, turn, then sl st through **both** loops of each sc around to within the sts of last row. Break off and fasten. Press lightly. Fasten with pin.

31

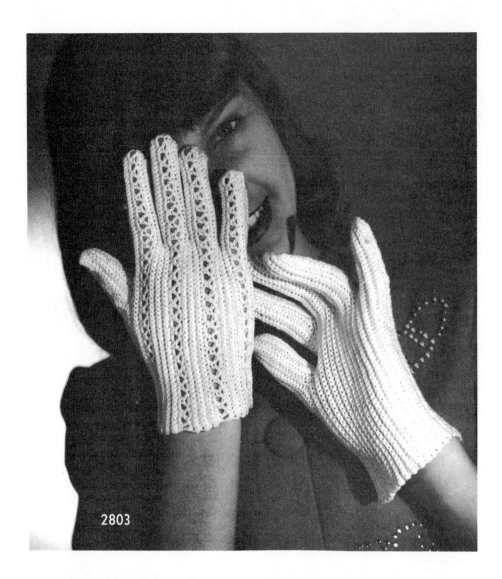

2803

2803 . . . Materials: Pearl Cotton, Size 5, 5 balls for *Small Size; 6 balls for Medium or Large Sizes . . . Steel Crochet Hook No. 7.*

GAUGE: 8 sc make 1 inch; 8 rows (stretched) make 1 inch.

Sizes	Small (6½″)	Medium (7″)	Large (7½″)

LEFT GLOVE—Back . . . Starting at Little Finger side, chain (not tightly)

	55 sts	61 sts	67 sts

1st row: Sc in 2nd ch from hook, sc in each ch across. There are on row

	54 sts	60 sts	66 sts

Ch 1, turn.

Hereafter, work only in the back loop of each sc on all sc rows.

2nd row: Sc in each sc across. Ch 3, turn.

3rd row: Work in both loops of each sc. Skip 2 sc, dc in next sc, * ch 2, holding back on hook the last loop of each dc make dc in same place where last dc was made, skip 2 sc, dc in next sc (3 loops left on hook), thread over and draw through all loops on hook—a joined dc made. Repeat from * across. Ch 1, turn.
4th row: * Sc in joined dc, 2 sc in next ch-2 sp. Repeat from * across, ending with sc in last dc, 2 sc in top of turning chain. There are on row

	54 sc	60 sc	66 sc

Ch 1, turn.

5th and 6th rows: Sc in each sc across. Ch 1, turn. **7th row:** Sc in

36 sc	39 sc	42 sc

chain (not tightly) for **Ring Finger**

22 sts	25 sts	28 sts

8th row: Sc in 2nd ch from hook, sc in next

20 ch	23 ch	26 ch

sc in each remaining sc. There are on row

57 sc	63 sc	69 sc

9th and 10th rows: Sc in each sc across. Ch 1, turn. At end of 10th row, ch 3, turn. **11th row:** Repeat 3rd row. **12th, 13th and 14th rows:** Repeat 4th, 5th and 6th rows. There are on row

57 sc	63 sc	69 sc

15th row: Sc in

39 sc	42 sc	45 sc

chain (not tightly) for **Middle Finger**

22 sts	25 sts	28 sts

16th row: Sc in 2nd ch from hook, sc in next

20 ch	23 ch	26 ch

sc in each remaining sc. There are on row

60 sc	66 sc	72 sc

Ch 1, turn.

17th to 22nd rows incl: Repeat 9th to 14th rows incl. **23rd row:** Sc in

39 sc	42 sc	45 sc

chain (not tightly) for **Index Finger**

19 sts	22 sts	25 sts

24th row: Sc in 2nd ch from hook, sc in next

17 ch	20 ch	23 ch

sc in each remaining sc. There are on row

57 sc	63 sc	69 sc

Ch 1, turn.

25th to 30th rows incl: Repeat 9th to 14th rows incl. Break off.

PALM . . . Starting at Little Finger side, chain

55 sts	61 sts	67 sts

1st row: Sc in 2nd ch from hook, sc in each ch across. There are on row

54 sts	60 sts	66 sts

Ch 1, turn.

Hereafter, work only in the back loop of each sc. 2nd to 6th rows incl: Sc in each sc across.

Ch 1, turn. **7th row:** Repeat 7th row of Back. **8th row:** Repeat 8th row of Back. **9th to 14th rows incl:** Sc in each sc across. Ch 1, turn. **15th row:** Repeat 15th row of Back. **16th row:** Repeat 16th row of Back. **17th to 22nd rows incl:** Sc in each sc across. Ch 1, turn. Then work as follows: **1st row:** Sc in

28 sc	30 sc	32 sc

Chain for front of Thumb

19 sts	21 sts	23 sts

2nd row: Sc in 2nd ch from hook, sc in next

17 ch	19 ch	21 ch

sc in each remaining sc. There are on row

46 sc	50 sc	54 sc

Ch 1, turn.

3rd to 7th rows incl: Sc in each sc across. Ch 1, turn. At end of 7th row, break off.

For back of Thumb and Index Finger work as follows: **1st row:** For back of Thumb chain

18 sts	20 sts	22 sts

on Palm work sc in next

11 sc	12 sc	13 sc

for Index Finger chain

19 sts	22 sts	25 sts

2nd row: Sc in 2nd ch from hook, sc in next

17 ch	20 ch	23 ch

sc in next

11 sc	12 sc	13 sc

sc in next

18 ch	20 ch	22 ch

There are on row

47 sc	53 sc	59 sc

Ch 1, turn.

3rd to 7th rows incl: Sc in each sc across. Ch 1, turn. At end of 7th row, break off.

Sew edges of Thumb together. Sew edges of Back and Palm together, leaving wrist edge open. Press through damp cloth.

RIGHT GLOVE—Back . . . Work exactly the same as Back of Left Glove (the wrong side of the joined dc's will be right side of Back).

PALM . . . Work exactly the same as Palm of Left Glove. When sewing Thumb seam, be sure Palm is for right hand.

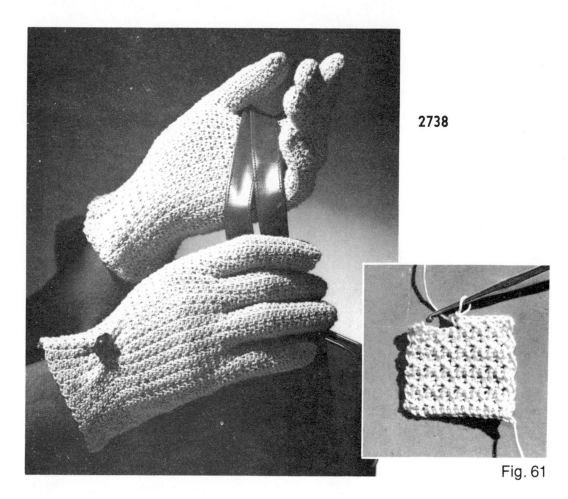

2738

Fig. 61

2738 . . . Materials: Knit-Cro-Sheen, *1 ball for Small Size, 2 balls for Medium and Large Sizes* . . . *Steel Crochet Hook No. 7.*

Sizes	Small	Medium	Large

GAUGE: 8 sc make 1 inch; 8 rows make 1 inch.

LEFT GLOVE—Back of Hand . . . Starting at Little Finger side, chain

	Small	Medium	Large
	59 sts	65 sts	71 sts

1st row: Sc in 2nd ch from hook and in each ch across. Ch 1, turn. Mark this end for tip of finger. **2nd row:** * Sc in back loop of next sc, sc in front loop of next sc. Repeat from * across. Ch 1, turn. Repeat the 2nd row throughout for pattern—**sc in back loop falls over sc in front loop and sc in front loop over sc in back loop of previous row** (Fig. 61). Now work in pattern, increasing 1 sc at tip of finger on 3rd row—*to inc 1 sc, make 2 sc in 1 sc*—and decreas-

ing 1 sc at tip of finger on 5th row—*to dec 1 sc, work off 2 sc as 1 sc.* Continue until 6 rows in all have been made—work is at wrist edge. **Measure glove against hand frequently to insure proper fit.**

RING FINGER . . . Work across to last

	Small	Medium	Large
	16 sc	18 sc	20 sc
chain	21 sts	23 sts	25 sts

Next row: Sc in 2nd ch from hook and in each ch across, sc in each sc across. Ch 1, turn. Work straight in pattern over these sts for 7 rows, increasing 1 sc at tip of finger on 2nd row and decreasing 1 sc at tip of finger on the 6th row. The 7th row brings work to wrist edge.

MIDDLE FINGER . . . Work across to last

	Small	Medium	Large
	20 sc	22 sc	24 sc
chain	23 sts	25 sts	27 sts

Work as for Ring Finger.

INDEX FINGER . . . Work across to last

	22 sc	24 sc	26 sc
chain	21 sts	23 sts	25 sts

Work as for Ring Finger. Break off.

PALM . . . Starting at Little Finger side, work as for Back of Hand until Middle Finger is complete. Work is at wrist edge.

FRONT of THUMB . . . Work in pattern over the next

	32 sc	34 sc	36 sc
chain	21 sts	23 sts	25 sts

Turn.

Next row: Sc in 2nd ch from hook and in each ch across, work in pattern over the next

	32 sc	34 sc	36 sc

Work over these

	52 sts	56 sts	60 sts

only as for Ring Finger, until 7 rows are made. Break off.

BACK of THUMB and INDEX FINGER . . . Attach thread to ch at tip of Thumb. Working along opposite side of Thumb chain, make sc in each ch across, work in pattern to within

	22 sc	24 sc	26 sc
from tip of Middle Finger, chain			
	21 sts	23 sts	25 sts

Sc in 2nd ch from hook and in each st across to tip of Thumb. Ch 1, turn. Work 6 more rows of pattern as before over these sts only, increasing and decreasing as before at tip of both Thumb and Index Finger. Break off at end of 7th row.

Hold Palm and Back pieces together and sew around edges. Make a small inverted pleat on back of hand at wrist. Sew button in center of pleat.

RIGHT GLOVE . . . Because this stitch is reversible both gloves are made exactly the same. Before sewing pieces together be sure you have a right- and a left-hand glove.

4335

Directions are given for Small Size (10–12). Changes for Medium Size (14–16) and Large Size (18–20) are in parentheses.

Materials: J. & P. Coats Metallic Knit-Cro-Sheen, *Art. A.64-M:* 7 (7, 8) balls of No. 90-B Gold . . . J. & P. Coats Knit-Cro-Sheen, *Art. A.64,* 1 ball each of No. 48 Hunter's Green and No. 122 Watermelon . . . Steel Crochet Hook No. 7 . . . 25 (25, 27) brass rings, ¾ inch in diameter; 25 (25, 27) rhinestones, about ⅝ inch in diameter; 11 (11, 12) drop crystal beads; 1 hook and 6 small gold buttons; ¾ yard gold chiffon for lining (optional).

GAUGE: 3 patterns make 2 inches; 4 rows make 1 inch.

BLOCKING MEASUREMENTS:

Sizes	Small	Medium	Large
Body Bust Size (In Inches)	30-32	34-36	38-40
Actual Crocheting Measurements			
Width around waist	28	30	32
Width before back shaping	32	34	36
Width of front above back shaping	13	15	17
Length of necklace	16	16	17
Length from front of neck to lower edge	16	17	18

NECKLACE

Cover 13 (13, 14) rings with Green and 12 (12, 13) with Watermelon as follows: Make a circle of thread over left forefinger, insert hook in circle and pull through a loop, ch 2, make 10 h dc in circle and draw up end of thread tightly. Join with sl st to first h dc. Hold a ring behind crocheted piece. Working over ring, ch 1, make 3 sc in joining and in each h dc around—30 sc. Join with sl st to first sc. Break off and fasten. Cover is wrong side of ring.

JOIN GREEN RINGS . . . With Gold and right side of rings facing sc in 15 sc of **each** Green ring; working around other side of rings and taking care not to twist row, * sc in next 3 sc, (in next sc make sc, ch 1 and sc, sc in next 3 sc) 3 times. Repeat from * across each ring; at end of row, ch 3 for eye, sl st in first sc on same ring. Break off and fasten.

JOIN WATERMELON RINGS . . . With Gold and right side of rings facing h dc in 4 sc on first Watermelon ring, sl st in center ch-1 on first Green ring, h dc in same sc on Watermelon ring, h dc in next 3 sc, * sl st in last

35

ch-1 on same Green ring, h dc in same sc as last h dc and in next 3 sc on same Watermelon ring, sl st in first ch-1 on next Green ring, h dc in same sc as last h dc and in next 3 sc on same Watermelon ring, sl st in center ch-1 of same Green ring, h dc in each of 4 sc on next Watermelon ring. Repeat from * until last Watermelon ring has been joined to center ch-1 of last Green ring, h dc in same sc and next 3 sc of last Watermelon ring. Working around other side of Watermelon rings, dc in next sc, * 2 dc in next sc, dc in next sc. Repeat from * around remaining sc on same ring, dc in first free sc on next ring. Continue in this way across all remaining rings. Join with sl st in first h dc of rnd. Break off and fasten.

HALTER

Starting at lower edge with Gold, ch 254 (272, 290) to measure, without stretching, 30 (32, 34) inches. **1st row:** Sc in 2nd ch from hook, * skip 2 ch, *in next ch make dc, ch 1, dc, ch 1, and dc*—shell made; skip 2 ch, sc in next ch. Repeat from * across—42 (45, 48) shells. Ch 6, turn. **2nd row:** Sc in center dc of first shell, * ch 3, dc in next sc, ch 3, sc in center dc of next shell. Repeat from * across, ch 3, dc in last sc. Ch 1, turn. **3rd row:** Sc in first dc, * shell in next

sc, sc in next dc. Repeat from * across, ending with sc in 4th ch of turning ch-6. Ch 6, turn. Repeat 2nd and 3rd rows for pattern. Work even in pattern for 4 more rows, ending with shell row. **First Increase Row:** Mark the 6th (7th, 8th) shell and the 16th (17th, 18th) shell from each edge. * Work in pattern to marked shell, ch 3, sc in first dc of shell, ch 3, dc in center dc of same shell, ch 3, sc in 3rd dc of same shell, ch 3. Repeat from * across markers —1 pattern increased over each marked shell; complete row in pattern. Work even in pattern on 46 (49, 52) patterns for 7 rows, ending with a shell row. **Second Increase Row:** Mark the 7th (8th, 9th) shell and the 18th (19th, 21st) shell from each edge. Inc 1 pattern over each marked shell. Work even on 50 (53, 56) patterns until total length is 5 inches, ending with a shell row. Ch 1, turn.

BACK SHAPING . . . **1st row:** Sl st to center of 4th shell, ch 3, dc in next sc and continue in pattern, ending with sc in 4th shell from end of row. Ch 1, turn. **2nd row:** Sl st to first dc, * shell in next sc, sc in next dc. Repeat from * across, ending with sc in last dc. Ch 1, turn. **3rd row:** Sl st to center of first shell, ch 3, dc in next sc and continue in pattern, ending with ch 3, sc in last shell. Ch 1, turn. Repeat 2nd and 3rd rows until 20 (23, 26) shells remain, ending with a shell row. Ch 6, turn, and work even in pattern until piece measures 6½ (7, 7½) inches above last dec row, ending with a shell row. Break off and fasten.

FINISHING . . . Block to measurements. Work 2 rows of sc evenly along each back edge, making 6 button loops, evenly spaced, on last row of right back edge. If lining is desired, cut paper pattern from crocheted halter. Place lining material over paper pattern and, before cutting lining, baste four ½-inch pleats evenly spaced on center front section (running from lower to neck edge). Allowing 1 inch extra all around, cut lining from pattern. Pin lining to wrong side of crocheted halter. Turn under raw edges and stitch in place. Remove basting of pleats. Gather top edge to measure about 5 (5½, 6) inches and sew under center of lower edge of necklace. Sew buttons on left back edge, sew hook to left side of necklace. Sew a rhinestone to center of each ring, sew drop crystals between scallops at lower edge of necklace.

CHAPTER THREE

Hats and Bags

HATS ARE FUN—and the more the merrier: tams, berets, big hats with floppy brims. A hat is the perfect accessory for casual or dressy events, an article of clothing that expresses your whim of the moment.

In this chapter we've shown hats to ward off winter winds and hats to shade you from the summer sun. You'll also discover a collection of handbags to suit every occasion—elegant clutch bags for evening, a commodious shoulder tote perfect for carrying all those miscellaneous, but necessary, items.

Whatever your taste or needs in hats and bags, you'll find something in this chapter that will fit the bill—beautifully!

4556 . . . Materials: COATS & CLARK'S O.N.T. RUG YARN (70-yard skeins), 2 skeins of No. 1 White, 1 skein each of No. 44 Rose, No. 45 Deep Rose, and No. 49 Chartreuse Green . . . Crochet Hook Size J.

GAUGE: 5 sc make 2 inches; 3 rnds make 1 inch.

Starting at center with White, ch. 2. **1st rnd:** 6 sc in 2nd ch from hook. Join with sl st to first sc. **2nd rnd:** Ch 1, 2 sc in joining, 2 sc in each st around—12 sc. Join as before. Drop White, attach Rose. **3rd rnd:** With Rose, ch 1, 2 sc in joining—1 sc increased; sc in next sc, (2 sc in next sc, sc in next sc) 5 times—18 sc. Join. **4th rnd:** Ch 1; being careful incs do not fall directly over previous incs, sc in each sc, increasing 6 sc evenly spaced around—24 sc. Join. Break off Rose, pick up White. Repeating 4th rnd, work 2 rnds with White; 2 rnds with Deep Rose and 2 rnds with White. Break off Deep Rose. There are 60 sc on last rnd. Drop White; attach Green. **11th rnd:** With Green ch 1, sc in each sc increasing 5 sc evenly spaced around—65 sc. Join. **12th rnd:** Ch 1, sc in each sc around. Join. Break off Green, pick up White. **13th and 14th rnds:** With White work as for 11th and 12th rnds—70 sc on last rnd. Piece measures about 9 inches in diameter. **15th through 18th rnd:** Omitting increases, work 2 rnds with Rose and 2 rnds with White. Drop White, attach Deep Rose. **19th rnd:** With Deep Rose ch 1, sc in each sc, decreasing 10 sc evenly spaced around—to dec 1 sc, *draw up a loop in each of the next 2 sc, yarn over and draw through all 3 loops on hook*—60 sc. Join. **20th rnd:** With Deep Rose repeat 12th rnd. Break off Deep Rose, pick up White. **21st rnd:** With White ch 1, being careful decreases do not fall over previous decreases, sc in each sc, decreasing 5 sc evenly spaced around—55 sc. Join. **22nd rnd:** Ch 1, sc in each sc around. Join. Break off White, attach Green. **Next 2 rnds:** With Green work as for 21st and 22nd rnds—50 sc. Break off and fasten.

POMPON . . . Cut 2 cardboard circles, each 4 inches in diameter. Cut a hole 1 inch in diameter in center of each circle. Cut 2 yards of each color. Place cardboard circles together, and holding the 4 strands of yarn (one strand

of each color) together, wind around the double circles, drawing yarn through center opening and over edge until center hole is filled. Cut yarn around outer edge between the 2 circles. Cut a ½-yard length of yarn, slip between the 2 cardboard circles and tie securely around strands of Pompon. Remove cardboard and trim ends evenly. Sew to center top as shown.

2795 . . . Materials: Knitting Worsted (3½-oz. skeins), 2 skeins . . . Aluminum or Plastic Crochet Hook F-5.

GAUGE: 5 star sts make 2 inches.

Starting at flap edge, make a chain about 15 inches long (5 ch sts to 1 inch). **1st row:** Sc (loosely) in 2nd ch from hook and in each ch across until row measures 12 inches. Cut off remaining chain. Ch 3, turn. **2nd row:** Insert hook in 2nd ch and pull loop through, insert hook in next ch and pull loop through, (insert

2795

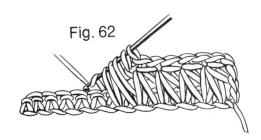

Fig. 62

hook at base of next sc and pull loop through) twice; yarn over and draw through all loops on hook, ch 1 to fasten (star st made—Fig. 62). * Insert hook in fastening ch and pull loop through, insert hook in last loop of last star st and pull loop through, insert hook where last loop of last star st was made and pull loop through, insert hook at base of next sc and pull loop through, yarn over and draw loop through all loops on hook, ch 1 to fasten (another star st made). Repeat from * across. Ch 1 more, turn. **3rd row:** Sc in fastening ch of each star st across, sc in top of turning chain. Ch 3, turn. Repeat 2nd and 3rd rows alternately until piece measures 21 inches, ending with the 3rd row. Break off.

GUSSET (Make 2) . . . Starting at bottom, ch 2. **1st rnd:** 7 sc in 2nd ch from hook. Sl st in 1st sc. **2nd rnd:** 2 sc in each sc around. Join. Work is now done in rows. **1st row:** Ch 24 (to measure 6 inches). Sc in 2nd ch from hook and in each ch across, sc in each sc around circular piece, increasing as necessary to keep work flat. Then work along opposite side of starting chain, making sc in each ch across. Turn. **2nd row:** Sl st in next 10 sc, sc in each sc across to within last 10 sc, increasing at curved end as before. Sl st in last 10 sc. Break off.

Block bag piece to measure 12 x 21 inches. Cut lining to correspond with crocheted pieces and line. Fold bag and sew Gussets in place. Trim flap as desired. Fasten with snap fasteners.

A-810 . . . Materials: Coats & Clark's O.N.T. Rug Yarn *(70-yard skeins), 4 skeins of No. 60 Straw . . . Crochet Hook, Size J . . . ½ yard of brass chain; 2 brass rings; 2 brass buttons . . . ⅓ yard beige felt for dining.*

GAUGE: 13 sts make 4 inches; 5 rnds make 2 inches.

POCKET (Make 2) . . . Starting at base ch 31, having 3 ch sts to 1 inch. **1st rnd:** Make 2 sc in 2nd ch from hook, sc in next ch and in each ch across to within last ch, 3 sc in last ch for corner; working along opposite side of starting chain, sc in each ch across, ending with sc in same ch where first 2 sc were made. Join with sl st to first sc. **2nd rnd:** Ch 1, 2 sc in each of first 2 sc, sc in each sc around, making 2 sc in each of the 3 sc at opposite corner and ending with 2 sc in last sc. Join to first sc. **3rd rnd:** Ch 1, *working in* back *loop only of each sc, draw up a loop in each of first 2 sc, yarn over and draw through all 3 loops on hook—joint sc made;* * ch 1, make a joint sc as before over next 2 sc. Repeat from * around. Join to first joint sc. **4th rnd:** Ch 1, *insert hook through* both *loops of first joint sc and draw up a loop, insert hook in* back *loop of next ch and draw up a loop, yarn over and draw through all 3 loops on hook—joint sc made* over joint sc and next ch; * ch 1, joint sc over next joint sc and following ch. Repeat from * around to within last joint sc, ch 1, make a joint sc through both loops of last joint sc and in back loop of next sl st. Join to first joint sc. Repeat 4th rnd 15 times more. Turn at end of last rnd. **Next rnd:** Sl st in each joint sc and in each ch around. Join. Break off and fasten.

BUTTONHOLE TAB . . . Starting at center, ch 24. **1st row:** Sl st in 10th ch from hook for buttonhole, ch 4, skip next 4 ch, sl st in next ch for another buttonhole, sl st in each remaining ch. Now work in rnds as follows: **1st rnd:** Working along opposite side of starting chain and sts of 1st row, make 3 sc in first ch, sc in each of next 17 ch, 2 sc in each of next 3 ch, sc in next 3 ch, sc in next sl st, sc in next 4 ch, sc in next 9 sl sts, 3 sc in next sl st. Join with sl st to first sc. **2nd rnd:** Ch 1, sc in joining, 3 sc in next sc, sc in next 19 sc, 2 sc in next sc, (sc in next sc, 2 sc in next sc) twice; sc in next 18 sc, 3 sc in next sc, sc in next sc. Join. Break off and fasten.

Sew narrow straight edge to one pocket, ½ inch down from top edge.

LINING . . . Cut a piece of felt, 10½ x 17 inches. Fold piece so that narrow edges meet. Sew a ¼-inch seam along both side edges. Insert lining in pocket and sew in place. Make lining for second pocket in same way.

Having buttonhole tab on the outside, sew the 2 adjacent top edges of pockets together. Sew 2 adjacent bottom corners of pockets together. Sew a ring to each end of joined pockets at top edge. Open last link at both ends of chain and attach to rings. Sew 2 buttons in place.

B-709 . . . Materials: COATS & CLARK'S RED HEART KNITTING WORSTED, 4-Ply ("Tangle-Proof" Pull-Out Skeins), 4 ounces of any color . . . Crochet Hook Size H . . . ¾ yard grosgrain ribbon, ¾ inch wide.

GAUGE: 4 sc make 1 inch; 9 rnds make 2 inches.

CROWN . . . Starting at center top, ch 4. Join with sl st to form ring. **1st rnd:** Make 6 sc in ring. Do not join rnds but carry a contrasting color thread up between last and first sts of every rnd to indicate beg of rnds. **2nd rnd:** * Sc in next sc of previous rnd, *insert hook in ring and draw up a loop to height of rnd, yarn over and complete an sc*—long sc made. Repeat from * around—12 sts. **3rd and all uneven rnds unless otherwise stated:** Sc in each st around. **4th rnd:** * Sc in next 2 sc of previous rnd, *insert hook through center of next long sc 1 rnd below and draw up loop to height of rnd, yarn over and complete an sc*—long sc

through long sc made. Repeat from * around—18 sts. **6th rnd:** * Sc in next 2 sc of previous rnd, *2 sc in next sc*—1 sc increased; long sc through next long sc. Repeat from * around—30 sts. **8th rnd:** * Sc in next 5 sc of previous rnd, long sc through next long sc. Repeat from * around—36 sts. **10th rnd:** * Sc in next 6 sc of previous rnd, long sc through next long sc. Repeat from * around—42 sts. **12th rnd:** * Sc in next 7 sc of previous rnd, long sc through next long sc. Repeat from * around—48 sts. **14th rnd:** * Sc in next 7 sc of previous rnd, inc 1 sc in next sc, long sc through next long sc. Repeat from * around—60 sts. **16th rnd:** * Sc in next 10 sc of previous rnd, long sc through next long sc. Repeat from * around—66 sts. **18th, 20th, and 22nd rnds:** Work as for 10th rnd, having 1 sc more between long sc's on each rnd. There are 84 sts on 22nd rnd. **23rd rnd:** * Sc in next 12 sts, *draw up a loop in each of next 2 sts, yarn over and draw through all loops on hook*—1 sc decreased. Repeat from * around—78 sts. **24th rnd:** * Sc in next 13 sc, long sc through next long sc. Repeat from * around—84 sts. **25th rnd:** * Dec 1 sc over next 2 sc, sc in next 12 sts. Repeat from * around—78 sts. **26th rnd:** Repeat 24th rnd—84 sts. Repeat last 4 rnds until total length is about 6½ inches, ending with an even-numbered rnd.

BRIM . . . 1st rnd—First Half of Rnd: Sl st in **front** loop of each st around. **Second Half of Rnd:** In **back** loop of each st on same rnd, * inc in next st, sc in next st. Repeat from * around—126 sts. **2nd rnd:** Working through **both** loops of each sc, sc in each sc around. **3rd rnd:** * Sc in next 20 sc, inc in next sc. Repeat from * around—6 sc increased. **4th rnd:** Repeat 2nd rnd. **5th rnd:** Being careful that incs do not fall over incs of previous rnd, sc in each sc around, increasing 6 sc evenly spaced. Repeat 2nd and 5th rnds alternately until there are 156 sc on rnd, ending with 2nd rnd. Brim measures about 2¾ inches. **Next rnd:** Ch 1, * **working from left to right,** insert hook in next sc to the **right** and complete an sc. Repeat from * around. Join, break off, and fasten.

Block. Sew ribbon in place on wrong side at base of crown for headband, adjusting to fit head size.

2785 . . . Materials: PEARL COTTON, *Size 5, 15 balls . . . Plastic Crochet Hook No. 4.*

GAUGE: 4 sts make 1 inch; 4½ rnds make 1 inch.

Use 3 threads throughout.

BAG PIECE . . . Starting at center, ch 4. Join with sl st. **1st rnd:** 8 sc in ring. **2nd rnd:** (3 sc in next sc, sc in next sc) 4 times. **3rd to 32nd rnds incl:** (Sc in each sc to center sc of next 3-sc group, 3 sc in center sc) 4 times; sc in each sc to end of rnd. At end of 32nd rnd, sl st in next sc. Break off.

HANDLE . . . Starting at center, ch 70. **1st rnd:** 3 sc in 2nd ch from hook, sc in each ch across, 3 sc in last ch; working along opposite side of starting chain, make sc in each ch across. **2nd rnd:** 2 sc in next 3 sc, sc in each sc to next 3-sc group, 2 sc in next 3 sc, sc in each sc to end of rnd. **3rd rnd:** Sc in each sc around. Sl st in next sc. Break off.

BUTTON LOOP TAB . . . Starting at center of one button loop, ch 9. Join with sl st, ch 16,

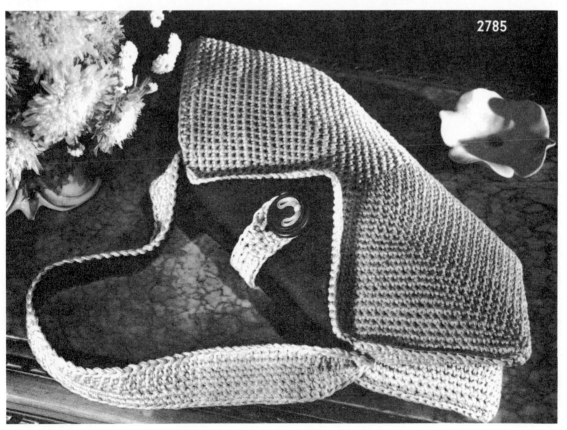

2785

sl st in 9th ch from hook. **1st rnd:** Sc in each ch around, working on both sides of center chain. **2nd rnd:** Sc in each sc around. Sl st in next sc. Break off.

Cut lining to correspond with Bag Piece and sew in place. Fold two diagonal points together and pin (top of bag). Measure 5 inches from points at top on each side. Pin free corners to each pin mark. Join sides by working sc through both thicknesses. Remove pins and turn top points back for flaps. Sew a **button on each flap and fasten Button Loop** Tab. Sew on Handle.

A-818 . . . Materials: COATS & CLARK'S O.N.T. RUG YARN *(70-yard skeins), 3 skeins of No. 138 Rusticana, 2 skeins of No. 139 Spring Green . . . Crochet Hook Size H . . . 4 buttons, 2 brass rings.*

GAUGE: 3 sc make 1 inch; 7 rows make 2 inches.

POCKET . . . Starting at lower edge with Green, ch 18. **1st row:** Sc in 2nd ch from hook and in each ch across—17 sc. Ch 1, turn. **2nd row:** Sc in each sc across. Ch 1, turn. Repeat 2nd row until 16 rows have been completed. Break off and fasten. Lay piece aside to be used later.

FRONT . . . Starting at lower edge, with Rusticana ch 35, drop Rusticana, (with Green, yarn over and draw through loop on hook) twice. **1st row—wrong side:** Insert hook in 2nd ch from hook and draw loop through, drop Green to front of work, pick up Rusticana, yarn over and draw through both loops on hook—color changed in first sc; with Rusticana, sc in each remaining ch across—36 sc. Ch 1, turn. **2nd row:** Sc in each sc across to within last 2 Rusticana sc, draw up a loop in next sc, drop Rusticana to back of work, pick up Green, yarn over and draw through both loops on hook—**always change color in this way;** with Green, sc in next 2 sc. Ch 1, turn. **3rd row:** With Green, sc in each Green sc, change color in next Rusticana sc and drop Green to front of work, with Rusticana sc in each remaining sc. Ch 1, turn. **4th row:** With Rusticana sc in each sc across to within last 2 Rusticana sc, change color in next sc and drop Rusticana to

back of work, with Green sc in each remaining sc. Ch 1, turn. Repeat 3rd and 4th rows alternately until there are 18 sc of each color. **Next row:** With Green sc in each Green sc, then continuing with Green, sc in each sc worked on last row of Pocket. Ch 1, turn. Continue to work over these 35 sc for 15 more rows. Drop Green. Now work over the Rusticana section as follows: **Next row:** Pick up Rusticana, *draw up a loop in each of first 2 sc, yarn over and draw through all loops on hook—1 sc decreased;* sc in each remaining sc. Ch 1, turn. **Following row:** Sc in each sc across to within last 2 Rusticana sc, dec 1 sc over the last 2 sc. Ch 1, turn. Repeat last 2 rows until 10 sc remain. Last st worked on last row is inner edge. Ch 10 for button loop, turn, then sl st in first ch of ch-10. **Next row:** Dec first sc, sc in each remaining sc. Ch 1, turn. Continue as before, decreasing 1 sc at inner edge on every row until 2 sc remain. Drop Rusticana loop, pick up Green at other end and ch 1, turn. **Next row:** Sc in each sc across to within last sc of Green section, draw up a loop in next sc, drop Green, pick up Rusticana, and draw dropped Rusticana loop through both loops on hook, with Rusticana draw up a loop in each of next 2 Rusticana sc, drop Rusticana, pick up Green and draw through all loops on hook. Ch 1, turn. **Following row:** Sc in each sc across. Break off and fasten.

BACK . . . Reversing colors, work same as for Pocket and Front.

BASE . . . Starting at center with Rusticana, ch 32. **1st rnd:** 2 sc in 2nd ch from hook, sc in each ch across to within last ch, 3 sc in last ch; working along opposite side of starting chain, sc in each ch, ending with sc in same ch where first 2 sc were made. Join with sl st to first sc. **2nd and 3rd rnds:** Ch 1, 2 sc in first sc, sc in each sc around, making 3 sc in center sc of the 3-sc group at opposite end and ending with 1 sc in same st where first 2 sc were made. Join. Break off and fasten.

SHOULDER STRAP . . . With Rusticana ch 125, having 3 ch sts to 1 inch. **1st row:** Sc in 2nd ch from hook and in each ch across. Ch 1, turn. **2nd row:** Sc in each sc across to within last 5 sc, ch 3 for buttonhole, skip next 3 sc, sc in last 2 sc. Ch 1, turn. **3rd row:** Sc in first 2 sc, sc in next 3 ch, sc in next sc and in each sc across. Break off and fasten.

Press pieces through a damp cloth. Sew the 3 edges of each pocket in place. Sew side seams. Sew base to lower edge of front and back. Sew 1 ring to top of each side seam. Draw shoulder strap through rings. Leaving buttonhole end free, sew opposite end in place 1 inch up from ring. Sew 1 button to strap 2 inches up from ring; sew 1 button at opposite end of strap 4 inches from buttonhole. Strap may be shortened by buttoning to other button. Sew a button opposite button loop on front and back.

2794 . . . Materials: KNITTING WORSTED (3½-ounce balls), 2 balls of Yellow . . . Aluminum or Plastic Crochet Hook F-5.

GAUGE: Side—4½ sc make 1 inch; 4 rows make 1 inch.

2794

BOTTOM . . . Chain 45 to measure 8½ inches. **1st row:** Sc in 2nd ch from hook and in each ch across. Ch 1, turn. **2nd to 12th rows incl:** Sc in each sc across. Ch 1, turn.

SIDE . . . **1st rnd:** Make sc in each sc around all edges of Bottom. **2nd rnd:** Sc in back loop of each sc around. Sl st in 1st sc. Repeat the 2nd rnd until Side measures 7 inches. Break off.

TRIMMING . . . With top of bag facing, attach yarn to 1st free loop on the 4th rnd of Side (counting from the Bottom), * ch 5, (yarn over hook, insert hook in 4th ch from hook and draw loop through) 3 times; yarn over hook (Fig. 63) and draw through all

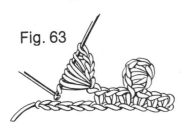

Fig. 63

loops on hook; sl st in next ch, sc in free loop of next 3 sc. Repeat from * around. Join and break off. Work 3 more rows of Trimming, spacing Trimming 4 rows apart.

BUTTON (Make 2) . . . **1st rnd:** Ch 2, make 6 sc in 2nd ch from hook. **2nd rnd:** Sc in each sc around. Break off.

Line bag with felt, inserting a cardboard at bottom. Fold Sides in at top, leaving 5 inches free at center of each Side. Insert buttons in crocheted pieces and sew at each end of one Side at top. Make two ch-9 loops opposite buttons. Cover three-quarters of 2 handles closely with sc. Sew handles in place.

2726 . . . Materials: Knit-Cro-Sheen, *5 balls* . . . *Steel Crochet Hook No. 5.*

GAUGE: Each motif measures about 1¾ inches square.

Use thread double throughout.

MOTIF . . . Ch 6. Join with sl st to form ring. **1st rnd:** Ch 3, 19 dc in ring. Sl st in top of ch-3. Ch 1, turn. **2nd rnd:** Sc in back loop of each dc around. Sl st in 1st sc. Ch 1, turn. **3rd rnd:** Sl st in back loop of st where sl st was made on 1st rnd, ch 3, in same place make dc, ch 3 and 2 dc, * dc in free loop of each of

next 4 sts on 1st rnd, in next free loop make 2 dc, ch 3 and 2 dc. Repeat from * around, ending with sl st in top st of starting ch-3. Ch 1, turn. **4th rnd:** Sc in back loop of each st around. Sl st in 1st sc. Break off. Make 80 motifs in all.

Sew motifs together, as shown on chart, catching only the free loop of sts on 3rd rnd. Cut 2 pieces of lining material same as crocheted piece. Cut crinoline ¼ inch smaller all around. Face crinoline with one piece of lining material. Cover other side of crinoline with lining material, turning in all edges and sewing with slip sts all around. Sew lining to wrong side of crocheted piece. Fold piece in half and pin top edges together. Fold in 4 motifs at each end to form gussets (see dotted lines on chart). Sew side edges. Sew zipper along opening.

LOOP . . . **1st row:** Ch 5. Sc in 2nd ch from hook and in next 3 ch. Ch 1, turn. **2nd row:** Sc in each sc across. Repeat 2nd row until piece measures 5 inches. Break off. Sew long edges together. Sew ends together, forming a loop. Sew this end of loop to zipper pull. Make 2 motifs and sew them together back to back. Sew one corner of joined motifs to free end of loop.

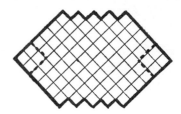

6002

To fit all sizes.

Materials: Knitting Worsted (*4-ounce skein*), *1 skein of Eggshell* . . . *Aluminum or Plastic Crochet Hook Size I-9* . . . *1½ yards round elastic.*

GAUGE: 7 sc make 2 inches; 4 rnds make 1 inch.

CROWN . . . Start at center top, ch 4. Join with sl st to form ring. **1st rnd:** Make 6 sc in ring. Join with sl st to first sc. **2nd rnd:** Ch 1,

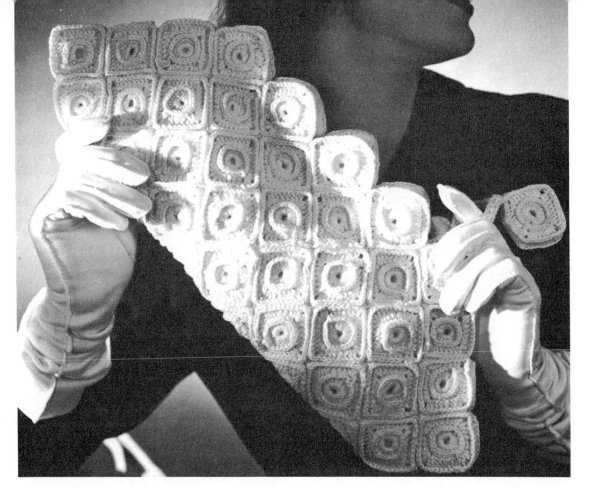

2 sc in same sc as joining, 2 sc in each sc around. Join. **3rd rnd:** Ch 1, sc in same sc as joining, * *2 sc in next sc—*inc **made;** sc in next sc. Repeat from * around, ending with 2 sc in last sc. Join—6 sc increased. **4th rnd:** Ch 1, sc in same sc as joining, increasing 6 sc evenly spaced around, sc in each sc. Join—24 sc. **5th through 10th rnds:** Being careful not to have incs fall directly over incs of previous rnd, repeat 4th rnd 6 times—60 sc. **11th rnd:** Ch 1, sc in same sc as joining, sc in each sc around. Join. Repeat last rnd until Crown measures 6½ inches from starting ring.

BRIM . . . 1st rnd: Repeat 4th rnd of Crown —66 sc: **2nd rnd:** Ch 1, sc in same sc as joining, sc in each sc. Join. Repeat last 2 rnds alternately 3 more times—84 sc on last rnd. Repeat 2nd rnd of Brim twice. **Last rnd:** Work from left to right, * insert hook in next sc to the right and complete an sc; repeat from * around. Join with sl st to first sc. Break off and fasten.

Double elastic and draw through last rnd of Crown, adjust to fit and sew ends together.

2796 . . . Materials: PEARL COTTON, *Size 5, 14 balls of Black . . . Steel Crochet Hook No. 5.*

Use thread double throughout.

GAUGE: 2 patterns make 2¼ inches.

Starting at top, make a chain about 10 inches long (5 ch sts to 1 inch). **1st row:** In 5th ch from hook make 4 tr, ch 1 and 4 tr (a shell); * skip 3 ch, dc in next ch, skip 3 ch, in next ch make 4 tr, ch 1 and 4 tr. Repeat from * across until row measures 9 inches, ending with 4 tr (half shell). Cut off remaining chain. Turn. **2nd row:** * Skip the half shell, in sp between 2nd and 3rd tr's of next shell make 4 tr. Now ch 1 and, working over 4 tr just completed, make 4 tr between 2nd and 3rd tr's of half shell just skipped; sc in next ch-1 sp (Fig. 64). Repeat from * across, ending with half shell in last half of last shell. Turn. Repeat the 2nd row until piece measures 16 inches in all. Break off.

GUSSET (Make 2) . . . Starting at bottom, ch 6. **1st row:** Sc in 2nd ch from hook and in each ch across. Ch 1, turn. **2nd row:** 2 sc in 1st sc (an inc), sc in each sc across. Ch 1, turn.

Repeat the 2nd row until there are 17 sc in row. Work 5 rows straight. **Next row:** Dec 1 sc —*to dec 1 sc, work off 2 sc as 1 sc*—sc in each sc across. Ch 1, turn. Repeat the last row until 5 sts remain. Break off. Sew Gussets in place, leaving a 3½ inch flap. With 4 strands, make a 2-inch chain loop and sew to center of flap. Fasten with a rhinestone button.

HANDLE . . . Ch 6. **1st row:** Sc in 2nd ch from hook and in each ch across. Ch 1, turn. **2nd row:** Sc in each sc across. Ch 1, turn. Repeat the 2nd row until piece measures 9 inches. Join Handle piece to form ring.

Line Bag and Handle with buckram and lining material and sew 4 inches of Handle to center back of Bag.

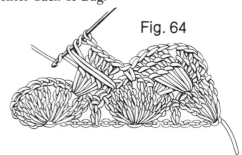

Fig. 64

B-713 . . . Materials: COATS & CLARK'S RED HEART WINTUK SPORT YARN, 2-Ply (2-ounce "Tangle-Proof" Pull-Out Skeins), 2 ounces of any color . . . Crochet Hook Size H . . . Elastic thread.

GAUGE: 4 sts make 1 inch; 3 rnds make 1 inch.

Note: The wrong side of work is the right side of the beret.

Starting at center top, ch 4. Join with sl st to form ring. **1st rnd:** Ch 1, in ring make (sc and tr) 4 times—each tr forms a popcorn—8 sts. Do not join rnds but carry a contrasting color thread up between last and first sts of each rnd to indicate beg of rnds (to be used later for marker). **2nd rnd:** Make sc and tr in each st around—16 sts. **3rd rnd:** Repeat 2nd rnd—32 sts. **4th rnd:** *In next sc make sc and tr*—one st **increased**; sc in next tr, tr in next sc, sc in next tr, (place a different color thread for marker between last st and next st; inc in next st as before, sc in next tr, tr in next sc, sc in next tr) 7 times—40 sts. **Always carry markers up. 5th rnd:** (Inc in next st, work in pattern of sc in next tr, tr in next sc alternately to next marker) 8 times. **6th rnd:** (Inc in next st, work in pattern of sc in next tr, tr in next sc alternately to within one st before next marker, sc in next tr) 8 times. **7th through 14th rnds:** Repeat 5th and 6th rnds alternately. There are 120 sts on 14th rnd. **15th rnd:** Repeat 5th rnd to within last st, in last st make tr and sc—129 sts. Remove all but first marker. **16th rnd:** Tr in next sc, * sc in next tr, tr in next sc. Repeat from * around. **17th rnd:** Sc in next tr, * tr in next sc, sc in next tr. Repeat from * around. **18th rnd:** Repeat 16th rnd. **19th rnd:** Repeat 17th rnd to within last st—this is now end of rnd. Move marker back one stitch. Now work dec rnds as follows: **1st dec rnd:** (*Draw up a loop in each of next tr, following sc and next tr; yarn over and draw through all 4 loops on hook*—2 sts decreased; work in pattern over next 13 sts, place a different color thread for marker) 7 times; dec 2 sts over next 3 sts as before, work in pattern over next 14 sts—113 sts. **2nd dec rnd:** (Dec 2 sts over next 3 sts as before, work in pattern to next marker) 8 times. **Next 2 rnds:** Repeat 2nd dec rnd. There are 65 sts on last rnd. Sl st in next st. Turn. **Following rnd:** With right side facing and **working from left to right,** * insert hook in next st to the **right** and complete an sc. Repeat from * around. Join to first sc. Break off and fasten.

Draw elastic thread through last rnd, adjusting to fit head size.

CHAPTER FOUR

Blouses and Vests

IT's A TWOSOME everywhere you look. In the deluxe magazines, on well-dressed women, morning, noon, and night, the two-are-better-than-one idea has become firmly established as America's favorite fashion. Youthful and wearable, the skirt-plus-top makes a versatile team, is blessed with a keen social sense, a knack for turning you out perfectly dressed for any occasion.

Take no more than three skirts—say a tweed, a gray flannel, and a slim black knit—to give you the basis for a town, country, and party-going wardrobe. Just add a selection of becoming, brightly styled vests and blouses: It makes wonderful figuring both ways—from the point of view of finance **and** fit.

In the chapter that follows you'll find a highly compatible collection that we think is **tops**—from vests for daytime wear to a cocktail blouse for gala PM's.

5853

Directions are given for Small (6-8) Size. Changes for Medium (10-12) and Large (14-16) Sizes are in parentheses.

Materials: COATS & CLARK'S RED HEART KNITTING WORSTED, 4 Ply ("Tangle-Proof" Pull-Out Skeins), 8 (10, 11) ounces of No. 360 Wood Brown, 2 ounces of No. 255 Burnt Orange, and 1 ounce each of No. 243 Mid Orange and No. 330 Sandstone for each size . . . Crochet Hook Size G.

GAUGE: 1 shell makes 1¼ inches; 3 rows make 2 inches.

BLOCKING MEASUREMENTS

Sizes	Small (6-8)	Medium (10-12)	Large (14-16)
Body Bust Size (In Inches)	30½-31½	32½-34	36-38
Actual Crocheting Measurements			
Bust	32½	35	39
Width across back at underarm	16¼	17½	19
Width across front at underarm	16¼	17½	20
Length from shoulder to lower edge (excluding border)	17	18	19½
Length of side seam (excluding borders)	10	10½	11

5853

TOP

BACK . . . Starting at lower edge with Brown, ch 56 (60, 64) to measure 17 (18¼, 19¾) inches. **1st row (right side):** In 6th ch from hook make *2 dc, ch 1 and 2 dc*—**first shell made;** * skip next 3 ch, in next ch make *2 dc, ch 1 and 2 dc*—**shell made.** Repeat from * across to within last 2 ch, skip next ch, dc in last ch. There are 13 (14, 15) shells and 1 dc at each end of row, counting chain at beg of row as 1 dc. Ch 3, turn. **2nd row:** * *In ch-1 sp of next shell make 2 dc, ch 1 and 2 dc*—**shell over shell made.** Repeat from * across, ending with dc in top of turning chain. Ch 3, turn. Repeat 2nd row for pattern. Work in pattern until total length is 10 (10½, 11) inches. Do not ch 3 at end of last row. Turn.

Armhole Shaping: 1st row: Sl st in each of first 3 dc, in ch st and in each of next 2 dc; sc between last dc used and next dc, ch 3, * shell over shell. Repeat from * across to within last shell, dc in space between last shell used and next shell. There are 11 (12, 13) shells. Ch 3, turn. Work in pattern over these sts until length is about 6½ (7, 8) inches from first row of armhole shaping. Ch 3, turn.

Neck and Shoulder Shaping: 1st row: Work in pattern until 3 (3, 4) shells have been completed; dc in ch-1 sp of next shell; do not work over remaining sts. Ch 4, turn. **2nd row:** Shell over next 1 (1, 2) shells, in ch-1 sp of next shell make 2 h dc, ch 1 and 2 sc; sl st in next sp between shells. Break off and fasten. **Next row:** Skip the center 3 (4, 3) shells on last row made before neck and shoulder shaping for center back of neck; attach Brown to ch-1 sp on next shell, ch 3, make shell over each remaining shell, dc in top of turning chain. Do not ch 3 at end of last row. Turn. **Following row:** Sl st in each of first 6 sts (including ch st), in next shell make 2 sc, ch 1 and 2 h dc, shell over next 1 (1, 2) shells, tr in top of ch-3. Break off and fasten.

FRONT . . . Starting at lower edge with Brown, ch 56 (60, 68) to measure 17 (18¼, 20¾) inches. **1st row:** Work same as for 1st row of Back. There are 13 (14, 16) shells. Ch 3, turn. Continue in pattern as for Back until total length is 10 (10½, 11) inches. Do not ch 3 at end of last row. Turn.

Armhole Shaping: 1st row: Work same as for 1st row of Back Armhole Shaping—11 (12, 14)

shells remain. **For Large Size only:** Turn. **2nd row:** Sl st in each of first 3 dc, sl st in next ch-1 sp, ch 3, (make shell over next shell) 12 times; dc in sp of last shell. **For All Sizes:** Ch 3, turn. Work 1 row in pattern. Ch 3, turn. There are 11 (12, 12) shells.

Neck Shaping: 1st row: Work in pattern until 3 (3, 4) shells have been completed; **for Small and Medium Sizes only,** dc in ch-1 sp of next shell; **for Large Size Only,** dc between last shell used and next shell. For All Sizes, ch 3, turn. Work in pattern over these 3 (3, 4) shells until length is about 7 (7½, 8) inches from first row of armhole shaping, ending at armhole edge. Turn.

Shoulder Shaping: Next row: Sl st in each of first 6 sts (including ch st), in next shell make 2 sc, ch 1 and 2 h dc, complete row in pattern. Break off and fasten. Skip next 3 (4, 4) shells on last row made before neck shaping for center front of neck; **for Small and Medium Sizes only,** attach yarn to ch-1 sp of next shell; **for Large Size only,** attach yarn between last shell used and next shell; **for All Sizes,** ch 3. Complete to correspond with opposite side, reversing shaping.

Block to measurements. Sew side and shoulder seams.

Bottom Border: With right side facing, attach Brown to lower end of a side seam. **1st rnd:** Working along opposite side of starting chain make sc in next sp, * sc in same ch st where next shell of first row was made, 3 sc in next sp between shells. Repeat from * around entire lower edge, ending with 2 sc in last sp. Join with sl st to first sc. Break off and fasten. Attach Mid Orange to same sc as joining. **2nd rnd:** With Mid Orange, ch 1, sc in same sc where yarn was attached, sc in each sc around. Join. Break off and fasten. **3rd rnd:** With Burnt Orange, repeat 2nd rnd. Break off and fasten. **4th rnd:** With Sandstone, repeat 2nd rnd. Break off and fasten.

Armhole Border: With right side facing, attach Brown to top end of a side seam. **1st rnd:** Ch 1, sc in same place where yarn was attached, sc evenly along entire armhole edge. Join to first sc. Break off and fasten. **Next 3 rnds:** Repeat 2nd, 3rd, and 4th rnds of Bottom Border.

Neck Border: 1st rnd: With right side facing, attach Brown to a shoulder seam, ch 1, sc in same place, sc evenly along entire neck edge, making 1 sc at each corner. Join. Break off and fasten. **Mark each corner sc. 2nd rnd:** Attach

Mid Orange to same sc as joining, ch 1, sc in same sc, * sc in each sc to within one sc before next corner st, *draw up a loop in each of next 3 sts, yarn over hook and draw through all 4 loops on hook—2 sc decreased at corner.* Repeat from * 3 more times; sc in each remaining sc. Join. Break off and fasten. **3rd rnd:** With Burnt Orange, repeat last rnd. Break off and fasten. **4th rnd:** With Sandstone, repeat same rnd. Break off and fasten.

HAT

CROWN . . . First Motif: Starting at center with Sandstone, ch 4. Joint with sl st to form ring. **1st rnd:** Ch 3, 11 dc in ring. Join with sl st to top of ch-3. Break off and fasten. **2nd rnd:** Attach Mid Orange to any dc on first rnd. Ch 1, sc in same st where yarn was attached, * ch 5, skip next dc, sc in next dc. Repeat from * around, ending with ch 5, skip last dc. Join with sl st to first sc. There are 6 ch-5 loops. **3rd rnd:** * In next ch-5 loop make *2 sc, 1 h dc, 2 dc, 1 h dc, and 2 sc*—shell made. Repeat from * around. Join. Break off and fasten. This is center motif.

Second Motif: Work same as for First Motif until first rnd has been completed. **2nd rnd:** Attach Burnt Orange to same sc as joining and with Burnt Orange repeat 2nd rnd of First Motif. **3rd rnd:** In next ch-5 loop make 2 sc and h dc; holding First Motif in back of work with wrong side facing, *sl st in first h dc on any shell on First Motif, dc in same loop on Second Motif, (sl st in next dc on First Motif, dc in same loop on Second Motif) twice; sl st in next h dc on First Motif*—motifs joined: make h dc and 2 sc in same loop on Second Motif to complete shell; in each remaining loop make 2 sc, h dc, 2 dc, h dc, and 2 sc. Join. Break off and fasten.

Third Motif: Using Burnt Orange instead of Mid Orange, work same as for First Motif until 2nd rnd has been completed. **3rd rnd:** In next loop make 2 sc and h dc, joining to shell preceding last joining of motifs, join to First Motif same as Second Motif was joined, make h dc and 2 sc in same loop on motif in work to complete shell, * 2 sc and h dc in next loop; joining as before, join to next free shell on last motif completed; h dc and 2 sc in same loop to complete shell. Repeat from * once more. Complete rnd as for Second Motif. Break off and fasten. Make and join 4 more motifs same as Third Motif, joining last motif to corre-

sponding shells on Second Motif. Now work as follows; **1st rnd:** Attach Brown to 2nd dc on free shell of any motif, ch 1, sc in same place where yarn was attached, * ch 4, sc in 2nd sc on next shell of same motif (before joining), ch 4, sc in first sc of next shell (after joining) on next motif; ch 4, sc in 2nd dc on next shell of same motif. Repeat from * around, ending with ch 4. Join with sl st to first sc—18 loops. Hereafter do not join rnds but carry a contrasting thread up between last and first sts of each rnd to indicate beg of rnds. **2nd rnd:** * Make 4 sc in next loop, 5 sc in next loop. Repeat from * around, ending with 4 sc in each of last 2 loops—80 sc. **3rd rnd:** Sc in each sc around. Repeat last rnd until length is 2 inches from edge of motifs. Break off Brown and fasten. **Next rnd:** Attach Mid Orange to last sc made and sc in each sc around. Break off and fasten. Working same as for last rnd, make one rnd in Burnt Orange and one rnd in Sandstone.

BRIM . . . Attach Brown to last sc made. **1st rnd:** * Sc in each of next 9 sc, *2 sc in next sc*—inc made. Repeat from * around—8 sc increased. **2nd rnd:** Sc in each sc around. **3rd rnd:** Increasing 8 sc evenly spaced around, sc in each sc around. Repeat 2nd and 3rd rnds alternately until there are 120 sc on rnd, then repeat 2nd rnd once more. **Next rnd:** Working over sts of last rnd, sc in each sc on 2nd rnd below. **Last rnd:** Sl st in each sc of last round. Join to first sl st. Break off and fasten.

4336

Directions are for Small Size (8-10). Changes for Medium (12-14) and Large (16-18) sizes are in parentheses.

Materials: COATS & CLARK'S SOCK AND SWEATER YARN, 3 Ply (2-ounce "Tangle-Proof" Pull-Out Skeins), 3 skeins for Small Size, 4 skeins for Medium or Large . . . Crochet Hook Size G.

GAUGE: 1 pattern makes 1½ inches; 10 rows make 3 inches.

—97 (105, 113) sc. Ch 1, turn. **2nd row:** Sc in first sc, * skip 3 sc, *dc in next sc, (ch 1, dc in same sc) 3 times*—**fan made;** skip 3 sc, sc in next sc. Repeat from * across—12 (13, 14) fans. Ch 4, turn. **3rd row:** In first sc make *dc, ch 1 and dc*—**½ fan made;** * sc in center ch-1 sp of next fan, fan in next sc. Repeat from * across, ending with *dc, (ch 1 and dc) twice in last sc*—**½ fan made.** Ch 1, turn. **4th row:** Sc in first ch-1 sp, * fan in next sc, sc in center sp of next fan. Repeat from * across, ending with sc in turning chain sp. Ch 4, turn. Repeat 3rd and 4th rows for pattern. Work even in pattern until piece measures 14 (14½, 15) inches, ending with 4th row of pattern. At end of last row, ch 1, turn.

Armhole Shaping: Next row: Sl st to center of first fan, sc in center sp of same fan, work in pattern across, ending with sc in center sp of last fan. Ch 1, turn—½ fan decreased at each edge. Repeat last row 2 more times—9 (10, 11) fans remain. Ch 4, turn. Work even in pattern until length from first row of Armhole Shaping is 5 (5½, 6) inches, ending with 3rd row of pattern.

Neck Shaping: Next row: Sc in first sp, (fan in next sc, sc in center sp of next fan) 3 (3, 4) times. Ch 1, turn. Dec ½ fan at neck edge on next 2 (2, 3) rows. Work even on remaining 2 (2, 2½) fans for 2 more rows. Break off and fasten. Skip 2 (3, 2) center fans, attach yarn to center sp of next fan and complete other side to correspond, reversing shaping.

FRONT . . . Work same as for Back but working 1 row less on each shoulder.

Block to measurements. Fitting fans between fans, sew shoulder seams. Sew side seams, matching rows.

Neck Edging: 1st rnd: With right side facing and holding in edge to fit, sc evenly around neck edge, join with sl st to first sc. Ch 1, but do not turn. **2nd rnd:** Insert hook in last sc made and draw up a loop, yarn over hook and draw through both loops on hook, * **working from left to right,** insert hook in next sc and draw up a loop, yarn over hook and draw through both loops on hook. Repeat from * around. Join. Break off and fasten.

Holding in edges to fit, finish armholes in same way. With right side facing, attach yarn to a side seam at lower edge and work as for 2nd rnd of Neck Edging around entire lower edge. Break off and fasten.

BLOCKING MEASUREMENTS:

Sizes	Small	Medium	Large
Body Bust Size (In Inches)			
	30-31	32-34	36-38
Actual Crocheting Measurements			
Bust	35	39	43
Width across back or front at underarm			
	17½	19½	21½
Length of side seam			
	14	14½	15
Length from shoulder to lower edge			
	20	21	22

BACK . . . Starting at lower edge, ch 98 (106, 114) to measure 18 (20, 22) inches. **1st row:** Sc in 2nd ch from hook and in each ch across

1269 . . . Materials: KNIT-CRO-SHEEN, *4 balls of Black, 1 ball of Violet, 2 balls each of Rose and Turquoise for Size 12; 5 balls of Black, 1 ball of Violet, 2 balls each of Rose and Turquoise for Sizes 14 and 16 . . . Steel Crochet Hook No. 4 or 5.*

GAUGE: 17 sts make 2 inches; 8 rows (2 dc rows and 6 sc rows) make 1¼ inches.

BLOCKING MEASUREMENTS:

Sizes	12	14	16
Bust	32″	34″	36″
Width across back at underarm	15″	16″	17″
Width across front at underarm	17″	18″	19″
Width across back between shoulders	13″	13½″	14″
Length of side seam	15″	15″	15″
Length from top of shoulder	23″	23½″	23½″
Length of sleeve seam	3¾″	3¾″	3¾″
Width across sleeve at upperarm	12½″	13½″	13½″

BACK . . . With Black make a chain 20 inches long (about 8 ch sts to 1 inch). **1st row:** Dc in 4th ch from hook and in each ch until there are on row (counting first ch-3 as 1 dc)

	136 sts	144 sts	153 sts

and row measures 16″ 17″ 18″ Cut off remaining chain. Ch 1, turn.

2nd and 3rd rows: Sc in each st across. There are on row   136 sts   144 sts   153 sts Ch 1, turn.

4th row: Sc in each st across. Ch 3, turn. **5th row:** Dc in next st and in each st across. There are on row   136 sts   144 sts   153 sts Ch 1, turn.

The last 4 rows (2nd to 5th rows incl) constitute the pattern. Repeat pattern until piece measures 1½ inches. Dec 1 st at end of each row—*to dec an sc, work off 2 sc as 1 sc; to dec a dc, (thread over, insert hook in next st and pull loop through, thread over and draw through 2 loops) twice; thread over and draw through all loops on hook*—until there remain   106 sts   114 sts   123 sts

Work straight until piece measures 8¾ inches in all. Inc 1 st at end of each row until piece measures 10 inches ending with 3rd sc row—*to inc, work 2 sts in 1 st*. Break off Black, attach Violet, and work next 4 rows in pattern, increasing as before. Break off Violet, attach Black, and work next 4 rows in pattern increasing as before. There are on row   **128 sts   136 sts   145 sts**

Break off Black, attach Rose, and work straight until piece measures 15 inches in all, ending with 3rd sc row.

To Shape Armholes: Sl st across 6 sts (thus decreasing 6 sts), work across to last 6 sts. Ch 1, turn (6 more sts decreased). Dec 1 st at both ends of each of the next 3 rows. There remain   **110 sts   118 sts   127 sts**

Break off Rose, attach Turquoise. **On Sizes 14 and 16 only,** continue decreasing 1 st at both ends of each row until there remain   **114 sts   119 sts**

On All Sizes: Work straight until piece measures 3¾ inches from 1st row of armhole shaping, ending with the 3rd sc row. Break off Turquoise, attach Black and work as follows: Work across   **55 sts   57 sts   59 sts** turn, thus starting back opening.

Work straight in pattern over these sts only until piece measures from 1st row of armhole shaping   **7″   7½″   7½″**

To Shape Shoulder: * Starting at armhole edge sl st across 12 sts, finish row and work back. Repeat from * once more. Then, starting at same edge, sl st across   **12 sts   14 sts   14 sts** Finish row and break off.

Attach Black where sts were divided—**on Size 16 only, dec 1 st**—and work to correspond. Break off.

FRONT . . . With Black make a chain 21 inches long (about 8 ch sts to 1 inch). **1st row:** Dc in 4th ch from hook and in each ch until there are on row, counting first ch-3 as 1 dc,   **145 sts   153 sts   162 sts**

Work as for Back until piece measures 2½ inches. Dec 1 st at both ends of each row until there remain   **107 sts   115 sts   124 sts**

1269

Work straight until piece measures 8¾ inches in all. Inc 1 st at both ends of each row until piece measures 10 inches, ending with the 3rd sc row. Break off Black, attach Violet and work next 4 rows in pattern increasing as before. Break off Violet, attach Black and work next 4 rows in pattern, increasing as before. There are on row | 145 sts | 153 sts | 162 sts

Break off Black, attach Rose and work straight until piece measures 15 inches in all ending with 3rd sc row.

To Shape Armholes: 1st row: Sl st across 6 sts, work across to last 6 sts. Ch 1, turn. **2nd and 3rd rows:** Sl st across 2 sts, work across to last 2 sts. Ch 1, turn. **4th row:** Sl st across 3 sts, work across to last 3 sts. Break off Rose, attach Turquoise, ch 3, turn. Now dec 1 st at both ends of each row until there remain

| | 111 sts | 115 sts | 120 sts |

Work straight until piece measures 3¾ inches from 1st row of armhole shaping ending with the 3rd sc row. Break off Turquoise, attach Black, and work straight until piece measures 6 inches from 1st row of armhole shaping.

To Shape Neck: Work across

| | 48 sts | 50 sts | 50 sts |

turn and work over these sts only, decreasing 2 sts at neck edge on each row until there remain | 36 sts | 38 sts | 38 sts

Work straight until piece measures from 1st row of armhole shaping | 7″ | 7½″ | 7½″

Shape shoulder same as Back shoulder. Break off. Skip next | 15 sts | 15 sts | 20 sts Attach Black in next st and work over remaining sts to correspond. Break off.

SLEEVES . . . With Black, make a chain 15 inches long (about 8 ch sts to 1 inch). **1st row:** Dc in 4th ch from hook and in each ch until there are on row | 98 sts | 106 sts | 106 sts

Work next 3 rows straight. Inc 1 st at end of next 4 rows. Break off Black, attach Rose, and continue increasing 1 st at end of each row until there are on row | 106 sts | 114 sts | 114 sts

Work straight until piece measures 3¾ inches in all, ending with the 3rd sc row.

To Shape Top: Sl st across 6 sts, work across to last 6 sts, turn. Dec 1 st at both ends of next 3 rows. Break off Rose, attach Turquoise,

and dec 1 st at both ends of each row until there remain | 56 sts | 64 sts | 64 sts

Break off Turquoise, attach Black, and continue decreasing 1 st at both ends of each row until 34 sts remain. Break off.

Sew underarm seams, leaving a 9-inch opening for zipper on left side, sew in zipper. Sew shoulder seams. Sew sleeve seams; sew sleeves in, matching stripes and gathering any extra fullness into top 5 inches at shoulder. With Black work a row of sc along back opening and around neck edge, holding neck edge in to fit snugly. Sew 4-inch zipper along back opening. Press through damp cloth.

1271 . . . Materials: KNIT-CRO-SHEEN, *3 balls of Ecru and 1 ball each of Light and Dark colors for Size 14; 4 balls of Ecru and 2 balls each of Light and Dark colors for Sizes 16 and 18* . . . *Steel Crochet Hook No. 4.*

GAUGE: 8 sts make 1 inch; 9 rows make 1 inch.

BLOCKING MEASUREMENTS:

Sizes	14	16	18
Bust (vest buttoned)	33½″	35½″	37½″
Width across back at underarm	16½″	17½″	18½″
Width across each front at underarm	9″	9½″	10″
Width across back between armholes (incl armbands)	12½″	13″	13½″
Length of side seam (incl bands)	11½″	11½″	12″
Length from top of shoulder.	19½″	20″	20½″

BACK . . . With Ecru	ch 129	ch 137	ch 145
to measure	16″	17″	18″

1st row: Sc in 2nd ch from hook and in each ch across. Ch 1, turn. **2nd row:** Sc in each st across. Ch 1, turn. Repeat 2nd row until piece measures | 1½″ | 1½″ | 2″

Dec 1 st at end of each row—*to dec 1 st, work off 2 sts as 1 st*—until there remain

| | 104 sts | 112 sts | 120 sts |

Work straight until piece measures in all | | 5″ | 5″ | 5½″ |

1271

Inc 1 st at end of each row—*to inc 1 st, work 2 sts in 1 st*—until there are

132 sts	140 sts	148 sts

Work straight until piece measures in all

10″	10″	10½″

To Shape Armholes: 1st row: Sl st across 8 sts, work across to last 8 sts (8 sts decreased at each end). Ch 1, turn. **2nd row:** Sl st across 2 sts, work across remainder of row. Ch 1, turn. Repeat 2nd row 9 more times. Dec 1 st at end of each row until there remain

88 sts	92 sts	96 sts

Work straight until piece measures from 1st row of armhole shaping

8¼″	8½″	9¼″

Shape shoulder and back of neck as follows:
1st row: Work across

33 sts	34 sts	34 sts

turn.

2nd row: Sl st across 4 sts, work across remainder of row. **3rd row:** Work across to last 4 sts, turn. **4th row:** Work across entire row. **5th row:** Starting at armhole edge, sl st across

6 sts	7 sts	7 sts

finish row.

6th row: Work across to last

6 sts	7 sts	7 sts

turn.

7th row: Repeat 5th row. Break off. Skip next

21 sts	23 sts	27 sts

attach thread in next st, ch 1 and work across remaining

33 sts	34 sts	34 sts

to correspond with other side. Break off.

RIGHT FRONT . . . With Ecru, ch 2. **1st row:** 2 sc in 2nd ch from hook. Ch 4, turn. **2nd row:** Sc in 2nd ch from hook, sc in 2 ch, sc in each st across. Ch 4, turn. **3rd row:** Repeat 2nd row. **4th row:** Sc in 2nd ch from hook, sc in 2 ch, sc in each st across. Break off Ecru, attach Light, ch 4, turn. **5th row:** Repeat 2nd row. **6th row:** Repeat 4th row. Break off Light, attach Dark, ch 4, turn. **7th row:** Sc in 2nd ch from hook, sc in 2 ch, sc in 11 sts, a long sc in next st—*to make a long sc, insert hook in base of next st 4 rows down, draw loop through and complete as for an sc*—skip sc behind long sc and finish row. Ch 4, turn. **8th row:** Repeat 2nd row. **9th row:** Repeat 2nd row only. Ch 5 and turn. **10th row:** Repeat 4th row. Break off Dark, attach Ecru, ch 5, turn. **11th row:** Sc in 2nd ch from hook, sc in 3 ch, (sc in 11 sts, long sc in next st 4 rows down, skip sc behind long

sc) twice; sc in 6 sts. Ch 5, turn. **12th row:** Sc in 2nd ch from hook, sc in 3 ch, finish row. Break off Ecru, attach Light. Ch 5, turn. **13th row:** Sc in 2nd ch from hook, sc in 3 ch, sc in 9 sts, (long sc in next st, skip sc behind long sc, sc in 11 sts) twice; long sc in next st, skip sc behind long sc, sc in 4 sts. Ch 5, turn. **14th, 15th and 16th rows:** Sc in 2nd ch from hook, sc in 3 ch, finish row. Ch 5, turn. At end of 16th row break off Light, attach Dark. Ch 5, turn. **17th row:** Sc in 2nd ch from hook, sc in 3 ch, (sc in 11 sts, long sc in next st) 4 times; sc in 6 sts. **On Size 14 only**—ch 1, turn; **on Sizes 16 and 18**—ch 5, turn. **18th row:** on Size 14 only—sc in each st across. **On Sizes 16 and 18**—same as 14th row. **All Sizes**—break off Dark, attach Ecru. Size 14 only—ch 1, turn; Sizes 16 and 18—ch 5, turn. **19th row:** On Size 14 only—sc in 9 sts, (long sc in next st, sc in 11 sts) 4 times; long sc in next st, sc in next sc. **On Sizes 16 and 18 only**—sc in 2nd ch from hook, sc in 3 ch, sc in 9 sts, (long sc in next st, sc in 11 sts) 4 times; long sc in next st, sc in remaining sts. **On Sizes 14 and 16 only**—ch 1, turn. **On Size 18 only**—ch 5, turn. **20th row: On Sizes 14 and 16 only**—sc in each st across. Ch 1, turn. **On Size 18 only**—sc in 2nd ch from hook, sc in 3 ch, finish row. Ch 1, turn. **21st and 22nd rows: All Sizes**—sc in each st across, ch 1, turn. At end of 22nd row, break off Ecru. Attach Light. Ch 1, turn.

Shaping of point is now complete. There are on row

58 sts	66 sts	70 sts

The last 18 rows (5th to 22nd rows incl) describe the color sequence and the position of the long sc's. Work straight in pattern until piece measures down center of piece to tip of point

3½″	3½″	3″

Now, keeping front edge straight dec 1 st at side edge on next row and every other row thereafter until there remain on row

48 sts	52 sts	56 sts

Work straight until piece measures straight up from point

6½″	7″	7½″

Now inc 1 st at side edge on next row and every other row thereafter until there are on row

62 sts	66 sts	70 sts

Work straight until piece measures straight up from point

12″	12″	12½″

To Shape Armhole: Starting at side edge, sl st across 8 sts, finish row. Starting at same edge sl st across 2 sts every other row 5 times. Continue armhole shaping and shape front simultaneously as follows: Dec 1 st at armhole edge every other row

4 times	6 times	8 times

At the Same Time, dec 1 st at front edge every other row until there remain

24 sts	28 sts	28 sts

Work straight until piece measures from 1st row of armhole shaping

8½″	9″	9½″

Starting at armhole edge sl st across

6 sts	7 sts	7 sts

every other row 4 times. Break off.

LEFT FRONT . . . Work to correspond with Right Front. Press pieces through damp cloth. Sew shoulder and underarm seams.

ARM BANDS . . . With Ecru, ch 7. **1st row:** Sc in 2nd ch from hook and in each ch across. Ch 1, turn. **2nd row:** Sc in each st across. Ch 1, turn. Repeat 2nd row until piece is 1 inch shorter than circumference of entire armhole. Break off. Make another piece same as this. Starting at underarm, pin band around armhole having band overlap on right side of vest for ⅛ inch and stretching band along curved edge to fit. Sew in place with invisible sts.

OUTSIDE BAND . . . Work as for Arm Band, making a buttonhole when piece measures

1¼″	1¼″	1½″

—to make a buttonhole, sc in 1st sc, ch 4, skip 4 sc, sc in last sc, ch 1, turn. On next row work sc in each sc and in each ch across. Ch 1, turn— and thereafter every

2¼″	2¼″	2½″

(measuring from the beginning of the 1st buttonhole) until 5 in all are made.

Then work straight until piece is long enough to go up Right Front, around back of Neck, down Left Front, along point of Left Front, around lower Back and along point of Right Front. Pin band in place, mitering at points if necessary and stretching band along back of neck to fit. Sew with invisible sts. Sew on buttons to correspond with buttonholes.

Ponchos and Shawls

Youthful and attractive, ponchos and shawls keep you warm with a flair. It's not without reason that these fashion items are so popular today with women of all ages—they look so graceful and allow you such freedom of movement.

Whether you plan on cheering the local football team to victory or spending a night on the town, you'll find just the right wrap in this chapter—big bulky ponchos with long fringe or a delicate and stunning flower-motif stole. You'll even find several ponchos for the younger set—take your pick!

5650 . . . Materials: J. & P. Coats Knit-Cro-Sheen, ART. A.64, *3 balls of No. 1 White, No. 61 Ecru, or No. 42 Cream, or 5 balls of any color for main color; 6 balls of any contrasting color* . . . Steel Crochet Hook No. 1.

GAUGE: 2 bls and 2 ch-1 sps make 1½ inches; 3 rnds make 1 inch.

Use 2 strands of same color held together throughout.

BLOCKING MEASUREMENTS:

Length from neck edge to lower edge at shoulders (In Inches)	17
Length at center front or back from neck edge to point	23
Width along entire lower edge	96

Starting at neck edge with 2 strands of main color held together, ch 138 to measure 22 inches. Being careful not to twist chain, join with sl st to first ch st. **1st rnd:** Ch 6, *dc in each of next 4 ch*—**bl made;** (ch 1, skip next ch, dc in each of next 4 ch) 13 times; ch 3, dc in each of next 4 ch, (ch 1, skip next ch, dc in each of next 4 ch) 12 times; ch 1, skip next ch, dc in next 3 ch. Join with sl st to 3rd ch of ch-6—28 bls. **2nd rnd:** Sl st in each of next 2 ch, *ch 6, 4 dc in same sp*—**starting sp and bl made over first sp,** * ch 1, skip 4 dc, *4 dc in next ch-1 sp*—**bl over sp made.** Repeat from * across to within next ch-3 sp; ch 1, skip 4 dc, *in next*

ch-3 sp make 4 dc, ch 3 and 4 dc—corner group made; make ch 1 and 4 dc in each remaining ch-1 sp, ending with ch 1, 3 dc in same sp where first bl was made, sl st in 3rd ch of ch-6 to complete another corner group—2 more bls than on previous rnd. The 2nd rnd establishes the pattern. 3rd through 9th rnds: Repeat 2nd rnd 7 times—44 bls on last rnd. Break off and fasten. 10th rnd: Attach 2 strands of contrasting color held together to starting sp on last rnd, ch 6, 4 dc in same sp, ch 1 and continue as for 2nd rnd. 11th through 15th rnds: With contrasting color, repeat 2nd rnd 5 times. At end of last rnd, break off and fasten. Attach double strand of main color to starting sp on last rnd.

Note: Hereafter, work first rnd of each stripe same as for 10th rnd. Break off and fasten at end of each stripe and attach next color, as before. With main color, work in pattern for 2 rnds. With contrasting color, work in pattern for 9 rnds. With main color, work in pattern for 6 rnds. With contrasting color, work in pattern for 2 rnds. With main color, work in pattern for 9 rnds. With contrasting color, work in pattern for 6 rnds. With main color, work in pattern for 2 rnds.

COLLAR . . . 1st rnd: With right side facing, attach double strand of contrasting color to joining stitch of starting chain, working along opposite side of starting chain, sc in joining, sc in each ch around. Join to first sc—138 sc. 2nd rnd: Ch 3, skip joining, dc in each of next 30 sc, holding back on hook last loop of each dc, make dc in each of next 2 sc, thread over hook and draw through all 3 loops on hook—1 dc decreased; (dc in each of next 33 sc, dec 1 dc over next 2 sc) 3 times. Join with sl st to top of ch-3. 3rd rnd: Ch 1, sc in same st as joining, * sc in each sc to within next dec, skip next st. Repeat from * around, ending with sl st in first sc—130 sc. 4th rnd: Ch 3, dc in each of next 28 sc, dec 1 dc over next 2 sc, (dc in 31 sc, dec 1 dc over next 2 sc) 3 times. Join to top of ch-3. 5th rnd: Repeat 3rd rnd. 6th rnd: Ch 3, dc in each sc. Join to top of ch-3. 7th rnd: Ch 1, sc in the joining, sc in each dc around. Join to first sc—122 sc. 8th through 11th rnds: Repeat 6th and 7th rnds. At end of 11th rnd, ch 3, turn. 12th rnd: Dc in each sc. Join to top of turning chain. 13th rnd: Repeat 7th rnd. Now repeat 6th and 7th rnds alternately 5 times or for desired length. At end of last rnd, break off and fasten.

FRINGE . . . Wind double strand of contrasting color 50 times around a 7½-inch square of cardboard. Cut at one edge, thus making 15-inch strands. Continue to cut fringe as needed. Hold eight 15-inch strands together. Fold these strands in half to form loop. With right side of poncho facing, insert hook from back to front into a sp along lower edge and draw loop through, then draw loose ends through the loop and pull up tightly. Knot eight 15-inch strands in each sp around entire lower edge in same way. Take 8 strands from first group and 8 strands from second group, holding these 16 strands together, tie a knot 1 inch from lower edge of crochet and in between previous knots. Pick up remaining 8 strands of second group and 8 strands of next group, tie these 16 strands together as before. Continue in this manner to tie second rnd of knots all around. Trim fringe evenly.

5719 . . . Materials: COATS & CLARK'S RED HEART KNITTING WORSTED, 4 Ply ("Tangle-Proof" Pull-Out Skeins), 20 ounces of No. 757 Wild Rose . . . Crochet Hook Size K.

GAUGE: 3 h dc make 1 inch; 5 rows make 3 inches.
Shawl measures 72 inches across top edge, 48 inches along each side edge, and 38 inches up center from point to top edge.

Starting at center of top edge, ch 3. 1st row: 5 h dc in 3rd ch from hook. Ch 2, turn. 2nd row: Working in the back loop only of each h dc, make 3 h dc in first h dc, h dc in next h dc, 3 h dc in next h dc, h dc in next h dc, 3 h dc in last h dc—11 h dc. Ch 2, turn. Do not count turning ch-2 as a st. Note: Hereafter work in back loop only of each h dc throughout. 3rd row: 3 h dc in first h dc, h dc in each of next 4 h dc, 3 h dc in next h dc, this is center st of center 3-h dc group of previous row, h dc in each of next 4 h dc, 3 h dc in last h dc. Ch 2, turn. 4th row: 3 h dc in first h dc, h dc in each h dc to within center st of next 3-h dc group, 3 h dc in center st, h dc in each h dc to within last h dc, 3 h dc in last h dc—6 sts increased. Ch 2, turn. Repeat 4th row until each side edge measures about 48 inches. Ch 1, do not turn.

5719

EDGING . . . In top of last st make sc, ch 1 and sc; working over ends of rows along top edge, * work ch 1, skip ½ inch, sc in edge. Repeat from * across to next corner, in corner st make sc, ch 1 and sc; ch 2, working along side edge, make sc and ch 2 in every other st across to center st of 3-h dc group, ch 2, in center h dc make (sc and ch 2) twice; then continue to make sc and ch 2 in every other st along remaining side edge, ending with ch 2. Join with sl st to first sc of edging. Break off and fasten.

FRINGE . . . Wind yarn about 50 times around a 6-inch square of cardboard. Cut at one edge, thus making 12-inch strands. Continue to cut strands as needed. Hold four 12-inch strands together, double these strands to form a loop. Insert hook in first ch-2 sp on one side edge and draw loop through. Draw loose ends through loop and pull up tightly to form a knot. Tie four 12-inch strands as before in every ch-2 sp along both side edges. Trim fringe evenly.

5598 . . . Materials: Coats & Clark's O.N.T. Speed-Cro-Sheen Mercerized Cotton, *14 balls of No. 122 Watermelon* . . . *Crochet Hook Size F* . . . *Small button.*

GAUGE: 9 dc make 2 inches; 6 rows of pattern make 2¼ inches.

BLOCKING MEASUREMENTS
Length from neck edge to lower edge (excluding neck ruffle)—21 inches; width around entire lower edge—100 inches.

Starting at neck edge, ch 93 to measure 21 inches. **1st row:** Dc in 4th ch from hook, dc in each ch across—91 dc, counting chain at beg of row as one dc. Ch 6, turn. **2nd row:** Skip first 2 dc, sc in each of next 2 dc, * ch 3, skip next dc, dc in next dc, ch 3, skip next dc, sc in each of next 2 dc. Repeat from * across, ending with ch 3, skip last dc, dc in next ch st. Ch 3, turn. **3rd row:** Dc in first dc, ch 3, sc in each of next 2 sc, * ch 3, 3 dc in next dc, ch 3, sc in each of next 2 sc. Repeat from * across, ending with ch 3, skip 3 ch sts, 2 dc in next ch st. Ch 3, turn. **4th row:** Skip first dc, 2 dc in next dc, ch 3, sc in next 2 sc, * ch 3, 2 dc in next dc, dc in next dc, 2 dc in next dc, ch 3, sc in

next 2 sc. Repeat from * across, ending with ch 3, 2 dc in last dc, dc in top of ch-3—17 scallops plus half a scallop at each end. Ch 1, turn. **5th row:** Sc in first 2 dc, * ch 3, skip next dc, 2 sc and dc; make sc in each of next 3 dc. Repeat from * across, ending with ch 3, skip next dc, 2 sc and dc; make sc in next dc, sc in top of ch-3. Ch 3, turn. **Hereafter, work is done in rnds; do not turn at end of each rnd. 1st rnd (right side):** Skip first sc, dc in next sc, * 3 dc in next sp, dc in each of next 3 sc. Repeat from * around, ending with 3 dc in last sp, skip next sc, dc in last sc. Join with sl st to top of ch-3 at beg of this rnd—108 dc, always counting the ch-3 as one dc. **2nd rnd:** Ch 3, increasing 7 dc evenly spaced around, work dc in each dc (**to inc 1 dc**—*work 2 dc in 1 dc*). Join to top of ch-3—115 dc. **3rd rnd:** Ch 6, skip next dc, sc in next 2 dc, * ch 3, skip next dc, dc in next dc, ch 3, skip next dc, sc in next 2 dc. Repeat from * around, ending with ch 3, skip last dc. Join with sl st to 3rd ch of ch-6—23 scallops started. **4th rnd:** Ch 3, dc in same st as joining, ch 3, sc in next 2 sc, * ch 3, 3 dc in next dc, ch 3, sc in next 2 sc. Repeat from * around, ending with ch 3, dc in same place as first dc. Join to top of ch-3. **5th rnd:** Ch 3, 2 dc in next dc, ch 3, sc in next 2 sc, * ch 3, 2 dc in next dc, dc in next dc, 2 dc in next dc, ch 3, sc in next 2 sc. Repeat from * around, ending with ch 3, 2 dc in last dc. Join. **6th rnd:** Ch 1, sc in same st as joining, sc in next dc, * ch 3, skip next dc, 2 sc and dc; make sc in each of next 3 dc. Repeat from * around, ending with ch 3, skip next dc, 2 sc and dc; sc in last dc. Join to first sc. **7th rnd:** Ch 3, dc in next sc, * 3 dc in next sp, dc in each of next 3 sc. Repeat from * around, ending with 3 dc in sp, dc in last sc. Join—138 dc. **8th rnd:** Ch 3, increasing 12 dc evenly spaced around, work dc in each dc. Join—150 dc. **9th through 12th rnd:** Repeat 3rd through 6th rnd—30 scallops. **13th rnd:** Repeat 7th rnd—180 dc. **14th rnd:** Ch 3, * 2 dc in next dc, dc in next 8 dc. Repeat from * around, ending with dc in last 7 dc. Join—200 dc. **15th, 16th, and 17th rnds:** Repeat 3rd, 4th, and 5th rnds—40 scallops. **18th rnd:** Ch 1, sc in same st as joining, sc in next dc, * ch 4, skip next dc, 2 sc and dc; make sc in each of next 3 dc. Repeat from * around, ending with ch 4. Join. **19th rnd:** Ch 3, dc in next sc, * 4 dc in next sp, dc in 3 sc. Repeat from * around, ending with 4 dc

in sp, dc in last sc. Join—280 dc. **20th rnd:** Ch 3, increasing 2 dc evenly spaced around, dc in each dc. Join—282 dc. **21st rnd:** Ch 6, skip next 2 dc, 2 sc in next dc; * ch 3, skip next 2 dc, dc in next dc, ch 3, skip next 2 dc, 2 sc in next dc. Repeat from * around, ending with ch 3, skip last 2 dc. Join to 3rd ch of ch-6 —47 scallops started. **22nd, 23rd, and 24th rnds:** Repeat 4th, 5th, and 18th rnds. **25th rnd:** Repeat 19th rnd—329 dc. **26th rnd:** Ch 3, increasing 21 dc evenly spaced around, dc in each dc around—350 dc. **27th rnd:** Ch 6, skip next 2 dc, sc in next 2 dc, * ch 3, skip next 2 dc, dc in next dc, ch 3, skip next 2 dc, sc in next 2 dc. Repeat from * around, ending with ch 3, skip last 2 dc. Join to 3rd ch of ch-6— 50 scallops started. **28th, 29th, and 30th rnds:** Repeat 4th, 5th, and 18th rnds. **31st rnd:** Repeat 19th rnd—350 dc. **32nd rnd:** Ch 3, dc in next dc, *holding back on hook the last loop of each dc, dc in next 2 dc, yarn over and draw through all 3 loops on hook*—1 dc decreased; dc in 172 dc. Repeat from * once—348 dc. **33rd rnd:** Repeat 21st rnd—58 scallops started. **34th, 35th, and 36th rnds:** Repeat 4th, 5th, and 18th rnds. **37th rnd:** Repeat 19th rnd—406 dc. **38th rnd:** Ch 3, increasing 7 dc evenly spaced around, dc in each dc—413 dc. **39th through 42nd rnd:** Repeat 27th, 4th, 5th, and 18th rnds—59 scallops. **43rd rnd:** Repeat 19th rnd—413 dc. **44th rnd:** Ch 3, dc in 10 dc, * 2 dc in next dc, dc in 10 dc, 2 dc in next dc, dc in 11 dc. Repeat from * around, ending with 2 dc in next dc, dc in 10 dc. Join—448 dc. **45th through 48th rnd:** Repeat 27th, 4th, 5th, and 18th rnds—64 scallops. **49th rnd:** Repeat 19th rnd—448 dc. **50th rnd:** Ch 3, dc in each dc around. Join—448 dc. **51st, 52nd, and 53rd rnds:** Repeat 27th, 4th, and 5th rnds: Join. Break off and fasten.

NECK RUFFLE . . . Working along opposite side of starting chain at neck edge, attach thread to last ch st of chain. **1st row:** Ch 6, skip next ch, sc in next 2 ch, * ch 3, skip next ch, dc in next ch, ch 3, skip next ch, sc in next 2 ch. Repeat from * across, ending with ch 3, skip next ch, dc in next ch. Ch 3, turn. **2nd and 3rd rows:** Repeat 3rd and 4th rows of Poncho. Break off and fasten.

Press through damp cloth. Sew button to first row of Poncho; use sp between dc's at opposite side as buttonhole.

B-775

Directions are given for Small Size. Changes for Medium and Large Sizes are in parentheses.

Materials: COATS & CLARK'S RED HEART KNITTING WORSTED, *4 Ply ("Tangle-Proof" Pull-Out Skeins), 10 (11, 12) ounces of No. 603 Lt. Gold . . . Crochet Hook Size H.*

GAUGE: 3 dc make 1 inch.

Starting at neck edge, ch 77 (84, 91) having 3 ch sts to 1 inch. Join with sl st to form a ring, being careful not to twist sts. **1st rnd:** Ch 3, skip joining, dc in next ch and in each ch around. Join to top of ch-3—77 (84, 91) dc, counting ch-3 as 1 dc. **2nd rnd:** Ch 3, 2 dc in joining * ch 1, skip next 2 dc, dc in next dc, ch 1, dc in next dc, ch 1, skip next 2 dc, 3 dc in next dc. Repeat from * around to within last 6 sts, ch 1, skip next 2 dc, dc in next dc, ch 1, dc in next dc, ch 1, skip last 2 dc. Join to top of ch-3. **3rd rnd:** Ch 3, skip joining, dc in each dc and in each ch around. Join as before—88 (96, 104) dc. **4th rnd:** Ch 4, skip joining and next dc; dc in next dc, ch 3, skip next 2 dc, 3 dc in next dc, * ch 3, skip next 2 dc, dc in next dc, ch 1, skip next dc, dc in next dc, ch 3, skip next 2 dc, 3 dc in next dc. Repeat from * around to within last 2 dc, ch 3. Join to 3rd ch of ch-4. **5th rnd:** Ch 1, sc in joining and in each st around. Join to first sc—132 (144, 156) sc.

Now work in loop pattern as follows: **1st rnd:** Ch 1, sc in joining, * ch 5, skip next 2 sc, sc in next sc. Repeat from * around to within last 2 sc, ch 2, skip last 2 sc, dc in first sc to form last loop—44 (48, 52) loops. **2nd rnd:** Sc in loop just formed, * ch 5, sc in center ch of next loop. Repeat from * around, ending with ch 2, dc in first sc. **3rd through 7th rnd:** Sc in loop just formed, * ch 7, sc in center ch of next loop. Repeat from * around, ending with ch 3, tr in first sc. **8th rnd:** Sc in loop just formed, * ch 8, sc in center ch of next loop. Repeat from * around, ending with ch 4, tr in first sc. **9th through 13th rnd:** Sc in loop just formed, ch 8, sc in 4th ch of next loop. Repeat from * around, ending with ch 4, tr in first sc. **14th rnd:** Sc in loop just formed, * ch 9, sc in 4th ch of next loop. Repeat from * around, ending with ch 4, d tr in first sc. **15th rnd:** Sc in loop just formed, * ch 9, sc in center ch

of next loop. Repeat from * around, ending with ch 4, d tr in first sc. Repeat 15th rnd 4 (5, 6) times more. Break off and fasten.

FRINGE . . . Cut 8 strands of yarn, each 19 inches long. Double these strands to form a loop. Insert hook in any loop of last rnd and draw loop through. Draw ends through loop and pull up tightly to form a knot. Knot strands as before in each loop of last rnd. Trim ends evenly.

4925 . . . Materials: COATS & CLARK'S RED HEART KNITTING WORSTED, *4 Ply ("Tangle-Proof" Pull-Out Skeins), 16 ounces of No. 584 Lavender . . . Crochet Hook Size G.*

GAUGE: Each motif measures 3 inches from point to point.
Stole measures 21 inches deep at center.

CENTER ROW OF 8 MOTIFS . . . First Motif: Starting at center, ch 4. Join with sl st to form ring. **1st rnd:** Ch 1, (sc in ring, ch 5) 6 times. Join with sl st to first sc—6 loops. **2nd rnd:** Ch 1, sc in joining, * ch 5, sc in 5th ch from hook—picot made; ch 5, complete another picot, sc in next sc. Repeat from * around, ending with (ch 5, complete picot) twice. Join to first sc. **3rd rnd:** (Ch 7, holding next 2 picots forward, sl st in next sc between picots) 5 times; ch 3, tr in joining of last rnd to form last loop. **4th rnd:** Ch 1, sc in loop just formed, * ch 7, sc in next loop. Repeat from * around. Join last ch-7 to first sc. Break off and fasten. **Mark this motif with a colored thread.**
Second Motif: Work as for First Motif until 3rd rnd has been completed. **4th rnd:** Ch 1, sc in loop just formed, ch 7, sc in next loop, ch 3; with wrong side of First Motif facing, sl st in any loop on First Motif, ch 3, sc in next loop on Second Motif, ch 3, sl st in next loop on First Motif, ch 3, sc in next loop on Second Motif, ch 7, and complete motif same as for First Motif—no more joinings. Break off and fasten.
Third Motif: Work as for First Motif until 3rd rnd has been completed. **4th rnd:** Ch 1, sc in loop just formed, ch 7, sc in next loop, ch 3, with wrong side of last motif facing, skip the ch-7 loop preceding joining of motifs on last motif made, sl st in next loop, ch 3, sc in next loop on Third Motif, ch 3, sl st in next loop

on previous motif, ch 3, sc in next loop on Third Motif, ch 7, and complete motif as before—no more joinings.

Make and join 5 more motifs, joining each motif to previous motif as Third Motif was joined to Second Motif.

NEXT ROW OF MOTIFS . . . First Motif: Work as for First Motif of Center Row until 3rd rnd has been completed. 4th rnd: Ch 1, sc in loop just formed, ch 7, sc in next loop, ch 3, with wrong side of joined motifs facing, sl st in ch-7 loop on **marked motif** of last row of motifs preceding the joining of motifs, ch 3, sc in next loop of motif in work, ch 3, sl st in next sl st joining motifs on last row of motifs, ch 3, sc in next loop of motif in work, ch 3, sl st in next free ch-7 loop on next motif on last row of motifs, ch 3, sc in next loop of motif in work, ch 7, and complete motif as before. Break off and fasten. **Mark this motif with a colored thread. Note: Hereafter mark first motif of each row.**

Second Motif: Work as for First Motif of Center Row until 3rd rnd has been completed. **4th rnd:** Ch 1, sc in loop just formed, ch 7, sc in next loop, ch 3, with wrong side of joined motifs facing, sl st in free ch-7 loop preceding joining of motifs on last motif made, (ch 3, sc in next loop on motif in work, ch 3, sl st in next sl st joining motifs) twice; ch 3, sc in next loop on motif in work, ch 3, sl st in next free ch-7 loop on next motif on last row of motifs, ch 3, sc in next loop of motif in work, ch 7, and complete motif as before. Make and join 5 more motifs, joining each motif to last motif made and to motifs of last row (same as last motif made)—7 motifs on row.

FOLLOWING ROW OF MOTIFS . . . Work as for last row of motifs until 6 motifs have been made and joined.

Last Motif: Work as for First Motif of Center Row until 3rd rnd has been completed. **4th rnd:** Ch 1, sc in loop just formed, ch 7, sc in next loop, ch 3, with wrong side of joined motifs facing, sl st in ch-7 loop preceding last joining of motifs on last motif, ch 3, sc in next loop on motif in work, ch 3, sl st in next sl st joining motifs, ch 3, sc in next loop on motif in work, ch 3, sl st in next ch-7 loop on last motif on last row of motifs, ch 3, sc in next loop of motif in work, ch 7, and complete motif as before—7 motifs on row.

NEXT 11 ROWS OF MOTIFS . . . Working as for last 2 rows of motifs, work 2 rows of 6 motifs on each row; 2 rows of 5 motifs; 2 rows of 4; 2 rows of 3 and 2 rows of 2; make and join 1 motif to last row.

Work 13 rows of motifs on opposite side of Center Row to correspond with opposite side, being sure to have all marked motifs on same edge (uneven edge is neck edge).

FILL-IN MOTIF . . . Starting at center, ch 4. Join with sl st to form ring. **1st row:** Ch 1, sc in ring (ch 5, sc in ring) 3 times—3 loops. Ch 1, turn. **2nd row:** Sc in first sc, (make 2 picots, sc in next sc) 3 times. Ch 1, turn. **3rd row:** Sc in first sc, (ch 7, skip next 2 picots, sc in next sc) 3 times. Ch 1, turn. **4th row:** Sc in first sc, ch 3, with wrong side of joined motifs facing, sl st in ch-7 loop preceding joining of motifs on last 2-motif row at neck edge, (ch 3, sc in next loop on motif in work, ch 3, sl st in next sl st joining motifs) twice; ch 3, sc in next loop on motif in work, ch 3, sl st in next free ch-7 loop on next motif, ch 3, sc in last sc.

Break off and fasten. Make and join 11 more Fill-in Motifs along uneven edge (see diagram).

EDGING . . . **1st rnd:** With right side facing, attach yarn in the end sc on last row of Fill-In Motif at right end of neck edge. Ch 1, sc where yarn was attached, * ch 7, sc in starting ring of same motif, ch 7, sc in the sc at opposite end of last row on same motif, ch 7, sc in next sc on next motif, ch 7, sc in the end sc on last row of next Fill-In Motif. Repeat from * across neck edge to last sc on last Fill-In Motif at other end, ch 7, work sc, and ch 7 in each free sc on each remaining motif around, ending with ch 7. Join with sl st to first sc. **2nd rnd:** Sl st in next 3 ch, ch 1, sc in same loop, * (ch 5, sc in 3rd ch from hook) twice; ch 1, sc in next loop. Repeat from * around. Join. Break off and fasten.

Press through damp cloth.

5487 . . . **Materials:** COATS & CLARK'S RED HEART KNITTING WORSTED, 4 Ply ("Tangle-Proof" Pull-Out Skeins), 3 (3, 4) ounces of No. 909 Scarlet, 1 (2, 2) ounces each of No. 111 Eggshell, No. 326 Dk. Camel and No. 491 Pearl Grey, and 2 ounces of No. 358 Med. Brown for each size . . . Crochet Hook Size G.

GAUGE: 7 dc make 2 inches; 2 dc rows make 1 inch.

Directions are given for Small Size. Changes for Medium and Large Sizes are in parentheses.

PONCHO

FIRST HALF . . . Starting at narrow edge with Scarlet, ch 32 (36, 40), having 7 ch sts to 2 inches. **1st row:** Dc in 4th ch from hook and in each ch across—30 (34, 38) dc, counting chain at beg of row as 1 dc. Ch 3, turn. **2nd row:** Skip first dc, dc in each dc across, dc in top of ch-3—30 (34, 38) dc, counting turning chain as 1 dc. Break off and fasten. Attach Brown to last st made, then ch 3, turn. **3rd row:** Skip dc where yarn was attached, dc in each dc across, dc in top of ch-3. Ch 3, turn. **4th row:** Repeat 2nd row. Break off and fasten. Attach Camel to last st made, then ch 3, turn. Repeating last 2 rows alternately, work 2 rows of each color in the following order: Camel, Grey, Eggshell, Scarlet, Brown, Camel, Eggshell, Grey, Scarlet, Brown, Eggshell, Camel, Grey, and Brown. **For Medium Size only:** Work 2 rows with Eggshell. **For Large Size only:** Work 2 rows with Eggshell and 2 rows with Camel. **For All Sizes:** Break off and fasten.

SECOND HALF . . . Starting with Brown, work as for First Half, making 2 rows of each color in the following order: Brown, Scarlet, Eggshell, Camel, Grey, Brown, Scarlet, Camel, Eggshell, Brown, Scarlet, Eggshell, Grey, Camel, Brown, and Scarlet. **For Medium Size only:** Work 2 rows with Eggshell. **For Large Size only:** Work 2 rows with Eggshell and 2 rows with Grey. **For All Sizes:** Break off and fasten.

Starting at right-hand lower corner of Second Half, sew entire starting chain of First Half to first 8½ (9¾, 11) inches of long edge of Second Half, leaving remainder of edge free for neck edge; starting at corner of last row of First Half, sew entire last row of Second

Half to inner long edge of First Half for the same length as before.

Neckband: With right side facing and working along inner end sts of both halves, attach Scarlet to end st of center row between seams —shoulder. **1st rnd:** Ch 1, sc evenly around entire neck edge, being careful to keep work flat. Join with sl st to first sc. **Next 3 rnds:** Ch 1, sc in each sc around, decreasing 1 sc directly above each seam. **To dec 1 sc**—*draw up a loop in each of 2 sc, yarn over hook and draw through all 3 loops on hook.* Join each rnd with sl st to first sc. At end of last rnd, break off and fasten.

Lower Band: 1st rnd: With Scarlet, sc along entire lower edge, making 3 sc in each of the 2 corners. Join. **Next 3 rnds:** Sc in each sc around, making 3 sc in center sc of each 3-sc group. Join. At end of last rnd, break off and fasten.

FRINGE . . . Wind Scarlet about 50 times around a 5½-inch piece of cardboard. Cut at one edge, thus making 11-inch strands. Continue to cut strands as needed. Hold four 11-inch strands together and double them to form a loop, insert hook in center sc of a 3-sc group and draw loop through. Draw loose ends through loop and pull up tightly to form a knot. * Skip 3 sc, tie four 11-inch strands to next sc as before. Repeat from * around last rnd. Trim evenly.

HEADBAND

Starting at a long edge, with Scarlet make a chain to fit around head. Being careful not to twist chain, join with sl st to first ch to form a circle. **1st rnd:** Ch 1, sc in each ch around. Join with sl st to first sc. Break off and fasten. **2nd rnd:** Attach Eggshell to joining, ch 1, sc in same st and in each st around. Break off and fasten. **3rd rnd:** With right side facing, Grey and working along opposite side of starting chain, sc in each ch around. Join. Break off and fasten. **4th rnd:** Repeat 2nd rnd. Break off and fasten.

Motif: Starting at center with Eggshell, ch 2. **1st rnd:** Ch 1, make 6 sc in 2nd ch from hook, join to first sc. **2nd rnd:** Ch 1, make 2 sc in each sc around. Join. Break off and fasten. **3rd rnd:** Attach Camel to joining, ch 1, 2 sc in same place, sc in next sc, * 2 sc in next sc— 1 sc increased; sc in next sc. Repeat from * around. Join—18 sc. Break off and fasten. **4th rnd:** Attach Grey to joining, ch 1, increasing

6 sc evenly spaced, sc in each sc around. Join. Break off and fasten. **5th rnd:** With Brown repeat 4th rnd—30 sc. Break off and fasten. Sew motif to band.

Button (Make 4): With Scarlet, ch 2. **1st rnd:** 6 sc in 2nd ch from hook. Join. **Next 2 rnds:** Ch 1, sc in each sc around. Join. At end of last rnd, break off, leaving a 6-inch length of yarn. Thread this end of yarn into a darning needle and gather sts of last rnd together.

Sew the 4 buttons evenly spaced along 3rd rnd of motif.

6139 . . . Materials: Coats & Clark's Red Heart Knitting Worsted, *4 Ply ("Tangle-Proof" Pull-Out Skeins), 14 ounces of No. 588 Amethyst and 6 ounces of No. 243 Mid Orange . . . Crochet Hook Size H.*

GAUGE: 7 sc make 2 inches; 4 rows make 1 inch.

Shawl measures 63 inches across long edge and 27½ inches at center back (excluding fringe).

Starting at point with Amethyst, ch 2. **1st row:** Make 3 sc in 2nd ch from hook. Ch 1, turn. **2nd row:** 2 sc in first sc—1 sc increased; sc in next sc, 2 sc in last sc—5 sc. Ch 1, turn. **3rd row:** Sc in each sc across. Ch 1, turn. **4th row:** Increasing 1 sc at both ends of row, sc in each sc across. Repeat last row until there are 179 sc on row and total length from point is about 22½ inches. Break off Amethyst; attach Orange and ch 1, turn. Continue in sc, increasing 1 sc at both ends of every row as before until total length from point is about 27½ inches. Ch 1, turn. **Last row:** Sl st in each sc across. Break off and fasten.

FRINGE . . . Wind Amethyst several times around a 6½-inch square of cardboard; cut at one edge, thus making 13-inch strands. Continue to cut strands as needed. Hold three 13-inch strands together and fold in half to form a loop, insert hook in ch st at point and draw loop through; draw loose ends through loop on hook, pull tightly to form a knot. Working along ends of rows, tie three 13-inch Amethyst strands in same way in end st of each Amethyst row. With Orange, tie strands as before in end st of each Orange row. Tie fringe along other side edge in same way. Trim evenly.

Steam lightly through a damp cloth.

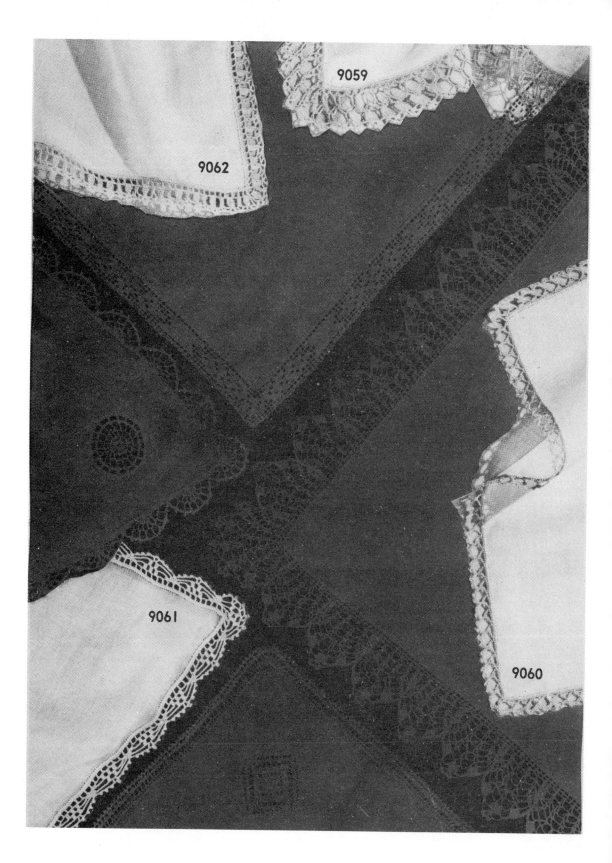

9059

9062

9061

9060

CHAPTER SIX

Edgings

A WOMAN WITH A TALENT for gracious living enjoys adding the small personal touches that add immeasurably to the atmosphere of a home and make it a place to be proud of. In her efforts she may want to add a graceful handmade edging to her pillow slips and her linen towels.

Thanks to her facility with the crochet hook, her own personal possessions acquire a dainty look. Her slips, panties, and nightgowns wear expensive-looking edgings; a simple white handkerchief takes on a new decorative importance thanks to a touch of handmade trimming. Easy to make, these little niceties add the prized touch of glamour to everyday things, make an impression entirely out of proportion to size, show you and your home off to advantage.

9062 . . . Materials: TATTING COTTON, *Size 70, 2 balls* . . . *Steel Crochet Hook No. 13* . . . *A rolled edge handkerchief, 12½ inches square.*

1st rnd: Attach thread to one corner and work sc evenly around, making 3 sc in each corner. Join with sl st. **2nd rnd:** (Spaces on this rnd should be a multiple of 3 plus 1—excluding ch-5 sp at each corner.) Ch 5, ** dc in next sc, ch 5, dc in next sc, ch 2, skip 1 sc, dc in next sc, * ch 2, skip 2 sc, dc in next sc. Repeat from * across to 3 sc of next corner, ch 2. Repeat from ** around. Join last ch-2 with sl st in 3rd ch of ch-5. **3rd rnd:** * Ch 7, 4-tr cluster in next sp—*to make a 4-tr cluster, holding back on hook the last loop of each tr, make 4 tr in sp, thread over and draw through all loops on hook*—ch 7, sc in next 2 sps. Repeat from * around. Join and break off. **4th rnd:** Attach thread to tip of 1st cluster, ch 6, dc in 3rd ch from hook, dc in same place where thread was attached, * ch 2, dc in next two ch-7 loops, ch 2, dc in tip of next cluster, ch 3, dc in last dc, dc in tip of same cluster. Repeat from * around. Join and break off.

9059 . . . Materials: TATTING COTTON, *Size 70, 2 balls* . . . *Steel Crochet Hook No. 13* . . . *A rolled edge handkerchief, 12½ inches square.*

1st rnd: Attach thread at one corner and work sc closely around, making 3 sc in each corner. Sl st in 1st sc. **2nd rnd:** Sc in next sc, ch 5, sc in same place where last sc was made, * ch 5, skip 3 sc, sc in next sc. Repeat from * around, making sc, ch 5 and sc in each corner sc and ending with ch 2, dc in 1st sc. (There must be an even number of loops on each side—not counting corner loops.) **3rd rnd:** Ch 5, tr under dc, (ch 7, in next loop make tr, ch 1 and tr) twice; * ch 7, tr in next loop, ch 1, tr in next loop. Repeat from * around, making other corners to correspond, ending with ch 7, sl st in 4th st of ch-5. **4th rnd:** * Sc in next ch-1 sp, ch 5, sc in next loop, ch 5. Repeat from * around, ending with sl st in 1st sc. **5th rnd:** Sl st in each of the next 4 ch, ch 5, * tr in next ch-5 loop, ch 7, tr in next ch-5 loop, ch 1. Repeat from * around, ending with ch 7, sl st in 4th st of ch-5. **6th rnd:** * Sc in next ch-1 sp, ch 4, in 4th st of next ch-7 make dc, ch 4, dc in top of last dc (a picot

made) and dc; ch 4. Repeat from * around, sl st in 1st sc. Break off.

9061 . . . Materials: TATTING COTTON, *Size 70, 1 ball* . . . *Steel Crochet Hook No. 13* . . . *A rolled edge handkerchief, 12½ inches square.*

1st rnd: Attach thread to one corner and work sc closely around, making 3 sc in each corner, sl st in 1st sc. **2nd rnd:** Sl st in next sc (center sc of corner group), ch 8, dc in center sc, ch 2, dc in next sc, * ch 2, skip 2 sc, dc in next sc. Repeat from * across to within corner sc, ch 2, dc in next (corner) sc, ch 5, dc in same sc. There must be a multiple of 8 plus 5 sps on each side, not counting the ch-5 sp at each corner. Work across other sides in similar manner, ending with ch 2, sl st in 3rd st of ch-8. **3rd rnd:** Sl st in each of the next 3 ch, ch 3, dc in corner sp, ** ch 2, make 2 dc in same sp, * ch 5, skip 1 sp, (2 sc in next sp, sc in next dc) twice; 2 sc in next sp, ch 5, skip 1 sp, 2 dc in next sp, (ch 2, make 2 dc in next sp) twice. Repeat from * across to within 1 sp of corner, ch 5, skip 1 sp, in corner sp make 2 dc. Repeat from ** around, ending with sl st in top st of ch-3. **4th rnd:** Sl st in next dc and in sp, ch 3, dc in same sp, ** ch 2, make 2 dc in next ch-5 loop, * ch 7, skip 2 sc, sc in next 4 sc, ch 7, 2 dc in next ch-2 sp, ch 2, make 2 dc in next ch-2 sp. Repeat from * across to sc group before corner, ch 7, skip 2 sc, sc in next 4 sc, ch 7, make 2 dc in next ch-5 loop, ch 2, make 2 dc in next ch-2 sp. Repeat from ** around, joining with sl st in top st of ch-3. **5th rnd:** Sl st in next dc and in sp, ch 6, sc in 3rd ch from hook (a picot made), dc in same sp as sl st, ** ch 2, in next ch-7 loop make dc, ch 3, p and dc; (ch 1, p) twice, * ch 1, skip 1 sc, sc in next 2 sc, (ch 1, p) 3 times; ch 1, in next ch-2 sp make dc, p and dc; (ch 1, p) 3 times. Repeat from * across to sc group before corner, skip 1 sc, sc in 2 sc, (ch 1, p) twice; ch 1, in next ch-7 loop make dc, p and dc; (ch 2, in next ch-2 sp make dc, p and dc) twice. Repeat from ** around, ending with ch 2, sl st in 3rd st of ch-6. Break off.

9060 . . . Materials: TATTING COTTON, *Size 70, 1 ball* . . . *Steel Crochet Hook No. 13* . . . *A rolled edge handkerchief, 12½ inches square.*

1st rnd: Attach thread to one corner of handkerchief and work sc closely around, making 3 sc in each corner. Join. **2nd rnd:** Ch 4, skip 1 sc, tr in next sc, * ch 7, tr in same place as last tr, skip 5 sc, tr in next sc. Repeat from * around, skipping only 1 sc between tr's (instead of 5) at corners. Join last ch-7 with sl st to 4th ch of starting ch-4. **3rd rnd:** In each loop around make (3 sc, ch 3) twice and 3 sc. Join and break off.

9012 . . . Materials: BEST SIX CORD MERCERIZED CROCHET, *Size 30* . . . *Steel Crochet Hook No. 10.*

Make a chain the length desired. **1st row:** Sc in 2nd ch from hook, sc in next 4 ch, * (ch 4, sc in 3rd ch from hook) 3 times; ch 1, skip 2 ch, sc in next 5 ch. Repeat from * across. Break off.

9010 . . . Materials: BEST SIX CORD MERCERIZED CROCHET, *Size 30* . . . *Steel Crochet Hook No. 10.*

Make a chain the length desired. **1st row:** In 7th ch from hook make (dc, ch 2, sc in last dc) 3 times and dc; * ch 2, skip 2 ch, sc in next ch, ch 2, skip 2 ch, in next ch make (dc, ch 2, sc in last dc) 3 times and dc. Repeat from * across. Break off. ·

9015 . . . Materials: BEST SIX CORD MERCERIZED CROCHET, *Size 30* . . . *Steel Crochet Hook No. 10.*

Make a chain the length desired. **1st row:** Dc in 4th ch from hook, dc in each ch across. Ch 3, turn. **2nd row:** * Ch 3, holding back on hook the last loop of each dc, make dc in next 2 dc, thread over and draw through all loops on hook, ch 3, sc at tip of cluster just made, ch 3, sc in next dc, ch 3, sc in 3rd ch from hook, skip 1 dc, sc in next 2 dc. Repeat from * across. Break off.

9026 . . . Materials: BEST SIX CORD MERCERIZED CROCHET, *Size 30* . . . *Steel Crochet Hook No. 10.*

1st row: * Ch 13, sc in 9th ch from hook. Repeat from * for length desired, ending with a loop. Ch 1, turn. **2nd row:** * 11 sc in next loop, sc under ch-4 between loops, in next loop make 8 dc, ch 5 and 8 dc; sc under next ch-4. Repeat from * across. Do not break off but work across long side as follows: Ch 5, * dc in center of next ring, ch 3, dc in next sc, ch 3. Repeat from * across. Break off.

9013 . . . Materials: BEST SIX CORD MERCERIZED CROCHET, *Size 30* . . . *Steel Crochet Hook No. 10.*

Make a chain the length desired. **1st row:** Holding back on hook the last loop of each dc make 2 dc in 4th ch from hook, thread over and draw through all loops on hook (cluster); * ch 1, skip 1 ch, make a cluster in next ch, ch 3, skip 3 ch, cluster in next ch. Repeat from * across, ending with cluster, ch 1 and cluster. Ch 1, turn. **2nd row:** * Sc in ch-1 sp, in ch-3 sp make sc, half dc, 5 dc, half dc, and sc. Repeat from * across. Break off.

9021 . . . Materials: BEST SIX CORD MERCERIZED CROCHET, *Size 30* . . . *Steel Crochet Hook No. 10.*

1st row: Ch 5; 2 dc in 5th ch from hook, ch 3, sl st in last dc (a picot made), dc in same ch as last dc; ch 2, in same ch make 2 dc, p and dc. Ch 5, turn. **2nd row:** In ch-2 sp make dc, ch 3 and dc. Ch 4, turn. **3rd row:** In ch-3 sp make 2 dc, p, dc, ch 2, 2 dc, p and dc. Ch 5, turn. Repeat 2nd and 3rd rows alternately for length desired. Do not break off but work along side where ch-5's appear as follows: * In loop formed by next turning ch-5 make dc, ch 3 and dc; ch 3. Repeat from * across. Break off.

9018 . . . Materials: BEST SIX CORD MERCERIZED CROCHET, *Size 30* . . . *Steel Crochet Hook No. 10.*

Make a chain slightly longer than length desired. **1st row:** * Holding back on hook the last loop of each tr, make 3 tr in 5th ch from hook, thread over and draw through all loops on hook, ch 7, skip 2 ch, sl st in next ch, turn; make 15 sc in ch-7 loop, turn; (ch 3, skip 2 sc, sc in next sc) 5 times; sc in next 5 ch, ch 5. Repeat from * across. Break off.

9012
9010
9015
9026
9013
9021
9018
9028
9009
9022
9016
9027
9019
8046

9008
9020
9006
9014
9011
9007
8969
9023
8961
9017

9028 . . . Materials: THREE CORD MERCER-IZED CROCHET, *Size 50 . . . Steel Crochet Hook No. 12.*

1st row: Ch 8, dc in 6th ch from hook, ch 1, skip 1 ch, dc in next ch. Ch 4, turn. **2nd row:** Dc in next dc, ch 1, skip 1 ch of turning chain, dc in next ch. Ch 7, do not turn work. **3rd row:** Dc in 4th ch from hook, dc in next 3 ch. Ch 3, turn. **4th row:** Dc in 3 dc, dc in top st of turning chain. Repeat these 4 rows for length desired. Do not break off but work along one long side as follows: Ch 7, sc in free tip of same square, * ch 7, sc in free tip of next square. Repeat from * across. Ch 1, turn and make 10 sc in each ch-7 loop across. Then sl st to remaining free tip of first square on opposite long side, * ch 7, sc in free tip of next square. Repeat from * across. Break off.

9009 . . . Materials: BEST SIX CORD MER-CERIZED CROCHET, *Size 30 . . . Steel Crochet Hook No. 10.*

Make a chain slightly longer than length desired. **1st row:** In 4th ch from hook make dc, ch 2 and dc; * skip 2 ch, in next ch make dc, ch 2 and dc. Repeat from * across. Ch 3, turn. **2nd row:** * Skip the ch-2, sc in next dc, ch 3. Repeat from * across. Ch 1, turn. **3rd row:** 5 sc in each ch-3 loop across. Break off.

9022 . . . Materials: BEST SIX CORD MER-CERIZED CROCHET, *Size 30 . . . Steel Crochet Hook No. 10.*

1st row: Ch 6, dc in 6th ch from hook. Ch 3, turn. **2nd row:** 13 dc in sp just made. Ch 7, turn. **3rd row:** Skip 6 dc, in next dc make dc, ch 5 and dc. Ch 3, turn. **4th row:** 13 dc in ch-5 loop, dc in turning ch-7 loop. Ch 7, turn. Repeat the 3rd and 4th rows alternately for length desired. Break off.

9016 . . . Materials: BEST SIX CORD MER-CERIZED CROCHET, *Size 30 . . . Steel Crochet Hook No. 10.*

Make a chain the length desired. **1st row:** Holding back on hook the last loop of each dc make 2 dc in 4th ch from hook, thread over and draw through all loops on hook (a cluster made), * ch 3, cluster in same place as last cluster, skip 2 ch, cluster in next ch. Repeat from * across. Break off. **2nd row:** Attach

thread to 1st cluster made, in each ch-3 sp across make 2 sc, ch 2, sl st in last sc (picot) and 2 sc. Break off.

9027 . . . Materials: THREE CORD MERCER-IZED CROCHET, *Size 50 . . . Steel Crochet Hook No. 12.*

Ch 12. **1st row:** Make 5 dc in 9th ch from hook. Ch 5, turn. **2nd row:** Dc in next dc. Ch 8, turn. **3rd row:** 5 dc in last dc made. Ch 5, turn. Repeat the 2nd and 3rd rows alternately for length desired. Do not break off but work along the long side with the turning ch-5 as follows: * Sc in next ch-5, ch 5. Repeat from * across. Break off. **4th row:** Attach thread to base of 1st 5-dc group made, * in next loop make (2 sc, ch 3, sc in last sc) 3 times and 2 sc; 5 sc in next ch-8 loop. Repeat from * across. Break off.

9019 . . . Materials: BEST SIX CORD MER-CERIZED CROCHET, *Size 30 . . . Steel Crochet Hook No. 10.*

Make a chain the length desired. **1st row:** Sc in 2nd ch from hook, * ch 5, skip 2 ch, sc in next 5 ch. Repeat from * across, ending with 2 sc. Ch 4, turn. **2nd row:** * In next loop make 3 tr, ch 5 and 3 tr; ch 2, sc in next loop, ch 2. Repeat from * across. Break off.

8046 . . . Materials: THREE CORD MERCER-IZED CROCHET, *Size 50 . . . Steel Crochet Hook No. 12.*

To make braid, ch 11, tr in first st of chain, * ch 7, turn, skip 2 sts of last loop, tr in next st. Repeat from * for length desired. Ch 1, do not turn. **1st row:** * In next sp work half dc, 5 dc and half dc, sc in next st. Repeat from * along braid. Repeat row on other side of braid. Break off.

Heading . . . Attach thread to 3rd dc of 1st scallop on one long side, ch 10, tr in 3rd dc of next scallop, * ch 5, tr in 3rd dc of next scallop. Repeat from * across. Break off.

9008 . . . Materials: BEST SIX CORD MER-CERIZED CROCHET, *Size 30 . . . Steel Crochet Hook No. 10.*

Make a chain the length desired. **1st row:** Dc in 5th ch from hook, * ch 1, skip 1 ch, dc in next ch. Repeat from * across. Ch 1, turn. **2nd row:** * In next sp make sc, ch 3, sl st in 3rd ch from hook, and sc; 2 sc in next sp. Repeat from * across. Break off.

9020 . . . Materials: BEST SIX CORD MERCERIZED CROCHET, *Size 30* . . . *Steel Crochet Hook No. 10.*

1st row: * Ch 5, dc in 5th ch from hook. Repeat from * for length desired. Ch 5, turn. **2nd row:** * Sc in next loop, ch 5. Repeat from * across. Ch 1, turn. **3rd row:** * 3 sc in next ch-5 loop, (ch 2, sl st in 2nd ch from hook) twice; 3 sc in same loop, 5 sc in next loop. Repeat from * across. Break off.

9006 . . . Materials: BEST SIX CORD MERCERIZED CROCHET, *Size 30* . . . *Steel Crochet Hook No. 10.*

Make a chain slightly longer than length desired. **1st row:** Sc in 9th ch from hook, * ch 5, skip 3 ch, sc in next ch. Repeat from * across. Ch 5, turn. **2nd row:** * Sc in 3rd ch from hook (a picot made), ch 3, sc in next loop, ch 5. Repeat from * across. Break off.

9014 . . . Materials: BEST SIX CORD MERCERIZED CROCHET, *Size 30* . . . *Steel Crochet Hook No. 10.*

1st row: Ch 3, (thread over hook, insert hook in 3rd ch from hook and draw a loop through) twice; * thread over and draw through all loops on hook (cluster made), ch 1. Pull loop on hook out to measure 1/8 inch, (thread over, insert hook in ch-1 and draw a loop through) twice. Repeat from * for length desired. Ch 5, turn. **2nd row:** * Skip 1 cluster, sc on side of next cluster, ch 5. Repeat from * across. Ch 1, turn. **3rd row:** In each ch-5 loop across make (sc, ch 2) 3 times and sc. Break off.

9011. . . Materials: BEST SIX CORD MERCERIZED CROCHET, *Size 30* . . . *Steel Crochet Hook No. 10.*

1st row: * Ch 6; sc in 2nd ch from hook, half dc in next ch, dc in next ch. Repeat from * for length desired. Break off. **2nd row:** Attach thread in 1st sc made, sc in place where thread was attached, * sc in next half dc, sc in dc, sc under ch-2 (between groups); ch 3, in next sc make sc, ch 3 and sc. Repeat from * across. Break off.

9007 . . . Materials: THREE CORD MERCERIZED CROCHET, *Size 50* . . . *Steel Crochet Hook No. 12.*

Make a chain slightly longer than desired length. **1st row:** Sc in 9th ch from hook, * ch 5, skip 3 ch, sc in next ch. Repeat from * across. Ch 3, turn. **2nd row:** * Sc in 3rd ch from hook, (ch 3, sc in 3rd ch from hook) twice; sc in next loop, 5 dc in sc between 2 loops, sc in next loop, ch 3. Repeat from * across, ending with sc in last loop. Break off.

8969 . . . Materials: BEST SIX CORD MERCERIZED CROCHET, *Size 30* . . . *Steel Crochet Hook No. 10.*

Make a chain the length desired. **1st row:** In 4th ch from hook make 4 dc, ch 2 and 4 dc; * skip 2 ch, sc in next ch, skip 2 ch, in next ch make 4 dc, ch 2 and 4 dc. Repeat from * across, ending with an sc. Ch 5, turn. **2nd row:** * In ch-2 sp make sc, ch 3 and sc; ch 5, sc in next sc, ch 5. Repeat from * across. Break off.

9023 . . . Materials: THREE CORD MERCERIZED CROCHET, *Size 50* . . . *Steel Crochet Hook No. 12.*

Make a chain slightly longer than length desired. **1st row:** Sc in 2nd ch from hook, * (ch 3, sc in 3rd ch from hook) 3 times (3 picots made), skip 2 ch, sc in next 7 ch. Repeat from * across, ending with 3 p's, skip 2 ch, sc in next ch. Ch 5, turn. **2nd row:** * Tr between 1st and 2nd p's of next loop, ch 5, tr between 2nd and 3rd p's of same loop, ch 5, skip 1 sc, sc in next 5 sc, ch 5. Repeat from * across, ending with ch 5, sl st in last sc. Ch 1, turn. **3rd row:** * In next loop make 2 sc, p and 2 sc; in next loop make (2 sc, p) twice and 2 sc; in next loop make 2 sc, p and 2 sc; ch 2, skip 2 sc, sc in next sc, ch 2. Repeat from * across. Break off.

8961 . . . Materials: BEST SIX CORD MERCERIZED CROCHET, *Size 30* . . . *Steel Crochet Hook No. 10.*

1st row: Ch 4, 5 dc in 4th ch from hook. Ch 3, turn. **2nd row:** Sc in 1st dc, ch 3, holding back on hook the last loop of each dc make dc in next 4 dc and in turning chain, thread over and draw through all loops on hook, ch 1 to fasten (a cluster made). Ch 3, turn. **3rd row:** 5 dc in fastening ch-1, ch 4, sc in ch-3 loop of previous row. Ch 4, turn. **4th row:** In next dc make sc, ch 3 and sc; ch 3, cluster over next 5 dc. Ch 3, turn. Repeat 3rd and 4th rows alternately for length desired. Break off.

9017 . . . Materials: THREE CORD MERCERIZED CROCHET, *Size 50* . . . *Steel Crochet Hook No. 12.*

Make a chain slightly longer than length desired. **1st row:** Dc in 4th ch from hook, dc in next ch, * ch 4, skip 4 ch, dc in next 3 ch. Repeat from * across. Ch 1, turn. **2nd row:** Sc in 3 dc, * ch 7, sc in next 3 dc. Repeat from * across. Ch 1, turn. **3rd row:** * Sc in center sc of 3-sc group, in ch-7 loop make (3 sc, ch 3) 3 times and 3 sc. Repeat from * across. Break off.

8871 . . . Materials: THREE CORD MERCERIZED CROCHET, *Size 50* . . . *Steel Crochet Hook No. 12.*

Make a chain 1½ times longer than length desired. **1st row:** Sc in 2nd ch from hook, sc in next 6 ch, * ch 7, skip 4 ch, sc in next 7 ch. Repeat from * across until 1st row is length desired. Cut off remaining chain. Ch 1, turn. **2nd row:** Skip 1st sc, sc in next 5 sc, * ch 5, sc in loop. Ch 5, skip next sc, sc in next 5 sc. Repeat from * across. Ch 1, turn. **3rd row:** Skip 1st sc, sc in next 3 sc, * ch 7, skip next sc, sc in next sc, ch 7, skip next sc, sc in next 3 sc. Repeat from * across. Ch 1, turn. **4th row:** Skip 1st sc, sc in next sc, * ch 5, sc in next loop, (ch 3, sc in 3rd ch from hook) 3 times; sc in next loop, ch 5, skip 1 sc, sc in next sc. Repeat from * across. Break off.

8878 . . . Materials: THREE CORD MERCERIZED CROCHET, *Size 50* . . . *Steel Crochet Hook No. 12.*

Make a chain 1½ times longer than length desired. **1st row:** Sc in 2nd ch from hook and in each ch across until 1st row is length desired,

having a multiple of 20 plus 9 sc's. Cut off remaining chain. Ch 1, turn. **2nd row:** Sc in 1st sc, * ch 7, skip 3 sc, sc in next sc, (ch 7, skip 3 sc, sc in next 5 sc) twice. Repeat from * across, ending with (ch 7, skip 3 sc, sc in next sc) twice. Ch 1, turn. **3rd row:** * In next loop make (3 sc, ch 3, sc in 3rd ch from hook—picot made) twice and 3 sc; in next loop make 3 sc, p, 1 sc, ch 10, turn, sl st in center sc (between p's) of last loop, turn. In ch-10 loop make (3 sc, p) 3 times and 3 sc; make 1 sc, p and 3 sc in last ch-7 loop, skip 1 sc, sc in next 3 sc, in next loop make (3 sc, p) twice and 3 sc; skip 1 sc, sc in next 3 sc. Repeat from * across. Break off.

8846 . . . Materials: THREE CORD MERCERIZED CROCHET, *Size 50* . . . *Steel Crochet Hook No. 12.*

First Flower . . . Ch 8, join with sl st to form ring. **1st rnd:** Ch 3, make 2 dc in ring, (ch 5, sc in 3rd ch from hook, ch 2, make 3 dc in ring) 6 times; ch 5, sc in 3rd ch from hook, ch 2, sl st in top st of ch-3. **2nd rnd:** Sc in next dc, (ch 10, sc in center dc of next group) 6 times; ch 10, sl st in 1st sc. Break off.

Second Flower . . . Work as for 1st flower until 1st rnd is complete. **2nd rnd:** Sc in next dc, ch 5, sc in any ch-10 loop on 1st flower, ch 5, sc in center dc of next group on 2nd flower. Finish 2nd rnd as before (no more joinings). Break off.

Make necessary number of flowers, joining them as 2nd was joined to 1st, having two ch-10 loops free on upper edge and 3 loops free on lower edge.

Heading . . . With right side facing, attach thread in 2nd loop to the right of 1st joining. **1st row:** Ch 1, sc in same place where thread was attached, * ch 5, sc in next loop, ch 5, holding back on hook the last loop of each d tr make d tr in each of next 2 (joined) loops, thread over and draw through all loops on hook, ch 5, sc in next loop on next flower. Repeat from * across. Ch 9, turn. **2nd row:** * (Dc in next sc, ch 5) twice; dc in top of joined tr's, ch 5. Repeat from * across. Break off.

8879 . . . Materials: THREE CORD MERCERIZED CROCHET, *Size 50* . . . *Steel Crochet Hook No. 12.*

Make a chain 1¼ times longer than length desired. **1st row:** Sc in 2nd ch from hook, * ch 10, skip 7 ch, sc in next ch. Repeat from * until 1st row is length desired, having a multiple of 3 plus 2 loops. Cut off remaining chain. Ch 1, turn. **2nd row:** * 7 sc in next loop, ch 10, sc in next loop, ch 1, turn. Make 14 sc over ch-10 loop, sl st in next sc. Ch 1, turn; sc in 14 sc. Turn; (ch 7, skip 4 sc, sc in next sc) twice; ch 7, sc in sl st. Ch 1, turn. In each ch-7 loop make sc, half dc, 7 dc, half dc and sc, sl st in next sc. Make 7 sc in same loop on 1st row, 7 sc in next loop, ch 8, sc in 8th ch from hook, (ch 7, sc in same place as last sc) twice; 7 sc in same loop. Repeat from * across. Break off.

Heading . . . With right side facing, attach thread to end of starting chain. Ch 3, dc in same place, ch 6, dc in each of next 2 loops, * ch 6, dc in same loop as last dc, dc in next loop. Repeat from * across. Break off.

8854 . . . Materials: KNIT-CRO-SHEEN, *light and dark colors* . . . *Steel Crochet Hook No. 7.*

1st row: Starting at one end with Light, ch 6, dc in 6th ch from hook, * ch 5, turn, dc in dc. Repeat from * for length desired, having a multiple of 4 plus 1 dc groups. Break off. **2nd row:** Attach Light in 1st ch-5 loop, ch 1, sc in same loop, * ch 1, in next loop make 7 tr with ch 1 between, ch 1, sc in next loop. Repeat from * across. Break off. **3rd row:** Turn, attach Dark in last ch-1 sp made on last row, sc in same place, * sc in next sp between tr's, (ch 3, sc in next sp) 5 times; sc in each of next 2 sps. Repeat from * across, ending with sc in last sp. Ch 4, turn. **4th row:** * (Dc in next ch-3 loop, ch 1) twice; in next loop make 4 dc with ch 1 between, (ch 1, dc in next loop) twice. Repeat from * across, ending with dc in last loop, tr in last sc. Break off. **5th row:** Turn, attach Light to tr, sc in ch-1 sp between dc's, * (ch 3, sc in next sp) 3 times; ch 3, sc where last sc was made, (ch 3, sc in next sp) 3 times; skip 2 dc, sc in next sp. Repeat from * across. Ch 1, turn. **6th row:** * Sc in next loop, (ch 3, sc in next loop) 3 times; ch 3, sc where last sc was made, (ch 3, sc in next loop) 3 times. Repeat from * across. Break off.

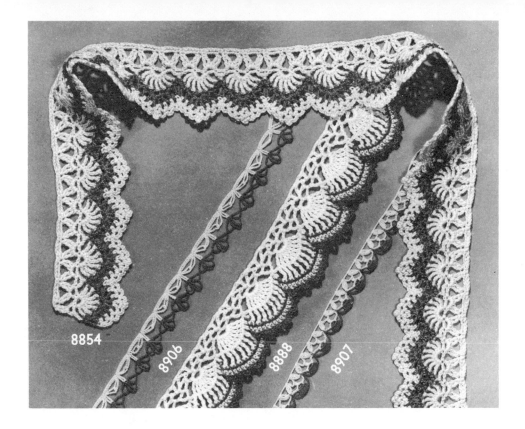

Heading . . . 1st row: Attach Light to 1st free ch-5 loop on opposite edge, ch 4, tr in same place, ch 4, holding back on hook the last loop of each tr, make 2 tr in same loop, thread over and draw through all loops on hook (cluster made), * in next loop make cluster, ch 4 and cluster. Repeat from * across. Ch 1, turn. **2nd row:** Sc in tip of 1st cluster, * ch 4, sc in tip of next 2 clusters. Repeat from * across, ending with sc in tip of last cluster. Break off.

8906 . . . Materials: BEST SIX CORD MERCERIZED CROCHET, *Size 30, White and Ecru . . . Steel Crochet Hook No. 10.*

With White make a chain 1¼ times longer than length desired. **1st row:** Sc in 2nd ch from hook, ch 9, sc in same ch, ch 13, sc in same ch, * sc in next 9 ch, ch 6, sl st in last ch-13 loop, ch 6, in same ch as last sc make sc, ch 9, sc, ch 13 and sc. Repeat from * across until row is length desired, ending with sc in next 9 ch, ch 6, sl st in last ch-13 loop, ch 6, in same ch as last sc make sc, ch 9 and sc. Break off. Cut off remaining chain. **2nd row:** Attach Ecru in center st of 1st ch-9 loop, ch 8, in same center st of loop make tr, ch 4, d tr, ch 4, tr, ch 4 and d tr, * in center st of next free ch-9 loop make

(d tr, ch 4, tr, ch 4) twice and d tr. Repeat from * across. Break off.

8888 . . . Materials: PEARL COTTON, *Size 5, light and dark colors . . . Steel Crochet Hook No. 7.*

Starting at one narrow end with Light, ch 6. **1st row:** Dc in 6th ch from hook, ch 3, dc in same ch. Ch 5, turn. **2nd row:** In ch-3 sp make dc, ch 3 and dc. Ch 5, turn. Repeat the 2nd row for length desired (there must be an even number of ch-5 loops on one side and one additional loop on other side). Do not ch to turn at end of last row. Work along end with odd number of loops as follows: **1st row:** Turn, sl st in next 3 ch, in next dc and in next 2 ch Sc in loop, * ch 1, 9 tr in next ch-5 loop, ch 1 sc in next ch-5 loop. Repeat from * across, ending with sc. Ch 3, turn. **2nd row:** * Tr in next tr, (ch 1, tr in next tr) 8 times, ch 3, sc in next sc, ch 3. Repeat from * across. Break off. Turn. **3rd row:** Attach Dark in last sc of last row. Work 2 sc in ch-3 loop, * (sc in next tr, sc in next sp) 8 times; sc in next tr, 2 sc in each of next 2 sps. Repeat from * across. Break off. **4th row:** Working in same direction as last row, attach Light to 2nd st. Work sc in same place, sc in next 18 sc, * skip 2 sc, sc in next 19 sc. Repeat from * across. Break off. **5th row:** Working in same direction as last row attach Dark to 1st sc. Work sc in same place and in next 2 sts, * (ch 3, sc in next 3 sts) twice; ch 3, sc in next st, (ch 3, sc in next 3 sts) twice; ch 3, sc in next 6 sts. Repeat from * across. Break off.

Heading . . . Attach Light to 1st free ch-5 loop, sc in same loop, * ch 2, dc over next dc (between ch-5 loops), ch 2, sc in next ch-5 loop. Repeat from * across. Break off.

8907 . . . Materials: BEST SIX CORD MERCERIZED CROCHET, Size 30, White and Ecru . . . Steel Crochet Hook No. 10.

With White make a chain slightly longer than length desired. **1st row:** Holding back on hook the last loop of each tr, make 2 tr in 5th ch from hook, thread over and draw through all loops on hook (cluster made), * skip 5 ch, make a 2-tr cluster in next ch, ch 4, sc at base of 2-tr cluster, ch 7, skip 3 ch, sc in next ch, ch 4, then holding back on hook the last loop of each tr make 2 tr in same place as last sc and complete a cluster as before. Repeat from * across for length desired, ending with ch-7 and cluster, then skip 5 ch and make a 3-tr

cluster in next ch. Ch 1, turn. Cut off remaining chain. **2nd row:** Sc between 2 clusters, * ch 4, thread over twice, insert hook in next ch-7 and draw loop through, thread over and draw through 2 loops on hook, thread over, insert hook in same ch-7 and draw loop through, (thread over and draw through 2 loops) 4 times (a long cluster made), ch 5, dc in center of long cluster, ch 4, sc between next 2 clusters. Repeat from * across. Break off. Turn. Attach Ecru to last sc of previous row. * Sc between clusters on 1st row (working over the sc of previous row), ch 5, skip next sp, 7 dc in next loop, ch 5. Repeat from * across. Break off.

8904 . . . Materials: THREE CORD MERCERIZED CROCHET, Size 50 . . . Steel Crochet Hook No. 12.

Starting at narrow end, ch 18. **1st row:** 2 dc in 8th ch from hook, ch 2, make 2 dc in next ch, ch 5, skip 7 ch, 2 dc in next ch, ch 2, make 2 dc in next ch. Ch 7, turn. **2nd row:** In next ch-2 sp make 2 dc, ch 2 and 2 dc (shell over shell), ch 5, shell over shell. Ch 7, turn. **3rd row:** Shell over shell, ch 3, sc over both chains below, ch 3, shell over shell. Ch 7, turn. **4th and 5th rows:** Shell over shell, ch 5, shell over shell. Ch 7, turn. **6th row:** Shell over shell,

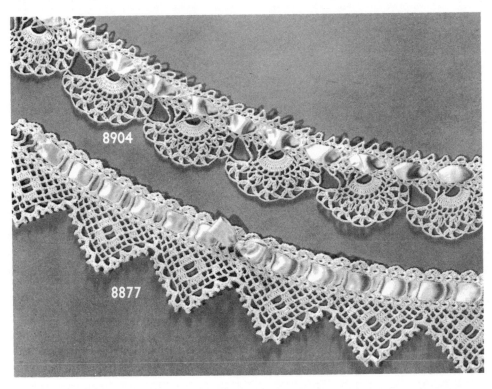

ch 3, sc over both chains below, ch 3, shell over shell. Ch 10, do not turn but work sc in next loop on this side; ch 4, tr in next loop on this side. Turn. **7th row:** Make 18 tr in ch-10 loop, ch 1, shell over shell, ch 5, shell over shell. Ch 7, turn. **8th row:** Shell over shell, ch 5, shell over shell, ch 1, dc in next tr, (ch 2, skip next tr, dc in next tr) 8 times; ch 2, dc in top st of ch-4, tr tr in next loop on this side. Ch 5, turn. **9th row:** Sc in next ch-2 sp, (ch 5, sc in next ch-2 sp) 8 times; ch 3, shell over shell, ch 3, sc over both chains below, ch 3, shell over shell. Ch 7, turn. **10th row:** Shell over shell, ch 5, shell over shell, ch 1, * holding back on hook the last loop of each tr make 2 tr in next ch-5 loop, thread over and draw through all loops on hook (cluster made), ch 5, cluster in same loop, ch 3, sc in next loop, ch 3. Repeat from * 3 more times; in next loop make cluster, ch 5 and cluster. Ch 9, turn. **11th row:** (In next ch-5 sp make 3 clusters with ch 5 between) 5 times; ch 3, shell over shell, ch 5, shell over shell. Ch 7, turn. **12th to 17th rows incl:** Repeat 3rd, 4th and 5th rows respectively, twice. **18th to 21st rows incl:** Repeat 6th to 9th rows incl. **22nd row:** Repeat 10th row, but end with ch 4, sc in top of center cluster of adjoining 3-cluster group. Ch 4, turn. **23rd row:** Repeat 11th row. Repeat last 12 rows (12th to 23rd rows incl) for length desired. Break off.

8877 . . . Materials: BEST SIX CORD MERCERIZED CROCHET, Size 30 . . . *Steel Crochet Hook No. 10.*

Starting at narrow end, ch 17. **1st row:** 2 dc in 4th ch from hook, ch 2, make 3 dc in next ch (shell made), ch 5, skip 7 ch, 3 dc in next ch, ch 2, make 3 dc in next ch (shell), ch 2, skip 2 ch, dc in next ch. Ch 5, turn. **2nd row:** Dc in 1st dc of shell, ch 2, in ch-2 sp of shell below make 3 dc, ch 2 and 3 dc (shell over shell), ch 5, shell over shell. Ch 3, turn. **3rd row:** Shell over shell, ch 5, shell over shell, ch 2, skip 2 dc, dc in next dc (sp made), ch 2, dc in next dc, ch 2, dc in 3rd st of turning chain (2 more sps made). Ch 5, turn. **4th row:** Dc in next dc (sp made), 2 dc in sp, dc in next dc (bl made), ch 2, dc in next dc, ch 2, shell over shell, ch 5, shell over shell. Ch 3, turn. **5th row:** Shell, ch 5, shell, 5 sps. Ch 5, turn.

6th row: Make 2 sps, 2 bls, 1 sp, ch 2, shell, ch 5, shell. Ch 3, turn. **7th row:** Shell, ch 5, shell, 2 sps, 1 bl, ch 4, skip 5 dc, dc in next dc, 1 bl, 1 sp. Ch 5, turn. **8th row:** 1 sp, 1 bl, ch 4, dc in next dc, 1 bl, 2 sps, ch 2, shell, ch 5, shell. Ch 3, turn. **9th row:** Shell, ch 5, shell, 2 sps, 1 bl, 2 sps, 5 dc over ch-4, dc in next dc, 2 sps. Ch 5, turn. **10th row:** Make 9 sps, ch 2, shell, ch 5, shell. Ch 3, turn. **11th row:** Shell, ch 5, shell, ch 2, skip 2 dc, dc in next dc. Ch 5, turn. Repeat last 10 rows (2nd to 11th rows incl) for length desired. Break off.

Edging . . . **1st row:** Attach thread in end sp (next to shell) on scalloped edge, ch 10, * skip 1 sp, sc in next sp, (ch 7, skip 1 sp, sc in next sp) 3 times; (ch 7, sc in next sp) twice; (ch 7, skip 1 sp, sc in next sp) 3 times; ch 3, skip 1 sp, holding back on hook the last loop of each tr make tr in each of the next 2 sps, thread over and draw through all loops on hook, ch 3. Repeat from * across. Ch 1, turn. **2nd row:** Make 3 sc in each ch-3 loop and in each ch-7 loop make (3 sc, ch 3, sc in 3rd ch from hook) twice and 3 sc. Break off.

8887 . . . Materials: THREE CORD MERCERIZED CROCHET, Size 50 . . . *Steel Crochet Hook No. 12.*

First Motif . . . Starting at center ch 10. Join with sl st to form ring. **1st rnd:** Ch 1, work 18 sc in ring. Join with sl st in 1st sc made. **2nd rnd:** Ch 4 (to count as tr), holding back on hook the last loop of each tr make 2 tr in same place as sl st, thread over and draw through all loops on hook (3-tr cluster made), * ch 10, skip 2 sc, 3-tr cluster in next sc. Repeat from * around, joining last ch-10 with sl st in top of 1st cluster made. **3rd rnd:** * In next loop make 3 sc, (ch 3, 3 sc) 3 times. Repeat from * around. Join and break off.

Second Motif . . . Work as for First Motif until 2nd rnd is complete. **3rd rnd:** In 1st loop make 3 sc, (ch 3, 3 sc) twice; ch 1, sc in corresponding picot on First Motif, ch 1, 3 sc in same loop on Second Motif, 3 sc in next loop, ch 1, sc in next p on First Motif, ch 1, in same loop on Second Motif make 3 sc, (ch 3, 3 sc) twice; and complete motif with no more joinings. Break off. Make and join a number of motifs as second was joined to first (there are 7 free p's between joinings).

81

Corner Motif . . . Work another motif until the 2nd rnd is complete. Join as follows: **3rd rnd:** In 1st loop make 3 sc, ch 3, 3 sc, ch 1, skip 6 p's on last motif (inner edge), sc in next p, ch 1, 3 sc in same loop on Corner Motif, ch 1, sc in next p on last motif, ch 1, 3 sc in same loop on Corner Motif. Complete motif as before (no more joinings). Break off.

Next Motif . . . Work as for First Motif until 2nd rnd is complete. **3rd rnd:** In 1st loop make 3 sc, ch 3, 3 sc, ch 1, skip 2 p's on Corner Motif (inner edge), sc in next p, ch 1, 3 sc in same loop on motif in work, ch 1, sc in next p on Corner Motif, ch 1, 3 sc in same loop. Complete motif as before. Continue thus, joining motifs as second was joined to first, along straight edges and turning corners as described.

Inner Edge of Motifs . . . With right side facing, attach thread in the 3rd free p to the left of a corner. **1st rnd:** Ch 1, sc in same place where thread was attached, * ch 6, skip 1 p, tr in next p, ch 6, skip 2 p's, tr in next p, ch 6, skip 1 p, sc in next p. Repeat from * across until the last sc made is on the motif before the corner, ch 6, skip next p, holding back on hook the last loop of each d tr, make d tr in each of next 4 free p's, thread over and draw through all loops on hook, ch 6, skip next p, sc in next p. Continue thus around. Join. **2nd rnd:** Ch 1 and work 7 sc over each ch-6 loop. Join. **3rd rnd:** Ch 4, * skip 1 sc, dc in next sc, ch 1. Repeat from * to 2 sts before next corner, holding back on hook the last loop of each dc, make dc in next st, skip 4 sts, dc in next st, thread over and draw through all loops on hook, ch 1, skip 1 st, dc in next st and continue thus around. Join last ch-1 with sl st in 3rd st of starting chain. **4th rnd:** Ch 1, sc in same place as sl st, * sc in next sp, sc in next st. Repeat from * around. Join and break off.

8886 . . . Materials: BEST SIX CORD MER-CERIZED CROCHET, *Size 30* . . . *Steel Crochet Hook No. 10.*

Make a tight chain 1½ times longer than length desired. **1st rnd:** Dc in 8th ch from hook, (ch 2, skip 2 ch, dc in next ch) 18 times; (ch 2, dc in same place as last dc) twice (2 sps made for corner); * ch 2, skip 2 ch, dc in next ch. Repeat from * across to next corner, being sure to have a multiple of 12 plus 8 sps, excluding 2 sps for corner, for side of lace make another corner. Continue thus around until all corners are made and all sides are complete. Join with sl st in 5th st of starting chain. Cut off remainder of starting chain. **2nd rnd:** Sl st in next sp, ch 5, dc in next sp, (ch 2, dc in next sp) 4 times; ch 4, skip 2 sps, 5 tr in next sp, ch 2, make 5 tr in next sp, ch 4, skip 2 sps, dc in next sp, (ch 2, dc in next sp) 5 times; ch 4, skip 1 sp, 5 tr in 1st sp of corner, ch 2, make 5 tr in 2nd sp of corner, ch 4 skip 1 sp, * dc in next sp, (ch 2, dc in next sp) 5 times; ch 4, skip 2 sps, 5 tr in next sp, ch 2, make 5 tr in next sp, ch 4, skip 2 sps. Repeat from * across to next corner. Turn corner as before and continue around, joining last ch-4 with sl st in 3rd st of starting chain. **3rd rnd:** Sl st in next sp, ch 5, dc in next sp, (ch 2, dc in next sp) 3 times; ch 4, (tr in next 3 tr, ch 2, tr in same place as last tr, tr in next 2 tr, ch 2) twice; ch 2 more, skip next sp, dc in next sp, (ch 2, dc in next sp) 4 times; ch 4, tr in next 3 tr, ch 2, tr in same place as last tr, tr in next 2 tr, ch 5, work over the next 5 tr as before, ch 4, skip next sp, dc in next sp and continue around. Join as before. **4th rnd:** Sl st to center of 2nd sp, ch 5, dc in next sp, ch 4, make 2 tr in next tr, tr in next 5 tr, ch 3, tr in ch-2 sp, ch 3, tr in next 5 tr, 2 tr in next tr, ch 6, skip 2 sps, dc in next sp, ch 2, dc in next sp, ch 6, make 2 tr in next tr, tr in next 4 tr, 2 tr in next tr, ch 3, make 4 tr in corner loop, ch 3, make 2 tr in next tr, tr in next 4 tr, make 2 tr in next tr, ch 6, skip 2 sps, dc in next sp and continue around. Join.

5th rnd: Sl st in next sp, ch 12, holding back on hook the last loop of each tr make tr in 7 tr, thread over and draw through all loops on hook (cluster made), ch 5, make 5 tr in next tr, ch 5, make a cluster over the next 7 tr, ch 9, skip 1 sp, dc in next sp, ch 9, make a cluster over the next 8 tr, ch 5, (make a 3-tr cluster in the next tr, ch 2) 3 times; make a 3-tr cluster in the next tr, ch 5, make a cluster over the next 8 tr, ch 9, skip 1 sp, dc in next sp and continue around. Join. **6th rnd:** Sl st in next 2 ch, ch 8, tr in top of cluster, ch 6, make a 3-tr cluster in next tr, (ch 2, skip next tr, 3-tr cluster in next tr) twice; ch 6, tr in top of next

cluster, ch 6, dc in next loop, ch 3, dc in next loop, ch 5, dc in same loop, ch 5, tr in top of cluster, ch 5, (2-tr cluster in next cluster, ch 4, sc in 4th ch from hook—picot made—make another 2-tr cluster in same place as last cluster, ch 1) 4 times; ch 4 more, tr in top of next cluster, ch 5, dc in next loop, ch 5, dc in same loop, ch 3, dc in next loop and continue around. Join. **7th rnd:** Sl st in next sp, ch 1, sc in same sp, ch 7, tr in next tr, ch 6, (in top of next cluster make 2-tr cluster, p and 2-tr cluster, ch 1) 3 times; ch 5 more, tr in next tr, ch 7, sc in next ch-3 sp, ch 7, dc in next loop, ch 5, tr in next loop, ch 5, (2-tr cluster in next cluster, p, 2-tr cluster in next cluster, ch 3) 4 times; ch 2 more, skip next loop, tr in next loop, ch 5, dc in next loop, ch 7, sc in next ch-3 sp and continue around. Join and break off.

8885 . . . Materials: Best Six Cord Mercerized Crochet, *Size 30* . . . *Steel Crochet Hook No. 10.*

Starting where indicated on chart, ch 47. **1st row:** Dc in 8th ch from hook, dc in next 9 ch, (ch 2, skip 2 ch, dc in next ch) 3 times; dc in next 9 ch, (ch 2, skip 2 ch, dc in next ch) 4 times. Ch 5, turn. **2nd row:** Dc in next dc, (ch 2, dc in next dc) 3 times (4 sps over 4 sps

made); dc in next 9 dc (3 bls over 3 bls made), make 3 sps, ch 2, skip 2 dc, dc in next dc (sp over bl made); make 2 bls, ch 2, skip 2 ch, dc in next ch. Ch 5, turn. **3rd row:** Make 1 sp, 2 bls, 2 sps, 2 dc in next sp, dc in next dc (bl over sp made), make 5 more bls, 3 sps, ch 5, dc in same place as last dc (1 sp increased). Turn, sl st in 3 ch, ch 7, do not turn. **4th row:** Dc in same place as last sl st (1 sp increased), make 3 sps, 3 bls, 1 sp, 3 bls, 2 sps, 2 bls, 1 sp. Ch 5, turn. **Follow chart until 11th row is completed. Turn. 12th row:** Sl st in 2 ch, sl st in dc (1 sp decreased), ch 5 and follow chart across. Ch 5, turn. Now follow chart until 17th row is complete. Ch 13, turn. **18th row:** Dc in 8th ch from hook, ch 2, skip 2 ch, dc in next ch, ch 2, dc in next dc (3 sps increased), ch 2 and follow chart across. Ch 5, turn. Now follow chart to top. Do not break off but continue on until corner is complete. Break off. Attach thread at X and follow chart for other side of lace. Repeat these last 2 scallops alternately for straight part of pattern. Turn corners as before. Work sc evenly along both straight and scalloped edges. Break off.

8953 . . . Materials: Three Cord Mercerized Crochet, *Size 50* . . . *Steel Crochet Hook No. 12.*

Starting at bottom of chart, ch 29. **1st row:** Dc in 8th ch from hook, (ch 2, skip 2 ch, dc in next ch) 4 times; dc in next 3 ch, ch 2, skip 2 ch, dc in next 4 ch. Ch 3, turn. **2nd row:** Dc in 3 dc (bl over bl made), ch 2, dc in next 4 dc

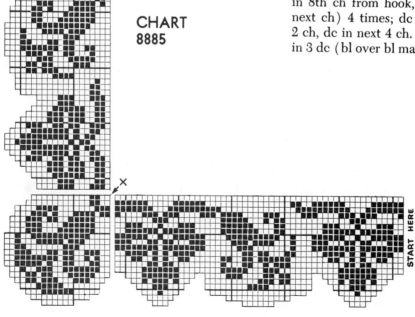

CHART
8885

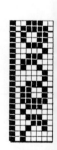

CHART
8953

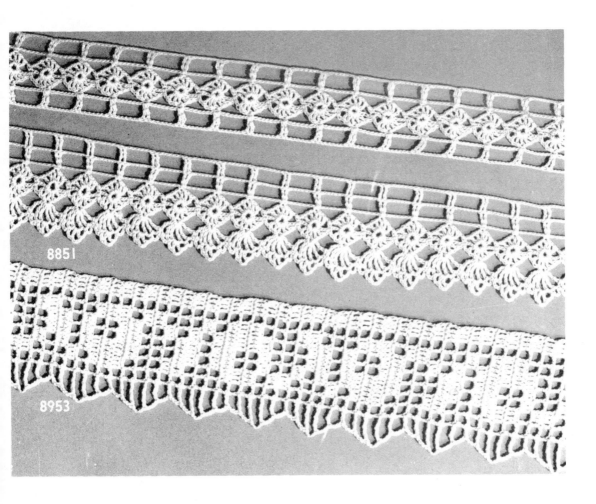

8851

8953

(sp over sp and bl over bl made), (ch 2, dc in next dc) 4 times; ch 2, skip 2 ch, dc in next ch (5 sps over 5 sps made). Ch 5, turn. **3rd row:** Dc in next dc, 2 dc in next sp, dc in dc (bl over sp made), make 2 sps, 1 bl, ch 2, skip 2 dc, dc in next dc (sp over bl made), make 1 more sp, 1 bl. Ch 3, turn. Starting with 4th row, follow chart to top. Repeat entire chart for length desired. Break off.

Edging . . . Attach thread in corner sp at one end, ch 6, * tr in end of next row, (ch 3, d tr in end of next row) twice; ch 3, tr in end of next row, ch 3, dc in end of next row, ch 3. Repeat from * across. Break off.

8851 . . . Materials: BEST SIX CORD MERCERIZED CROCHET, *Size 30* . . . *Steel Crochet Hook No. 10.*

Edging . . . 1st row: Ch 6, sl st in 6th ch from hook, * ch 11, dc in 4th ch from hook (sp made). Repeat from * for slightly longer than length desired. **2nd row:** Ch 4, * 5 dc with ch 1 between in next sp, ch 1, skip 3 ch, sc in next ch, ch 1. Repeat from * across to last sp. In last sp make 11 dc with ch 1 between. Now work along opposite side as follows: ** Ch 1, sc in base of next sc, ch 1, in next sp make 5 dc with ch 1 between. Repeat from ** across. Join with sl st in 3rd st of starting ch-4. Do not turn.

3rd row: Ch 9, * sc in center dc of next group, ch 7. Repeat from * across, ending with ch 5, skip 2 dc, tr in next dc. Ch 9, turn. **4th row:** * 2 tr in next sc, ch 6. Repeat from * across, ending with ch 5, skip 5 ch, tr in next ch. Ch 9, turn. **5th row:** * Tr in next 2 tr, ch 6. Repeat from * across, ending with ch 5, skip 5 ch, tr in next ch. Break off. **Next row:** Attach thread in same dc where tr at end of 3rd row was made and work along other long edge as follows: Ch 6, * in center dc of next group make 6 tr with ch 2 between. Repeat from * across, ending with ch 6, skip 2 dc, sl st in next dc.

Break off. **Last row:** With right side facing attach thread in 1st ch-2 sp of last row, ch 1, sc in same sp, * ch 3, sc in next sp, ch 2, in next sp make dc, ch 3 and dc; ch 2, sc in next sp, ch 3, sc in each of next 2 sps. Repeat from * across. Break off.

Insertion . . . 1st to 4th rows incl: Same as 1st to 4th rows incl of Edging. Break off. Attach thread on other end and work 3rd and 4th rows along other long edge in same way. Break off.

CHAPTER SEVEN

Pot Holders
and Hot Plate Mats

Wʜᴀᴛ's ᴛʜᴇ ʙᴜsɪᴇsᴛ and most popular spot in your home? Your kitchen, of course! It's the core of the household. From it come all good things, such as turkey and cranberry sauce for Thanksgiving dinner, all sorts of enticing delightful smells . . . ginger and cinnamon and Irish stew and freshly brewed coffee, and bacon crisping in the oven. From it comes the endless parade of meals—1,095 (excluding snacks)—that every member of your family eats during the year.

Let's make it as attractive as it deserves to be. Our collection of pot holders and hot plate mats will go a long way toward reaching this goal as well as making your cooking and serving chores easier.

Hot plate mats come in practically every size and shape you can think of to accommodate platters, teapots, vegetable plates, tureens—absolutely everything that's hot stuff. They come in pairs and sets, oval and square and round, and will keep your precious table safe. As for the pot holders—they come in fun-making disguises like sugar and creamer and cup, or there's a whole family to hang over your stove— Ma, Pa, and Susie—along with that must for every good cook—a pair of mittens made for grasping the roaster.

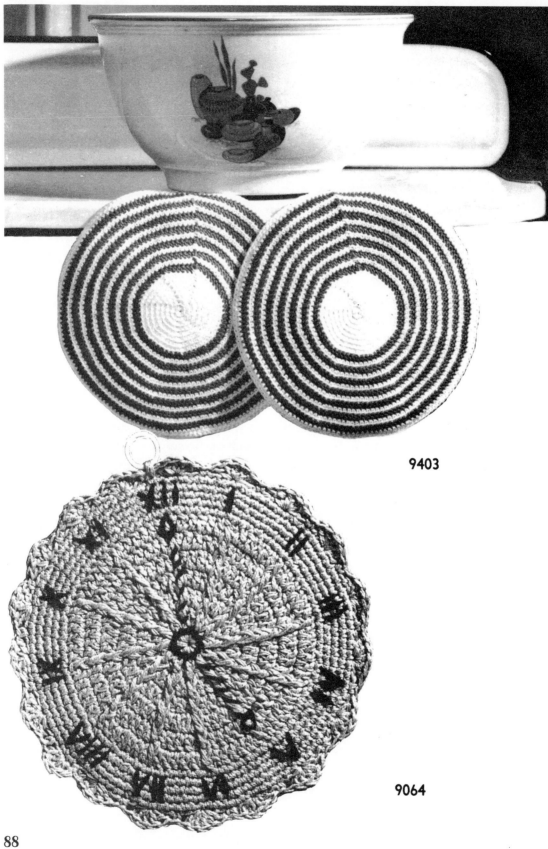

9403

9064

9403 . . . Materials: KNIT-CRO-SHEEN, *1 ball of White or Ecru for main color, 1 ball each of 2 contrasting colors (to be referred to as Light and Dark)* . . . *Steel Crochet Hook No. 7* . . . *2 plastic rings.*

Starting at center with main color, ch 2. **1st rnd:** 7 sc in 2nd ch from hook. **2nd rnd:** 2 sc in back loop of each sc around. **3rd rnd:** * Sc in back loop of next sc, 2 sc in back loop of next sc. Repeat from * around. **4th rnd:** * Sc in back loop of next 2 sc, 2 sc in next sc. Repeat from * around. Continue thus working in the back loop, increasing as necessary to keep work flat until piece measures 2 inches in diameter. Drop main color. Attach Light and ch 2. **Next rnd:** Half dc in back loop of each sc around increasing as necessary. Join with sl st in top st of starting chain. Drop Light. Pick up main color and ch 1. **Following rnd:** Sc in each half dc around (through both loops) increasing as necessary. Join with sl st in 1st sc. Drop main color. Attach Dark and ch 2. **Next rnd:** Half dc in back loop of each sc around increasing as necessary. Join with sl st in top st of starting chain. Drop Dark, pick up main color and ch 1. Work another sc rnd as before. Drop main color, pick up Light, and ch 2. Repeat these last 4 rnds for stripe pattern until piece measures 6 inches in diameter, ending with an sc rnd. Break off. Make another piece same as this.

For padding see chapter on General Information. Work a rnd of sc all around through the 2 pieces. Sew on ring. Make other pot holder same as this.

9064 . . . Materials: PEARL COTTON, *Size 5, 3 balls* . . . SIX STRAND EMBROIDERY FLOSS, *1 skein of Black* . . . *Steel Crochet Hook No. 7* . . . *A plastic ring.*

Use double thread throughout.

1st rnd: Ch 4, 11 dc in 4th ch from hook. Join. **2nd rnd:** Ch 3 (to count as dc), dc under ch on 1st rnd (a raised st); * dc in next dc, dc under bar of same st where last dc was made. Repeat from * around (12 dc and 12 raised sts). Join. Make a raised st over each raised st and dc over each dc, increasing 1 dc in each dc-section, until piece measures 5½ inches in diameter. Now make sc in each st around, in-

creasing as necessary to keep work flat, until piece measures 7 inches in diameter. Break off.

With 2 full strands of Six Strand, embroider Roman numerals on sc-section. Embroider a circle at center, with over-and-over stitches embroider over any 2 lines of raised sts, making one slightly shorter than the other, and ending each in a triangle (see illustration).

SCALLOPED EDGE . . . Attach thread in any sc and * skip 2 sc; in next sc make 5 dc with ch-1 between, skip 2 sc, sc in next sc. Repeat from * around. Break off. Sew ring to scallop.

For padding, see chapter on General Information.

9362 . . . Materials: KNIT-CRO-SHEEN, *1 ball* . . . *Steel Crochet Hook No. 7.*

Starting at center, ch 2. **1st rnd:** 6 sc in 2nd ch from hook. **2nd rnd:** 2 sc in each sc around. **3rd rnd:** * Sc in next sc, 2 sc in next sc. Repeat from * around. **4th rnd:** * Sc in next 2 sc, 2 sc in next sc. Repeat from * around. **5th rnd:** * Sc in next 3 sc, 2 sc in next sc. Repeat from * around. Continue thus, increasing 6 sc evenly on each rnd until there are 108 sc on rnd. Now work as follows: **1st rnd:** Sl st in next sc, ch 3, 2 dc in same place as sl st, thread over, insert hook in next st and pull loop through (to height of st on hook), (thread over, insert hook in same place and pull loop through) 3 times; thread over and draw through all loops on hook (cluster is made), * (dc in next st, make a cluster in next st) 8 times; 3 dc in next sc, cluster in next st. Repeat from * around, ending with a cluster, sl st in top st of ch-3. **2nd, 3rd and 4th rnds:** Sl st in next dc, ch 3, 2 dc in same place, * dc in each st across to center dc of next 3-dc group, 3 dc in next dc. Repeat from * around. Join.

5th rnd: Sl st in next dc, ch 3, 2 dc in same place, * cluster in next st, dc in next st. Repeat from * across to center dc of next 3-dc group, 3 dc in next st, cluster in next st, dc in next st and continue thus around, always making 3 dc in center dc of each 3-dc group. Join. **6th rnd:** Sl st in next dc, ch 1, 3 sc in same place as sl st, sc in each st around, making 3 sc in center dc of each 3-dc group. Sl st in 1st sc made. **7th rnd:** Sl st in next sc, ch 3, 2 dc in same place as sl st, * dc in next 5 sts, half dc in next 5 sts, sc in

9362

9378

each st to 10 sts from center sc of 3-sc group, half dc in next 5 sts, dc in next 5 sts, 3 dc in next st. Repeat from * around. Join. **8th rnd:** Same as previous rnd, only making sl st in each sc of rnd below. Join and break off.

Make another piece same as this. For padding see chapter on General Information. Sew edges together.

RING . . . Ch 16, join with sl st to form ring. Work sc closely over ring. Join with sl st in 1st sc made. Break off. Sew ring to pot holder.

9378 . . . Materials: KNIT-CRO-SHEEN, *1 ball* . . . *Steel Crochet Hook No. 7 . . . 1 plastic ring.*

Starting at center, ch 6. Join with sl st to form ring. **1st rnd:** Ch 1, 15 sc in ring. Join with sl st in 1st sc. **2nd rnd:** Ch 3 (to count as 1 dc), dc in same place as sl st, 2 dc in each st around (30 sts). Join with sl st in top st of 1st ch-3. **3rd rnd:** Ch 1, sc in same place as sl st, * half dc in front loop of next st, 5 dc in front loop of next st, half dc in front loop of next st, sc in front loop of next 2 sts. Repeat from * around. Join last sc in same place as 1st sc. **4th rnd:** Ch 3, dc in remaining loop of each st of rnd before last, increasing 15 sts evenly around (45 sts). Join. Repeat 3rd and 4th rnds alternately until piece measures 6¼ inches, ending with the 3rd rnd. Break off.

Make another piece same as this, sew these 2 pieces together along outer edges of last dc-rnd, having petals on outside. Sew on plastic ring.

7172 . . . Materials: KNIT-CRO-SHEEN, *1 ball each of Green, Blue, and Yellow* . . . *Steel Crochet Hook No. 6 or 7 . . . 3 hooks.*

7172-A (Left) . . . Starting at one side, with Green ch 60 (to measure about 7 inches). **1st row:** Sc in 2nd ch from hook, sc in each ch across. Ch 1, turn. **2nd row:** Sc in each sc across. Ch 1, turn. **3rd row:** Picking up only the front loop of each sc, make sc in each sc across. Ch 1, turn. **4th, 5th, and 6th rows:** Repeat 2nd, 3rd, and 2nd rows. Break off Green, attach Blue, and repeat 3rd and 2nd rows alternately 3 times. Break off Blue, attach Yellow, and repeat 3rd and 2nd rows alternately 3 more times. These 18 rows constitute the pattern (3 stripes). Work in pattern until piece is perfectly square. Break off. With Yellow ch 60 (to measure about 7 inches), and work another piece same as this, working entirely in Yellow. For padding see chapter on General Information. Join the 2 pieces by working sc

7172

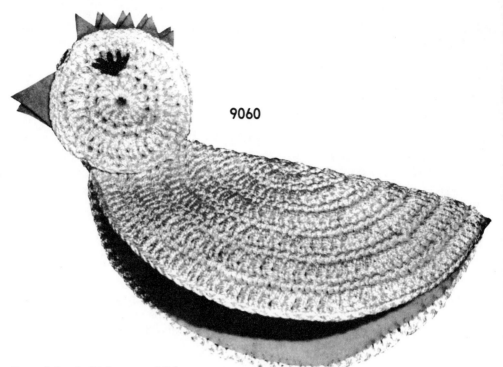

9060

with Yellow through both thicknesses. Make a ch-24 loop at one corner; work sc closely over loop. Break off.

7172-B (Center) . . . Starting at one corner, with Green ch 2. **1st row:** 3 sc in 2nd ch from hook. Ch 1, turn. **2nd row:** 2 sc in 1st sc (an inc), sc in each sc across, 2 sc in last sc (another inc). Ch 1, turn. **3rd row:** Picking up only the front loop of each sc, make 2 sc in 1st sc, sc in each sc across, 2 sc in last sc. Ch 1, turn. **4th, 5th, and 6th rows:** Repeat 2nd, 3rd, and 2nd rows. Break off Green, attach Blue and repeat 3rd and 2nd rows alternately 3 times. Break off Blue, attach Yellow, and repeat 3rd and 2nd rows alternately 3 more times. These 18 rows constitute pattern (3 stripes). Work in pattern until each increase-edge measures 6½ inches. Then, continuing in stripe pattern, dec 1 sc at both ends of each row until 3 sc remain (*to dec, work off 2 sc as 1 sc*). Break off. Make another piece same as this, working entirely in Blue. Make padding as before; then join pieces and make loop with Blue. Break off.

7172-C (Right) . . . Starting at top corner, with Green ch 2. **1st row:** 3 sc in 2nd ch from hook. Ch 1, turn. **2nd row:** Sc in each sc to center sc, 3 sc in center sc, sc in each sc across. Ch 1, turn. **3rd row:** Picking up only the front loop of each sc, make sc in each sc to center sc, 3 sc in center sc, sc in each sc across. Ch 1, turn. **4th, 5th and 6th rows:** Repeat 2nd, 3rd and 2nd rows. Break off Green, attach Blue, and repeat 3rd and 2nd rows alternately 3 times. Break off Blue, attach Yellow, and repeat 3rd and 2nd rows alternately 3 more times. These 18 rows constitute pattern (3 stripes). Work in pattern until each side measures 6½ inches. Break off. Make another piece same as this, working entirely in Green. Make padding as before; then join pieces and make loop with Green. Break off.

7172-D RACK . . . Starting at bottom, with Green make a chain 14 inches long. **1st row:** Sc in 2nd ch from hook, sc in each ch across until row measures 10 inches. Cut off remaining chain. Ch 1, turn. Hereafter work in stripe pattern as for Pot Holder 7172-A until 6 stripes are completed. Break off. Fold this piece in half, attach Blue at one corner and, working through the two thicknesses, work a row of sc closely together across one short side. Break off. Work other side to correspond.

Cut 2 pieces of wood or cardboard, each 2½ x 10 inches, and insert between the two thicknesses of crocheted piece. With Blue work a row of sc to join the 2 long sides together. Break off.

CORD . . . Measure off 6 strands of each color, each 1 yard long. Twist strands tightly, double the twisted strands and give them a second twist in the opposite direction. Tie a strand of Blue 1½ inches up from one end, and fasten securely. Finish opposite end in same way. Trim ends evenly. Sew one end of cord to each top corner of rack.

Attach 3 screw hooks at equal distances at center of lower stripe. Hang pot holders on hooks.

9060 . . . Materials: PEARL COTTON, *Size 5, 2 balls . . . Steel Crochet Hook No. 4 . . . 10 square inches of felt.*

Use double thread throughout.

BODY . . . Starting at center, ch 4. **1st rnd:** 14 dc in 4th ch from hook. Join with sl st in top st of ch-4. **2nd rnd:** Ch 1, 2 sc in same place as sl st, * sc in next 2 dc, 2 sc in next dc. Repeat from * around, join (20 sc). **3rd rnd:** Ch 3 (to count as dc), dc in same place as sl st, * dc in next sc, 2 dc in next sc. Repeat from * around, join. **4th rnd:** Ch 1, 2 sc in same place as sl st, * sc in next 2 dc, 2 sc in next dc. Repeat from * around, join (40 sc). Work in this manner, alternating sc-rnds and dc-rnds, increasing as necessary to keep work flat—*to inc, make 2 sts in 1 st*—until piece is 7 inches in diameter. Break off.

HEAD (Make 2) . . . Work as for Body until piece measures 2¼ inches in diameter. Break off.

Trace one 6¾-inch circle (body) and two 2-inch circles (head) on felt. Mark 5 points, ½ inch deep, along a 2-inch area at edges of small circles (comb), and 1 larger point 1 inch away from last point of comb (beak). Cut out pieces. Sew crocheted and felt body pieces together along outer edge. Fold in half. Place felt head pieces between crocheted head pieces and sew all together from bottom of beak to end of comb. Slip head over one end of folded body, and sew each side of head individually to body. Use small buttons or embroider eyes, as desired.

9387

9387 . . . Materials: RUG YARN, *1 70-yard skein . . . SIX STRAND EMBROIDERY FLOSS, 1 skein each of Green and Black . . . Crochet Hook Size G . . . A plastic ring.*

Starting at center, ch 2. **1st rnd:** 7 sc in 2nd ch from hook. Join with sl st in 1st sc made. **2nd and all even rnds:** Sl st in each st around. **3rd rnd:** 2 sc in back loop of each sc of 1st rnd. Join. **5th rnd:** * Sc in back loop of next sc of 3rd rnd, 2 sc in back loop of next sc of 3rd rnd. Repeat from * around. Join. **7th rnd:** * Sc in back loop of next 2 sc, 2 sc in back loop of next sc. Repeat from * around. Join. Continue thus, increasing 7 sts evenly on each sc rnd until piece measures 6½ inches in diameter, ending with a sl st rnd. Now work ears as follows: Working in *both loops* of each sc, make * sc in next sc, half dc in next sc; in next sc make dc and tr; in next st make tr and dc; half dc in next sc, sc in next sc, sl st in 9 sc. Repeat from * once more; then continue sl st to end of rnd. Break off.

Using wrong side of crochet for face, embroider cat's features, having green eyes, and black nose, mouth and whiskers. Sew ring between the ears.

9388 . . . Materials: Rug Yarn, *1 70-yard skein* . . . *Crochet Hook Size G* . . . *A plastic ring.*

Starting at center, ch 11. **1st rnd:** 3 sc in 2nd ch from hook, sc in each ch across to last ch, 5 sc in last ch; then, working along opposite side of starting chain, make sc in each ch and 2 sc in same place where first 3 sc were made. **2nd rnd:** 2 ch-sc in each of the next 3 sts—*to make a ch-sc, insert hook in st and pull loop through, yarn over and draw through 1 loop, yarn over and draw through 2 loops.* Ch-sc in each of 8 sts; 2 ch-sc in each of following 5 sts; ch-sc in each of next 8 sts, 2 ch-sc in each of next 2 sts. Continue thus working rnds of ch-sc, increasing as necessary around ends of oval to keep work flat, until piece measures about 5 x 7 inches (there must be a multiple of 8 sts on last rnd). Now work scallops as follows: * Sc in next st, skip 2 sts, 3 tr in each of next 3 sts, skip 2 sts. Repeat from * around. Join last tr with sl st in 1st sc made. Break off. Sew on ring.

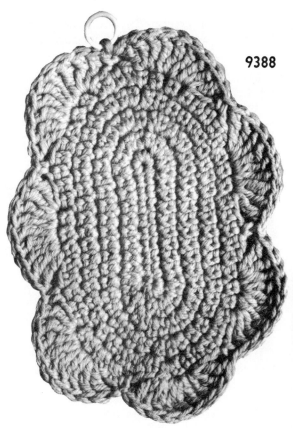

9388

9349 . . . Materials: Rug Yarn, *1 70-yard skein* . . . *Crochet Hook Size G.*

Starting at thumb, ch 8. **1st rnd:** Dc in 4th ch from hook and in each ch across; now, working along opposite side of starting chain, make dc in each ch across. Sl st in top st of starting chain. **2nd and 3rd rnds:** Ch 3 (to count as dc), dc in each st around. Join and break off. Lay this piece aside. Starting at finger tips, ch 13. **1st rnd:** Dc in 4th ch from hook and in each ch across. Now, working along the opposite side of starting chain, make dc in each st across (22 sts on rnd). Sl st in top st of starting chain. **2nd rnd:** Ch 3, dc in each dc around. Join. Repeat this rnd 3 more times. **6th rnd:** Ch 3, dc in each dc around, pick up thumb piece, insert hook in same place as last sl st on thumb piece, insert hook in top st of starting chain on last rnd of finger piece, yarn over and pull loop through (thus joining thumb and finger piece). Ch 3 and work in dc rnds (over both thumb and finger piece) as before, until piece measures 8½ inches from finger tip. Break off.

9349

94

9386 . . . Materials: RUG YARN, *1 70-yard skein each of White and any color . . . Crochet Hook Size G.*

POT HOLDER . . . Starting at center with Color, ch 4. **1st rnd:** 15 dc in 4th ch from hook. Join with sl st in top st of starting chain. Break off. Attach White in same place as sl st. **2nd rnd:** Ch 2, half dc in same place as sl st, * 2 half dc in next st (an inc is made), half dc in next st. Repeat from * around. Join with sl st in 1st half dc. Continue thus, increasing as necessary to keep work flat until piece measures about 5¾ inches in diameter. Join and break off White. Attach Color and work 1 more half dc rnd as before. Join and break off.

CENTER . . . With Color, ch 4 and work 1st rnd of Pot Holder. Break off.

SPOKE (Make 8) . . . With Color make a chain 6 inches long. Work sc in 2nd ch from hook and in each ch across. Break off.

Divide pot holder into 8 equal parts. Have one end of each spoke at outer edge of colored center and have spoke extend beyond edge of pot holder. Fold spoke to bring other end to corresponding position on other side. Sew spokes in place, whipping together the edges of each spoke-extension. Sew Center in center of piece. Make another pot holder same as this.

CORD . . . Cut 4 strands of Color each 1½ yards long. Twist tightly, then double the twisted strands and give them a second twist in the opposite direction. Knot loose ends and trim.

Sew a pot holder to each end of cord.

9370 . . . Materials: KNIT-CRO-SHEEN, *2 balls of Brown* . . . SIX STRAND EMBROIDERY FLOSS, *1 skein each of Black, Red, White, and Yellow* . . . *Steel Crochet Hook No. 7* . . . *3 plastic rings.*

HOLDER . . . Starting at center, ch 2. **1st rnd:** 7 sc in 2nd ch from hook. **2nd rnd:** 2 sc in each sc around. **3rd rnd:** * Sc in next sc, 2 sc in next sc. Repeat from * around. **4th rnd:** * Sc in next 2 sc, 2 sc in next sc. Repeat from * around. Continue thus, increasing as necessary to keep work flat, until piece measures 5¾ inches in diameter. Then work 2 rnds without increasing. Break off. Make 5 more pieces same as this.

Embroider features on 3 pieces in chain and back stitch as in illustration, using Black and Red for eyes, noses and lips. Use White for hair and eyebrows on Pa; Red and Yellow for bandanna on Ma, and Black for hair and eyebrows on Baby. For padding, see chapter on General Information. Sew back and face pieces together around edge. Sew ring to back at top.

9385 . . . Materials: KNIT-CRO-SHEEN, *2 balls each of 2 colors* . . . *Steel Crochet Hook No. 6.*

Starting at bottom with 1st color, ch 29 to measure 3 inches. **1st row:** Half dc in 3rd ch from hook, sc in same ch, sc in each ch across, in last ch make sc and half dc (29 sts). Ch 3, turn. **2nd, 3rd,** and **4th rows:** In first st make half dc and sc; sc in each st across, making sc, half dc and dc in last st or turning chain, as the case may be. Ch 3, turn. There are 41 sts at end of 4th row. Ch 1, turn. **5th row:** 2 sc in 1st st, sc in each st across. Ch 1, turn. Repeat 5th row until there are 61 sts on row. Work straight until piece measures 3 inches. Break off. Attach 2nd color. Ch 3, turn.

BAND . . . **1st row:** 2 dc in same place where

9370

2nd color was attached (half shell), * skip 2 sts, sc in next st, skip 2 sts, 5 dc in next st (shell). Repeat from * across, ending with 3 dc in last st (half shell). Ch 1, turn. **2nd row:** Sc in 1st dc, * shell in next sc, sc in center st of next shell. Repeat from * across, ending with sc in top st of turning chain. Ch 3, turn. **3rd row:** Half shell in sc, * sc in center st of next shell, shell in next sc. Repeat from * across, ending with half shell. Ch 1, turn. Repeat 2nd and 3rd rows alternately until piece measures 4¼ inches. Break off 2nd color. Attach 1st color, ch 2, turn. **Next row:** Work sc in each dc and half dc in each sc across (61 sts). Ch 1, turn. **Following row:** Sc in each st across. Ch 1, turn. Repeat last row until piece measures 5 inches. Break off.

Embroider lazy daisy flowers on edges of band as in illustration. Make another piece same as this.

HANDLE . . . With 1st color ch 6. **1st row:** Sc in 2nd ch from hook and in each ch across (5 sts). Ch 1, turn. **2nd row:** Sc in each st across. Ch 1, turn. Repeat 2nd row until piece measures 4½ inches. Break off. Fold in half and whip long edges together.

For padding see chapter on General Information. Pin ends of handle in place. Whip edges together neatly, using self colors. Make other pot holder same as this, reversing colors.

9228 . . . Materials: KNIT-CRO-SHEEN, *1 ball each of light and dark colors* . . . Steel Crochet Hook No. 7.

SUGAR BOWL . . . Starting at bottom, with Light ch 58 to measure 6½ inches. **1st row:** Sc in 2nd ch from hook, sc in each ch across. Ch 1, turn. **2nd, 3rd, and 4th rows:** Sc in each sc across. Ch 1, turn. At end of 4th row, break off. Turn. **5th row:** (Right side) Attach Dark, ch 1, sc in 1st sc, * insert hook in next sc 2 rows down and pull loop through, thread over and draw through 2 loops on hook (a long sc made); sc in next sc. Repeat from * across. Break off, do not turn. **6th row:** Attach Light in 1st sc of last row, ch 1, sc in 1st sc, sc in each st across. Ch 1, turn. **7th row:** Sc in each sc across. Break off. Turn. **8th to 13th rows incl:** Repeat 5th, 6th and 7th rows twice. At the end of the 13th row ch 3, turn. **14th row:** Dc in each sc across. Ch 3, turn. **15th row:** Dc in each dc across, dc in top st of turning chain. Ch 3, turn. Repeat 15th row until piece measures 4½ inches in all. Ch 3, turn.

To Shape Top: 1st row: (Holding back on hook the last loop of each dc, make dc in 3 dc, thread over and draw through all loops on hook) twice (4 dc decreased). Dc in each dc

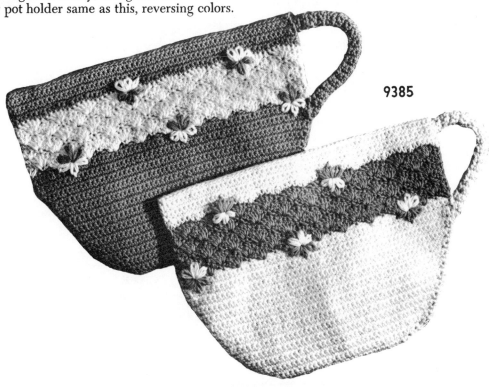

9385

97

9228

across to last 5 dc, work off next 3 dc as 1 dc (2 dc decreased); holding back on hook the last loop of each dc make dc in last 2 dc, dc in top st of turning chain, thread over and draw through all loops on hook (4 more dc decreased). Ch 3, turn. **2nd and 3rd rows:** Repeat 1st row. At end of 3rd row, ch 1, turn. **4th, 5th, and 6th rows:** Sc in each st across. Ch 1, turn. At end of 6th row, break off. **7th row:** With right side facing attach Dark, ch 1, sc in 1st sc, * long sc in next sc, sc in next sc. Repeat from * across. Break off Dark, attach Light and repeat 5th, 6th, and 7th rows once more. Break off Dark, attach Light. **Next row:** 2 sc in first st, sc in each st across, 2 sc in last st. Ch 1, turn. Repeat last row 4 more times. Work 1 row straight. Break off. Attach Dark and work sl st in each sc of last row. Break off. Make another piece same as this, only reversing colors.

HANDLE (Make 2) . . . With 2 strands of Dark, ch 5. Join with sl st. **1st rnd:** Sc in each ch around. **2nd rnd:** Sc in each sc around. Repeat last rnd until piece measures 2½ inches. Break off.

CORD . . . Cut 5 strands of Dark each 2½ yards long. Twist these strands tightly, then double the twisted strands and give them a second twist in the opposite direction. Knot free end. Trace outline of crocheted piece on paper. Write the word "Sugar" diagonally across outline. Pin paper to light colored crocheted piece, then sew cord to crochet through paper, following letters. Pull ends of cord through to wrong side and fasten. Remove paper. For padding see chapter on General Information. Sew edges of crocheted pieces together. Sew handles in place.

CREAM PITCHER . . . Work same as Sugar Bowl, making only one handle. Make Cord of light color and spell out "Cream" on dark colored crocheted piece. Finish same as Sugar Bowl.

98

9222 . . . **Materials:** KNIT-CRO-SHEEN, *3 balls* . . . SIX STRAND EMBROIDERY FLOSS, *1 skein each of a light and a dark color* . . . *Steel Crochet Hook No. 3.*

Using double thread, ch 29. **1st row:** Sc in 2nd ch from hook and in each ch across (28 sc). Ch 1, turn. **2nd row:** Sc in each sc across. Ch 1, turn. Repeat 2nd row until piece measures 1 inch. To shape for thumb, inc 1 st at same edge every other row until there are 37 sts. Starting at thumb edge, work across 9 sts. Ch 1, turn. Work over these 9 sts for 1 inch. Dec 1 st at both ends of each row until 3 sts remain. Break off. For palm, attach double thread where sts were divided and work over remaining 28 sts until piece measures 6½ inches from starting chain. Dec 1 st at both ends of each row until 10 sts remain. Break off. Make 3 more pieces same as this.

CORD . . . Cut 12 strands of thread, each 60 inches long. Twist these strands tightly; double twisted strands and give them a second twist in the opposite direction. Tie loose ends in a knot and trim.

Lay 2 pieces together (thumbs corresponding), and work a row of sc around through both thicknesses, leaving wrist edge open. Finish other mitt in same way. Sew an end of cord to wrist edge of each mitt.

Using Embroidery Floss double (12 strands) make 3 dark diagonal stripes across back of mitt in one direction. Cross the dark stripes with 3 stripes of light color as in illustration.

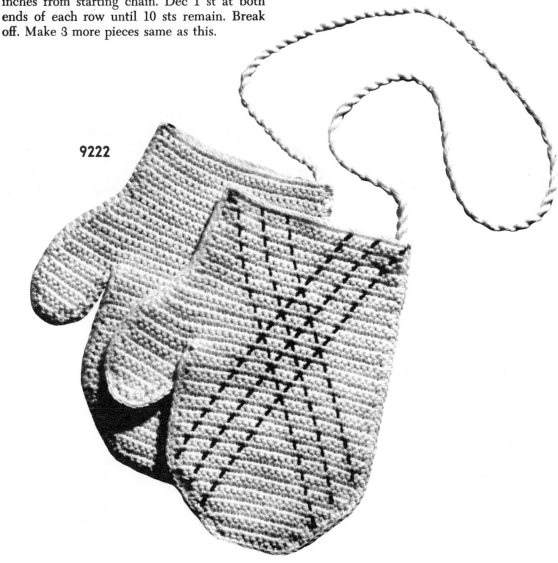

9222

9383

9383 . . . Materials: Rug Yarn, *3 70-yard skeins . . . Steel Crochet Hook No. 2/0 (double zero).*

Large mat measures about 9 inches square; medium mat 7½ inches square; small mat 5½ inches square.

LARGE MAT . . . Ch 36 (to measure 9 inches). **1st row:** Yarn over, insert hook in 4th ch from hook and pull loop through, yarn over, insert hook in same ch and pull loop through, * yarn over, skip 1 ch, insert hook in next ch and pull loop through, yarn over and draw through all 7 loops on hook, ch 1 (a V cluster made); (yarn over, insert hook where last loop was pulled through and pull loop through) twice. Repeat from * across, ending with ch 1 (16 V clusters). Ch 3 more, turn. **2nd row:** Yarn over, insert hook in 4th ch from hook and pull loop through, yarn over, insert hook in same ch and pull loop through, * yarn over, insert hook in next ch-1 and pull loop through, yarn over and draw through all 7 loops on hook, ch 1; (yarn over, insert hook in same ch-1 where last loop was pulled through and pull loop through) twice. Repeat from * across, ending with ch 1 (16 V clusters). Ch 3 more, turn. Repeat 2nd row until piece is square. Do not break off but work a row of sc evenly all around piece. Join with sl st in 1st sc made. Ch 1, turn. **2nd rnd:** Sc in front loop of each st around. Join. Ch 1, turn. **3rd rnd:** Sc in remaining loop of each sc of 1st rnd. Join and break off.

MEDIUM MAT . . . Ch 30. Work as for Large Mat, having 13 V clusters on row, until piece is square. Finish as for Large Mat.

SMALL MAT . . . Ch 22. Work as for Large Mat, having 9 V clusters on row, until piece is square. Finish as for Large Mat.

100

9233 . . . Materials: Rug Yarn, *1 70-yard skein . . . Crochet Hook Size G.*

Starting at center, ch 15. **1st rnd:** 2 dc in 4th ch from hook, dc in 10 ch, 5 dc in last ch; then, working along opposite side of starting chain, dc in 10 ch, 2 dc in last ch (30 sts). Join with sl st to top st of first ch-3. **2nd rnd:** Ch 1, * sc behind next dc—*to make an sc behind a dc, insert hook between next 2 sts from back to front of work, pass hook over next dc and insert hook between sts from front to back, yarn over, draw loop through and finish as for an sc (sc will be behind dc).* Repeat from * around (30 sts). Join to 1st sc made. **3rd rnd:** Ch 3 (to count as 1 dc), dc in same place as sl st, 2 dc in next st, dc in next 10 sts, 2 dc in next 5 sts, dc in next 10 sts, 2 dc in next 3 sts (40 sts). Join. **4th rnd:** Repeat 2nd rnd (40 sts).

Continue thus, increasing as necessary (on odd rnds only) at ends of oval to keep work flat, until piece measures about 6 x 8½ inches, ending with 2nd rnd. Break off. Make another piece same as this.

9079 . . . Materials: Pearl Cotton, *Size 5, 4 balls . . . Steel Crochet Hook No. 7 . . . 61 plastic rings, ⅞ inch in diameter.*

FIRST MOTIF . . . **1st rnd:** Make 36 sc over bone ring. Join. **2nd rnd:** Ch 1, * sc in next 5 sc, ch 3, skip 1 sc. Repeat from * around, ending with ch 3, join to 1st sc made. Break off.

SECOND MOTIF . . . **1st rnd:** Work as for First Motif. **2nd rnd:** Ch 1, sc in next 5 sc, ch 1, sl st in ch-3 loop on First Motif, ch 1, skip 1 sc of previous rnd, sc in next 5 sc, ch 1, sl st in corresponding loop on First Motif, ch 1, skip 1 sc, sc in next 5 sc; complete as for 2nd rnd of First Motif. Break off.

Work all other motifs as for previous motifs, joining corresponding ch-3's as illustrated.

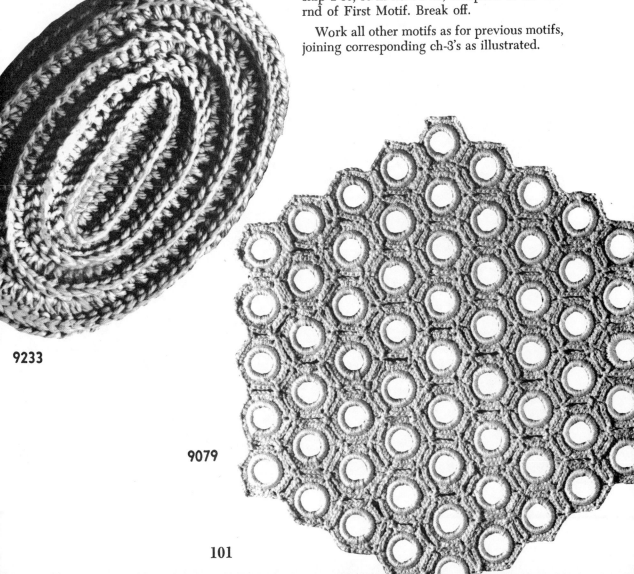

9233

9079

101

7715

CHAPTER EIGHT

Doilies

YOUR HOME REFLECTS you as accurately as any mirror. The arrangement of the furniture, the pictures on the wall, the titles of your books, all tell a true story about you . . . they're the telltales to your habits, your taste, your way of life.

Somehow it's the little things that are most revealing. It takes only a few minutes to make any one of the lovely doilies in this chapter. Decorative in every setting, invaluable to graceful entertaining, they serve a host of useful purposes, add a delicate note of beauty wherever you place them. They make bright table talk in the dining room, on the tea table . . . add a lovely note to dresser or dressing table . . . perfect under a lamp, vase, or bonbon dish . . . come in handy when serving refreshments. Gossamer or sturdy, plain or ruffled, there's a doily here for every purpose.

7715. . . . Materials: BEST SIX CORD MERCERIZED CROCHET, *Size 30: 3 balls* . . . *Steel Crochet Hook No. 10 or 11.*

Small mats measure about 5½ inches in diameter; large mat 11 inches in diameter.

LARGE MAT . . . Ch 8. Join with sl st. **1st rnd:** Ch 1, work 12 sc in ring. Join with sl st in 1st sc. **2nd rnd:** Ch 4, * dc in next sc, ch 1. Repeat from * around, joining last ch 1 with sl st in 3rd st of starting chain (12 sps). **3rd rnd:** Ch 6, dc in same place as sl st, * in next dc make dc, ch 3 and dc. Repeat from * around. Join with sl st in 3rd st of starting chain. **4th rnd:** Ch 1, make 5 sc in each ch-3 sp around. Join. **5th rnd:** Ch 7, * skip next sc, tr in next sc, ch 3. Repeat from * around. Join with sl st in 4th st of starting chain. **6th rnd:** Ch 4, tr in next tr, * ch 5, holding back on hook the last loop of each tr make tr in same place as last tr, tr in next tr, thread over and draw through all loops on hook (a joined tr made). Repeat from * around. Join. **7th rnd:** Make 5 sc in each ch-5 sp around. Join. **8th rnd:** Sl st in next

2 sc, ch 9, * skip 4 sc, tr in next sc, ch 5. Repeat from * around, joining last ch-5 with sl st in 4th st of starting chain. **9th rnd:** Repeat 6th rnd, having ch-7 sps instead of ch-5 sps. **10th rnd:** Make 9 sc in each ch-7 sp around. Join. **11th rnd:** Sl st in next 3 sc, ch 1, * sc in next sc, ch 11, skip 8 sc. Repeat from * around. Join. **12th rnd:** Make 13 sc in each sp around. Join. **13th rnd:** Sl st in next 5 sc, ch 1, * sc in next sc, ch 11, skip 12 sc. Repeat from * around. Join. **14th rnd:** Repeat 12th rnd.

15th rnd: Sl st in next 5 sc, ch 1, * sc in next sc, ch 13, skip 12 sc. Repeat from * around. Join. **16th rnd:** Make 15 sc in each sp around. Join. **17th rnd:** Sl st in next 7 sc, ch 4, holding back on hook the last loop of each tr, make 2 tr in same place as last sl st, thread over and draw through all loops on hook (a 2-tr cluster made); * (ch 5, make a 2-tr cluster in 5th ch from hook) twice; skip 14 sc, holding back on hook the last loop of each tr, make 3 tr in next sc, thread over and draw through all loops on hook (a 3-tr cluster made). Repeat from * around. Join. **18th rnd:** Ch 4, 2-tr cluster in same place as sl st, * ch 7, make a 2-tr cluster from hook, skip next cluster, 3-tr cluster in base of next cluster, ch 5, 2-tr cluster in 5th ch from hook, skip next cluster, 3-tr cluster in top of next cluster. Repeat from * around. Join. **19th rnd:** Ch 4, 2-tr cluster in same place as sl st, * ch 5, 2-tr cluster in 5th ch from hook, 3-tr cluster in top of next cluster. Repeat from * around. Join. **20th, 21st, and 22nd rnds:** Ch 4, 2-tr cluster in same place as sl st, * ch 6, 2-tr cluster in 5th ch from hook, ch 1, 3-tr cluster in top of next 3-tr cluster. Repeat from * around. Join. **23rd rnd:** Ch 4, 2-tr cluster in

same place as sl st, * ch 7, make a 2-tr cluster in 6th ch from hook, ch 1, 3-tr cluster in top of next 3-tr cluster. Repeat from * around. Join. **24th rnd:** Ch 1, sc in same place as sl st, * ch 11, sc in top of next 3-tr cluster. Repeat from * around. Join. **25th rnd:** Work 13 sc in each sp around. Join and break off.

SMALL MAT (Make 4) . . . **1st to 10th rnds incl:** Work 1st to 10th rnds incl of Large Mat. **11th rnd:** Sl st in next 4 sc, ch 4, 2-tr cluster in same place as last sl st, * ch 5, 2-tr cluster in 5th ch from hook, skip 8 sc, 3-tr cluster in next sc. Repeat from * around. Join. **12th rnd:** Re-

4038

peat 20th rnd of Large Mat. **13th rnd:** Repeat 24th rnd of Large Mat. **14th rnd:** Repeat 25th rnd of Large Mat. Starch lightly and press.

4038 . . . Materials: BEST SIX CORD MERCERIZED CROCHET, *Size 30: 2 balls . . . Steel Crochet Hook No. 10 or 11.*

Doily measures about 9 inches in diameter.

Ch 10. Join with sl st. **1st rnd:** Ch 3, make 23 dc in ring. Sl st in top st of ch-3. **2nd rnd:** Ch 8, * skip 1 dc, dc in next dc, ch 5. Repeat from * around, ending with ch 5, sl st in 3rd st of ch-8. **3rd rnd:** Sl st in next 2 ch, sc in sp, ch 8, * dc in next sp, ch 5. Repeat from * around. Join as before. **4th rnd:** Ch 3, * 7 dc in sp, dc in dc. Repeat from * around. Join. **5th rnd:** Sl st in next dc, ch 3, dc in next 14 dc, * ch 5, skip 1 dc, dc in next 15 dc. Repeat from * around. Join. **6th rnd:** Sl st in next dc, ch 3, * dc in each dc to last dc of this group—do not work in last dc—ch 5, sc in next loop, ch 5, skip next dc. Repeat from * around. Join. **7th rnd:** Sl st in next dc, ch 3, * dc in each dc to last dc of this group—do not work in last dc —(ch 5, sc in next loop) twice; ch 5, skip next dc. Repeat from * around. Join. **8th to 11th rnds incl:** Work as for previous rnd, having 1 more loop between dc-groups on each rnd. **12th rnd:** Sl st in next dc, ch 8, * sc in next loop, (ch 5, sc in next loop) 6 times; ch 5, skip 1 dc, dc in next dc, ch 5. Repeat from * around. Join. **13th rnd:** Sl st in next 3 ch, ch 8, * dc in next loop, ch 5. Repeat from * around. Join. **14th rnd:** Ch 3, * 5 dc in sp, dc in next dc. Repeat from * around. Join. **15th rnd:** Sc in same place as sl st, * ch 7, skip 1 dc, sc in next dc. Repeat from * around, ending with ch 3, tr in 1st sc. **16th to 19th rnds incl:** * Ch 7, sc in next loop. Repeat from * around, ending with ch 3, tr in tr. **20th rnd:** Repeat 19th rnd, making ch-8 (instead of ch-7) loops and ending with ch 4, tr in tr. **21st rnd:** Same as previous rnd, making ch-9 loops and ending with ch 4, d tr in tr. **22nd rnd:** Make ch-10 loops around, ending with ch 5, d tr in d tr. **23rd rnd:** Make ch-11 loops around, ending with ch 11, sl st in d tr. Break off.

A-619 . . . Materials: J. & P. COATS BIG BALL BEST SIX CORD MERCERIZED CROCHET, *Art. A.105, Size 30, 1 ball of No. 1 White or No. 61 Ecru; or* CLARK'S BIG BALL MERCERIZED CROCHET, *Art. B.34, Size 30, 1 ball of No. 1 White, No. 61 Ecru, or No. 42 Cream; or* CLARK'S BIG BALL MERCERIZED CROCHET, *Art. B.345, Size 30, 1 ball of No. 1 White or No. 61 Ecru . . . Steel Crochet Hook No. 10.*

Doily measures 14 inches in diameter.

Starting at center, ch 18. Join with sl st to form ring. **1st rnd:** Ch 4, *holding back on hook the last loop of each tr, make 2 tr in ring, thread over and draw through all loops on hook—starting cluster made;* (ch 5, *holding back on hook the last loop of each tr, make 3 tr in ring, thread over and draw through all loops on hook—cluster made*) 11 times; ch 2, dc in tip of first cluster to form last loop. **2nd rnd:** Ch 1, sc in loop just formed, * ch 12, sc in next loop, (ch 4, sc in next loop) twice. Repeat from * around, ending with ch 12, sc in next loop, ch 4, sc in next loop, tr in first sc. **3rd rnd:** * In next ch-12 loop make (cluster, ch 5) 7 times and cluster; skip next ch-4 loop, sc in next sc. Repeat from * around, ending with skip last ch-4 loop, join to tip of first cluster. **4th rnd:** Sl st to center of second ch-5 loop, ch 1, sc in same loop, * ch 12, sc in next loop, (ch 4, sc in next loop) twice; ch 12, sc in next loop, ch 9, skip next two loops, sc in next loop. Repeat from * around, ending with ch 4, d tr in first sc to form last ch-9 loop. **5th rnd:** Ch 1, sc in loop just formed, * in next ch-12 loop make (cluster, ch 5) 7 times and cluster; skip next ch-4 loop, sc in next sc, in next ch-12 loop make (cluster, ch 5) 7 times and cluster; sc in next ch-9 loop. Repeat from * around, joining last cluster to first sc. **6th rnd:** Sl st to center of second ch-5 loop, ch 1, sc in same loop, * (ch 9, skip next loop, sc in next loop) twice; ch 9, skip next 2 loops, sc in next loop. Repeat from * around, ending with ch 4, d tr in first sc—24 loops. **7th rnd:** Ch 1, sc in loop just formed, * ch 10, sc in next loop. Repeat from * around, ending with ch 5, d tr in first sc. **8th rnd:** Ch 1, sc in loop just formed, * ch 11, sc in next loop. Repeat from * around, ending with ch 6, d tr in first sc. **9th rnd:** Ch 1, sc in loop just formed, * ch 12, sc in next loop. Repeat from * around, ending with ch 12. Join to first sc. **10th rnd:** Ch 1, sc in joining, 15 sc in next loop, * sc in next sc, 15 sc in next loop. Repeat from * around. Join. **11th rnd:** Skip

joining, sl st in next 5 sc, * sc in next sc, ch 5, skip 3 sc, sc in next sc, ch 12, skip 11 sc. Repeat from * around. Join to first sc. **12th rnd:** Sl st to center of first ch-5 loop, sc in same loop, * *holding back on hook the last loop of each dc, make 3 dc in next ch-12 loop, thread over and draw through all loops on hook—3-dc* **cluster made;** ch 5, in same loop make (3-tr cluster, ch 5) 6 times and 3-dc cluster; sc in next ch-5 loop. Repeat from * around, ending with a 3-dc cluster. Join to first sc. **13th rnd:** Sl st to center of third ch-5 loop, sc in same loop, * ch 7, skip next loop, sc in next loop, ch 9, skip next 4 loops, sc in next loop. Repeat from * around, ending as on 6th rnd. **14th rnd:** Ch 1, sc in loop just formed, * ch 9, sc in next loop. Repeat from * around, ending as on 6th rnd. **15th rnd:** Ch 1, sc in loop just formed, * ch 12, sc in next loop, ch 7, sc in next loop. Repeat from * around, ending with ch 3, tr in first sc. **16th rnd:** Ch 1, sc in loop just formed, * in next loop make (3-tr cluster, ch 5) 7 times and 3-tr cluster; sc in next loop. Repeat from * around, joining last 3-tr cluster to first sc.

17th rnd: Sl st to center of third ch-5 loop, sc in same loop, * (ch 5, sc in next loop) twice; ch 14, skip next 4 loops, sc in next loop. Repeat from * around, ending with ch 14. Join to first sc. **18th rnd:** Sl st to center of first ch-5 loop, *draw up a loop in same ch-5 loop and next ch-5 loop, thread over and draw through all 3 loops on hook—group st made;* * in next ch-14 loop make (3-tr cluster, ch 5) 7 times and 3-tr cluster; *draw up a loop in each of next two ch-5 loops, thread over and draw through all 3 loops on hook—group st made.* Repeat from * around, joining last 3-tr cluster to first group st. **19th rnd:** Sl st to center of second loop, sc in same loop, * (ch 7, skip next loop, sc in next loop) twice; ch 9, skip next 2 loops, sc in next loop. Repeat from * around, ending as on 6th rnd. **20th and 21st rnds:** Repeat 14th and 7th rnds. **22nd rnd:** 5 sc in loop just formed, * sc in next sc, 10 sc in next loop. Repeat from * around, ending with 5 sc in last loop. Join. Break off and fasten. Starch lightly and press.

7256

7256 . . . Materials: Best Six Cord Mercerized Crochet, *Size 30: 1 ball* . . . *Steel
Crochet Hook No. 10 or 11.*

Doily measures about 18 inches in diameter.

Ch 10, join with sl st. **1st rnd:** Ch 6, * tr in ring,
ch 2. Repeat from * 10 more times; join to 4th
st of ch-6 (12 sps). **2nd rnd:** Ch 4 (to count
as tr), 3 tr in sp, * tr in tr, 3 tr in sp. Repeat
from * around. Join to top of ch-4 (48 tr). **3rd**
rnd: Ch 9, skip 2 tr, * tr in next tr, ch 5, skip
2 tr. Repeat from * around. Join to 4th st of
ch-9 (16 sps). **4th rnd:** Ch 4, tr in next 5 ch,
* tr in tr, tr in next 5 ch. Repeat from * around.
Join. **5th rnd:** Ch 12, * skip 5 tr, tr in next tr,
ch 8. Repeat from * around. Join to 4th st of
ch-12. **6th rnd:** Sl st in sp, ch 4, 7 tr in same sp;
* ch 2, 8 tr in next sp. Repeat from * around,
ending with ch 2, join (16 groups of 8 tr with
ch-2 between). **7th rnd:** Ch 4, tr in next 7 tr,

107

* ch 3, skip 2 ch, tr in each tr of next 8-tr group. Repeat from * around, ending with ch 3, join. **8th rnd:** Ch 4, tr in next 7 tr, * ch 4, skip ch-3, tr in each tr of next tr-group. Repeat from * around, ending with ch 4, join. **9th rnd:** Turn and sl st into last ch of previous rnd, ch 15, turn, * skip 8-tr group, tr in each of next 4 ch, ch 11. Repeat from * around, ending with tr in last 3 ch, join to 4th st of ch-15. **10th rnd:** Ch 10, * 2 sc in loop, ch 6, tr in each tr of 4-tr group, ch 6. Repeat from * around, ending with 2 sc in loop, ch 6, tr in each of next 3 tr, join to 4th ch of ch-10. **11th rnd:** Ch 16, * skip ch-6, the 2 sc and the ch-6; make tr in each tr of 4-tr group, ch 12. Repeat from * around, ending with tr in each of next 3 tr, join to 4th st of ch-16. **12th rnd:** Sl st in next ch, ch 4, tr in next 11 ch, * ch 5, skip 4 tr, tr in next 12 ch. Repeat from * around, ending with ch 5, join. **13th rnd:** Ch 4, holding back on hook the last loop of each tr make tr in next 3 tr, thread over and draw through all loops on hook (a cluster); tr in each of next 4 tr; holding back on hook the last loop of each tr make a tr in next 4 tr, complete a cluster as before. * Ch 13, skip ch-5, 4-tr cluster over next 4 tr, tr in each of next 4 tr, 4-tr cluster over last 4 tr. Repeat from * around, ending with ch 13, join to tip of 1st cluster. **14th rnd:** Ch 11, * skip 4 tr, tr in tip of next cluster, ch 3, skip 3 ch, tr in next ch, ch 7, skip 5 ch, tr in next ch, ch 3, skip 3 ch, tr in tip of next cluster, ch 7. Repeat from * around, ending with ch 3, join to 4th ch of ch-11.

15th rnd: Ch 6, * tr in ch-7 sp, ch 2, tr in same sp, ch 2, tr in tr, ch 3, tr in next tr, ch 2. Repeat from * around, ending with ch 3, join to 4th ch of ch-6. **16th rnd:** Turn and sl st in last ch-3 of previous rnd, ch 11, turn, skip 1 sp, * d tr in next sp, ch 6, skip 1 sp. Repeat from * around, ending with ch 6, join to 5th ch of ch-11. **17th rnd:** Ch 11, * d tr in d tr, ch 6. Repeat from * ending with ch 6, sl st in 5th ch of ch-11. **18th rnd:** Sl st in sp, ch 7, * tr in same sp, ch 3, tr in next sp, ch 3. Repeat from * around, ending with ch 3, join to 4th ch of ch-7. **19th rnd:** Sl st to top of next tr, ch 6, * dc in next tr, ch 15, skip 2 tr, dc in next tr, ch 3. Repeat from * around, ending with ch 15, join to 3rd ch of ch-6. **20th rnd:** Sl st in next 2 ch, ch 8, * skip dc and 5 ch, 3 tr in next ch; tr in each of next 3 ch, 3 tr in next ch (9 tr in

group). Ch 5, skip 5 ch and the dc, dc in center ch of ch-3 sp, ch 5. Repeat from * around, ending with ch 5, join to 3rd ch of ch-8. **21st rnd:** Sl st to top of 1st tr, ch 3 (to count as dc), dc in each of 8 tr, * ch 11, dc in each of 9 tr. Repeat from * around, ending with ch 11, join to top of ch-3. **22nd rnd:** Ch 4 (to count as tr), holding back on hook the last loop of each tr make tr in next 2 dc; complete cluster as before. * Tr in next 3 dc; then make a 3-tr cluster over next 3 dc. Ch 6, dc in center ch of next loop, ch 6, 3-tr cluster over next 3 dc. Repeat from *, ending with ch 6, join to tip of 1st cluster; turn. **23rd rnd:** Sl st in next 6 ch, turn, ch 17, * skip the tr-group; dc in ch preceding next dc, ch 3, skip dc, dc in next ch, ch 14. Repeat from * around, ending with ch 3, join to 3rd st of ch-17. **24th rnd:** Turn and sl st in last ch-3 of previous rnd, ch 8, turn, * skip dc and 4 ch, 3 tr in next ch, tr in each of next 4 ch, 3 tr in next ch (10-tr group). Ch 5, dc in center ch of ch-3 sp, ch 5. Repeat from * around, ending with ch 5, join to 3rd ch of ch-8. **25th rnd:** Repeat 21st rnd, making 10 dc in each group (instead of 9) and ch-13 loops (instead of ch-11). **26th rnd:** Repeat 22nd rnd, making 1 more tr in each group and ch-7 (instead of ch-6). Join and turn. **27th rnd:** Sl st in next 7 ch, turn, ch 20 (to count as dc and ch-17), turn and work in pattern as for 23rd rnd, making ch-17 loops (instead of ch-14). **28th rnd:** Turn and sl st in last ch-3 of previous rnd, ch 9, turn, skip 5 ch and work in pattern as for 24th rnd, having 11 tr in each group (instead of 10 tr) and making ch 6 (instead of ch 5). Join. **29th rnd:** Repeat 21st rnd, making 11 dc in each group (instead of 9), and ch-13 loops (instead of ch-11). **30th rnd:** Repeat 22nd rnd, making 2 more tr's in each group, and ch 7 instead of ch 6. Join to tip of 1st cluster. **31st rnd:** Ch 12, * skip 5 tr, d tr in tip of next cluster, ch 7, dc in next sp, ch 3, dc in next sp, ch 7, d tr in tip of next cluster, ch 7. Repeat from * around, ending with ch 7, sl st in 5th st of ch-12. **32nd rnd:** Sl st in next 2 ch, ch 9, dc in 6th ch from hook, tr in same sp. * (Ch 5, dc in last tr, tr in same sp as last tr) twice; dc in next sp; (ch 2, dc in same sp) twice; ch 2, sc in next sp, ch 2, dc in next sp; (ch 2, dc in same sp) twice; tr in next sp, ch 5, dc in last tr, tr in same sp as last tr. Repeat from * around, ending with (ch 2, dc in same sp) twice; join to 4th st of ch-9. Break off.

621 . . . **Materials:** BEST SIX CORD MERCER-
IZED CROCHET, *Size 30: 1 ball . . . Steel Crochet
Hook No. 10 or 11.*

Doily measures about 8½ inches in diameter.

Ch 8, join with sl st. **1st rnd:** Ch 5 (to count as
dc and ch 2), dc in ring, (ch 2, dc in ring) 6
times; ch 2, sl st in 3rd ch of ch-5. **2nd rnd:**
Ch 5 (to count as tr and ch 1), tr in same place
as sl st, * ch 1, in next sp make tr, ch 1 and tr;
ch 1, in next dc make tr, ch 1 and tr. Repeat
from * around. Join last ch-1 with sl st to 4th
ch of ch-5. **3rd rnd:** Sl st in next sp, ch 4, tr in
same place as sl st, * ch 4, skip 1 sp, in next
ch-1 sp make 2 tr. Repeat from * around. Join
(16 groups of 2 tr). **4th rnd:** Ch 4, tr in next
tr and in next ch, * ch 4, skip 2 ch, tr in next
ch, tr in next 2 tr, tr in next ch. Repeat from *
around, ending with ch 4, skip 2 ch, tr in next
ch. Join. **5th rnd:** Ch 4, tr in next 2 tr and in
next ch, * ch 2, skip 2 ch, tr in next ch, tr in
next 4 tr, tr in next ch. Repeat from * around,

ending with 2 tr. Join. **6th rnd:** Ch 5, * tr in
next 3 tr, ch 3, tr in next 3 tr, ch 1. Repeat
from * around, ending with 2 tr. Join to 4th
ch of ch-5. **7th rnd:** Ch 6, * tr in next 3 tr, ch 4,
tr in next 3 tr, ch 2. Repeat from * around,
ending with 2 tr. Join. **8th rnd:** Ch 7, * tr in
next 3 tr, ch 4, tr in next 3 tr, ch 3. Repeat
from * around, ending with 2 tr. Join. **9th rnd:**
Ch 7, * tr in next 3 tr, ch 5, tr in next 3 tr,
ch 3. Repeat from * around, ending and joining as before.

10th rnd: Ch 8, * tr in next 3 tr, ch 5, tr in
next 3 tr, ch 4. Repeat from * around, ending
and joining as before. **11th rnd:** Sl st in each
ch and in next tr, ch 4, holding back on hook
the last loop of each tr make tr in next 2 tr,
thread over and draw through all loops, ch 1
to fasten, * ch 1 more, holding back on hook
the last loop of each tr make tr in next 3 tr,
thread over and draw through all loops on
hook, ch 1 to fasten (a 3-tr cluster made).
Ch 4, in next sp make tr, ch 4 and tr; ch 4,

cluster over next 3 tr. Repeat from * around, ending with ch 4, sl st in tip of 1st cluster. **12th rnd:** Sl st in next sp, ch 6, * cluster in next sp, ch 2, in next sp make a cluster, ch 5 and a cluster; ch 2, cluster in next sp, ch 3, dc in next ch-1 sp, ch 3. Repeat from * around, ending with a cluster, dc in 3rd ch of ch 6, turn. **13th rnd:** Sl st in 3 ch, turn. Ch 4 and complete a cluster in this same sp, * skip 2 sps, cluster in next sp, ch 4, in next sp make (cluster, ch 3) twice and cluster; ch 4, cluster in next sp. Repeat from * around. Join last ch-4 to tip of 1st cluster. **14th rnd:** Sl st in next cluster and in next 2 ch, ch 1, sc in same sp, * ch 6, sc in next sp, ch 7, sc in next sp, ch 6, sc in next sp, ch 5, sc in next sp. Repeat from * around. Join last ch-5 to 1st sc made. **15th rnd:** Sl st to center ch of next loop, ch 1, sc in same loop, * ch 3, sl st in last sc, ch 5, in next loop make **tr, ch 7, and tr;** ch 5, sc in next loop, ch 3, sl st in last sc, ch 6, skip 1 loop, sc in next loop. Repeat from * around. Join last ch-6 with sl st to 1st sc made. **16th rnd:** Sl st in next 3 ch, ch 1, sc in same loop, * (ch 3, sl st in last sc— a p made—ch 5, sc in next loop) 3 times; ch 5, sc in next loop. Repeat from * around. Join last ch-5 to 1st sc made. Break off.

7690 . . . Materials: Best Six Cord Mercerized Crochet, *Size 30: 1 ball . . . Steel Crochet Hook No. 8 or 9.*

Doily measures about 11½ inches in diameter.

1st rnd: Ch 10, in 10th ch from hook make (tr, ch 5) 5 times. Join with sl st in 5th st of starting chain. **2nd rnd:** Ch 4, 2 tr in same place as sl st, * ch 5, 3 tr in next tr. Repeat from * around, ending with ch 5, sl st in 4th st of starting chain. **3rd rnd:** Sl st in next tr, ch 6, * 5 tr in next tr, ch 1, 5 tr in next tr, ch 2, tr in next tr, ch 2. Repeat from * around. Join. **4th rnd:** Ch 4, 2 tr in same place as sl st, * ch 3, tr in next 5 tr, ch 1, tr in next 5 tr, ch 3, 3 tr in next tr. Repeat from * around. Join. **5th rnd:** Sl st in next tr, ch 6, * 5 tr in next tr, ch 3, holding back on hook the last loop of each tr, make tr in next 5 tr, thread over and draw through all loops on hook (cluster made—Fig. 65); ch 3, make a cluster over next 5 tr, ch 3, 5 tr in next tr, ch 2, tr in next tr, ch 2. Repeat from * around. Join. **6th rnd:** Ch 4, 2 tr in same place as sl st, * ch 3, tr in next 5 tr, ch 5, skip next sp and cluster, sc in next sp, ch 5, skip next cluster and

sp, tr in next 5 tr, ch 3, 3 tr in next tr. Repeat from * around. Join. **7th rnd:** Sl st in next 2 tr, ch 4, 2 tr in same place as last sl st, * ch 3, make a cluster over next 5 tr, ch 5, sc in next loop, ch 7, sc in next loop, ch 5, cluster over next 5 tr, ch 3, 3 tr in next tr, ch 3, skip next tr, 3 tr in next tr. Repeat from * around. Join.

8th rnd: Ch 4, 4 tr in same place as sl st, * ch 2, tr in next tr, ch 2, 5 tr in next tr, ch 5, skip next cluster, sc in next loop, (ch 7, sc in next loop) twice; ch 5, 5 tr in next tr, ch 2, tr in next tr, (ch 2, 5 tr in next tr) twice. Repeat from * around. Join. **9th rnd:** Ch 4, tr in next 4 tr, * ch 2, tr in next tr, ch 2, tr in next 5 tr, ch 5, sc in next loop, (ch 7, sc in next loop) 3 times; ch 5, tr in next 5 tr, ch 2, tr in next tr, (ch 2, tr in next 5 tr) twice. Repeat from * around. Join. **10th rnd:** Ch 4, holding back on hook the last loop of each tr, make tr in next 4 tr and complete cluster, * ch 3, 3 tr in next tr, ch 3, cluster over next 5 tr, ch 5, skip next loop, sc in next loop, (ch 7, sc in next loop) twice, ch 5, cluster over next 5 tr, ch 3, 3 tr in next tr, ch 3, cluster over next 5 tr, ch 5, cluster over next 5 tr. Repeat from * around. Join last ch-5 to tip of 1st cluster made. **11th rnd:** Sl st in next 3 ch and in next tr, ch 4, 4 tr in same place as sl st, * ch 3, tr in next tr, ch 3, 5 tr in next tr, ch 5, skip next cluster, sc in next loop, (ch 7, sc in next loop) 3 times; ch 5, skip next cluster, 5 tr in next tr, ch 3, tr in next tr, ch 3, 5 tr in next tr, ch 5, 5 tr in 1st tr of next 3-tr group. Repeat from * around. Join.

12th rnd: Ch 4, tr in next 4 tr, * ch 3, 5 tr in next tr, ch 3, tr in next 5 tr, ch 5, skip 1 loop, sc in next loop, (ch 7, sc in next loop) twice; ch 5, tr in next 5 tr, ch 3, 5 tr in next tr, ch 3, tr in next 5 tr, ch 5, sc in next sp, ch 5, tr in next 5 tr. Repeat from * around. Join. **13th rnd:** Ch 4 and complete cluster, * ch 5, sc in next sp, ch 5, tr in next 5 tr, ch 5, sc in next sp, ch 5, cluster over next 5 tr, ch 5, skip next loop, sc in next loop, ch 7, sc in next loop, ch 5, clus-

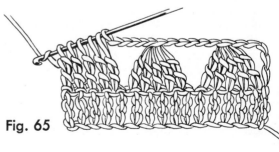

Fig. 65

110

ter over next 5 tr, ch 5, sc in next sp, ch 5, tr in next 5 tr, ch 5, sc in next sp, ch 5, cluster over next 5 tr, ch 5, sc in next loop, ch 7, sc in next loop, ch 5, cluster over next 5 tr. Repeat from * around. Join. **14th rnd:** Sl st in next 2 ch, sc in loop, ch 7, sc in next loop, * ch 5, cluster over next 5 tr, ch 5, sc in next loop, ch 7, sc in next loop, ch 7, skip 1 loop, sc in next loop, ch 7, skip next cluster, sc in next loop, ch 7, sc in next loop. Repeat from * around. Join last ch-7 with sl st to 1st sc. **15th rnd:** Sl st in next 3 ch, sc in loop, * ch 7, sc in next loop. Repeat from * around. Join.

16th rnd: Sl st in next 3 ch, sc in loop, * ch 5, in next loop make tr, ch 7 and tr; ch 5, 5 sc in each of next 5 loops, ch 25, turn, sl st in first sc of 25-sc group, turn, 33 sc in ch-25 loop, sl st in sc at base of ch-25. Repeat from * around. Join. **17th rnd:** Sl st in next 4 ch, sc in loop, * ch 5, in next loop make dc, ch 1 and dc, ch 5, sc in next loop, tr in each of the 33 sc, sc in next loop. Repeat from * around. Join. **18th rnd:** Sl st in next 4 ch, sc in loop, * sc in ch-1 sp, sc in next loop, cluster over next 5 tr, ** ch 7, make another 5-tr cluster (having 1st tr in same place where last tr of previous cluster was made). Repeat from ** until 8 clusters in all have been completed, sc in next loop. Repeat from * around. Join. **19th rnd:** * Sc in next sc, skip next sc, in each of next 7 loops make (2 sc, ch 3) 3 times and 2 sc; skip next sc. Repeat from * around. Join and break off.

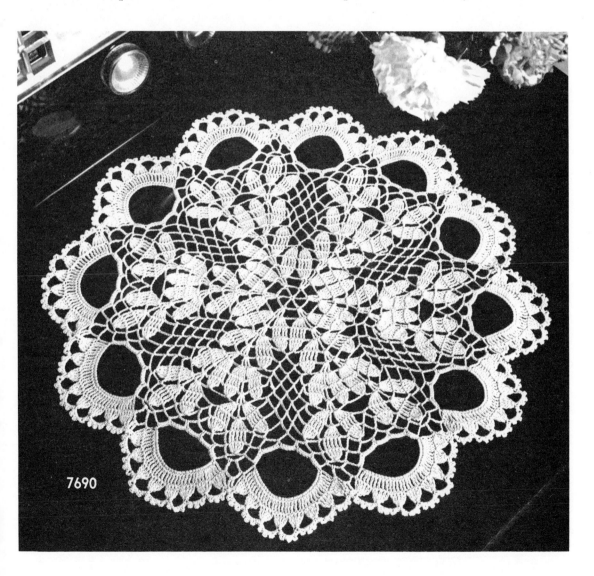

7690

7318

7318 . . . Materials: Coats & Clark's O.N.T.
Mercerized Crochet, *Size 70: 2 balls* . . .
Steel Crochet Hook No. 13.

Doily measures about 11 inches in diameter.

Ch 10, join with sl st. **1st rnd:** Ch 1, 16 sc in
ring, sl st in 1st sc made. **2nd rnd:** Ch 1, sc in
same place as sl st, * ch 5, skip 1 sc, sc in next
sc. Repeat from * around, ending with ch 5.
3rd rnd: * Sc in next sc, 2 sc in ch-5 sp, ch 5.
Repeat from * around. **4th to 17th rnds incl:**
* Skip 1st sc, sc in each remaining sc of sc-
group, 2 sc in ch-5 sp, ch 5. Repeat from *
around; on 17th rnd end with the 17 sc of last
group. **18th rnd:** Ch 5, * skip 1 sc, sc in next
15 sc, ch 5, sc in ch-5 sp, ch 5. Repeat from *
around. **19th rnd:** * Skip 1 sc, sc in next 13 sc;
(ch 5, sc in next loop) twice; ch 5. Repeat

from * around. Continue in this manner, having 2 sc less in each sc-group and 1 loop more
between sc-groups on each rnd, until 1 sc remains in each sc-group, and ending with ch 5,
sc in loop preceding 1st sc. Now work as
follows:

26th to 30th rnds incl: * Ch 6, sc in next
loop. Repeat from * around. **31st rnd:** * Make
ch-6 loops across to loop directly above last
sc of next point, ch 6, 9 dc in loop above sc.
Repeat from * around (1 group of 9 dc directly above each point). **32nd rnd:** * Make
ch-6 loops to next dc-group, ch 6, skip 4 dc of
group, sc in next dc, ch 6, sc in next loop. Repeat from * around. **33rd and 34th rnds:** Make
ch-6 loops around, ending with sc. **35th rnd:**
Ch 5, * 2 half dc in next loop, ch 3. Repeat
from * around, ending with ch 3, half dc in

last sc, sl st in 2nd ch of ch-5 (80 ch-3 sps). **36th rnd:** Ch 2, * 2 half dc in sp, half dc in next 2 half dc. Repeat from * around, ending with sl st in 2nd ch of ch-2 (320 half dc). **37th rnd:** * Ch 4, skip 4 half dc, in next half dc make 2 dc, ch 2 and 2 dc (shell). Ch 4, skip 4 half dc, sc in next 17 half dc. Repeat from * around, but skip 5 half dc (instead of 4) before and after any 4 shells on rnd (12 groups of 17 sc, with a shell between each group). Join with sl st in 1st ch of ch-4. Hereafter work only in the back loop of each sc. **38th rnd:** * Ch 4, in ch-2 of shell make (2 dc, ch 2) 3 times and 2 dc. Ch 4, skip 1 sc, make sc in next 15 sc. Repeat from * around; join. **39th rnd:** * Ch 4, shell in next ch-2 sp, (ch 3, shell in next ch-2 sp) twice; ch 4, skip 1 sc, sc in next 13 sc. Repeat from * around; join.

40th rnd: * Ch 4, shell over next shell, ch 3; in next shell make (2 dc, ch 2) 3 times and 2 dc. Ch 3, shell over next shell, ch 4, skip 1 sc, sc in next 11 sc. Repeat from * around; join. **41st rnd:** * Ch 5, shell over next shell, ch 3; (shell in next ch-2 sp, ch 2) twice; shell in next ch-2 sp, ch 3, shell over next shell, ch 5, skip 1 sc, sc in next 9 sc. Repeat from * around; join. **42nd rnd:** * Ch 5, shell over next shell, ch 3, shell over next shell, ch 3. In ch-2 of next shell make (2 dc, ch 2) 3 times and 2 dc. (Ch 3, shell over next shell) twice, ch 5, skip 1 sc, sc in next 7 sc. Repeat from * around; join. **43rd rnd:** * Ch 5, shell over next shell, ch 4, shell over shell; (ch 3, shell in next ch-2 sp) 3 times; ch 3, shell over next shell, ch 4, shell over next shell, ch 5, skip 1 sc, sc in next 5 sc. Repeat from * around; join.

44th rnd: * Ch 5, shell over next shell, ch 4; (shell over next shell, ch 3) twice; in next ch-2 sp make (2 dc, ch 2) 3 times and 2 dc. (Ch 3, shell over next shell) twice, ch 4, shell over next shell, ch 5, skip 1 sc, sc in next 3 sc. Repeat from * around; join. **45th rnd:** * Ch 5, (shell over next shell, ch 4) 3 times; (shell in next ch-2 sp, ch 3) twice; shell in next ch-2 sp. (Ch 4, shell over next shell) 3 times; ch 5, skip 1 sc, sc in next sc. Repeat from * around. Do not join. **46th rnd:** Ch 5, * in next ch-2 sp make dc, ch 5, sl st in 4th ch from hook (a ch-4 picot made). Ch 1, dc in same place as last dc, ch 2, sc in next sp between shells, ch 1, ch-4 p, ch 1. Repeat from * across shell pattern, skip the ch-5, the sc, and the ch-5, and continue thus around. Join and break off.

7186 . . . Materials: THREE CORD MERCERIZED CROCHET, *Size 50: 1 ball . . . Steel Crochet Hook No. 13.*

Doily measures about 10½ x 13½ inches across center. Center of doily is made of 3 individual motifs joined while working.

FIRST MOTIF . . . Ch 10, join with sl st. **1st rnd:** Ch 6, make 19 d tr in ring with ch-1 between. Join to 5th st of ch-6. **2nd rnd:** Ch 1, * sc in next sp, ch 5. Repeat from * around, ending with sl st in 1st sc made (20 loops). **3rd rnd:** Sl st to center of next loop, ch 1, sc in same loop, * ch 5, sc in next loop. Repeat from * around. Break off.

SECOND MOTIF . . . Work first 2 rnds as for First Motif. **3rd rnd:** Sl st to center of next loop, sc in same loop, ch 5, sc in next loop, ch 2, tr in a loop on First Motif, ch 2, sc in next loop on Second Motif, * ch 2, sc in next loop on First Motif, ch 2, sc in next loop on Second Motif. Repeat from * 3 more times, ch 2, tr in next loop on First Motif, ch 2, sc in next loop on Second Motif and complete rnd as for First Motif with no more joinings.

THIRD MOTIF . . . Join to Second Motif on 3rd rnd, leaving 4 loops free between joinings on each side of Second Motif. Join; do not break off, but sl st to top of next loop and work around all 3 motifs as follows:

1st rnd: Sc in same loop, * ch 5, tr in tr-sp at next joining, ch 5, tr in same sp; (ch 5, sc in next free ch-5 loop) 4 times. Repeat from * once more; make 10 more ch-5 loops, ch 5, tr in next tr-sp and continue thus around, working other half to correspond and ending rnd with sl st in 1st sc made. **2nd rnd:** Sl st in each of first 2 ch of next loop, ch 1, sc in loop, * ch 5, sc in next loop. Repeat from * around; join. **3rd rnd:** Sl st in next 2 ch, sc in loop, ch 10 (to count as d tr and ch-5), * d tr in next loop, ch 5. Repeat from * around. Join to 5th ch of ch-10. **4th rnd:** Sc in next sp, ch 6 (to count as dc and ch-3), in same sp make dc, ch 3 and dc; in each of next 9 sps make 3 dc with ch-3 between. In each of following 9 sps (at curve), make dc, ch 3, (tr, ch 3) twice and dc. In each of next 13 sps make 3 dc with ch-3 between. In each of next 9 sps (at curve), make dc, ch 3, (tr, ch 3) twice and dc. In each of remaining 3 sps make 3 dc with ch-3 between. Join to 3rd st of ch-6 first

7186

made. **5th rnd:** * Sc in next sp, ch 3, sc in following sp, skip 2 dc; in next sp make sc, ch 3, 2 tr, ch 3, and sc (a petal); ch 3, 2 tr in next dc, ch 3; in next sp make sc, ch 3, 2 tr, ch 3 and sc; skip 2 dc. Repeat from * 4 more times. ** Ch 3, sc in next ch-3 sp, sc in following sp (between tr's) and complete 3 petals in this sp, sc in next sp. Repeat from ** 8 more times; ch 3, skip 2 dc. *** Sc in next sp and complete a petal, ch 3, 2 tr in next dc, ch 3, sc in next sp and complete a petal; skip 2 dc, sc in next sp, ch 3, sc in next sp, skip 2 dc. Repeat from *** 5 more times; sc in next sp and complete a petal, ch 3, 2 tr in dc, ch 3, sc in next sp and complete a petal; ch 3, skip 2 dc, sc in next sp, sc in following sp (between tr's) and complete 3 petals; continue thus around, working remainder of rnd to correspond.

6th rnd: Sl st to center of next petal, sc between 2 tr's, ch 10, * d tr between 2 tr's of next petal, ch 5, d tr between tr's of next petal, d tr between tr's of next petal, ch 5. Repeat from * around, ending with d tr in last petal, sl st in 5th st of ch-10 first made. **7th rnd:** * In next sp make sc, ch 5, and sc; ch 5; in next sp make sc, ch 5, and sc; skip 2 d tr. Repeat from * around. **8th rnd:** Sl st to tip of next loop, sc in loop, * ch 5, sc in next loop. Repeat from * around. **9th rnd:** Sl st to center of next loop, sc in loop, * ch 3, sc in next loop. Repeat from * around, ending with sl st in 1st sc made. **10th rnd:** Sc in sp. ch 8, skip 1 sp; make d tr, ch 5, and d tr in next sp, ch 8, skip the ch-3 of next sp, sc in the sc of same sp (between 2 sps). * Ch 8, skip next sp; make d tr, ch 5, and d tr in next sp, ch 8, skip 1 sp, sc in next sp. Repeat from * 2 more times. ** Ch 8, skip next sp; in next sp make d tr, ch 5 and d tr; ch 8, skip the ch-3 of next sp, sc in the sc of same sp. Repeat from ** 6 more times. *** Ch 8, skip next sp; in next sp make d tr, ch 5 and d tr; ch 8, skip 1 sp, sc in next sp. Repeat from *** 2 more times. Repeat from the beginning of the rnd once more, omitting the 1st sc in sp, and ending with sl st in 1st sc made. **11th, 12th, and**

13th rnds: Sl st to center of next ch, sc in sp, ch 10, * in next sp make d tr, ch 5, and d tr; ch 5, d tr in each of next 2 sps, ch 5. Repeat from * around, ending with d tr, sl st in 5th st of ch-10 first made. **14th rnd:** Sl st to center of next ch, sc in sp, ch 10; * in next sp make 3 d tr with ch-5 between, ch 5, d tr in each of next 2 sps, ch 5. Repeat from * around, ending with d tr, sl st in 5th st of ch-10.

15th rnd: Sl st to center of next ch, sc in sp, ch 10, * d tr, ch 5, and d tr in next sp; ch 5; d tr, ch 5 and d tr in next sp; ch 5, d tr in each of next 2 sps, ch 5. Repeat from * around, ending with d tr in last sp, sl st in 5th st of ch-10 first made. **16th rnd:** * 5 sc in each of next 2 sps, ch 4, sc in 4th st from hook (p); dc in next ch-5 sp; (p, dc in same sp) 6 times; p, 5 sc in each of next 2 sps. Repeat from * around. Break off.

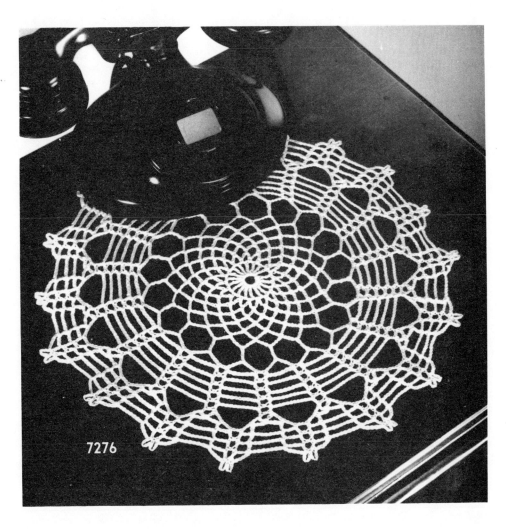

7276

7276 . . . Materials: KNIT-CRO-SHEEN, *1 ball* . . . *Steel Crochet Hook No. 7.*

Doily measures about 11½ inches in diameter.

Ch 12, join with sl st. **1st rnd:** Ch 5 (to count as tr and ch-1), * tr in ring, ch 1. Repeat from * 16 more times; join with sl st in 4th st of ch-5. **2nd rnd:** Ch 1, sc in sp; (ch 5, sc in next sp) 17 times; ch 2, join with dc in 1st sc of rnd (18 loops). **3rd rnd:** Ch 1, sc under dc, * ch 5, sc in next loop. Repeat from * around, ending with ch 2, join with dc. **4th rnd:** Repeat 3rd rnd. **5th rnd:** Make ch-6 loops (instead of ch-5), ending with ch 3, join with tr. **6th rnd:** Repeat 5th rnd, making ch-7 loops instead of ch-6. **7th rnd:** Make ch-8 loops instead of ch-7, ending with ch 4, join with tr. **8th rnd:** Ch 15 (to count as tr and ch-11), * tr in next loop, ch 11. Repeat from * around. Join to 4th st of ch-15. **9th rnd:** Sl st in next 4 ch, ch 1, sc in next ch; * ch 5, skip 1 ch, sc in next ch, ch 6, sc in 5th st of next ch-11 loop. Repeat from * around. Join to 1st sc made. **10th rnd:** Sl st in 1st ch, sc in next ch, * ch 5, skip 1 ch, sc in next ch, ch 7, skip ch-6 loop, sc in 2nd ch of next ch-5 loop. Repeat from * around. Join. **11th rnd:** Repeat 10th rnd, making ch-8 loops instead of ch-7. **12th rnd:** Repeat 11th rnd, making ch-9 loops instead of ch-8. **13th rnd:** Repeat 12th rnd, making ch-10 loops instead of ch-9. **14th rnd:** Repeat 13th rnd, making ch-14 loops instead of ch-10. Join and turn. **15th rnd:** Sl st in first 3 ch, ch 1, turn and work sc in same place as last sl st, * ch 3, sc in center ch of ch-5 loop, ch 3, sc in 3rd ch of next ch-14 loop, (ch 5, skip 2 ch, sc in next ch) 3 times. Repeat from * around. Join and turn. **16th rnd:** Sl st in first 3 ch, ch 1, turn and work sc in same place as last sl st, * ch 6, sc in 3rd ch of next ch-5 loop, ch 5, sc in 2nd ch of next loop, ch 5, skip 1 ch, sc in next ch of same loop, ch 5, sc in 3rd ch of next loop. Repeat from * around. Join and turn. **17th rnd:** Repeat 16th rnd, making ch-7 loops instead of ch-6 loops. **18th rnd:** Sl st in first 3 ch, ch 1, turn and work sc in same place as last sl st, * ch 7, sc in 3rd ch of next ch-5 loop, ch 5, sc in 2nd ch of next loop; (ch 4, sc in next ch) twice; ch 5, sc in 3rd ch of next loop. Repeat from * around. Join and break off.

7699 . . . Materials: BEST SIX CORD MERCERIZED CROCHET, *Size 30: 3 balls* . . . *Steel Crochet Hook No. 10 or 11.*

Large doily measures about 15 inches in diameter; small doily measures 9 inches in diameter.

LARGE DOILY . . . Ch 8, join with sl st. **1st rnd:** Ch 1, 12 sc in ring. Sl st in 1st sc made. **2nd rnd:** Ch 5, * dc in next sc, ch 2. Repeat from * around, ending with sl st in 3rd st of ch-5. **3rd rnd:** Ch 4, holding back on hook the last loop of each tr, make 2 tr in same place as sl st, thread over and draw through all loops on hook (cluster made), * ch 4, holding back on hook the last loop of each tr make 3 tr in next dc, thread over and draw through all loops on hook (a 3-tr cluster made). Repeat from * around, ending with ch 4, sl st in tip of 1st cluster. **4th rnd:** Ch 7, * tr in next sp, ch 3, tr in tip of next cluster, ch 3. Repeat from * around, ending with ch 3, tr in last sp, ch 3, sl st in 4th st of ch-7. **5th rnd:** Ch 1, sc in same place as sl st, * ch 10, sc in next tr, 2 sc in sp, sc in next tr. Repeat from * around, ending with sl st in 1st sc made.

6th rnd: * In next loop make sc, half dc and 8 dc; make 3 p's—*to make a p, ch 5, sl st in 5th ch from hook;* ch 3, make 3 more p's, sl st in last dc made; in same ch-10 loop make 8 dc, half dc and sc; skip 1 sc, sl st in each of next 2 sc. Repeat from * around (12 picot-loops in all). Join and break off. **7th rnd:** Attach thread in tip of any picot-loop, ch 6, dc in same place where thread was attached, * ch 13, in tip of next picot-loop make dc, ch 3 and dc. Repeat from * around, ending with ch 13, sl st in 3rd st of ch-6. **8th rnd:** Ch 1, 3 sc in 1st sp, * 17 sc over next ch-13, 3 sc in next ch-3 sp. Repeat from * around, ending with 17 sc over last ch-13. Join with sl st. **9th rnd:** Sl st in next sc (center of 3-sc group), ch 6, dc in same place as sl st, * ch 7, in center sc of next sp make dc, ch 3, and dc; ch 7, in center sc of next 3-sc group make dc, ch 3, and dc. Repeat from * around. Join with sl st as before.

10th rnd: Ch 1, * 3 sc in next ch-3 sp, 7 sc in next sp. Repeat from * around. Join as before. **11th rnd:** Sl st in next sc, ch 6, dc in same place as sl st, * ch 8, in center st of next 3-sc

7699

group make dc, ch 3 and dc. Repeat from * around. Join. **12th rnd:** Repeat 10th rnd, only having 8 sc over ch-8. **13th rnd:** Repeat 11th rnd, only making ch 9 instead of ch-8. **14th rnd:** Repeat 10th rnd, only having 9 sc over ch-9. **15th rnd:** Repeat 11th rnd, only making ch 10 instead of ch-8. **16th rnd:** Repeat 10th rnd, only having 11 sc over ch-10. **17th rnd:** Sl st in next sc, ch 4, * skip 1 sc, dc in next sc, ch 1. Repeat from * ending with sl st in 3rd st of ch-4. **18th rnd:** Ch 4, holding back on hook the last loop of each tr make 2 tr in same place as sl st, thread over and draw through all loops on hook (cluster made), * ch 4, skip next dc, in next dc make a 3-tr cluster. Repeat from * around, ending with ch-4, sl st in tip of 1st cluster. **19th rnd:** Ch 9, * tr in tip of next cluster, ch 5. Repeat from * ending with sl st in 4th st of ch-9.

20th rnd: Ch 1, sc in same place as sl st, * ch 10, sc in next tr, (4 sc in ch-5 sp, sc in next tr) twice. Repeat from * around, ending with sl st in 1st sc. **21st rnd:** Sl st in ch-10 loop, ch 3, 9 dc in same loop, * make 3 p's, ch 3 and 3 p's, sl st in last dc made, 10 dc in same ch-10 loop, skip 4 sc, sc in next 3 sc, 10 dc in next loop. Repeat from * around, ending with sl st in top st of starting ch-3. Join and break off. **22nd to 29th rnds incl:** Repeat 7th to 14th rnds incl. **30th and 31st rnds:** Repeat 13th and 14th rnds. **32nd to 35th rnds incl:** Repeat 17th to 20th rnds incl. **36th rnd:** Sl st in ch-10 loop, ch 3, 19 dc in same loop, * skip 4 sc, sc in next 3 sc, 20 dc in next loop. Repeat from * around. Join and break off.

SMALL DOILY (Make 2) . . . Work as for Large Doily to 20th rnd incl. **Last rnd:** Work as for last rnd of Large Doily.

7269 . . . Materials: Coats & Clark's O.N.T.
Mercerized Crochet, *Size 70: 1 ball . . .*
Steel Crochet Hook No. 14.

Doily measures about 10 inches in diameter.

MOTIF . . . Ch 10, join with sl st. **1st rnd:**
Ch 7 (to count as dc and ch-4), * dc in ring,
ch 4. Repeat from * 4 more times. Sl st in 3rd st
of.ch-7 first made (6 sps). **2nd rnd:** In each sp
around make sc, half dc, 5 dc, half dc and sc.
Sl st in sl st (6 petals). **3rd rnd:** * Ch 5, insert
hook between next 2 petals from back of work
and bring it out in following sp; thread over
and draw loop through; thread over and draw
through both loops on hook. Repeat from * 5
more times. **4th rnd:** Repeat 2nd rnd, making
7 dc (instead of 5 dc) in center of each petal.
5th rnd: Repeat 3rd rnd. **6th rnd:** Ch 3 (to
count as dc), 11 dc in next ch-5 loop, 12 dc in
each loop around. Sl st in 3rd st of ch-3 first
made. **7th rnd:** Ch 11 (to count as tr and
ch-7), skip 5 dc, tr between this and next dc
(5th and 6th dc), * ch 7, skip 6 dc, tr between
this and next dc (6th and 7th dc). Repeat
from * around, ending with ch 7, sl st in 4th

ch of ch-11 first made (12 sps). **8th rnd:** Ch 1,
* 9 sc in sp, sc in next tr. Repeat from *
around; join. **9th rnd:** Ch 12, sl st in 2nd ch
from hook and in each ch across; sl st in sl st.
* Ch 5, turn, skip 2 sts, dc in next st; (ch 2,
skip 2 sts, dc in next st) 3 times. Repeat from *
3 more times (a square completed). ** Ch 11,
sc in sc directly over next tr below, ch 5, turn;
skip 2 sts, dc in next st, ch 2, skip 2 sts, dc in
next st and complete a square as before. Repeat from ** around (12 squares). Join with
sl st to tip of first ch-12 made. **10th rnd:** * 2 sc
in next sp, sc in next st, 2 sc in next sp, sc in
next st, ch 3, sl st in 3rd ch from hook (p);
2 sc in next sp, sc in next st, 3 sc in next sp,
p, 2 sc in same sp, sc in next st, 2 sc in next sp,
sc in next st, p, 2 sc in next sp, sc in next st,
2 sc in next sp. Repeat from * around. Join and
break off.

Make 6 more motifs. Place these 6 motifs
around 1st motif and sew together 2 points of
each motif to 2 points of center motif. Join
adjacent motifs at 2 corresponding points in
same manner.

7269

7572 . . . Materials: THREE CORD MERCERIZED CROCHET, *Size 50: 1 ball . . . Steel Crochet Hook No. 12.*

Each doily measures about 6 inches in diameter:

DOILY (Make 6) . . . Ch 8, join with sl st. **1st rnd:** Ch 1, 16 sc in ring. Join with sl st to 1st sc made. **2nd rnd:** Ch 1, sc in same place as sl st, * ch 5, skip 1 sc, sc in next sc. Repeat from * around, joining last ch-5 to 1st sc made. **3rd rnd:** Ch 1, * in next loop make 3 sc, ch 1 and 3 sc. Repeat from * around. Join. **4th rnd:** Sl st to 1st ch-1 sp, ch 1, sc in same sp, * ch 9, sc in next ch-1 sp. Repeat from * around, joining last ch-9 to 1st sc. **5th rnd:** Ch 1, sc in same place as sl st, * in next loop make 4 sc, ch 3, sl st in 3rd ch from hook (a ch-3 p made), and 4 sc, sc in next sc. Repeat from * around. Join. **6th rnd:** Sl st in 3 sc, ch 1, sc in next sc, * ch 9, skip p, sc in next sc, ch 9, skip 7 sc, sc in next sc. Repeat from * around. Join. **7th rnd:** Sl st in 3 ch, ch 1, 4 sc in same loop, * ch 3, 3 sc in next loop, ch 3, 4 sc in next loop. Repeat from * around. Join. **8th rnd:** Sl st in 3 sc, sl st in next ch, ch 5, holding back on hook the last loop of each d tr, make 2 d tr in next ch, thread over and draw through all loops on hook, * ch 15, skip 1 ch, 3 sc and 1 ch, holding back on hook the last loop of each d tr, make 3 d tr in next ch, thread over and draw through all loops on hook (3-d tr cluster made), ch 1, skip 1 ch, 4 sc and 1 ch, cluster in next ch. Repeat from * around, ending with cluster, ch 1, sl st in top of 1st cluster made. **9th rnd:** Ch 5, dc in next loop, (ch 1, dc in same loop) 10 times; * (ch 2, dc in top of next cluster) twice; ch 2, in next loop make 11 dc with ch-1 between. Repeat from * around, joining last ch-2 with sl st in 3rd st of 1st ch-5. Turn, sl st in last sp, turn.

10th rnd: Ch 5, dc in next sp, * (ch 2, skip 1 dc, dc in next dc) 5 times; (ch 2, dc in next sp) 3 times. Repeat from * around. Join. **11th rnd:** Sl st in next sp, ch 5, * dc in next sp, ch 2. Repeat from * around. Join, turn, sl st in last sp, turn. **12th rnd:** Ch 6, * dc in next sp, ch 3. Repeat from * around. Join. **13th rnd:** Sl st in next sp, ch 3, 2 dc in same sp, * 3 dc in next sp. Repeat from * around. Join. **14th rnd:** Ch 1, sc in same place as sl st, ch 5, skip 5 dc, between 5th and 6th dc make 2 d tr, ch 5 and 2 d tr, * ch 5, skip 6 dc, sc between 6th and 7th dc, ch 5, skip 6 dc, between 6th and 7th dc make 2 d tr, ch 5 and 2 d tr. Repeat from * around. Join. **15th rnd:** Ch 1, * in next loop make 3 sc, ch-3 p, and 2 sc, sc in 2 d tr, in next loop make 2 sc, p, and 2 sc; sc in next d tr, ch 15, turn, skip 2 sc, p and 2 sc, sl st in next sc, turn. Working over last chain make 4 sc, (p, 2 sc) twice; p, 4 sc, sc in next d tr, in next loop make 2 sc, p and 3 sc. Repeat from * around. Join and break off.

7642 . . . Materials: BEST SIX CORD MERCERIZED CROCHET, *Size 20: 3 balls . . . Steel Crochet Hook No. 8 or 9.*

Doily measures about 19 inches in diameter.

Ch 12. Join with sl st. **1st rnd:** Ch 3 (to count as 1 dc), 31 dc in ring. Join with sl st in top st of starting chain. **2nd rnd:** Ch 1, sc in same place as sl st, sc in each dc around. Join. **3rd rnd:** Ch 1, sc in same place as sl st, * ch 1, sc in next sc. Repeat from * around, joining last ch-1 with sl st in 1st sc. **4th rnd:** Sl st in next sp, ch 4 (to count as dc and ch 1), * dc in next sp, ch 1. Repeat from * around, joining last ch-1 with sl st in 3rd st of ch-4. **5th rnd:** Sl st in next sp, ch 6 (to count as tr and ch 2), * tr in next sp, ch 2. Repeat from * around, joining last ch-2 with sl st in 4th st of ch-6. **6th rnd:** Sl st in next sp, ch 7, tr in same sp, * ch 3, skip 1 sp, in next sp make tr, ch 3 and tr. Repeat from * around. Join. **7th rnd:** Sl st in sp, ch 4, in same sp make tr, ch 2 and 2 tr (4-tr shell made); * ch 1, tr in next sp, ch 1, in next sp make 2 tr, ch 2 and 2 tr (another 4-tr shell made). Repeat from * around. Join. **8th rnd:** Sl st in next tr and in next sp, ch 4 and complete a 4-tr shell as before (shell over shell made), * ch 2, tr in next tr, ch 2, shell over shell. Repeat from * around. Join. **9th rnd:** Sl st in next tr and in next sp, ch 4, in same sp make 2 tr, ch 3 and 3 tr (6-tr shell made); * ch 2, tr in next tr, ch 2, in sp of next shell make a 6-tr shell. Repeat from * around. Join. **10th rnd:** Repeat 9th rnd, only having ch 3 between shell and tr, instead of ch-2. Join.

11th rnd: Sl st in next 2 tr and in sp, ch 4, in same sp make 3 tr, ch 5 and 4 tr (8-tr shell made); * ch 3, make 3 tr in next tr, ch 3, in sp of next shell make an 8-tr shell. Repeat from * around. Join. **12th rnd:** Sl st in next 3 tr and in sp, ch 4, in same sp make 7 tr, ch 3 and 8 tr (16-tr shell made); * ch 3, tr in center st of

119

7572

7642

121

3-tr group, ch 3, in sp of next shell make a 16-tr shell. Repeat from * around. Join. **13th rnd:** Ch 4, tr in next 3 tr, * ch 2, in next sp make an 8-tr shell, ch 2, skip 4 tr, tr in next 4 tr, ch 2, skip next sp, the tr and the following sp, tr in next 4 tr. Repeat from * around. Join. **14th rnd:** Sl st across to sp of next shell, sl st in sp, ch 4, make an 8-tr shell, * ch 6, skip next sp and following 2 tr, tr in next 2 tr, tr in each of next 2 ch, tr in next 2 tr, ch 6, make an 8-tr shell over next shell. Repeat from * around. Join. **15th rnd:** Sl st across to sp of next shell, sl st in sp, ch 4, make an 8-tr shell. * Ch 7, skip next sp and 1 tr, tr in next 4 tr, ch 7, make an 8-tr shell over next shell. Repeat from * around. Join. **16th rnd:** Ch 4, tr in next 3 tr, * in next sp make 4 tr, ch 3 and 4 tr; tr in next 4 tr, ch 6, skip next sp and 1 tr, tr in next 2 tr, ch 6, skip next sp, tr in next 4 tr. Repeat from * around. Join. **17th rnd:** Ch 4, tr in next 3 tr, * ch 2, make an 8-tr shell over next shell, ch 2, skip 4 tr, tr in next 4 tr, ch 6, skip next 2 sps, tr in next 4 tr. Repeat from * around. Join. **18th rnd:** Ch 4, tr in next 3 tr, * tr in next ch, ch 3, make an 8-tr shell over shell, ch 3, skip 1 ch of next ch-2, tr in next ch, tr in next 4 tr, ch 5, tr in next 4 tr. Repeat from * around. Join. **19th rnd:** Ch 4, tr in next 4 tr, * ch 6, make an 8-tr shell over next shell, ch 6, skip next sp, tr in next 5 tr, ch 3, tr in next 5 tr. Repeat from * around. Join. **20th rnd:** Ch 4, tr in next 3 tr, * ch 9, make an 8-tr shell over next shell, ch 9, skip next sp and 1 tr, tr in next 4 tr, ch 2, tr in next 4 tr. Repeat from * around. Join. **21st rnd:** Ch 4, tr in next 2 tr, * ch 10, make an 8-tr shell over next shell, ch 10, skip next sp and 1 tr, tr in next 3 tr, ch 2, tr in next 3 tr. Repeat from * around. Join.

22nd rnd: Ch 4, tr in next 2 tr, * ch 12, make an 8-tr shell over next shell, ch 10, skip next sp, tr in next 3 tr, ch 2, tr in next 3 tr. Repeat from * around. Join. **23rd rnd:** Ch 3, tr in next 2 tr, * ch 8, tr in next 4 tr, in next sp make 4 tr, ch 3 and 4 tr, tr in next 4 tr, ch 8, tr in next 3 tr, ch 2, tr in next 3 tr. Repeat from * around. Join. **24th rnd:** Sl st in next tr, ch 9 (to count as tr and ch 5), * tr in next 8 tr with ch 1 between; in ch-3 sp make (ch 1, tr) twice; ch 1, tr in next 8 tr with ch 1 between, ch 5, tr in center st of next 3-tr group, ch 2, tr in center st of next tr-group, ch 5. Repeat from * around. Join. **25th rnd:** Sl st in next ch, sl st in sp, * ch 4, tr in next tr, (ch 1, tr in next ch-1 sp) 8 times; ch 1, in center sp make tr, ch 1 and tr, (ch 1, tr in next sp) 8 times; ch 1, tr in next tr, (ch 4, sc in next sp) 3 times. Repeat from * around. Join. **26th rnd:** Sl st across to 1st tr, ch 5, * (tr in next sp, ch 1) 9 times; in center sp make tr, ch 1 and tr, (ch 1, tr in next sp) 9 times; ch 1, tr in next tr, ch 3, skip 1 sp, 2 tr in next sp, ch 1, 2 tr in next sp, ch 3, tr in next tr. Repeat from * around. Join. **27th rnd:** Sl st in next sp, ch 1, sc in same sp, * (ch 3, sc in next sp) 20 times; ch 4, sc in next ch-1 sp (between the two 2-tr groups), ch 4, sc in next ch-1 sp. Repeat from * around. Join. **28th rnd:** Sl st in next loop, ch 1, sc in same loop, * (ch 3, sc in next loop) 19 times; ch 3, skip ch 4, sc in next sc, ch 3, skip ch 4, sc in next loop. Repeat from * around. Join. **29th rnd:** Sl st in next loop, ch 1, sc in same loop, * (ch 3, sc in next loop) 18 times; ch 2, skip ch 3, sc in next sc, ch 2, skip ch 3, sc in next loop. Repeat from * around. Join. **30th rnd:** Sl st in next loop, ch 1, sc in same loop, * (ch 3, sc in next loop) 17 times; ch 1, skip ch 2, sc in next sc, ch 1, skip ch 2, sc in next loop. Repeat from * around. Join. **31st rnd:** Sl st in next loop, ch 1, sc in same loop, * (ch 4, sc in next loop) 16 times; skip next sc, sc in next sc, sc in next ch-3 loop. Repeat from * around. Join and break off.

CHAPTER NINE

Luncheon Sets

Iᴛ's ɴᴏᴛ sᴏ ᴍᴜᴄʜ what you serve as how it looks . . . the fruit cup crowned with cherry and mint . . . the lovely old tureen in which the shrimp curry or the minced chicken is served . . . the lace-edged napkin keeping the biscuits hot . . . or a handsome luncheon set completing the picture, making it a "feast for the eyes."

Somehow we've come to associate certain niceties of dining with a certain degree of taste and culture. A household with lovely linen, where a beautifully set table is a habit and meals a pleasant ritual is—generally speaking—a house where the people have cultivated tastes, attractive manners. Make sure when you have guests that your home—and table—reflect you as attractively as possible.

4041 . . . Materials: Pᴇᴀʀʟ Cᴏᴛᴛᴏɴ, *Size 5, 33 balls . . . Steel Crochet Hook No. 7.*

Place Mat measures about 11 x 17 inches; runner about 11 x 27 inches.

PLACE MAT (Make 4) . . . 1st row: Ch 11 drop loop from hook, holding chain just made with forefinger and thumb of left hand insert hook in 1st ch made and draw dropped loop through; * in ring just made make 4 sc, ch 3 and 4 sc; ch 10, drop loop from hook, holding the ch-10 with left hand as before insert hook in last sc made and draw dropped loop through. Repeat from * across, until row measures 11 inches, making (4 sc, ch 3) 3 times and 4 sc in last ring. Make 4 sc, ch 3 and 4 sc in remaining half of each ring; ch 3, sl st in 1st sc made. Break off. **2nd row:** Work 1st half of this row same as 1st half of 1st row, ending with (4 sc, ch 3) twice and 4 sc in last ring. Work other half as follows: Ch 1, sc in corresponding ch-3 loop of last ring on previous row, * ch 1, 4 sc in same ring on 2nd row, 4 sc in next ring, ch 1, sc in corresponding loop of next ring on previous row. Repeat from * across, ending row as before. Break off. Repeat 2nd row until piece measures 17 inches.

RUNNER . . . Work as for Place Mat until piece measures 27 inches long.

4041

7193

7193 . . . Materials: THREE CORD MERCER-IZED CROCHET, *Size 50: 5 balls . . . Steel Crochet Hook No. 12 or 13.*

Runner measures about 13½ x 31½ inches; each place mat, about 12¼ x 12¼ inches. Each motif measures 1¾ inches in diameter.

PLACE MAT—First Motif . . . Ch 10, join with sl st. **1st rnd:** Ch 3, 23 dc in ring. Join with sl st to top st of ch-3. **2nd rnd:** Ch 4, * dc in next dc, ch 1. Repeat from * around. Join. **3rd rnd:** Sl st in next sp, ch 10, * skip 1 sp, tr in next sp, ch 6. Repeat from * around. Join last ch-6 with sl st to 4th st of ch-10. **4th rnd:** Ch 1, sc in same place as sl st, * ch 2, skip 2 ch, dc in next ch, ch 2, dc in next ch, ch 2, sc in next tr. Repeat from * around. Join. **5th rnd:** Ch 1, sc in same place as sl st, * ch 2, dc in next dc, ch 2, dc in ch-2 sp, ch 2, dc in next dc, ch 2, sc in next sc. Repeat from * around. Join and break off.

SECOND MOTIF . . . Work 4 rnds as for First Motif. **5th rnd:** Ch 1, sc in same place as sl st, ch 2, dc in next dc, * ch 1, sl st in corresponding sp on First Motif, ch 1, dc in next sp on Second Motif, ch 1, sl st in next sp on First Motif, ch 1, dc in next dc on Second Motif, ch 2, sc in next sc, ch 2, dc in next dc. Repeat from * once more; complete rnd as for First Motif.

Make 2 more motifs, leaving 4 points free between joinings and joining as Second Motif was joined to First Motif. This completes one strip. Make another strip of 5 motifs, joining points of each motif to corresponding points of adjacent motifs as before (motifs fall between those of previous strip). Continue thus, making 1 strip of 6 motifs, 1 strip of 7 motifs, then 1 strip of 6 motifs, 1 strip of 5 motifs, and 1 strip of 4 motifs.

RUNNER . . . Make 1st strip of 14 motifs, then 1 strip of 15 motifs, 1 strip of 16 motifs, 1 strip of 17 motifs, 1 strip of 18 motifs, 1 strip of 17 motifs, 1 strip of 16 motifs, 1 strip of 15 motifs, and last strip of 14 motifs.

7444

7444 . . . Materials: BEST SIX CORD MERCERIZED CROCHET, *Size 20: 8 balls* . . . *Steel Crochet Hook No. 9 or 10.*

Centerpiece measures about 16 inches in diameter; place doily 13½ inches in diameter; bread and butter plate doily 8 inches in diameter, and glass doily 6 inches in diameter.

PLACE DOILY (Make 4) . . . Wind thread 10 times around forefinger. Slip strands off finger. 1st rnd: 32 sc in ring. Sl st in 1st sc made. 2nd rnd: Ch 5, skip 1 sc, dc in next sc, * ch 2, skip 1 sc, dc in next sc. Repeat from * around, ending with ch 2, sl st in 3rd st of ch-5. 3rd rnd: * Ch 10, sc in 2nd ch from hook, half dc in next ch, dc in next 7 ch, sc in next dc of 2nd rnd (a spoke made). Repeat from * around ending with sc at base of ch-10 first made (16 spokes in all). 4th rnd: Sl st to tip of 1st spoke, ch 1, sc in tip of same spoke, * ch 7, sc in tip of next spoke. Repeat from * around, ending with sl st in 1st sc made. 5th rnd: Ch 5, dc in same place as sl st, * ch 3, sc in next sp, ch 3, in next sc make dc, ch 2 and dc (shell made). Repeat from * around, ending with ch 3, sl st in 3rd st of ch-5. 6th rnd: Sl st in sp, ch 5, dc in same sp, * ch 4, sc in next sc, ch 4, make a shell in sp of next shell. Repeat from * around, ending with ch 4, sl st in 3rd st of ch-5 first made.

Continue in this manner, making shell over shell and sc over sc, having 1 additional st in ch's between sc's and shells on each successive rnd, until there are 20 ch between sc's and shells. Break off.

CENTERPIECE . . . Work as for Place Doily, but omit increases in ch's on 10th and 12th rnds. When there are 18 ch's work 7 rnds more, making 2 extra ch's between sc's and shells on each successive rnd (32 ch's). Break off.

BREAD and BUTTER PLATE DOILY (Make 4) . . . Work as for Place Doily to 13th rnd incl. Break off.

GLASS DOILY (Make 4) . . . Work as for Place Doily to 9th rnd incl. Break off.

7718 . . . Materials: KNIT-CRO-SHEEN, *3 balls.* . . . *Steel Crochet Hook No. 6 or 7.*

Place Mat measures about 12½ x 16½ inches; runner about 12½ x 24 inches.

PLACE MAT (Make 2) . . . Ch 139 to measure 15 inches. 1st row: Sc in 14th ch from hook, sc in next ch, * ch 6, skip 3 ch, tr in next 2 ch, ch 6, skip 3 ch, sc in next 2 ch. Repeat from * across, ending with ch 6, skip 3 ch, tr in last ch. Ch 1, turn. 2nd row: Sc in tr, * ch 6, sc in next 2 sc, ch 6, sc in next 2 tr. Repeat from * across, ending with ch 6, skip 6 sts of turning chain, sc in next ch. Ch 18, turn. 3rd row: * Skip next 2 sc, tr in next 2 sc, ch 14. Repeat from * across, ending with ch 14, skip next 2 sc, tr in last sc. Ch 1, turn. 4th row: Sc in 1st sc, * ch 6, skip 6 sts of next ch-14, sc in next 2 ch, ch 6, sc in next 2 tr. Repeat from * across, ending with ch 6, skip 6 sts of turning chain, sc in next 2 ch, ch 6, skip 6 more sts of turning chain, sc in next ch. Ch 7, turn. 5th row: Skip 1st sc, * sc in next 2 sc, ch 3, tr in next 2 sc, ch 3. Repeat from * across, ending with ch 3, tr in last sc. Ch 1, turn. 6th row: Sc in tr, * ch 3, sc in next 2 sc, ch 3, sc in next 2 tr. Repeat from * across, ending with ch 3, skip 3 ch, sc in next ch. Ch 10, turn. 7th row: * Sc in next 2 sc, ch 6, tr in next 2 sc, ch 6. Repeat from * across, ending with ch 6, tr in last sc. Ch 1, turn. Repeat 2nd to 7th rows incl 4 more times; then repeat 2nd to 5th rows incl once more.

Now work Border as follows: 1st rnd: Ch 3, 4 dc in tr just made, * 3 dc in next sp, dc at ends of each of next 2 chains. Repeat from * across narrow edge of mat. Make 5 dc in corner, ** 3 dc in next sp, dc in same place as next 2 sc. Repeat from ** across wide edge of mat. Complete remaining edges to correspond. Join with sl st in 3rd st of starting chain. 2nd rnd: Ch 3, dc in next dc, * 5 dc in next dc, dc in each dc across to center dc of next corner. Repeat from * around. Join. 3rd rnd: Ch 4, tr in 3 dc, ** make 5 tr in corner dc, tr in next 4 dc, * ch 6, skip 3 dc, sc in next 2 dc, ch 6, skip 3 dc, tr in next 2 dc. Repeat from * across

127

7718

to 7 sts from corner dc, skip 3 dc, tr in next 4 dc. Repeat from ** around, joining last ch-6 with sl st in 4th st of starting chain. **4th rnd:** Ch 1, sc in same place as sl st, sc in next 5 tr, ** 3 sc in corner tr, sc in next 6 tr, * ch 6, sc in next 2 sc, ch 6, sc in next 2 tr. Repeat from * across to next corner, sc in next 6 tr. Repeat from ** around. Join. **5th rnd:** ** Sc in each sc to corner sc, in corner sc make sc, ch 5 and sc; sc in each sc to next chain, * sc in each ch, sc in 2 sc, sc in each ch, sc in next sc, ch 5, sc in next sc. Repeat from * across to next corner. Repeat from ** around. Break off.

RUNNER . . . Ch 89 to measure 10 inches. Work 1st to 7th rows incl same as Place Mat. Repeat 2nd to 7th rows incl 11 more times; then repeat 2nd to 5th rows incl once more. Work Border same as Border of Place Mat.

7558 . . . Materials: BEST SIX CORD MERCERIZED CROCHET, *Size 20: 6 balls . . . Steel Crochet Hook No. 9 or 10.*

Centerpiece measures about 16 inches in diameter; place doily, 12 inches in diameter; bread and butter plate doily, 6½ inches in diameter, and glass doily, 5 inches in diameter.

CENTERPIECE . . . Ch 12. Join with sl st. **1st rnd:** Ch 4, 21 tr in ring. Join with sl st to top st of ch-4. **2nd rnd:** Ch 5, tr in same place as sl st, * ch 1, in next st make tr, ch 1 and tr. Repeat from * around, ending with ch 1, sl st in 4th st of ch-5. **3rd rnd:** Sl st in next sp, ch 4, * dc in next sp, ch 1. Repeat from * around. Join to 3rd st of ch-4. **4th rnd:** Sl st in next sp, ch 5, * dc in next sp, ch 2. Repeat from * around. Join to 3rd st of ch-5. **5th rnd:** Ch 6, dc in same place as sl st, * in next dc make dc, ch 3 and dc (shell made). Repeat from * around. Join with sl st in 3rd st of ch-6. **6th, 7th and 8th rnds:** Sl st in next ch, sl st in sp, ch 6, dc in same sp, * in next ch-3 sp make dc, ch 3 and dc (shell). Repeat from * around. Join. **9th rnd:** Sl st in next ch, sl st in sp, ch 6, dc in same sp, make 2 more shells as before (3 shells made), * ch 5, skip 1 shell, shell in next 3 shells. Repeat from * around (each 3-shell group is the base of a spoke; there are 11 spokes in all). **10th rnd:** Sl st in next ch, sl st in sp, ch 6, work 3 shells over 3 shells having 2 additional sts in ch-bars between shell groups.

Join. **11th rnd:** Same as previous rnd, having 1 additional st on ch-bars between shell groups. **12th to 23rd rnds incl:** Repeat the 10th and 11th rnds alternately (26 sts in ch-bars between shell groups on 23rd rnd). **24th rnd:** Same as 11th rnd (27 ch between shell groups). **25th rnd:** Sl st across to sp of center shell of this group, ch 6, dc in same sp, * ch 43, in sp of center shell of next group make a shell as before. Repeat from * around, joining last ch-43 to 3rd st of ch-6 (this begins scalloped edge). **26th rnd:** Sl st in next sp, ch 5, dc in same sp, * ch 1, in next (ch-43) sp make dc, ch 2 and dc; ch 17, working over the ch-bar below, make sc in center st of ch on 24th rnd, ch 17, in next sp make dc, ch 2, and dc; ch 1, in sp of next shell make dc, ch 2, and dc. Repeat from * around. Join.

Hereafter shells will be made of dc, ch 2, and dc. **27th rnd:** Sl st in next sp, ch 5, dc in same sp, ch 1, shell in sp of next shell; * ch 1, in next sp make dc, ch 2, and dc; ch 27, in next sp make dc, ch 2, and dc, (ch 1, shell in sp of next shell) 3 times. Repeat from * around. Join. **28th rnd:** Sl st in next sp, ch 5, dc in same sp, (ch 2, shell in sp of next shell) twice; * ch 25, (shell in sp of next shell, ch 2) 4 times; shell in sp of next shell. Repeat from * around. Join. **29th rnd:** Sl st in next sp, ch 5, dc in same sp, (ch 3, shell in next shell) twice; * ch 12, working over the ch-bar below, sc in center st of chain on 2nd rnd below, ch 12, (shell in next shell, ch 3) 4 times; shell in next shell. Repeat from * around. Join. **30th and 31st rnds:** Same as 27th and 28th rnds respectively having ch-4 between shells; between scallops make ch 21 on 30th rnd and ch 19 on 31st rnd. **32nd rnd:** Same as 29th rnd, having ch 5 between shells and ch 9 on both sides of the sc (between scallops). **33rd and 34th rnds:** Same as 30th and 31st rnds, having ch 5 between shells on 33rd rnd and ch 6 on 34th rnd; between scallops make ch 16 on 33rd rnd and ch 15 on 34th rnd. **35th rnd:** Same as 32nd rnd having ch 7 between shells and ch 7 on both sides of the sc between scallops. **36th and 37th rnds:** Same as 33rd and 34th rnds, having ch 8 between shells on 36th rnd and ch 9 on 37th rnd; between scallops make ch 11 on 36th rnd and ch 9 on 37th rnd. **38th rnd:** Sl st in next sp, ch 10, sc in 7th ch from hook, (ch 7, sc in same place as last sc) twice (triple p made);

7558

dc in same sp, (ch 10, dc in sp of next shell, ch 7, complete a triple p, dc in same sp) twice; * ch 7, working over the ch-bar below, sc in center st of ch on 36th rnd, ch 7, (dc in sp of next shell, ch 7; complete a triple p, dc in same sp, ch 10) 4 times; dc in next sp, complete a triple p, dc in same sp. Repeat from * around. Join and break off.

PLACE DOILY (Make 4) . . . Ch 10. Join. **1st rnd:** Ch 3, 17 dc in ring. Join with sl st to 3rd st of ch-3. **2nd to 7th rnds incl:** Work as for 2nd to 7th rnds of Centerpiece. **8th to 17th rnds incl:** Same as 9th to 18th rnds incl of Centerpiece (9 spokes). **18th rnd:** Same as 25th rnd of Centerpiece, making ch 35 (instead of 43). **19th rnd:** Same as 26th rnd of Centerpiece, making ch 15 (instead of 17). **20th to 27th rnds incl:** Same as 27th to 34th rnds incl of Centerpiece, having 1, 2, 3, 4, 4, 5, 6, 7 ch's respectively between shells; between scallops make 23 ch for 20th rnd, 21 for 21st rnd, ch 10 on both sides of the sc on the 22nd rnd; ch 17 for 23rd rnd, ch 15 for 24th rnd, ch 7 on both sides of the sc on the 25th rnd, ch 12 for 26th rnd and ch 11 for 27th rnd. **28th rnd:** Sl st in next sp, ch 10, sc in 7th ch from hook, (ch 7, sc in same place as last sc) twice (triple p made); dc in same sp, (ch 8, dc in next sp, ch 7, complete a triple p, dc in same sp) twice; * ch 5, working over the ch-bar below, sc in center st of ch on 26th rnd, ch 5, (dc in sp of next shell, ch 7; complete a triple p, dc in same sp, ch 8) 4 times; dc in next sp, complete a triple p, dc in same sp. Repeat from * around. Join and break off.

BREAD AND BUTTER PLATE DOILY (Make 4) . . . Ch 8. Join. **1st rnd:** Ch 3, 13 dc in ring. Join. **2nd rnd:** Ch 3, dc in same place as sl st, 2 dc in each dc around. Join (28 dc on rnd including starting chain). **3rd and 4th rnds:** Same as 5th and 6th rnds of Centerpiece. **5th to 10th rnds incl:** Repeat 9th to 14th rnds incl of Centerpiece, always having 2 additional ch's between spokes on each successive rnd (7 spokes). **11th rnd:** Same as 25th rnd of Centerpiece, making ch-25 (instead of ch-43). Shells of scalloped edge are made of dc, ch-3 and dc on this piece. **12th rnd:** Same as 26th rnd of Centerpiece, making ch-10 (instead of ch-17) on both sides of sc at center of scallops. **13th and 14th rnds:** Same as 27th and 28th rnds

of Centerpiece, having ch-2 and ch-3 respectively between shells; between scallops make ch 9 for 13th rnd and ch 7 for 14th rnd. **15th rnd:** Same as 38th rnd of Centerpiece, having ch-5 between shells and ch-5 on both sides of sc between scallops. Break off.

Note: Shells throughout are dc, ch 3 and dc.

GLASS DOILY (Make 4) . . . Ch 8. Join. **1st rnd:** Ch 3, 19 dc in ring. Join. **2nd to 6th rnds incl:** Repeat 3rd to 7th rnds incl of Bread and Butter Plate Doily having 3 additional ch's (instead of 2) between spokes on each successive rnd (5 spokes). **7th rnd:** Same as 25th rnd of Centerpiece, having 21 (instead of 43) ch's. **8th rnd:** Same as 26th rnd of Centerpiece, making ch 7 (instead of ch 17). **9th, 10th, and 11th rnds:** Repeat the last 3 rnds of Bread and Butter Plate Doily. Break off.

7712 . . . Materials: THREE CORD MERCERIZED CROCHET, *Size 50: 6 balls . . . Steel Crochet Hook No. 12.*

Place mat measures about 11 x 16½ inches; runner measures about 11 x 22 inches.

PLACE MAT (Make 4)—Motif . . . Ch 8. Join with sl st. **1st rnd:** Ch 6 to count as tr and ch 1, (tr in ring, ch 1) 15 times, sl st in 5th st of starting ch-6 (16 sps). **2nd rnd:** Ch 1, sc in same place as sl st, * 2 sc in next sp, sc in next tr. Repeat from * around, sl st in 1st sc (48 sc). **3rd rnd:** Ch 3 (to count as 1 dc), dc in next sc, * ch 2, skip next sc, dc in next 2 sc. Repeat from * around, joining last ch-2 with sl st in 3rd st of starting ch-3. **4th rnd:** Sl st between the ch-3 and dc, ch 6, dc in same place as last sl st, * skip next sp, between next 2 dc make dc, ch 3 and dc. Repeat from * around. Join. **5th rnd:** Ch 1, sc in same place as last sl st, * 3 sc in next ch-3 sp, sc between next 2 dc. Repeat from * around. Join (64 sc). **6th rnd:** Ch 7, skip 3 sc, sc in next sc, ch 4, skip 3 sc, sc in next sc, * ch 4, skip 3 sc, in next sc make dc, ch 4 and d tr; skip 3 sc, in next sc make d tr, ch 4 and dc, (ch 4, skip 3 sc, sc in next sc) twice. Repeat from * around, ending with d tr in base of starting ch-7, ch 4, sl st in 3rd st of starting ch-7. **7th rnd:** Ch 5, sc in next sp, ch 2, dc in next sc, * ch 4, dc in next sc (bar made), ch 2, sc in next sp, ch 2, dc in next dc (lacet

7712

made), 6 dc in next sp, skip next d tr, in next d tr make 3 dc, ch 5 and 3 dc, 6 dc in next sp, dc in next dc, ch 2, sc in next sp, ch 2, dc in next sc (another lacet made). Repeat from * around, ending with 6 dc in last sp, join with sl st in 3rd st of starting ch-5. **8th rnd:** Ch 7, dc in next dc, * ch 2, sc in next sp, ch 2, dc in next dc (lacet made over bar), ch 4, dc in 10 dc, in corner ch-5 sp make 2 dc, ch 5 and 2 dc; dc in next 10 dc, ch 4, dc in next dc (bar made over lacet). Repeat from * around, ending with dc in last 9 dc. Join.

9th rnd: Ch 5, sc in next sp, ch 2, dc in next dc (lacet), * make a bar over next lacet and a lacet over next bar, dc in each dc to next corner, in corner ch-5 sp make 2 dc, ch 5 and 2 dc; dc in each dc of next dc group, make a lacet over next bar. Repeat from * around. Join. **10th rnd:** Ch 7, dc in next dc (bar), * make 1 lacet and 1 bar, ch 2; skip next dc, sc in next dc, ch 2, skip next dc, dc in next dc (lacet made), ch 4, skip 4 dc, dc in next dc (bar made); make 1 lacet, in corner ch-5 sp make 3 dc, ch 5 and 3 dc; make (1 lacet, 1 bar) twice. Repeat from * around. Join. **11th rnd:** Make (1 lacet, 1 bar) 3 times; * dc in 3 dc, in corner sp make 3 dc, ch 5 and 3 dc; dc in 4 dc, (1 bar, 1 lacet) 4 times; 1 bar. Repeat from * around. Join. **12th rnd:** Make (1 bar, 1 lacet) 3 times; * dc in each dc to corner sp, in corner sp make 3 dc, ch 5 and 3 dc; dc in each dc of next dc group, (1 lacet, 1 bar) 4 times; 1 bar. Repeat from * around. Join. **13th rnd:** * Make (1 lacet, 1 bar) 4 times; turn corner as before, (1 bar, 1 lacet) twice; 1 bar. Repeat from * around. Join. **14th and 15th rnds:** Make bar over lacet and lacet over bar, work corner same as on 11th and 12th rnds. **16th rnd:** * Make (1 bar, 1 lacet) 5 times; turn corner as before, (1 lacet, 1 bar) 3 times; 1 lacet. Repeat from * around. Join. **17th rnd:** Make lacet over bar and bar over lacet, work corners same as on 11th rnd. **18th rnd:** Ch 7, dc in next dc, (ch 4, dc in next dc) 9 times; * turn corner as on 12th rnd, (ch 4, dc in next dc) 17 times. Repeat from * around. Join and break off. Make 5 more motifs. Sew 2 x 3 motifs together with neat over-and-over stitches.

EDGING . . . **1st rnd:** Attach thread in a corner sp, ch 1, 5 sc in sp, sc in each dc, (3 sc in next sp, sc in next dc) 17 times; sc in each dc, 2 sc in corner sp, sc in joining of motifs, 2 sc

in next corner sp. Continue thus around. Join. **2nd rnd:** Sl st in next 2 sc, ch 6, in same place as sl st make (dc, ch 3) twice and dc; * skip 3 sc, in next sc make dc, ch 3 and dc. Repeat from * across to next corner of mat, in corner sc make (dc, ch 3) 3 times and dc. Continue thus around. Join. **3rd rnd:** Ch 6, dc in same place as sl st, (dc, ch 3 and dc in next dc) twice; * skip ch 3 and 1 dc, in next dc make dc, ch 3 and dc. Repeat from * across to next corner. Work corner as before. Continue thus around. Join. **4th rnd:** Ch 1, sc in same place as sl st, 4 sc in each sp around. Join.

RUNNER . . . Make 8 motifs. Sew 2 x 4 motifs together. Finish with Edging same as Edging on Place Mats.

7713 . . . Materials: Knit-Cro-Sheen, *3 balls of White* . . . *Steel Crochet Hook No. 6 or 7.*

Place mat measures about 13 x 18 inches; runner about 14 x 28 inches.

PLACE MAT (Make 2) . . . Ch 156 to measure 16¼ inches. **1st row:** Sc in 2nd ch from hook, (ch 19, skip 10 ch, sc in next ch) 14 times. Ch 1, turn. **2nd row:** Sl st in 1st sc, (sc in each of 19 ch, sl st in next sc) 14 times. Ch 25, turn. **3rd row:** * Skip 9 sc of next 19-sc loop, sc in next sc, ch 19. Repeat from * across, ending with ch 25, sl st in sc at end of previous sc row; turn. Sl st in each of 15 ch of ch-25. **4th row:** Sc in next 10 ch, (sl st in next sc, sc in next 19 ch) 13 times; sl st in next sc, sc in next 10 ch. Ch 1, turn. **5th row:** Sl st in 1st sc, (ch 19, sc in center sc of next loop) 13 times; ch 19, sc in last sc. Ch 1, turn. Repeat the 2nd to 5th rows incl until 12 rows of sc loops are made (24 rows in all). Ch 10 to turn at end of 24th row. **25th row:** * Skip 9 sc of next 19-sc loop, sc in next sc, ch 10. Repeat from * across, ending with ch 10, sc in last loop.

BORDER . . . **1st rnd:** 3 sc in corner sc, sc in each ch and in each sc around, making 3 sc at each corner.

Pick up only the back loop of each sc throughout.

2nd to 6th rnds incl: Sc in each sc around, making 3 sc in center sc of each corner. Break off.

7713

RUNNER . . . Ch 112 to measure 11¾ inches and work in pattern as for Place Mat, having 10-sc loops on the row instead of 14-sc loops, and working until 28 rows are completed (14 rows of sc loops). Work Border as for Border of Place Mat, making 10 rnds instead of 6 rnds.

744

CHAPTER TEN

Tablecloths

THE DINNER HOUR is one of the most pleasant interludes of the day. Work done, problems temporarily forgotten, the family gathered in a circle . . . it's an hour for sociability and relaxation, for hearing the day's news and telling it . . . for sharing fun and making plans.

It deserves the most attractive setting you can give it. There's no excuse for a nondescript looking table—inexpensive dishes come in so many pretty colorful patterns. Make a habit of arranging the table as attractively as possible, bright silver at each setting, a pretty cloth, a gay centerpiece—a bowl of fruit, an amusing pair of pottery figures . . . bright decorations lend a festive note to the dinner table.

Naturally, when you have guests for dinner you want your table to look its best . . . your best crystal, sparkling silver, flowers . . . and one of your loveliest, laciest, dressed-for-dinner cloths . . . take your choice of the eight beauties in this chapter, making a handsome background for a table that looks "just like a picture."

744 . . . Materials: Best Six Cord Mercer-ized Crochet, *Size 20: 36 balls . . . Steel Crochet Hook No. 8 or 9.*

Motif measures about 4¼ inches in diameter. Tablecloth measures about 68 x 85 inches.

FIRST MOTIF . . . Ch 10. Join with sl st. **1st rnd:** Ch 3, 23 dc in ring. Join with sl st to top of ch-3 first made. **2nd rnd:** Ch 10, and complete a cross st as follows: Thread over twice, insert hook in 8th ch from hook, pull loop through—4 loops on hook—thread over once, skip 1 dc and insert hook in next dc, pull loop through—6 loops on hook—(thread over and draw through 2 loops) 5 times. * Ch 3, thread over 4 times, insert hook in next dc and pull loop through—6 loops on hook—(thread over and draw through 2 loops) twice; then thread over, skip 1 dc, insert hook in next dc, pull loop through—6 loops on hook—(thread over and draw through 2 loops) 5 times; ch 3, dc in center point of the cross, thus completing the cross. (See Figs. 59, 60 and 61.) Repeat from * around (8 cross sts). Join last ch-3 with sl st in 7th st of ch-10 first made. **3rd rnd:** 5 sc in each sp. **4th to 7th rnds incl:** Sc in each sc of previous rnd. **8th rnd:** Ch 4, dc in next sc, * ch 1, dc in next sc. Repeat from * around. Join last ch-1 with sl st in 3rd st of ch-4 first made. **9th rnd:** Sl st in next sp, ch 10, and complete cross st as before, skipping 2 dc between each leg of cross st and inserting hook in ch-1 sp. Make ch 3 and skip 2 dc between cross sts (20 cross sts). Join last ch-3 with sl st to 7th st of ch-10 first made. **10th rnd:** Sl st in 2 ch of 1st sp, ch 5, * dc in same sp, ch 3, sc in next sp, ch 3, dc in next sp, ch 2. Repeat from * around. Join. **11th rnd:** Sl st in next sp, ch 6, dc in same sp, * ch 4, sc in next sc, ch 4, dc in next ch-2 sp, ch 3, dc in same sp. Repeat from * around. Join and break off.

SECOND MOTIF . . . Work same as First Motif until 10th rnd is complete. **11th rnd:** Sl st in next sp, ch 6, dc in same sp, * ch 4, sc in next sc, ch 4, dc in next ch-2 sp, ch 1, sc in corresponding sp on First Motif, ch 1, dc in same sp on Second Motif. Repeat from * twice; complete rnd same as First Motif (no more joinings). Break off.

Make 16 x 20 motifs, joining 3 points of one motif to corresponding 3 points of the adjacent motif as Second Motif was joined to First Mo-tif and leaving 2 points free between joinings on each motif.

FILL-IN-LACE . . . Ch 4, join with sl st. ** Ch 15, sc in joining of two motifs, ch 15, sc in center ring, * ch 9, sc in point of next scallop, ch 9, sc in center ring. Repeat from * once more. Then repeat from ** 3 more times. Break off. Fill in all sps between motifs in this way.

7050 . . . Materials: Three Cord Mercer-ized Crochet, *Size 20: 24 balls . . . Steel Crochet Hook No. 8 or 9.*

Motif measures about 4¾ inches in diameter. Tablecloth measures about 62 x 80 inches.

FIRST MOTIF . . . Ch 6. Join with sl st. **1st rnd:** Ch 6, * tr in ring, ch 2. Repeat from * 6 more times, join to 4th st of ch-6 (8 sps). **2nd rnd:** Sl st in next sp, ch 4, 4 tr in same sp, * ch 2, 5 tr in next sp. Repeat from * around. Join last ch-2 to 4th st of ch-4. **3rd rnd:** Ch 4, tr in same place as sl st, tr in next 4 tr, * tr in 1st ch of ch-2, ch 3, tr in next ch of same ch-2, tr in next 5 tr. Repeat from * around. Join. Sl st in 1st tr of group. **4th rnd:** Ch 4, holding back on hook the last loop of each tr, make tr in next 4 tr, thread over and draw through all loops on hook (a cluster made); * ch 4, 5 tr in next ch-3 sp, ch 4, skip 1st tr of next group; holding back on hook the last loop of each tr, make tr in next 5 tr, thread over and draw through all loops on hook (cluster). Repeat from * around. Join last ch-4 to tip of 1st cluster. **5th rnd:** Ch 8, * skip first 3 ch of ch-4, tr in next ch, tr in next 5 tr, tr in 1st ch of next ch-4, ch 4, tr in tip of cluster, ch 4. Repeat from * around. Join to 4th st of ch-8. **6th rnd:** Ch 1, sc in same place as sl st, * ch 12, skip 1st tr of next group, make a cluster over next 5 tr, ch 12, sc in the single tr between groups. Repeat from * around. Join last ch-12 to 1st sc (16 loops). Break off.

SECOND MOTIF . . . Work first 5 rnds as for First Motif. **6th rnd:** Ch 12, skip 1st tr of next group; make a cluster over next 5 tr, ch 6, sl st in first ch-12 loop on First Motif, ch 6, sc in next single tr on Second Motif, ch 6, sl st in next ch-12 loop on First Motif, ch 6, make a cluster on Second Motif. Complete rnd same as First Motif (no more joinings).

Make 13 x 17 motifs, joining 2 ch-loops of

7050

each motif to corresponding loops of adjacent motifs as Second Motif was joined to First Motif, leaving 2 loops free between joinings.

FILL-IN-MOTIF . . . **1st rnd:** Ch 8, tr in 8th ch from hook, make (tr, ch 4) 3 times, join to 4th ch of ch-8 (4 sps). **2nd rnd:** Sl st in 1st sp, ch 4, 6 tr in same sp, * ch 5, 7 tr in next sp. Repeat from * around, ch 5, join to 4th st of ch-4; sl st in 1st tr. **3rd rnd:** Ch 4, make a cluster over next 4 tr, ch 5, join to first ch-12 loop of a large motif, * ch 5, sc in next ch-5 loop on Fill-in motif, ch 5, join to second ch-12 loop of same large motif, ch 5, work a 5-tr cluster on Fill-in motif, ch 5, join to first loop of next large motif. Repeat from * around. Break off. Fill in all sps between motifs in same way.

EDGING . . . Attach thread to joining between any 2 large motifs, * 7 sc in 1st loop of next motif; in each remaining loop of same motif make sc, half dc, 5 dc, 4 tr, 5 dc, half dc, sc; 7 sc in last loop. Repeat from * around. Break off.

7471 . . . Materials: BEST SIX CORD MER-CERIZED CROCHET, *Size 30: 33 balls . . . Steel Crochet Hook No. 10 or 11.*

Motif measures about 2½ inches in diameter. Tablecloth measures about 62 x 72 inches.

FIRST MOTIF . . . Ch 12. Join with sl st. **1st rnd:** Ch 7 (to count as dc and ch-4), dc in ring, (ch 4, dc in ring) 6 times; ch 4, join with sl st to 3rd st of ch-7 (8 sps). **2nd rnd:** Ch 3 (to count as dc), * 5 dc in next sp, dc in next dc. Repeat from * around (48 dc). Join with sl st to top of ch-3. **3rd rnd:** Ch 3, dc in next 7 dc, ch 5, * dc in next 8 dc, ch 5. Repeat from * around. Join (6 groups of dc with ch-5 between groups). **4th rnd:** Sl st in next dc, ch 3, dc in next 5 dc, * ch 5, sc in loop, ch 5, skip 1 dc, dc in next 6 dc. Repeat from * around, ending with ch 5, sc in loop, ch 5. Join. **5th rnd:** Sl st in next dc, ch 3, dc in next 3 dc, * (ch 5, sc in next loop) twice; ch 5, skip 1 dc, dc in next 4 dc. Repeat from * around. Join.

6th rnd: Sl st in next dc, ch 3, dc in next dc, * (ch 5, sc in next loop) 3 times; ch 5, skip 1 dc, dc in next 2 dc. Repeat from * around. Join. **7th rnd:** Sl st between ch-3 and dc, ch 8, * (sc in next loop, ch 5) 4 times; dc between next 2 dc, ch 5. Repeat from * around. Join last ch-5 to 3rd st of ch-8. Break off.

SECOND MOTIF . . . Work as for First Motif until 6th rnd is complete. **7th rnd:** Sl st between ch-3 and dc, ch 8, (sc in next loop, ch 5) 4 times; dc between next 2 dc, (ch 2, sc in corresponding loop on First Motif, ch 2, sc in next loop on Second Motif) 4 times; ch 2, sc in next loop on First Motif, ch 2, dc between next 2 dc on Second Motif. Complete rnd as for First Motif (no more joinings). Break off.

Make 712 motifs and join them as in diagram for joining hexagon motifs—see chapter on General Information—having 25 motifs from A to B, and 29 motifs from A to C.

BORDER . . . **1st rnd:** With right side facing, attach thread to any loop. Ch 3, 3 dc in same loop, then work 4 dc in each loop around. Join. **2nd rnd:** Ch 3, make dc in each dc around, increasing 1 dc at each of the outside points of each motif—*to inc, make 2 dc in 1 dc*—and decreasing 2 dc at joinings of motifs—*to dec, skip 2 dc.* Join. **3rd and 4th rnds:** Repeat 2nd rnd, making increases directly over increases and decreases over decreases of previous rnd. Break off.

7471

141

7144 . . . Materials: THREE CORD MERCER-
IZED CROCHET, *Size 20: 48 balls* . . . *Steel
Crochet Hook No. 8 or 9.*

Motif measures about 4½ inches in diameter.
Tablecloth measures about 72 x 90 inches.

FIRST MOTIF . . . Ch 8, join with sl st. **1st
rnd:** Ch 5, * dc in ring, ch 2. Repeat from *
6 more times. Join last ch-2 with sl st to 3rd st
of ch-5 first made (8 sps). **2nd rnd:** Sl st in sp,
ch 3, 2 dc in same sp, ch 2, * 3 dc in next sp,
ch 2. Repeat from * around. Join with sl st to
top of ch-3 first made. **3rd rnd:** Ch 3, dc in
same place as sl st, * dc in next dc, 2 dc in
next dc, ch 2, 2 dc in next dc. Repeat from *
around, ending with ch 2. Join. **4th rnd:** Ch 3,
dc in same place as sl st, * dc in 3 dc, 2 dc in
next dc, ch 2, 2 dc in next dc. Repeat from *
around. Join. **5th rnd:** Ch 3, dc in same place
as sl st, * dc in 5 dc, 2 dc in next dc, ch 3, 2 dc
in next dc. Repeat from * around. Join. **6th
rnd:** Sl st in next dc, ch 3, * dc in 6 dc, ch 3,
sc in sp, ch 3, skip 1 dc, dc in next dc. Repeat
from * around. Join. **7th rnd:** Sl st in next dc,
ch 3, * dc in 4 dc, ch 4, sc in sp, sc in next sc,
sc in next sp, ch 4, skip 1 dc, dc in next dc.
Repeat from * around. Join. **8th rnd:** Sl st
in next dc, ch 3, * dc in 2 dc, ch 5, sc in
sp, sc in 3 sc, sc in next sp, ch 5, skip 1 dc,
dc in next dc. Repeat from * around. Join. **9th
rnd:** Sl st in next dc, ch 3, holding back on
hook the last loop of each dc make 2 dc in
same place as sl st; thread over and draw
through all loops on hook, ch 1 to fasten (a
3-dc cluster made—counting ch-3 as 1 dc);
* ch 6, sc in loop, sc in 5 sc, sc in next loop,
ch 6, skip 1 dc, 3-dc cluster in next dc. Repeat
from * around, ending with ch 6, sl st in tip of
1st cluster made. **10th rnd:** Ch 1, sc in same
place as sl st, ** ch 5, skip 3 sc, tr in next sc,
* ch 2, tr in same sc. Repeat from * 2 more
times; ch 5, sc in tip of next cluster. Repeat
from ** around, ending with ch 5. Join. **11th
rnd:** Ch 6, dc in same place as sl st, * ch 3,
4 sc in next loop, sc in ch-2 sp, ch 3; in next
ch-2 sp make dc, ch 3 and dc; ch 3, sc in next
ch-2 sp, 4 sc in next loop, ch 3; in next sc make
dc, ch 3 and dc. Repeat from * around, ending
with ch 3. Join with sl st in 3rd st of ch-6 first

made. **12th rnd:** Sl st in next sp, ch 6, dc in
same sp, * ch 3, sc in next sp, ch 2, skip 2 sc,
sc in next sc, ch 2, sc in next sp, ch 3; in next
sp make dc, ch 3 and dc. Repeat from *
around, ending with ch 3, sl st in 3rd st of ch-6
first made. Break off.

SECOND MOTIF . . . Work same as First
Motif until 11th rnd is complete. **12th rnd:**
Sl st in next sp, ch 6, dc in same sp, * ch 3, sc
in next sp, ch 2, skip 2 sc, sc in next sc, ch 2,
sc in next sp, ch 3, dc in next sp, ch 1, sc in
corresponding sp on First Motif, ch 1, dc in
same sp on Second Motif. Repeat from * once
more; ch 3, sc in next sp. Complete rnd same
as for First Motif (no more joinings). Break
off.

Make 16 x 20 motifs, joining 2 points of each
motif to 2 points of adjacent motifs as Second
Motif was joined to First Motif, leaving 2
points free on each motif between joinings.

FILL-IN-LACE . . . Ch 8, join with sl st. **1st
rnd:** Ch 5, * dc in ring, ch 2. Repeat from *
6 more times. Join with sl st to 3rd st of ch-5
first made (8 sps). **2nd rnd:** Ch 1, sc in same
place as sl st, * ch 18, sc in joining of 2 motifs,
ch 18, sc in same place where 1st sc was made,
sc in next sp, ch 9, sc in next point on motif,
ch 9, sc in same sp on ring where last sc was
made, sc in next sp, ch 9, sc in next point, ch 9,
sc in same sp on ring where last sc was made,
sc in next dc. Repeat from * around. Join with
sl st. Break off. Fill in all sps between motifs
in this way.

142

7144

7015 . . . Materials: BEST SIX CORD MER-CERIZED CROCHET, *Size 30: 30 balls* . . . *Steel Crochet Hook No. 10.*

Motif measures about 4 inches square. Table-cloth measures about 64 x 80 inches.

FIRST MOTIF . . . Ch 6. Join with sl st to form ring. **1st rnd:** * Ch 7, sc in ring. Repeat from * 3 more times. **2nd rnd:** * Ch 6, 3 sc in next loop. Repeat from * 3 more times. **3rd rnd:** Hereafter work in the back loop only of each sc throughout. * Ch 6, 3 sc in next ch-6 loop, sc in next 2 sc. Repeat from * 3 more times. **4th to 8th rnds incl:** * Ch 6, 3 sc in next loop, sc in each sc to last sc of this group (do not work in last sc). Repeat from * 3 more times. There are 15 sc in each group at end of 8th rnd. **9th rnd:** * Ch 6, sc in next loop, ch 6, skip 1st sc of group, sc in next 13 sc. Repeat from * around. **10th rnd:** * (Ch 6, sc in next loop) twice; ch 6, skip 1st sc of group, sc in 11 sc. Repeat from * around. **11th rnd:** * Ch 6, sc in next loop, ch 6, 4 dc in next loop, ch 6, sc in next loop, ch 6, skip next sc, sc in 9 sc. Repeat from * around. **12th rnd:** * Ch 6, sc in next loop, ch 6, 3 sc in next loop, ch 3, skip 4 dc, 3 sc in next loop, ch 6, sc in next loop, ch 6, skip next sc, sc in 7 sc. Repeat from * around. **13th rnd:** * Ch 6, sc in next loop, ch 6, 3 sc in next loop, ch 10, skip the 3 sc, ch-3 and

3 sc, then make 3 sc in next loop, ch 6, sc in next loop, ch 6, skip next sc, sc in 5 sc. Repeat from * around. **14th rnd:** * Ch 6, sc in next loop, ch 6, 3 sc in next loop, ch 6, 4 dc in ch-10 loop, ch 6, 3 sc in next loop, ch 6, sc in next loop, ch 6, skip next sc, sc in 3 sc. Repeat from * around. **15th rnd:** Ch 6, sc in next loop, * ch 6, 3 sc in next loop, ch 6, 4 dc in next loop, ch 14, 4 dc in next loop, ch 6, 3 sc in next loop, ch 6, sc in next loop, ch 3, sc in next loop. Repeat from * around. **16th rnd:** Ch 5, sc in next loop, * ch 10, sc in next loop, (ch 10, skip 4 ch of corner loop, sc in next ch) twice; (ch 10, sc in next loop) twice; ch 10, skip ch-3, sc in next loop. Repeat from * around. Join last ch-10 with sl st to 1st sc. Break off.

SECOND MOTIF . . . Work as for First Motif until 15th rnd is completed. **16th rnd:** Ch 5, sc in next loop, ch 10, sc in next loop, ch 10, sc in 5th ch of corner loop, ch 5, sc in corner loop of First Motif, ch 5, skip 4 ch of corner loop on Second Motif, sc in next ch, (ch 5, sc in corresponding loop of First Motif, ch 5, sc in next loop on Second Motif) 6 times; join corners as before. Complete rnd same as First Motif (no more joinings). Break off.

Make 16 x 20 motifs, joining adjacent sides as Second Motif was joined to First Motif (where 4 corners meet, join the last 2 corners to joining of 2 previous corners).

EDGING . . . **1st rnd:** With right side facing, attach thread to the center st of any corner loop, ch 7, dc in same place, ch 5, * sc in next sc, ch 8, in next sc make dc, ch 6 and dc; ch 8. Skipping all joinings of motifs, repeat from * across this side of piece to last motif. Now work into joining of last 2 motifs, treating joining as an sc, and continue to corner loop of piece, ch 5, in center st of corner loop make dc, ch 4 and dc; ch 5, sc in next sc. Ch 8, and continue thus around, ending with ch 5, sl st in 3rd st of ch-7 first made. **2nd rnd:** Ch 7, in loop make 4 dc, ch 3 and dc; ch 6, * 2 sc in next sc, ch 8, in next loop make dc, ch 3, 4 dc, ch 3 and dc, ch 8. Repeat from * all around, ending with ch 6, sl st in 3rd st of ch-7 first made. **3rd rnd:** Sl st in loop, ch 3, 3 dc in same loop, * ch 5, skip 4-dc group, 4 dc in next loop, ch 9, sc in next sc, ch 9, 4 dc in loop preceding next 4-dc group. Repeat from * around, ending with ch 9, sl st in 3rd st of ch-3 first made. Break off.

7015

7463 . . . **Materials:** Best Six Cord Mercerized Crochet, *Size 20: 30 balls* . . . *Steel Crochet Hook No. 8 or 9.*

Motif measures about 4½ inches in diameter. Tablecloth measures about 60 x 80 inches.

FIRST MOTIF . . . Ch 10, join with sl st. **1st rnd:** Ch 1, 16 sc in ring. Join with sl st in 1st sc made. **2nd rnd:** Ch 1, sc in same place as sl st, * ch 7, 2 dc in same place as last sc, skip 1 sc, sc in next sc. Repeat from * around, ending with 2 dc, skip 1 sc. Join. **3rd rnd:** Sl st in next 4 ch, sc in loop, * ch 7, sc in next loop. Repeat from * around. Join. **4th rnd:** Ch 1, make 9 sc in each ch-7 sp around. Join. **5th rnd:** Ch 1, sc in same place as sl st, sc in each sc around. Join. **6th rnd:** Ch 1, sc in same place as sl st, * ch 5, 2 dc in same place as last sc, skip 3 sc, sc in next sc. Repeat from * around. Join. **7th rnd:** Sl st in next 2 ch, ch 1, sc in loop, * ch 7, sc in next loop. Repeat from * around. Join. **8th rnd:** Sl st in next 3 ch, ch 1, sc in loop, * ch 5, 3 dc in same loop, sc in next loop, ch 8, sc in next loop. Repeat from * around. Join. **9th rnd:** Sl st in next 3 ch, ch 1, sc in loop, * ch 8, sc in next loop. Repeat from * around. Join. **10th rnd:** Ch 1, 8 sc in each loop around. Join. **11th rnd:** Ch 1, sc in same place as sl st, sc in each sc around. Join. **12th rnd:** Ch 1, sc in same place as sl st, * ch 5, 2 dc in same place as last sc, skip 3 sc, sc in next sc. Repeat from * around. Join. **13th rnd:** Sl st in first 2 ch, ch 1, sc in loop, * ch 7, sc in next loop. Repeat from * around. Join. **14th rnd:** Sl st in next 3 ch, ch 1, sc in loop, * ch 7, 3 dc in same loop, sc in next loop. Repeat from * around. Join and break off.

SECOND MOTIF . . . Work as for First Motif until 13th rnd is complete. **14th rnd:** Sl st in next 2 ch, ch 1, sc in loop, * ch 3, sc in corresponding loop on First Motif; ch 3, 3 dc in same loop on Second Motif where last sc was made, sc in next loop. Repeat from * 4 more times (5 loops joined). Complete rnd as for First Motif (no more joinings).

Make 13 x 17 motifs, joining them as Second Motif was joined to First Motif, having 4 free loops between joinings.

FILL-IN-MOTIF . . . **1st rnd:** Attach thread to a free loop immediately preceding a joining, ch 7 (to count as tr and ch-3), * d tr in joining, (ch 3, tr in next free loop) 4 times; ch 3. Repeat from * around, ending with ch-3, sl st in 4th st of ch-7 first made. **2nd rnd:** Sl st in next sp, ch 5 (to count as d tr), holding back on hook the last loop of each d tr make 2 d tr in same sp, thread over and draw through all loops on hook (cluster made), holding back on hook the last loop of each d tr make 3 d tr in next sp, thread over and draw through all loops on hook (another cluster made), * ch 5, skip 3 sps, cluster in each of next 2 sps. Repeat from * around, ending with sl st in tip of 1st cluster made. Break off. Fill in all sps between motifs in this manner.

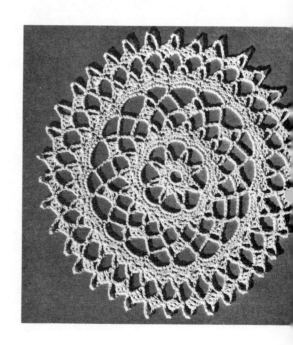

7463

7644 . . . Materials: THREE CORD MERCER-IZED CROCHET, *Size 20: 24 balls . . . Steel Crochet Hook No. 8 or 9.*

Motif measures 4½ inches in diameter. Table-cloth measures about 63 x 82 inches.

FIRST MOTIF . . . Ch 8. Join with sl st. **1st rnd:** Ch 3 (to count as 1 dc), 23 dc in ring. Join with sl st in top st of ch-3. **2nd rnd:** Ch 3, dc in next 3 dc, * ch 4, dc in next 4 dc. Repeat from * around, joining last ch-4 with sl st in top st of ch-3. **3rd rnd:** Ch 3, dc in same place as sl st, * dc in next 2 dc, 2 dc in next dc, ch 5, 2 dc in next dc. Repeat from * around. Join. **4th rnd:** Ch 3, dc in same place as sl st, * dc in next 2 dc, ch 3, dc in next 2 dc, 2 dc in next dc, ch 6, 2 dc in next dc. Repeat from * around. Join. **5th rnd:** Ch 3, dc in same place as sl st, * dc in next 2 dc, ch 5, skip 2 dc, dc in next 2 dc, 2 dc in next dc, ch 7, 2 dc in next dc. Repeat from * around. Join. **6th rnd:** Sl st in next dc, ch 3, dc in next 2 dc, * ch 3, dc in next 3 dc, ch 5, 4 dc in next loop, ch 5, skip next dc, dc in next 3 dc. Repeat from * around. Join. **7th rnd:** Sl st in next dc, ch 3, dc in next dc, * 2 dc in next sp, dc in next 2 dc, ch 6, skip next dc, 2 dc in next dc, dc in next 2 dc, 2 dc in next dc, ch 6, skip next dc, dc in next 2 dc. Repeat from * around. Join. **8th rnd:** Sl st in

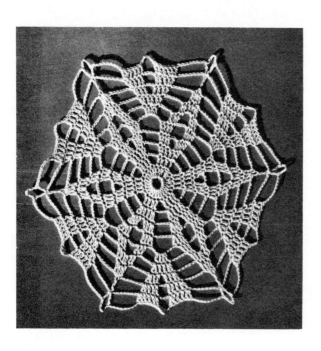

next dc, ch 3, dc in next 3 dc, * ch 7, skip next dc, 2 dc in next dc, dc in next 2 dc, ch 3, dc in next 2 dc, 2 dc in next dc, ch 7, skip next dc, dc in next 4 dc. Repeat from * around. Join. **9th rnd:** Sl st in next 2 dc, ch 11, * skip next dc, 2 dc in next dc, dc in next 3 dc, ch 4, dc in next 3 dc, 2 dc in next dc, ch 8, skip 2 dc, dc in next dc, ch 8. Repeat from * around. Join last ch-8 with sl st in 3rd st of ch-11. **10th rnd:** Ch 8, dc in same place as sl st, * ch 9, 2 dc in next dc, dc in next 4 dc, ch 5, dc in next 4 dc, 2 dc in next dc, ch 9; in next dc make dc, ch 5 and dc. Repeat from * around. Join and break off.

SECOND MOTIF . . . Work as for First Motif until 9th rnd is complete. **10th rnd:** Ch 8, dc in same place as sl st, ch 5, sc in 5th st of corresponding ch-9 on First Motif, ch 3, 2 dc in next dc on Second Motif, dc in next 4 dc, ch 2, sc in center ch of next ch-5 on First Motif, ch 2, dc in next 4 dc on Second Motif, 2 dc in next dc, ch 3, sc in 3rd st of corresponding ch-9 on First Motif, ch 5, in next dc on Second Motif make dc, ch 5 and dc and complete rnd as for First Motif (no more joinings).

Make 364 motifs and join them as in diagram for joining hexagon motifs—see chapter on General Information—having 27 motifs from A to B and 13 motifs from A to C.

EDGING . . . With right side facing, attach thread in first ch-5 sp (from joining) on end motif of narrow edge. **1st rnd:** Ch 6 (to count as tr and ch 2), in same sp make 5 tr with ch 2 between (6-tr shell made), * (sc in next loop, tr in next 6 dc, ch 2, make a 6-tr shell in next sp, ch 2, tr in next 6 dc, sc in next loop, make a 6-tr shell in next sp) 3 times, making last sc in joining of motifs, shell in next sp. Repeat from * across narrow end, then continue in this manner all around cloth. Join with sl st in 4th st of starting chain. **2nd rnd:** Sl st across to second ch-2 sp, ch 1, sc in same sp, ** (ch 5, sc in next sp) 3 times; * ch 5, skip 2 dc, sc in next dc, (ch 5, sc in next sp) 7 times; ch 5, skip 3 dc, sc in next dc, (ch 5, sc in next sp) 5 times. Repeat from * once more, ch 5, skip 2 dc, sc in next dc, (ch 5, sc in next sp) 7 times; ch 5, skip 3 dc, sc in next dc, (ch 5, sc in next sp) 4 times; sc in 2nd sp on next shell. Repeat from ** across narrow end, then continue in this manner all around cloth. Join and break off.

7644

7597

7597 . . . Materials: Best Six Cord Mercerized Crochet, *Size 30: 24 balls* . . . *Steel Crochet Hook No. 10 or 11.*

Motif measures about 3⅜ inches in diameter. Tablecloth measures about 54 x 74 inches.

FIRST MOTIF . . . Ch 7. Join with sl st. **1st rnd:** Ch 3 (to count as 1 dc), 23 dc in ring. Join with sl st in top of first ch-3. **2nd rnd:** (Ch 5, skip next dc, sc in next dc) 11 times; ch 2, skip next dc, dc in next dc. **3rd rnd:** (Ch 5, sc in next loop) 11 times; ch 2, dc in next dc. **4th rnd:** Repeat last rnd, only ending with ch 5, sl st in dc. **5th rnd:** Ch 1, work 7 sc in each loop around. Join with sl st in 1st sc. **6th rnd:** Sl st across to 4th sc of scallop, * ch 8, 5 dc in 3rd ch from hook, ch 2, sl st in same ch where dc's were made, ch 5, sc in 4th sc of next scallop. Repeat from * around, joining last ch-5 to base of 1st ch. Break off. **7th rnd:** Attach thread to center st of any dc group on last rnd, ch 1, sc in same place where thread was attached, * ch 11, sc in center st of next dc group. Repeat from * around. Join. **8th rnd:** Ch 1, work 15 sc in each loop around. Join. **9th rnd:** Skip 1st sc, * sc in next 6 sc, in next sc make sc, ch 3 and sc; sc in next 6 sc, skip 2 sc. Repeat from * around. Join. **10th rnd:** Skip 1st sc, * sc in next 6 sc, in ch-3 sp make sc, ch 3 and sc; sc in next 6 sc, skip 2 sc. Repeat from * around. Join and break off.

SECOND MOTIF . . . Work as for First Motif until 9th rnd is complete. **10th rnd:** Skip 1st sc, * sc in next 6 sc, ch 1, sc in corresponding sp on First Motif, ch 1, sc in next 6 sc on Second Motif, skip 2 sc. Repeat from * once more. Complete Second Motif same as First Motif (no more joinings). Break off.

Make 16 x 22 motifs, joining them as Second Motif was joined to First Motif, having one point free between joinings on each motif.

FILL-IN-LACE . . . Ch 5. Join with sl st. **1st rnd:** Ch 1, 16 sc in ring. Join. **2nd rnd:** (Ch 5, skip next sc, sc in next sc) 7 times; ch 2, skip next sc, dc in next sc. **3rd rnd:** (Ch 5, sc in next loop) 7 times; ch 2, dc in next loop. **4th rnd:** Ch 1, * 3 sc in next loop, ch 12, sl st in joining of two motifs, ch 12, 3 sc in same loop on Fill-in-lace, 3 sc in next loop, ch 5, sl st in ch-3 sp on next free point of motif, ch 5, 3 sc in same loop on Fill-in-Lace. Repeat from * around. Join and break off. Fill in all sps between motifs in this way.

6074

CHAPTER ELEVEN

Bedspreads

BEEN ANXIOUS to "do something" to the bedroom, give it a glamour treatment? Well, what are you waiting for? Why not start right away? Fortunately, there's no other room in the house that lends itself so readily—*and inexpensively*—to an attractive transformation.

One of the most dramatic ways to do this is to add the bedspread of your dreams, the one with that coveted hand-made look. Any one in the chapter that follows will be a treasure you'll cherish for years, with all the more pride and pleasure because you've made it yourself. . . . It's all in your own hands!

6074 . . . Materials: KNIT-CRO-SHEEN: *80 balls for Single Size; 98 balls for Double Size . . . Steel Crochet Hook No. 7 or 8.*

Motif measures about 5¾ inches from point to opposite point, and about 5 inches from side to opposite side before blocking. For single size spread, about 72 x 105 inches, make 348 motifs; for double size spread, about 90 x 105 inches, make 430 motifs.

MOTIF . . . Ch 10. Join with sl st. **1st rnd:** Ch 3 (to count as dc), 23 dc in ring. Join with sl st in top st of ch-3. **2nd rnd:** Ch 4 (to count as dc and ch 1), * dc in next dc, ch 1. Repeat from * around. Join with sl st to 3rd st of ch-4. **3rd rnd:** Sl st in next sp, ch 3 to count as dc, in same sp make 2 dc, ch 3 and 3 dc (shell made); * ch 2, skip 1 sp, dc in next sp, ch 2, skip 1 sp, in next sp make 3 dc, ch 3 and 3 dc (another shell made). Repeat from * around. Join. **4th rnd:** Sl st in next 2 sts, sl st in next sp, ch 3, complete a shell in same sp; * (ch 2, dc in next sp) twice; ch 2, shell in sp of next shell. Repeat from * around. Join. **5th rnd:** Sl st in next 2 sts, sl st in next sp, ch 3, shell in same sp; * ch 2, dc in next sp, ch 2, make a pc st in next sp—*to make a pc st, ch 1, 5 dc in next sp, drop loop from hook, insert hook in ch-1 preceding 1st dc of this group, and pull dropped loop through;* ch 2, dc in next sp, ch 2, shell in sp of next shell. Repeat from * around. Join.

6th rnd: Sl st in next 2 sts, sl st in next sp, ch 3, shell in same sp; * ch 2, dc in next sp, (ch 2, pc st in next sp) twice; ch 2, dc in next sp, ch 2, shell in sp of next shell. Repeat from * around. Join. **7th rnd:** Sl st in next dc, ch 3, pc st in top of next dc, in next sp make dc, ch 3 and dc; pc st in top of next dc, dc in next dc, * ch 2, dc in next sp, ch 2, (pc st in next sp, ch 2) 3 times; dc in next sp, ch 2, skip 1 dc, dc in next dc, pc st in top of next dc, in next sp make dc, ch 3 and dc; pc st in top of next dc, dc in next dc. Repeat from * around. Join. **8th rnd:** Ch 3, pc st in same place as sl st, dc in top of pc st, dc in next dc, in next sp make dc, ch 3 and dc; dc in next dc, dc in top of pc st, pc st in top of next dc, * (dc in next sp, ch 2) twice; (pc st in next sp, ch 2) twice; dc in next sp, ch 2, dc in next sp, pc st in top of next dc, dc in top of pc st, dc in next dc, in next sp make dc, ch 3 and dc; dc in next dc, dc in top

of next pc st, pc st in top of next dc. Repeat from * around, ending with dc in last sp. Join. **9th rnd:** Ch 3, dc in top of pc st, dc in next 3 dc, in next sp make dc, ch 3 and dc; dc in next 3 dc, dc in top of pc st, pc st in next dc, * (dc in next sp, ch 2) twice; pc st in next sp, (ch 2, dc in next sp) twice; pc st in next dc, dc in top of next pc st, dc in next 3 dc, in next sp make dc, ch 3 and dc; dc in next 3 dc, dc in top of pc st, pc st in next dc. Repeat from * around, ending with dc in last sp, pc st in last dc. Join and break off.

Make necessary number of motifs and sew together on wrong side with neat over-and-over sts, joining them as in diagram for joining hexagon motifs—see chapter on General Information. For single size spread make 17 motifs from A to B and 20 motifs from A to C; for double size spread make 21 motifs from A to B and 20 motifs from A to C.

6063 . . . Materials: BEST SIX CORD MERCERIZED CROCHET, *Size 20: 70 balls for Single Size; 86 balls for Double Size . . . Steel Crochet Hook No. 8 or 9.*

Motif measures 3¼ inches in diameter after blocking. For a single size spread 72 x 105 inches, make 22 x 32 motifs. For a double size spread about 88 x 105 inches, make 27 x 32 motifs.

MOTIF . . . Ch 10. Join with sl st. **1st rnd:** Ch 1, 18 sc in ring. Sl st in 1st sc made. **2nd rnd:** Ch 1, sc in same place as sl st, * ch 5, skip 2 sc, sc in next sc. Repeat from * 5 more times; ch 5, join with sl st in 1st sc. **3rd rnd:** Ch 1, in each loop around make sc, half dc, 5 dc, half dc and sc (6 petals). Join. **4th rnd:** Ch 1, sc in same place as sl st, * ch 7, insert hook in next loop from back to front of work, bring it out in next loop from front to back of work; thread over, draw loop through, thread over and draw through all loops on hook. Repeat from * around. Join (6 loops). **5th rnd:** in each loop around make sc, half dc, dc, 7 tr, dc, half dc and sc (6 petals). **6th rnd:** Repeat 4th rnd. **7th rnd:** Sl st in 1st loop, ch 3, 7 dc in same loop, 8 dc in each loop around (48 dc on rnd). Join with sl st in 3rd st of ch-3. **8th rnd:** Ch 3, dc in next 2 dc, * ch 2, dc in next 3 dc, ch 4, sc in 4th ch from hook (p made), dc in next 3 dc. Repeat from * around. Join. **9th**

6063

rnd: Ch 3, dc in next 2 dc, * ch 2, dc in next 3 dc, ch 1, p, ch 1, dc in next 3 dc. Repeat from * around. Join. **10th rnd:** Ch 3, dc in next 2 dc, * ch 2, dc in next 3 dc, ch 2, p, ch 2, dc in next 3 dc. Repeat from * around. Join. **11th rnd:** Ch 3, dc in next 2 dc, * ch 2, dc in next 3 dc, ch 11, dc in next 3 dc. Repeat from * around. Join. **12th rnd:** Ch 3, dc in next 2 dc, * ch 2, dc in next 3 dc, 11 dc in next sp, dc in next 3 dc. Repeat from * around. Join and break off.

Make necessary number of motifs and sew corresponding (9 dc, ch 2 and 9 dc) sides of adjacent motifs together with neat over-and-over sts on wrong side. There will be one group of 8 dc, ch 2 and 8 dc free between joinings.

FILL-IN-MOTIF . . . Ch 7, join with sl st. **1st rnd:** Ch 3, 15 dc in ring. Join with sl st to top st of ch-3. **2nd rnd:** Ch 7, * skip 1 dc, dc in next dc, ch 4. Repeat from * around, joining last ch-4 with sl st in 3rd st of ch-7 (8 sps). **3rd rnd:** Sl st in sp, ch 3, 7 dc in same sp, 8 dc in each following sp around. Join and break off.

Sew 8 dc of Fill-in-motif to center 3 dc, ch 2 and 3 dc of free group on large motif. Sew 3 adjacent groups in this manner, leaving 4 groups of 8 dc free on Fill-in-motif. Fill in all sps between motifs in same way.

6035 . . . Materials: Knit-Cro-Sheen: 74 balls for Single Size; 90 balls for Double Size . . . Steel Crochet Hook No. 7.

Each block measures about 5 inches square. For a single size spread 72 x 108 inches, including fringe, make 13 x 20 blocks. For a double size spread, 90 x 108 inches, including fringe, make 16 x 20 blocks.

BLOCK . . . Starting at center, ch 10. Join with sl st. **1st rnd:** Ch 3 (to count as dc), * make a pc st in ring—to make a pc st, ch 1, make 5 dc in ring, drop loop from hook, insert hook in ch-1 preceding 5 dc and draw dropped loop through—Fig. 66; make dc in ring. Repeat from * until 8 pc sts are complete. Join to top of ch-3. **2nd rnd:** Ch 3 (to count as 1 dc), holding back on hook the last loop of next 2 dc, make 2 dc in same place as sl st, thread over and draw through all loops on hook (a 3-dc clus-

ter made); ch 3, holding back on hook the last loop of next 3 dc, make 3 dc in same place as last cluster; thread over and draw through all loops on hook (another 3-dc cluster made). * Ch 2, skip next pc st, 3 dc in next dc, ch 2, skip next pc st, in next dc make a cluster, ch 3 and a cluster. Repeat from * around. Join last ch-2 to top of 1st cluster. **3rd rnd:** Sl st in next sp, ch 3 (to count as dc), in same sp make cluster, ch 3 and cluster, * ch 2, 2 dc in next sp, dc in next 3 dc, 2 dc in next sp, ch 2, in next sp (corner sp) make cluster, ch 3, and cluster. Repeat from * around. Join last ch-2 to top of 1st cluster. **4th rnd:** Sl st in next sp, ch 3 (to count as dc), in same sp make cluster, ch 3, and cluster. * Ch 2, 2 dc in next sp, dc in next 7 dc, 2 dc in next sp, ch 2, in corner sp make cluster, ch 3 and cluster. Repeat from * around. Join last ch-2 to 1st cluster.

5th rnd: Sl st in next sp, ch 3 (to count as dc), in same sp make cluster, ch 3 and cluster. * ch 2, 2 dc in next sp, dc in next 5 dc, pc st in next dc, dc in next 5 dc, 2 dc in next sp, ch 2; in corner sp make cluster, ch-3, and cluster. Repeat from * around. Join. **6th rnd:** Sl st in next sp, ch 3 (to count as dc), in same sp make cluster, ch 3 and cluster. * Ch 2, 2 dc in next sp, dc in next 5 dc, pc st in next dc, dc in next dc, dc back of next pc st and in following dc, pc st in next dc, dc in next 5 dc, 2 dc in next sp, ch 2; in corner sp make cluster, ch 3, and cluster. Repeat from * around. Join. **7th**

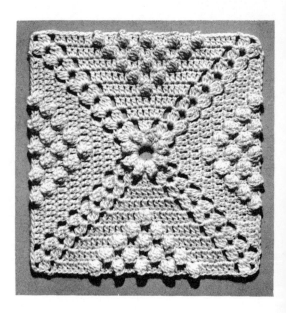

156

6035

rnd: Sl st in next sp, ch 3, in same sp make cluster, ch 3 and cluster. * Ch 2, 2 dc in next sp, dc in next 5 dc, pc st in next dc, (dc in next dc, dc in back of pc st and in following dc, pc st in next dc) twice; dc in next 5 dc,

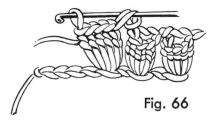

Fig. 66

2 dc in next sp, ch 2; in corner sp make cluster, ch 3 and cluster. Repeat from * around. Join. **8th rnd:** Sl st in next sp, ch 3, in same sp make cluster, ch 3 and cluster, * ch 2, 2 dc in next sp, dc in next 5 dc, pc st in next dc, (dc in next dc, dc in back of pc st, dc in next dc, pc st in next dc) 3 times; dc in next 5 dc, 2 dc in next sp; in corner sp make cluster, ch 3 and cluster. Repeat from * around. Join. **9th rnd:** Sl st in next sp, ch 3, in same sp make cluster, ch 3 and cluster; * ch 2, 2 dc in next sp, dc in next 5 dc, pc st in next dc, (dc in next dc, dc in back of pc st, dc in next dc, pc st in next

157

dc) 4 times; dc in next 5 dc, 2 dc in next sp, ch 2, in corner sp make cluster, ch 3 and cluster. Repeat from * around. Join and break off.

Make the necessary number of blocks and sew together neatly with over-and-over sts on wrong side.

FRINGE . . . Work a row of ch-2 sps (ch 2 and dc) along two long sides and one short side. Then make fringe in each sp along these 3 sides as follows: Cut 8 strands, each 12 inches long. Double these strands, forming a loop. Pull loop through a sp, then draw loose ends through loop. Pull tight. Trim fringe evenly to 4 inches. Block bedspread to measurements given.

6048 . . . Materials: KNIT-CRO-SHEEN: *80 balls for Single Size; 93 balls for Double Size . . . Steel Crochet Hook No. 7.*

Motif measures about 7 inches from side to side; 8 inches from point to point diagonally. For a single size spread, about 75 x 108 inches (including fringe), make 148 motifs. For a double size spread, about 90 x 108 inches (including fringe), make 175 motifs.

MOTIF . . . Ch 8. Join with sl st. **1st rnd:** Ch 3, 17 dc in ring. Sl st in top of ch-3. **2nd rnd:** Ch 3, 4 dc in same place as sl st, drop loop from hook, insert hook in top of ch-3 and draw dropped loop through (a starting pc st made), * ch 4, skip 2 dc, pc st in next dc— *to make a pc st, ch 1, make 5 dc in same place, drop loop from hook, insert hook in ch-1 preceding the 5 dc and draw dropped loop through.* Repeat from * around, ending with ch 4, join with sl st in top of 1st pc st made. **3rd rnd:** Ch 3 and complete a starting pc st in same place as sl st, * ch 3, dc in next sp, ch 3, pc st in top of next pc st. Repeat from * around, ending with ch 3. Join. **4th rnd:** Ch 3, and complete a starting pc st in same place as sl st, * (ch 2, dc in next sp) twice; ch 2, pc st in top of next pc st. Repeat from * around, ending with ch 2. Join. **5th rnd:** Ch 3, 7 dc in

same place as sl st (this is base of pineapple), * (ch 2, dc in next dc) twice; ch 2, 8 dc in top of next pc st. Repeat from * around, ending with ch 2. Join. **6th rnd:** Ch 4, (dc in next dc, ch 1) 6 times; dc in next 2 dc, * ch 2, dc in next 2 dc, (ch 1, dc in next dc) 7 times; dc in next dc. Repeat from * around. Join.

7th rnd: Sl st in sp, ch 3 and complete a starting pc st in same place, (ch 1, pc st in next sp) 6 times; * ch 2, skip next dc, dc in next dc, ch 2, dc in next dc, ch 2, skip next dc, (pc st in next sp, ch 1) 6 times; pc st in next sp. Repeat from * around, ending with ch 2. Join. **8th rnd:** Sl st in sp, ch 3 and complete a starting pc st, (ch 2, pc st in next sp) 5 times (6 pc sts in pineapple). * (Ch 2, dc in next sp) 3 times, (ch 2, pc st in next sp) 6 times. Repeat from * around, ending with ch 2. Join. **9th rnd:** Work as for 8th rnd, having 5 pc sts in each pineapple, and 5 ch-2 sps between pineapples. **10th rnd:** * Make 4 pc sts, (ch 2, dc in next sp) 3 times; ch 2, dc in same sp (increase sp made), make (ch 2, dc in next sp) twice; ch 2. Repeat from * around. Join. **11th, 12th, and 13th rnds:** Work as for 10th rnd, making 1 pc st less on each pineapple on each rnd, and working dc, ch 2 and dc in each increase sp. Join. **14th rnd:** Sl st in next ch, sc in sp, ch 5, * dc in next sp, ch 2. Repeat from * to the increase sp, in increase sp make 3 dc, ch 2 and 3 dc; ch 2, dc in next sp. Continue thus around. Join with sl st to 3rd st of ch-5. Break off.

Make necessary number of motifs and sew together on wrong side with neat over-and-over sts, joining them as in diagram for joining hexagon motifs—see chapter on General Information. For single size spread make 11 motifs from A to B and 13 motifs from A to C; for double size spread make 13 motifs from A to B and 13 motifs from A to C.

FRINGE . . . Make fringe in each sp around as follows: Cut 8 strands, each 12 inches long. Double these strands, forming a loop. Pull loop through sp and draw loose ends through loop. Pull tight. Trim evenly.

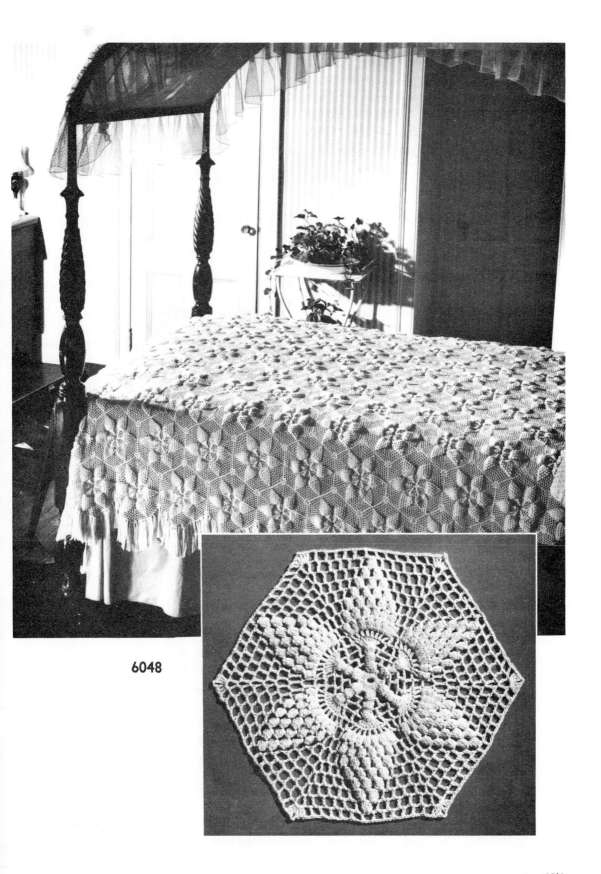

6048

6033 . . . Materials: THREE CORD MERCER-IZED CROCHET, *Size 20: 23 balls of White or Ecru for Single Size; 29 balls of White or Ecru for Double Size* . . . *Steel Crochet Hook No. 9.*

Motif measures 3½ inches square when blocked. For a single size spread, about 70 x 105 inches, make 20 x 30 motifs. For a double size spread, about 88 x 105 inches, make 25 x 30 motifs.

FIRST MOTIF . . . Starting at center, ch 10, join with sl st. **1st rnd:** Ch 3, 23 dc in ring; join. **2nd rnd:** Sc in same place as sl st, * ch 3, sc in next 3 sc. Repeat from * around, ending with sc in last 2 dc, sl st in 1st sc made. **3rd rnd:** Sl st in next ch-3 loop, ch 4, holding back on hook the last loop of each tr make 2 tr in same ch-3 sp, thread over and draw through all loops on hook (a 2-tr cluster made). * Ch 7, holding back on hook the last loop of each tr make 3 tr in next ch-3 and complete as for a cluster. Repeat from * around, ending with ch 7, sl st in top of 1st cluster. **4th rnd:** Sl st in ch-7 loop, ch 4, in same place as last sl st make 2-tr cluster, ch 4, 3-tr cluster, ch 4 and 3-tr cluster; * ch 4, 9 tr in next ch-7 loop, ch 4, in next ch-7 loop make three 3-tr clusters with ch-4 between each cluster. Repeat from * around. Join last ch-4 to top of 1st cluster.

5th rnd: Sl st in next 2 ch, sc in ch-4 sp, ch 4, 2-tr cluster in last sc, * ch 4, 3-tr cluster in next ch-4 sp, ch 7, tr in next sp, tr in next 9 tr, tr in next sp, ch 7, 3-tr cluster in next ch-4 sp. Repeat from * around. Join last ch-7 to top of 1st cluster. **6th rnd:** Sl st in next loop, ch 4, 2-tr cluster in same loop. * Ch 5, 3-tr cluster in same loop, ch 7, sc in next loop, ch 7, skip 1 tr, tr in next 9 tr, ch 7, sc in next loop, ch 7, 3-tr cluster in next loop. Repeat from * around. Join and break off.

SECOND MOTIF . . . Work first 5 rnds as for First Motif. **6th rnd:** Sl st in next loop, ch 4, 2-tr cluster in same loop. Ch 2, sl st in corresponding loop of First Motif, ch 2, 3-tr cluster back in same place as last cluster on Second Motif, ch 3, sc in next loop on First Motif, ch 3, sc back in next loop on Second Motif, ch 3, sc in next loop on First Motif, ch 3, skip 1 tr on Second Motif, tr in next 4 tr, sl st in 5th tr on First Motif, tr in next 5 tr back on Second Motif, and continue as for First Motif, joining next 3 loops to corresponding loops of First Motif as first 3 loops were joined. Complete rnd as for First Motif.

Make necessary number of motifs, joining adjacent sides as Second Motif was joined to First Motif (whenever 4 corners meet, join 3rd and 4th corners to joining of other corners). Block to measurements given.

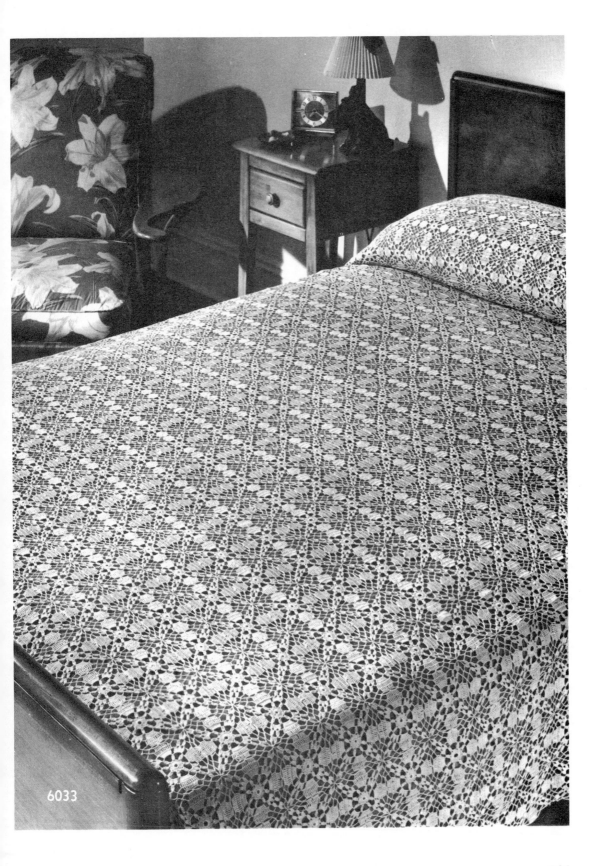

6033

6062 . . . Materials: BEST SIX CORD MERCERIZED CROCHET, *Size 20: 44 balls for Single Size; 58 balls for Double Size . . . Steel Crochet Hook No. 8 or 9.*

Motif measures 4 inches in diameter after blocking. For a single size spread, about 68 x 104 inches, make 17 x 26 motifs. For a double size spread, about 92 x 104 inches, make 23 x 26 motifs.

MOTIF . . . Starting at center, ch 8. Join with sl st. **1st rnd:** Ch 3 (to count as 1 dc), 19 dc in ring. Join with sl st to top st of ch-3. **2nd rnd:** Ch 3, dc in same place as sl st, 2 dc in each dc around. Join with sl st (40 sts). **3rd rnd:** Ch 1, sc in same place as sl st, * ch 7, skip 3 dc, sc in next dc. Repeat from * around, ending with ch 3, skip 3 dc, tr in 1st sc (10 loops). **4th rnd:** Ch 6, dc in top of tr, * ch 3, in center ch of next ch-7 loop make dc, ch 3 and dc. Repeat from * around, ending with ch 3, sl st in 3rd st of ch-6. **5th rnd:** Ch 3, * 4 dc in next ch-3 sp, dc in next dc, ch 3, dc in next dc. Repeat from * around, ending with ch 3, sl st in 3rd st of ch-3. **6th rnd:** Ch 3, dc in next 5 dc, * ch 3, sc in next sp, ch 3, dc in next 6 dc. Repeat from * around. Join. **7th rnd:** Ch 1, sc in same place as sl st, * ch 7, skip 4 dc, sc in next dc, ch 7, sc in next dc Repeat from * around, ending with ch 3, tr in 1st sc. **8th rnd:** Ch 3, 4 dc in top of tr, * ch 2, 5 dc in center st of next loop. Repeat from * around, ending with half dc in top st of ch-3 first made. **9th rnd:** Ch 1, sc in sp, ch 1, dc between ch-3 and following dc of 1st dc-group, * ch 1, dc between 2nd and 3rd dc of same group, ch 1, dc between 3rd and 4th dc, ch 1, dc between 4th and 5th dc, ch 1, sc in next sp (between groups), ch 1, dc between 1st and 2nd dc of next dc-group. Repeat from * around, ending with ch 1, sl st in sc first made. **10th rnd:** Ch 1, sc in same place as sl st, * ch 5, skip 2 dc, in next sp make dc, ch 3 and dc; ch 5, skip 2 dc, sc in next sc. Repeat from * around, ending with ch 5, sl st in 1st sc. Break off.

SECOND MOTIF . . . Work as for First Motif until 9th rnd is complete. **10th rnd:** Ch 1, sc in same place as sl st, ch 5, skip 2 dc, dc in next sp, ch 1, sl st in a point on First Motif, * ch 1, dc in same sp on Second Motif where last dc was made, ch 5, skip 2 dc, sc in next sc, ch 5, skip 2 dc, dc in next sp, ch 1, sl st in next point on First Motif. Repeat from * once more; ch 1, dc in same sp on Second Motif where last dc was made. Complete rnd as for First Motif (no more joinings). Break off.

Make necessary number of motifs, joining corresponding points as Second Motif was joined to First Motif, leaving 2 points free between joinings.

FILL-IN-LACE . . . Starting at center, ch 8. Join with sl st. Ch 5, holding back on hook the last loop of each d tr make 2 d tr in ring, thread over and draw through all loops on hook (a cluster), sl st in a free point (between motifs), * ch 6, sc in ring, ch 5, and complete another cluster in ring, sl st in next free point. Repeat from * around, ending with ch 6, sl st in base of ch-5 first made. Break off. Fill in all sps between motifs in this manner.

6062

6053 . . . Materials: "SOUTH MAID" CROCHET COTTON (ART. D54): *35 balls of White or Ecru for Single Size; 48 balls of White or Ecru for Double Size . . . Steel Crochet Hook No. 6.*

Motif measures about 7 inches from edge to edge, and 7¾ inches from point to point, before blocking. For a single size spread, about 70 x 102 inches, make 161 motifs. For a double size spread, about 91 x 102 inches, make 212 motifs.

FIRST MOTIF . . . Starting at center, ch 8. Join with sl st. **1st rnd:** Ch 3, 23 dc in ring. Join with sl st to top of first ch-3. **2nd rnd:** Ch 3, 4 dc in same place as sl st, drop loop from hook, insert hook in top st of ch-3 and pull loop through (a starting pc st), * ch 2, skip 1 dc, dc in next dc, ch 2, skip 1 dc, in next dc make 5 dc, drop loop from hook, insert hook in top of the 1st dc of this group and pull loop through (pc st). Repeat from * around. Join to top of 1st pc st. **3rd rnd:** Ch 3, starting pc st in top of 1st pc st, * ch 3, dc in next dc, ch 3, pc st in top of next pc st. Repeat from * around. Join. **4th rnd:** Ch 3, 4 dc in top of pc st, * ch 2, dc in next dc, ch 2, 5 dc in top of next pc st. Repeat from * around. Join. **5th rnd:** Ch 5, (dc in next dc, ch 2) 4 times; * in next dc make dc, ch 3 and dc; (ch 2, dc in next dc) 5 times; ch 2. Repeat from * around. Join with sl st in 3rd st of first ch-5. **6th rnd:** Sl st in next sp, ch 3, starting pc st in same sp, (ch 2, pc st in next sp) 3 times; ch 2, * in next ch-3 sp make dc, ch 3 and dc; ch 2, skip 1 sp, (pc st in next sp, ch 2) 4 times. Repeat from * around. Join.

7th rnd: Ch 3, starting pc st in top of 1st pc st, * (ch 2, pc st in next sp) 3 times; ch 2, pc st in top of next pc st, ch 2, in next ch-3 sp make dc, ch 3 and dc; ch 2, pc st in top of next pc st. Repeat from * around. Join. **8th rnd:** Ch 3, starting pc st in top of 1st pc st, * (ch 2, pc st in next sp) 4 times; ch 2, pc st in top of next pc st, ch 2, in next ch-3 sp make dc, ch 3 and dc; ch 2, pc st in top of next pc st. Repeat from * around. Join. **9th rnd:** Ch 3, starting

pc st in top of 1st pc st, * (ch 2, pc st in next sp) 5 times; ch 2, pc st in top of next pc st, ch 2, in next ch-3 sp make dc, ch 3 and dc; ch 2, pc st in top of next pc st. Repeat from * around. Join. **10th rnd:** Sl st to next sp, ch 3, starting pc st in same sp, * (ch 4, sc in next sp, ch 4, pc st in next sp, ch 2, pc st in next sp) twice; ch 2, in next ch-3 sp make dc, ch 3 and dc; (ch 2, pc st in next sp) twice. Repeat from * around, joining last ch-2 to top of 1st pc st. **11th rnd:** Ch 6, * (sc in next loop, ch 4) twice; pc st in next sp, (ch 4, sc in next loop) twice; ch 4, (pc st in next sp, ch 2) twice; in next ch-3 sp make dc, ch 3 and dc; (ch 2, pc st in next sp) twice; ch 4. Repeat from * around. Join to 3rd st of first ch-6. **12th rnd:** Sl st in next loop, ch 1, sc in same loop, (ch 4, sc in next loop) 6 times; * ch 4, pc st in next sp, ch 4, sc in next ch-3 sp, ch 4, pc st in next sp, (ch 4, sc in next loop) 8 times. Repeat from * around. Join with sl st to 1st sc made. **13th rnd:** Sl st to center of next loop, ch 1, sc in same loop, * ch 5, sc in next loop. Repeat from * around. Join and break off.

SECOND MOTIF . . . Work as for First Motif until 12th rnd is complete. **13th rnd:** Sl st to center of next loop, ch 1, sc in same loop, (ch 5, sc in next loop) 9 times; (ch 2, sl st in corresponding loop on First Motif, ch 2, sc in next loop on Second Motif) 8 times; ch 5, sc in next loop on Second Motif. Finish Second Motif with no more joinings. Break off.

Make necessary number of motifs and join them as in diagram for joining hexagon motifs —see chapter on General Information. For single size bedspread, make 17 motifs from A to B and 9 motifs from A to C; for double size spread, make 17 motifs from A to B and 12 motifs from A to C.

FRINGE . . . Make fringe in every other loop between scallops on both long sides as follows: Cut 20 strands, each 9 inches long. Double these strands forming a loop. Pull loop through 1st sp and draw loose ends through loop. Pull tight (there should be 7 groups of fringe between scallops). Trim evenly.

6053

6103 . . . Materials: BEST SIX CORD MER-
CERIZED CROCHET, *Size 20: 47 balls for Single
Size; 60 balls for Double Size . . . Steel Crochet
Hook No. 8 or 9.*

**Motif measures 4¾ inches in diameter before
blocking. For a single size spread, about 71 x
104 inches, make 15 x 22 motifs. For a double
size spread, about 90 x 104 inches, make 19 x
22 motifs.**

FIRST MOTIF . . . Starting at center ch 10.
Join with sl st. **1st rnd:** Ch 3, dc in ring,
(ch 3, 2 dc in ring) 7 times; ch 3, sl st in 3rd
st of ch-3. **2nd rnd:** Ch 3, dc in next dc, (ch 5,
dc in next 2 dc) 7 times; ch 5. Join. **3rd rnd:**
Ch 3, dc in next dc, * in next sp make 3 dc,
ch 2 and 3 dc; dc in next 2 dc. Repeat from *
around. Join. **4th rnd:** Ch 3, dc in next 2 dc,
* in next sp make 2 dc, ch 5 and 2 dc; skip
2 dc, dc in next 4 dc. Repeat from * around.
Join. **5th rnd:** Ch 3, dc in next 2 dc, * ch 3,
6 tr in next sp, ch 3, skip 2 dc, dc in next 4 dc.
Repeat from * around. Join. **6th rnd:** Ch 3,
dc in next 2 dc, * ch 4, (dc in next tr, ch 2)
5 times; dc in next tr, ch 4, dc in next 4 dc.
Repeat from * around. Join. **7th rnd:** Ch 3,
dc in next 2 dc, * ch 5, skip next sp, sc in
next sp, (ch 3, sc in next sp) 4 times; ch 5,
skip next sp, dc in next 4 dc. Repeat from *

around. Join. **8th rnd:** Ch 3, dc in next 2 dc,
* ch 6, sc in next ch-3 loop, (ch 3, sc in next
loop) 3 times; ch 6, dc in next 4 dc. Repeat
from * around. Join. **9th rnd:** Ch 3, dc in next
2 dc, 2 dc in next sp, * ch 6, sc in next loop,
(ch 3, sc in next loop) twice; ch 6, 2 dc in sp,
dc in next 4 dc, 2 dc in next sp. Repeat from *
around. Join. **10th rnd:** Sl st in next 3 dc, ch 3,
dc in next dc, 2 dc in next sp, * ch 6, sc in
next loop, ch 3, sc in next loop, ch 6, 2 dc in
next sp, dc in next 2 dc, ch 4, skip 4 dc, dc in
next 2 dc, 2 dc in next sp. Repeat from *
around. Join. **11th rnd:** Sl st in next 2 dc, ch 3,
dc in next dc, 2 dc in next sp, * ch 6, sc in next
loop, ch 6, 2 dc in next sp, dc in next 2 dc,
ch 6, sc in next sp, ch 6, skip 2 dc, dc in next
2 dc, 2 dc in next sp. Repeat from * around.
Join and break off.

SECOND MOTIF . . . Work as for First
Motif until 10th rnd is complete. **11th rnd:**
Sl st in next 2 dc, ch 3, dc in next dc, 2 dc in
next sp, ch 6, sc in next loop, ch 6, 2 dc in next
sp, dc in next 2 dc, ch 3, sl st in correspond-
ing sp on First Motif, ch 3, sc in next sp on
Second Motif, ch 3, sc in corresponding sp on
First Motif, ch 3, dc in next 2 dc on Second
Motif, 2 dc in next sp and complete rnd as
for First Motif (no more joinings).

Make necessary number of motifs, joining
adjacent sides as Second Motif was joined to
First Motif, leaving 6 sps free between joinings.

FILL-IN-MOTIF . . . Work first 2 rnds as for
First Motif. **3rd rnd:** Ch 3, dc in next dc,
* dc in next sp, ch 5, dc in same sp, dc in next
2 dc. Repeat from * around. Join. **4th rnd:**
Ch 3, dc in next 2 dc, ch 3, sl st in 3rd free
sp from joining of motifs, * ch 3, sc in next
sp on Fill-in-motif, ch 3, sl st in next sp on
large motif, ch 3, dc in next 4 dc on Fill-in-
motif, ch 3, tr in next 4 sps on large motif (2
preceding and 2 following joining), ch 3, dc in
next 4 dc on Fill-in-motif, ch 3, sl st in next
sp on large motif. Repeat from * around. Join.
Fill in all sps between motifs in this manner.

6103

6111 . . . Materials: KNIT-CRO-SHEEN: *43 balls for Single Size; 60 balls for Double Size . . . Steel Crochet Hook No. 7.*

GAUGE: 4 bls or sps make 1 inch; 4 rows make 1 inch; each strip measures 13½ inches wide.

For a single size spread, about 67½ x 107 inches, make 5 strips. For a double size spread, about 94½ x 107 inches, make 7 strips.

STRIP . . . Starting at the bottom, make a chain 20 inches long (about 12 ch sts to 1 inch). **1st row:** Dc in 4th ch from hook and in next 5 ch, (ch 3, skip 2 ch, sc in next ch, ch 3, skip 2 ch, dc in next ch) twice; (ch 2, skip 2 ch, dc in next ch) 3 times; dc in next 6 ch, ch 2, skip 2 ch, dc in next ch (sp made), dc in next 6 ch. Make 15 sps, dc in next 3 ch (bl made), make 10 sps, dc in next 6 ch, 1 sp, dc in next 6 ch, 3 sps, ch 3, skip 2 ch, sc in next ch, ch 3, skip 2 ch, dc in next ch (lacet made). Make 1 more lacet, dc in next 6 ch.

Cut off remaining chain. Ch 5, turn. **2nd row:** Skip 2 dc, dc in next dc, ch 2, skip 2 dc, dc in next dc (2 sps made over 2 bls), ch 5, dc in next dc (bar made over lacet). Make 1 more bar, ch 2, dc in next dc (sp made over sp), make 2 more sps, dc in next 3 dc (bl made over bl). Make 1 sp, 2 dc in next sp, dc in next dc (bl made over sp). Make 13 sps, 1 bl, 16 sps, 1 bl, 1 sp, 1 bl, 3 sps, 2 bars, 1 sp, ch 2, skip 2 dc, dc in top st of turning chain. Ch 3, turn. **3rd row:** 2 bls, ch 3, skip 2 ch, sc in next ch, ch 3, dc in next dc (lacet made over bar). Make 3 sps, 2 bls, 1 sp, 4 bls, 13 sps, 1 bl, 12 sps, 4 bls, 1 sp, 2 bls, 3 sps, 1 lacet, 1 bl, then make 2 dc in next sp, dc in 3rd st of turning chain. Ch 5, turn. Starting with 4th row, follow chart to top. Repeat 1st to 88th rows incl of chart 3 more times; then work the 1st to 78th rows once more. Break off.

Make the necessary number of strips and sew them together with neat over-and-over sts on wrong side.

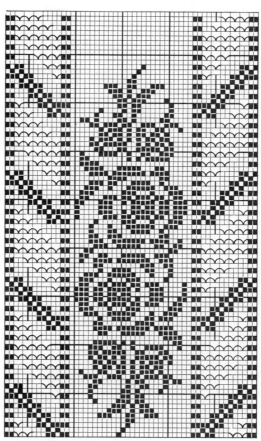

There are 10 spaces between heavy lines

START HERE

6111

7650-A

CHAPTER TWELVE

Pineapples

THERE'S CERTAINLY NO NEED to take a poll to determine America's most popular fruit—at least when it comes to crochet. It so happens there are excellent reasons for the popularity of the pineapple. Decoratively, it blends with any period; beautiful with Colonial furniture, it's very much at home with eighteenth-century English, has exactly the right flair for modern, graces with equal charm formal and informal settings. Then, too, from the point of view of design, it lends itself to endless lovely variations.

As you see, we've picked as choice a crop of pineapple beauties as ever set a crochet needle whirring through the thread—a dinner cloth, handsome enough to grace the most important occasions, a matching runner to set off a gleaming copper bowl or your best candlesticks, a luncheon set your friends will admire, and a trio of lacy doilies for the daintiest of undercover work.

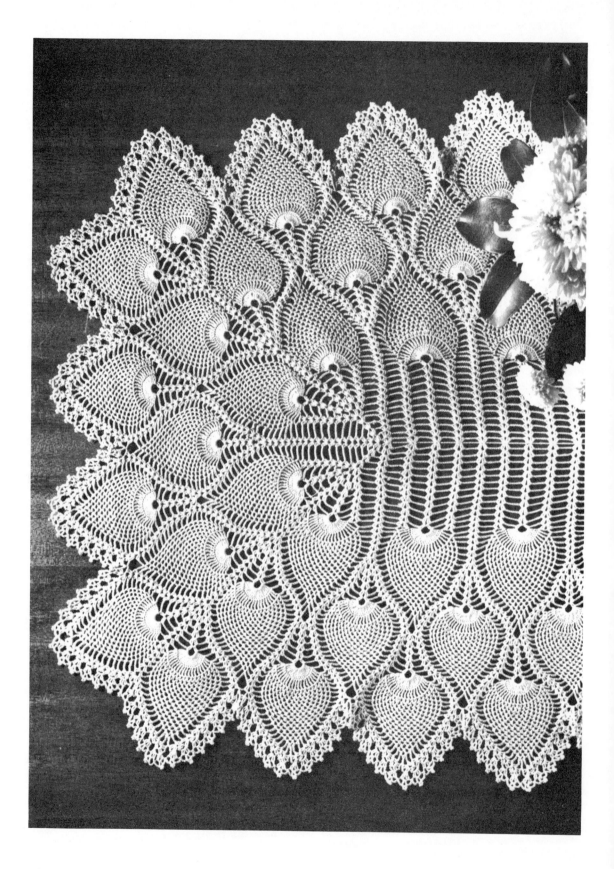

172

7650-A . . . Materials: BEST SIX CORD MERCERIZED CROCHET, *Size 30: 48 balls of White or Ecru . . . Steel Crochet Hook No. 10 or 11.*

Tablecloth measures 65 x 84 inches.

GAUGE: 3 shells and 3 ch-6 sps make 2 inches; 5 rows of shells make 1 inch.

Starting at center, make a chain about 25 inches long (13 ch sts to 1 inch). **1st rnd:** In 4th ch from hook make dc, ch 2 and 2 dc (shell made); * ch 6, skip 10 ch, in next ch make 2 dc, ch 2 and 2 dc (another shell). Repeat from * across until 29 shells are complete. Cut off remaining chain, ch 6, and, working along opposite side of starting chain, * make a shell at base of next shell, ch 6. Repeat from * across, ending with ch 6, sl st in top of turning chain. **2nd rnd:** Sl st in next dc and in sp, ch 3, in same sp make dc, ch 2 and 2 dc; * ch 6, shell in sp of next shell (shell over shell made). Repeat from * across one side, ch 2, in end ch-6 sp make 2 dc, ch 3, 2 dc, ch 2, 2 dc, ch 3 and 2 dc; ch 2, shell in sp of next shell, ch 6 and work across other side to correspond. Make end as before. Join. **3rd rnd:** Sl st in next dc and in next sp, in same sp make dc, ch 2 and 2 dc—each rnd begins in this way and this will be referred to as shell over shell. Ch 6, shell over shell, ch 3, shell over corner shell, ch 3, shell in sp between shells, ch 3, shell in next corner shell, ch 3 and work remainder of rnd to correspond. Join. **4th rnd:** * Shell over shell, ch 6. Repeat from * to corner; (ch 4, shell in next shell) 3 times; ch 4 and work remainder of rnd to correspond. Join. **5th rnd:** * Shell over shell, ch 6. Repeat from * around. Join. **6th rnd:** * Shell over shell, ch 6. Repeat from * across to corner shell; in corner shell make shell, ch 3 and shell; ch 6, shell over shell, ch 6, in corner shell make shell, ch 3 and shell. Complete rnd to correspond. Join. **7th rnd:** Work as for last rnd to corner, ch 6, shell over shell, ch 2, shell in ch-3 sp (between shells), ch 2, shell over shell, ch 6 and continue as before making all corners to correspond. Join. **8th rnd:** Work as before to corner, ch 6, (shell over shell, ch 1, shell in sp between shells, ch 1) twice; shell over shell (5 shells in corner). Ch 6 and work as before making all corners correspond. Join. **9th rnd:** Work as before to corner, ch 6, shell over corner shell, (ch 3, shell over shell) 4

times; ch 6 and work as before, making all corners to correspond. Join. **10th rnd:** Repeat 9th rnd, making ch 4 over each ch-3 sp. Join. **11th rnd:** Repeat 10th rnd, making ch-5 over each ch-4 sp. Join. Repeat 6th to 11th rnds incl 5 more times (41 rnds completed).

42nd rnd: Sl st in next dc and in next sp, ch 3, in same sp make dc, ch 7 and 2 dc; * (ch 6, shell over shell) 3 times; ch 6, in sp of next shell make 2 dc, ch 7 and 2 dc. Repeat from * 9 more times; ch 6, shell in center shell of corner, ch 6, in next shell make 2 dc, ch 7 and 2 dc; ch 6 and work in the same manner over remaining 3 sides, making all corners to correspond. Join. **43rd rnd:** Sl st in next dc and in sp, ch 4 (to count as tr), 19 tr in same sp, * shell over shell, (ch 6, shell over shell) twice; 20 tr in ch-7 sp of next shell. Repeat from * to corner shell, ch 2, shell in corner shell, ch 2, 20 tr in ch-7 loop and work remainder of rnd to correspond. Join (42 pineapples started on rnd). **44th rnd:** Ch 5, (tr in next tr, ch 1) 18 times; tr in next tr, * dc in sp of next shell, ch 6, shell over shell, ch 6, dc in sp of next shell (tr in next tr, ch 1) 19 times; tr in next tr. Repeat from * to corner shell, ch 2, shell over corner shell, ch 2, complete rnd to correspond, making corners as before. Join. **45th rnd:** Sc in next ch-1 sp, * (ch 3, sc in next ch-1 sp) 18 times; ch 6, shell over shell, ch 6, sc in next ch-1 sp. Repeat from * across to corner shell, ch 2, shell over corner shell, ch 2, sc in next ch-1 sp and complete rnd to correspond, making corners as before. Join. **46th rnd:** Sl st in next ch, sc in loop, * (ch 3, sc in next loop) 17 times; ch 5, shell over shell, ch 5, sc in next ch-3 loop. Repeat from * across to corner shell, ch 2, shell over corner shell, ch 2, sc in next ch-3 loop and complete rnd to correspond, making corners as before. Join. **47th rnd:** Sl st in next ch, sc in loop, * (ch 3, sc in next loop) 16 times; ch 4, shell over shell, ch 4, sc in next ch-3 loop. Repeat from * across to corner shell, ch 2, shell over corner shell, ch 2, sc in next ch-3 loop on next pineapple and complete to correspond. Join. **48th rnd:** Sl st in next ch, sc in loop, * (ch 3, sc in next loop) 15 times; ch 4, shell over shell, ch 4, sc in next ch-3 loop. Repeat from * across to corner shell, ch 2, shell over corner shell, ch 2, complete rnd to correspond. Join.

49th rnd: Sl st in next ch, sc in loop, * (ch 3,

sc in next loop) 14 times; ch 4, shell over shell, ch 4, sc in next ch-3 loop. Repeat from * across to corner shell, ch 2, shell over corner shell, ch 2, complete rnd to correspond. Join. **50th rnd:** Sl st in next ch, sc in loop, * (ch 3, sc in next loop) 13 times; ch 4, in sp of next shell make (2 dc, ch 2) twice and 2 dc; ch 4, sc in next ch-3 loop. Repeat from * across to corner shell, ch 2, in corner shell make (2 dc, ch 2) 3 times and 2 dc; ch 2, complete rnd to correspond. Join. **51st rnd:** Sl st in next ch, sc in loop, * (ch 3, sc in next loop) 12 times; ch 4, shell in next ch-2 sp, ch 2, shell in next ch-2 sp, ch 4, sc in next ch-3 loop. Repeat from * across to corner shell, ch 2, skip next ch-2, (shell in next sp, ch 2) 3 times; sc in next ch-3 loop and complete rnd to correspond. Join. **52nd rnd:** Sl st in next ch, sc in loop, * (ch 3, sc in next loop) 11 times; ch 4, shell over shell, shell in ch-2 sp between shells, shell over shell, ch 4, sc in next ch-3 loop. Repeat from * across to corner shell, ch 2, (shell over shell, shell in next sp) twice and shell over shell; ch 2, sc in next ch-3 loop and complete rnd to correspond. Join.

53rd rnd: Sl st in next ch, sc in loop, * (ch 3, sc in next loop) 10 times; ch 4, shell over shell, (ch 2, shell over shell) twice; ch 4, sc in next ch-3 loop. Repeat from * across to corner shell, (ch 2, shell over shell) 5 times; ch 2, sc in next ch-3 loop and complete rnd to correspond. Join. **54th rnd:** Sl st in next ch, sc in loop, * (ch 3, sc in next loop) 9 times; ch 4, shell over shell, (ch 3, shell over shell) twice; ch 4, sc in next ch-3 loop. Repeat from * across to corner shell, ch 2, (shell over shell, ch 3) 4 times and shell over shell; ch 2, sc in next ch-3 loop and complete rnd to correspond. Join. **55th rnd:** Sl st in next ch, sc in loop, * (ch 3, sc in next loop) 8 times; (ch 4, shell over shell) 3 times; ch 4, sc in next ch-3 loop. Repeat from * across to corner shell, ch 2, (shell over shell, ch 4) 4 times and shell over shell; ch 2, sc in next ch-3 loop and complete rnd to correspond. Join. **56th rnd:** Sl st in next ch, sc in loop, * (ch 3, sc in next loop) 7 times; ch 4, shell over shell, ch 5, in sp of next shell make 2 dc, ch 7 and 2 dc; ch 5, shell over shell, ch 4, sc in next ch-3 loop. Repeat from * across to corner shell, ch 3, shell over shell, ch 5, in sp of next shell make 2 dc, ch 7 and 2 dc; ch 5, shell over corner shell, ch 5, in sp of next shell make 2 dc, ch 7 and 2 dc; ch 5, shell over shell,

ch 3, sc in next ch-3 loop and complete rnd to correspond. Join.

57th rnd: Sl st in next ch, sc in loop, * (ch 3, sc in next loop) 6 times; ch 4, shell over shell, ch 4, 20 tr in ch-7 loop, ch 4, shell over shell, ch 4, sc in next ch-3 loop. Repeat from * across to corner shell, ch 4, shell over shell, ch 4, 20 tr in next ch-7 sp, ch 2, shell over shell, ch 2, 20 tr in next ch-7 sp, ch 4, shell over shell, ch 4, sc in next ch-3 loop and complete rnd to correspond. Join. **58th rnd:** Sl st in next ch, sc in loop, * (ch 3, sc in next loop) 5 times; ch 4, shell over shell, ch 4, (tr in next tr, ch 1) 19 times and tr; ch 4, shell over shell, ch 4, sc in next ch-3 loop. Repeat from * across to corner shell, ch 2, shell over corner shell, ch 2, complete rnd to correspond. Join. **59th rnd:** Sl st in next ch, sc in loop, * (ch 3, sc in next loop) 4 times; ch 4, shell over shell, ch 4, sc in next ch-1 sp, (ch 3, sc in next ch-1 sp) 18 times; ch 4, shell over shell, ch 4, sc in next ch-3 loop. Repeat from * across to corner shell, ch 2, shell over shell, ch 2, sc in next ch-1 sp and complete rnd to correspond. Join. **60th rnd:** Sl st in next ch, sc in loop, * (ch 3, sc in next loop) 3 times; ch 4, shell over shell, ch 4, sc in next ch-3 loop, (ch 3, sc in next ch-1 sp) 17 times; ch 4, shell over shell, ch 4, sc in next ch-3 loop. Repeat from * around, working over corners in established pattern and ending rnd as before. **61st rnd:** Sl st in next ch, sc in loop, * (ch 3, sc in next loop) twice; ch 4, shell over shell, ch 4, sc in next ch-3 loop, (ch 3, sc in next loop) 16 times; ch 4, shell over shell, ch 4, sc in next ch-3 loop. Repeat from * around, working over corners in established pattern. Join. **62nd rnd:** Sl st in next ch, sc in loop, * ch 3, sc in next loop, ch 4, shell over shell, ch 4, sc in next ch-3 loop, (ch 3, sc in next loop) 15 times; ch 4, shell over shell, ch 4, sc in next ch-3 loop. Repeat from * around, working over corners in established pattern. Join.

Note: Increases at corners are always worked in the same manner. Work over corners in pattern as established.

63rd rnd: Sl st in next ch, sc in loop, * ch 4, shell over shell, ch 4, sc in next ch-3 loop, (ch 3, sc in next loop) 14 times; ch 4, shell over shell, ch 4, sc in next ch-3 loop. Repeat from * around. Join. **64th rnd:** Sl st in next

4 ch and the following 2 dc, sl st in sp of shell, ch 3 (to count as dc), in same sp make dc, ch 2 and 2 dc; * ch 4, sc in next ch-3 loop, (ch 3, sc in next loop) 13 times; ch 4, shell over shell, ch 1, shell over shell. Repeat from * around, ending with ch 1. Join. **65th rnd:** Shell over shell, * ch 4, sc in next ch-3 loop, (ch 3, sc in next loop) 12 times; ch 4, shell over shell, shell in next ch-1, shell over shell. Repeat from * around, ending with shell in last ch-1. Join. **66th rnd:** * Shell over shell, ch 4, sc in next ch-3 loop, (ch 3, sc in next loop) 11 times; ch 4, (shell over shell, ch 1) twice. Repeat from * around. Join. **67th rnd:** * Shell over shell, ch 4, sc in next ch-3 loop, (ch 3, sc in next loop) 10 times; ch 4, (shell over shell, ch 2) twice. Repeat from * around. Join. **68th rnd:** Same as previous rnd, making 9 loops over pineapples and ch-3 (instead of ch-2) between shells. **69th rnd:** Same as previous rnd, making 8 loops over pineapples and ch-4 between shells. **70th rnd:** * Shell over shell, ch 4, make 7 loops over pineapple, ch 4, shell over shell, ch 5, in sp of next shell make 2 dc, ch 7 and 2 dc; ch 5. Repeat from * around. Join.

71st rnd: * Shell over shell, ch 4, make 6 loops over pineapple, ch 4, shell over shell, ch 4, 20 tr in next ch-7 sp, ch 4. Repeat from * around. Join. **72nd rnd:** * Shell over shell, ch 4, make 5 loops over pineapple, ch 4, shell over shell, ch 4, (tr in next tr, ch 1) 19 times and tr ch 4. Repeat from * around. Join. **73rd rnd:** * Shell over shell, ch 4, make 4 loops over pineapple, ch 4, shell over shell, ch 4, sc in next ch-1 sp, (ch 3, sc in next ch-1 sp) 18 times; ch 4. Repeat from * around. Join. **74th rnd:** * Shell over shell, ch 4, make 3 loops over pineapple, ch 4, shell over shell, ch 4, make 17 loops over pineapple, ch 4. Repeat from * around. Join. **75th rnd:** * Shell over shell, ch 4, make 2 loops over pineapple, ch 4, shell over shell, ch 4, make 16 loops over pineapple, ch 4. Repeat from * around. Join. **76th rnd:** * Shell over shell, ch 4, make 1 loop over pineapple, ch 4, shell over shell, ch 4, make 15 loops over pineapple, ch 4. Repeat from * around. Join. **77th rnd:** * Shell over shell, ch 4, sc in loop, ch 4, shell over shell, ch 4, make 14 loops over pineapple, ch 4. Repeat from * around. Join. **78th rnd:** * Shell over shell, ch 1, shell over shell, ch 4, make 13 loops over pineapple, ch 4. Repeat from * around. Join. **79th rnd:** * Shell over shell, shell in ch-1, shell over shell, ch 4, make 12 loops over pineapple, ch 4. Repeat from * around. Join. **80th rnd:** * (Shell over shell, ch 1) twice; shell over shell, ch 4, make 11 loops over pineapple, ch 4. Repeat from * around. Join. **81st rnd:** Same as previous rnd, making ch-2 (instead of ch-1) between shells and 10 loops over pineapples.

Continue thus in established pattern, until 10 rnds of pineapples have been completed, ending with the 78th rnd but making shell, ch 1 and shell in each corner shell on last rnd (13 loops across pineapples).

To Make Points: Now work pineapples individually as follows: **1st row:** Sl st in next dc and in sp, turn, shell over shell, ch 4, 12 loops over pineapple, ch 4, shell over shell. Ch 5, turn. **2nd row:** Shell over shell, ch 4, 11 loops over pineapple, ch 4, shell over shell. Ch 5, turn. Work in this manner, having 1 loop less over pineapple on each row until 1 loop remains. Ch 5, turn. **Next row:** Shell over shell, ch 4, sc in loop, ch 4, shell over shell. Ch 5, turn; (shell over shell) twice. Break off. Attach thread to 1st shell of next pineapple and complete in same manner. Continue thus until all points have been worked.

EDGING . . . 1st rnd: Attach thread in ch-1 sp between shells (at base of points), sc in same place, ch 3, * shell in turning ch-3 of next shell, ch 2. Repeat from * around pineapple, ch 3, sc in next ch-1 sp between shells (at base of points), ch 3, and continue thus around. Join. **2nd rnd:** Sl st to center of next shell, ch 5, * sc in next ch-2 sp, ch 2, in sp of next shell make dc, ch 4, sc in 4th ch from hook (picot made) and dc, ch 2. Repeat from * around pineapple, ending with dc in sp of last shell, then make a picot, dc in sp of 1st shell on next pineapple, ch 2, sc in next ch-2 sp, ch 2, and continue thus around. Break off.

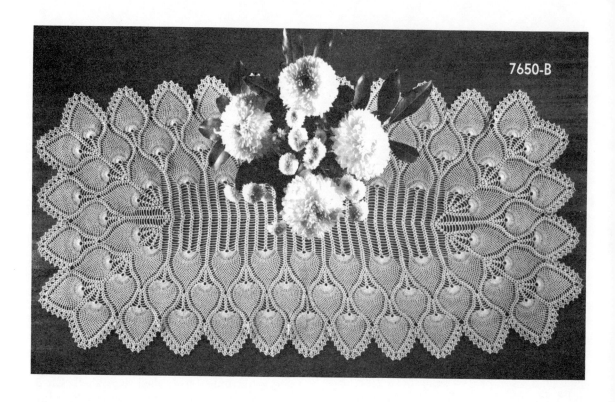

7650-B . . . Materials: Best Six Cord Mercerized Crochet, *Size 30: 12 balls . . . Steel
Crochet Hook No. 10.*

Runner measures 18 x 38 inches.

Work exactly as for Tablecloth 7650-A until
6th rnd is completed. **7th rnd:** * Shell over
shell, ch 6. Repeat from * across to corner
shell, (ch 6, shell over shell, ch 2, shell in next
sp—this is corner shell—ch 2, shell over shell,
ch 6, shell over shell) twice; ch 6 and complete rnd to correspond. Join. **8th rnd:** * Shell
over shell, ch 6. Repeat from * across to corner, (ch 6, shell over shell, ch 1, shell in next sp,
ch 1, shell over corner shell, ch 1, shell in next
sp, ch 1, shell over shell, ch 6, shell over shell)
twice. Complete rnd to correspond. Join. **9th,
10th and 11th rnds:** * Shell over shell, ch 6.
Repeat from * across to corner shell; ch 6,
shell over each corner shell but make ch 3
between corner shells (instead of ch-1) on 9th
rnd; ch 4 (instead of ch-3) on 10th rnd and
ch 5 (instead of ch-4) on 11th rnd. Break off
at end of 11th rnd. **12th rnd:** Attach thread in
sp of 5th shell on long side, counting from the
corner shell but do not count corner shell, ch 3,
in same sp make dc, ch 7 and 2 dc; * (ch 6,

shell over shell) 3 times; in next sp make 2 dc,
ch 7 and 2 dc. Repeat from * 6 more times,
ch 6, shell in center shell of corner, ch 6, in
next shell make 2 dc, ch 7 and 2 dc. Ch 6, and
work in the same manner over remaining 3
sides, making all corners to correspond. Join.
13th to 48th rnds incl: Repeat 43rd to 78th
rnds of Tablecloth 7650-A, pages 173–175, but
on last rnd make shell, ch 1 and shell in each
corner shell.

Now work Points and Edging as on Tablecloth 7650-A on page 175.

7335 . . . Materials: Best Six Cord Mercerized Crochet, *Size 50: 5 balls . . . Steel
Crochet Hook No. 12.*

**Centerpiece measures 14 inches in diameter;
each place doily 12 inches in diameter; each
bread and butter doily 7 inches in diameter;
and each glass doily 5½ inches in diameter.**

CENTERPIECE . . . Starting at center, ch 16,
join with sl st. **1st rnd:** Ch 3, 32 dc in ring, sl st
in top of ch-3. **2nd rnd:** Ch 3, dc in each dc
around: join. **3rd rnd:** Ch 3, dc in same place
as sl st, 2 dc in each dc around. join. **4th rnd:**

7335

Repeat 2nd rnd. **5th rnd:** Ch 3, dc in same place as sl st, * ch 3, skip 2 dc, 2 dc in next dc. Repeat from * around. Join last ch 3 to top of ch-3 (22 dc-groups). **6th rnd:** Sl st in next dc and in next sp, ch 3; in same sp make dc, ch 2 and 2 dc; in each ch-3 sp around make 2 dc, ch 2 and 2 dc; join. **7th rnd:** Sl st in next dc and in next ch-2 sp, ch 3, in same sp make dc, ch 2 and 2 dc; * ch 1, in next ch-2 sp make 2 dc, ch 2 and 2 dc (shell over shell). Repeat from * around. Join.

8th to 12th rnds incl: Repeat 7th rnd, having an extra ch between each shell in each rnd. **13th rnd:** Sl st in next dc and in next sp, ch 3; in same sp make dc, ch 5 and 2 dc. * Ch 6, in next ch-2 sp make 2 dc, ch 2 and 2 dc, ch 6; in next ch-2 sp make 2 dc, ch 5 and 2 dc. Repeat from * around. Join. **14th rnd:** Sl st in next dc and in next sp, ch 4, 12 tr in ch-5 of shell, * ch 5, in next ch-2 make 2 dc, ch 2 and 2 dc; ch 5, 13 tr in ch-5 of next shell. Repeat from * around. Join.

15th rnd: Ch 5 (to count as tr and ch-1), tr in the next tr; (ch 1, tr in next tr) 11 times; * ch 3, shell over next shell, ch 3, tr in next tr; (ch 1, tr in next tr) 12 times. Repeat from * around. Join to 4th st of ch-5 first made. **16th rnd:** Sl st in 1st ch-1 sp, sc in same sp; * (ch 3, sc in next ch-1 sp) 11 times, ch 3, shell over next shell, ch 3, sc in next ch-1 sp. Repeat from * around, ending with ch 3, sc in 1st ch-3 loop. **17th rnd:** (Ch 3, sc in next loop) 10 times, * ch 3, shell over next shell; (ch 3, sc in next loop) 11 times. Repeat from * around, ending as in 16th rnd. **18th rnd:** (Ch 3, sc in next loop) 9 times, * ch 3, in ch-2 of next shell make (2 dc, ch 2) twice, and 2 dc. (Ch 3, sc in next loop) 10 times. Repeat from * around, ending as before. **19th rnd:** (Ch 3, sc in next loop) 8 times, * ch 3, in next ch-2 make a shell, ch 2, shell in next ch-2. (Ch 3, sc in next loop) 9 times. Repeat from * around, ending as before. **20th rnd:** (Ch 3, sc in next loop) 7 times, * ch 3, shell over next shell, ch 1, shell in next ch-2 sp, ch 1, shell over next shell; (ch 3, sc in next loop) 8 times. Repeat from * around, ending as before. **21st rnd:** (Ch 3, sc in next loop) 6 times; * (ch 3, shell over next shell) 3 times; (ch 3, sc in next loop) 7 times. Repeat from * around, ending as before. **22nd rnd:** (Ch 3, sc in next loop) 5 times, * ch 3, shell over next shell; (ch 4, shell over next shell) twice; (ch 3, sc in next loop) 6 times. Repeat from * around. **23rd rnd:** (Ch 3, sc in next loop) 4 times; * ch 3, shell over next shell, ch 5; in next shell make 2 dc, ch 5 and 2 dc; ch 5, shell over next shell; (ch 3, sc in next loop) 5 times. Repeat from * around. **24th rnd:** (Ch 3, sc in next loop) 3 times; * ch 3, shell over next shell, ch 3, 14 tr in next shell, ch 3, shell over next shell; (ch 3, sc in next loop) 4 times. Repeat from * around. **25th rnd:** (Ch 3, sc in next loop) twice; * ch 3, shell over next shell, ch 3, tr in next tr; (ch 1, tr in next tr) 13 times; ch 3, shell over next shell; (ch 3, sc in next loop) 3 times. Repeat from * around.

26th rnd: Ch 3, sc in next loop, * ch 3, shell over next shell; (ch 3, sc in next ch-1 sp) 13 times; ch 3, shell over next shell; (ch 3, sc in next loop) twice. Repeat from * around. **27th rnd:** * Ch 4, shell over next shell; (ch 3, sc in next loop) 12 times; ch 3, shell over next shell; ch 4, sc in next loop. Repeat from * around, ending with ch 4, sl st in 1st sc.

To Make Points: 1st row: Sl st to ch-2 of next shell, sl st in sp, ch 3; make dc, ch 2 and 2 dc in same sp; (ch 3, sc in next loop) 11 times; ch 3, shell over next shell. Ch 3, turn. **2nd row:** Shell over shell; (ch 3, sc in next loop) 10 times; ch 3, shell over next shell. Ch 3, turn. Continue in this manner, having 1 ch-3 loop less on each row until 9th row is completed. **10th row:** Shell over shell; (ch 3, sc in next loop) twice; ch 3, shell over shell—1 loop remaining at point. Ch 3, turn. Make shell over shell, ch 4, sc in next loop, ch 4, 2 dc in next shell, ch 1, sl st back in ch-2 of last shell; ch 1, 2 dc where last 2 dc were made. Break off. * Attach thread to ch-2 of next shell of 27th rnd and complete the next point as before. Break off. Repeat from * until all points are completed.

EDGING . . . 1st rnd: Attach thread to tip of one point where shells were joined, ch 3, in same place make dc, ch 2 and 2 dc. * (Ch 3, shell in next turning chain between 2 rows) 5 times; ch 2, holding back the last loop of next 2 dc on hook, make dc in ch-2 of shell preceding ch 4 on 27th rnd, thread over and draw through all loops on hook; (ch 3, shell in turning chain between 2 rows) 5 times; ch 3, shell at tip of next point, where shells were joined.

Repeat from * around. Join. **2nd rnd:** Sl st in next dc and in next sp, ch 8, sc in 5th ch from hook (a picot made). Dc in same place as sl st, * ch 3, sc under next ch-3, ch 3; in next shell make dc, p and dc. Repeat from * 4 more times; ch 3, sc in next dc, ch 3; in next shell make dc, p and dc. Ch 3, sc under next ch-3. Continue thus around. Break off.

PLACE DOILY (Make 4) . . . Starting at center, ch 12. Join with sl st. **1st rnd:** Ch 3 (to count as dc), 26 dc in ring. Join with sl st in 3rd st of ch-3. **2nd rnd:** Ch 3, dc in same place as sl st, 2 dc in each dc around (54 dc). Join. **3rd to 9th rnds incl:** Same as 5th to 11th rnds incl of Centerpiece—18 dc-groups on 3rd rnd. **10th rnd:** Same as 13th rnd of Centerpiece, making ch-5 (instead of ch-6) between shells. **11th rnd:** Same as 14th rnd of Centerpiece, making ch-4 (instead of ch-5) between shells and tr-groups (9 tr-groups in rnd). Starting with 15th rnd of Centerpiece, work as for Centerpiece until Place Doily is completed.

BREAD and BUTTER DOILY (Make 4) . . . Ch 16, join with sl st. **1st rnd:** Ch 3 (to count as dc), 41 dc in ring. **2nd to 5th rnds incl:** Same as 5th to 8th rnds incl of Centerpiece (14 dc-groups on 2nd rnd). **6th rnd:** Sl st in next dc and in next sp, ch 3, in same sp make dc, ch 5 and 2 dc, * ch 4, shell over next shell, ch 4, in sp of next shell make 2 dc, ch 5 and 2 dc. Repeat from * around. Join. **7th rnd:** Sl st in next dc and in next sp, ch 4 (to count as tr), 10 tr in ch-5 sp, * ch 3, shell over shell, ch 3, 11 tr in next ch-5 sp. Repeat from * around, ending with ch 3, join (7 tr-groups in rnd). **8th rnd:** Ch 5 (to count as tr and ch-1), tr in next tr; (ch 1, tr in next tr) 9 times; * ch 3, shell over next shell, ch 3, tr in next tr; (ch 1, tr in next tr) 10 times. Repeat from * around. Join to 4th st of ch-5 first made. **9th rnd:** Same as 16th rnd of Centerpiece, making (ch-3, sc in next ch-1 sp) 9 times—instead of 11 times. **10th rnd:** (Ch 3, sc in next loop) 8 times, * ch 3, shell over next shell; (ch 3, sc in next loop) 9 times. Repeat from * around, ending with sl st in sc at base of 1st loop made. Break off.

To Make Points: 1st row: Attach thread to ch-2 of next shell of previous rnd, ch 3; make dc, ch 2 and 2 dc in same shell; (ch 3, sc in next loop) 8 times; ch 3, shell over next shell. Ch 3, turn. **2nd row:** Shell over shell, (ch 3, sc in next loop) 7 times; ch 3, shell over next shell. Ch 3, turn. Continue in this manner, having 1 ch-3 loop less on each row until 6th row is completed. **7th row:** Same as 10th row of Points of Centerpiece. Break off. Attach thread to ch-2 of next shell on 10th rnd and complete the next point in same manner. Continue thus until all 7 points have been worked. Break off.

EDGING . . . **1st rnd:** Attach thread to tip of any point where shells were joined, ch 3; in same place make dc, ch 2 and 2 dc. * (Ch 3, shell in next turning chain) 3 times, ch 2, dc in next turning chain, skip next shell, dc under starting chain of next shell, (ch 3, shell in next turning chain) 3 times; ch 3, shell in tip of point where shells meet. Repeat from * around. Join. **2nd rnd:** Sl st in next dc and in next sp, ch 8 (to count as dc and ch-5 for a picot), sc in 5th ch from hook (a picot made). Dc in same place as sl st, * ch 3, sc under next ch-3, ch 3; in next shell make dc, p and dc. Repeat from * 2 more times, ch 3, sc between next 2 dc, ch 3; in next shell make dc, p and dc. Ch 3, sc under next ch-3. Continue thus around. Join and break off.

GLASS DOILY (Make 4) . . . Starting at center, ch 8. Join. **1st rnd:** Ch 3, 19 dc in ring. Join. **2nd rnd:** Ch 3, dc in same place as sl st, * ch 2, skip 1 dc, 2 dc in next dc. Repeat from * around, ending with ch 2, sl st in top of ch-3 (10 dc-groups). **3rd rnd:** Sl st in next dc and in next sp, ch 3. In same sp make dc, ch 2 and 2 dc, * ch 3, shell in next sp. Repeat from * around, ending with ch 3, sl st in top st of ch-3. **4th rnd:** Sl st in next dc and in next sp, ch 3; in same sp make dc, ch 5 and 2 dc, * ch 4, shell in sp of next shell, ch 4. In sp of next shell make 2 dc, ch 5 and 2 dc. Repeat from * around, ending with ch 4, sl st in top of ch-3. **5th rnd:** Repeat 7th rnd of Bread and Butter Doily (5 tr-groups in rnd). Work remainder of this doily as for Bread and Butter Doily. Block all pieces to measurements given.

7275-M

7275

7275-M . . . Materials: Best Six Cord Mercerized Crochet, *Size 30: 4 balls . . . Steel Crochet Hook No. 10.*

Doily measures 18 inches in diameter.

Work as for Centerpiece of 7335 (pages 176–178) until 27 rnds are complete. **28th rnd:** Sl st to sp of shell, ch 3, in same sp make dc, ch 2 and 2 dc; * (ch 3, sc in next loop) 11 times; (ch 3, shell over next shell) twice. Repeat from * around. Join. **29th rnd:** Sl st to sp of shell, ch 3, in same sp make dc, ch 2 and 2 dc; * (ch 3, sc in next loop) 10 times; ch 3, shell over next shell, ch 1, shell in next ch-3 sp, ch 1, shell over next shell. Repeat from * around. Join. **30th rnd:** Make a shell as before, * (ch 3, sc in next loop) 9 times; (ch 3, shell over next shell) 3 times. Repeat from * around. Join. **31st rnd:** Shell over shell, * (ch 3, sc in next loop) 8 times; ch 3, shell over shell, (ch 4, shell over next shell) twice. Repeat from * around. Join. **32nd rnd:** Shell over shell, * (ch 3, sc in next loop) 7 times; ch 3, shell over shell, ch 5, in next shell make 2 dc, ch 6 and 2 dc; ch 5, shell over shell. Repeat from * around. Join. **33rd rnd:** Shell over shell, * (ch 3, sc in next loop) 6 times; ch 3, shell over shell, ch 3, 16 tr in ch-6 loop, ch 3, shell over shell. Repeat from * around (3rd rnd of pineapples started). Continue to work around until only 1 loop remains at top of 2nd rnd of pineapples. **Next rnd:** Shell over shell, * ch 4, sc in next loop, ch 4, shell over shell, ch 4, sc in next loop, (ch 3, sc in next loop) 11 times; ch 4, shell over shell. Repeat from * around. Join.

To Make Points: 1st row: Ch 3, turn. Work shell over last shell, ch 4, sc in next loop, (ch 3, sc in next loop) 10 times; ch 4, shell over shell. Ch 3, turn. **2nd row:** Shell over shell, ch 4, sc in next loop, (ch 3, sc in next loop) 9 times; ch 4, shell over shell. Ch 3, turn. Continue in this manner, having one ch-3 loop less on each row until 1 loop remains at top of pineapple. Ch 3, turn. **Next row:** Make shell over shell, ch 4, sc in loop, ch 4, 2 dc in next shell, ch 1, sl st back in ch-2 of last shell, ch 1, 2 dc where last 2 dc were made. Break off. Attach thread to 1st shell of next pineapple and complete the point in same manner. Continue thus until all 11 points have been worked.

7275 . . . Materials: Three Cord Mercerized Crochet, *Size 50: 1 ball . . . Steel Crochet Hook No. 12.*

Follow directions for Centerpiece of Luncheon Set 7335, pages 176–178.

7714 . . . Materials: Best Six Cord Mercerized Crochet, *Size 20: 2 balls . . . Steel Crochet Hook No. 8.*

Doily measures 10 x 14 inches.

Starting at center, ch 8. Join with sl st to form a ring. **1st rnd:** Ch 3, 23 dc in ring. Join to top of ch-3. **2nd rnd:** Ch 3, dc in same place as sl st, (ch 2, skip 1 dc, 2 dc in next dc) 11 times; ch 2, sl st in top of ch-3. **3rd rnd:** Sl st in next dc and in next sp, ch 3, in same sp make dc, ch 2 and 2 dc (a starting shell). In each sp around make 2 dc, ch 2 and 2 dc (shell). Join. **4th rnd:** Sl st in next dc and in next sp, ch 3 and make a starting shell in same sp, (ch 2, shell over next shell) 11 times; ch 2. Join. **5th rnd:** Sl st in next dc and in next sp, ch 3 and make a starting shell over this starting shell, (ch 4, in sp of next shell make 2 dc, ch 5 and 2 dc; ch 4, shell over next shell) 5 times; ch 4, in next shell make 2 dc, ch 5 and 2 dc; ch 4. Join. **6th rnd:** Sl st in next dc and in next sp, * shell over shell, ch 3, 13 tr in next ch-5 loop, ch 3. Repeat from * around. Join. **7th rnd:** Sl st in next dc and in next sp, * shell over shell, ch 3, (tr in next tr, ch 1) 12 times; tr in next tr, ch 3. Repeat from * around. Join. **8th rnd:** Sl st in next dc and in next sp, * shell over shell, (ch 3, sc in next ch-1 sp) 12 times; ch 3. Repeat from * once more. In sp of next shell make (2 dc, ch 2) twice and 2 dc. ** (Ch 3, sc in next ch-1 sp) 12 times; ch 3, shell over shell. Repeat from ** 2 more times. Ch 2, 2 dc in same place as last shell, (ch 3, sc in next ch-1 sp) 12 times; ch 3. Join.

9th rnd: Sl st in next dc and in next sp, * shell over shell, ch 3, skip ch-3, sc in next loop, (ch 3, sc in next loop) 10 times; ch 3. Repeat from * once more; (shell in next ch-2 sp, ch 2) twice; ch 1 more, skip ch-3, sc in next loop. Work over remainder of rnd to correspond. **10th rnd:** Sl st in next dc and in next sp, * shell over shell, ch 3, skip ch-3, (sc in next loop, ch 3) 9 times; sc in next loop, ch 3. Repeat from * once more. Shell over shell,

7714

ch 2, shell in sp between shells, ch 2, shell over shell. Work over remainder of rnd to correspond, **making an increase, as before, directly opposite other increase. 11th rnd:** Sl st in next dc and in next sp, * shell over shell, ch 3, skip ch-3, sc in next loop, (ch 3, sc in next loop) 8 times; ch 3. Repeat from * once more. Shell over shell, (ch 3, shell over shell) twice; ch 3 and work over remainder of rnd to correspond. **12th rnd:** Shell over shell, * ch 3, skip next ch 3, sc in next loop, (ch 3, sc in next loop) 7 times; ch 3, in sp of next shell make (2 dc, ch 2) twice and 2 dc; ch 3, skip ch-3, sc in next loop, (ch 3, sc in next loop) 7 times; ch 3, shell over shell, ch 4, in sp of next shell make 2 dc, ch 5, and 2 dc; ch 4, shell over shell, ch 3, skip next ch 3, sc in next loop, (ch 3, sc in next loop) 7 times; ch 3, in sp of next shell make (2 dc, ch 2) twice and 2 dc. Repeat from * once more, but ending with 2 dc in same place as 1st shell, ch 2. Join.

Now work pineapples individually as fol-lows: **1st row:** Sl st in next dc and in sp, ch 3 and complete shell in same sp as last sl st, ch 3, skip next ch-3, make 6 loops across pineapple, ch 3, shell in next ch-2 sp. Ch 4, turn. **2nd row:** Shell over shell, ch 3, make 5 loops across pineapple, ch 3, shell over shell. Ch 4, turn. Repeat the 2nd row, making 1 loop less on each row until 1 loop remains. Ch 4, turn. **Next row:** Shell over shell, ch 4, sc in loop, ch 4, 2 dc in next shell, ch 1, sl st in sp of last complete shell, ch 1, 2 dc in same place as last 2 dc were made, ch 4, turn, sc in joining of shells. Break off.

Attach thread to next ch-2 sp on 12th rnd following pineapple just completed and work as follows: **1st row:** Shell in same sp as thread was attached, ch 3, skip the next ch 3, make 6 loops across pineapple, ch 3, shell over shell, ch 3, 13 tr in next ch-5 sp, ch 3, shell over shell, ch 3, make 6 loops across next pineapple, ch 3, shell in next ch-2 sp. Ch 4, turn. **2nd row:** Shell over shell, ch 3, make 5 loops across pineapple, ch 3, shell over shell, ch 3, (tr in next tr, ch 1) 12 times; tr in next tr; ch 3, shell over shell, ch 3, make 5 loops across pineapple, ch-3, shell over shell. Ch 4, turn. **3rd row:** Shell over shell, ch 3, make 4 loops across pineapple, ch 3, shell over shell, (ch 3, sc in next ch-! sp) 12 times; ch 3, shell over shell, ch 3, make 4 loops across pineapple, ch 3, shell over shell. Ch 4, turn. **4th row:** Shell over shell, ch 3, make 3 loops across pineapple, ch 3, in sp of next shell make (2 dc, ch 2) twice and 2 dc; ch 3, skip next ch 3, sc in loop, make 10 loops across pineapple, ch 3, in sp of next shell make (2 dc, ch 2) twice and 2 dc; ch 3, make 3 loops across pineapple, ch 3, shell over shell. Ch 4, turn. **5th row:** Shell over shell, ch 3, make 2

loops across pineapple, ch 3, shell over **next** ch-2 sp. Ch 4, turn and complete this pineapple as before. Complete other 2 pineapples in the same way. Complete other half of **doily** to correspond.

EDGING . . . 1st rnd: Attach thread to a ch-4 loop at tip of any pineapple, ch 3 and in same loop complete a shell, * ch 3, shell in next turning ch-4 loop. Repeat from * around, ending with dc in top of starting chain. **2nd rnd:** Sl st under the dc just made, sc in same **sp,** * ch 3, in sp of next shell make dc, ch 3, sc in 3rd ch from hook (a picot made) and dc. Ch 3, sc in next sp between shells. Repeat from * around, ending with ch 3, sl st in 1st sc made. Break off.

7592

7592 . . . Materials: BEST SIX CORD MERCERIZED CROCHET, Size 30: *7 balls of White or Ecru . . . Steel Crochet Hook No. 10 or 11.*

Tablecloth measures 41 inches in diameter.

Ch 15, join with sl st to form a ring. **1st rnd:** Ch 4, 43 tr in ring, sl st in top of ch-4. **2nd rnd:** Ch 5, * tr in next tr, ch 1. Repeat from * around, ch 1. Join. **3rd rnd:** Ch 6, * tr in next tr, ch 2. Repeat from * around, ch 2. Join. **4th rnd:** Sl st in next ch, sc in sp, * ch 4, sc in next sp. Repeat from * around, ending with ch 1, dc in 1st sc made. **5th, 6th and 7th rnds:** * Ch 4, sc in next loop. Repeat from * around, ending with ch 1, dc in dc. **8th rnd:** Sl st in loop just made, ch 4, tr in same loop, * ch 3, 2 tr in next loop. Repeat from * around. Join. **9th rnd:** Sl st in next tr and in next sp, ch 3, in same sp make dc, ch 2 and 2 dc (shell made); in each sp around make a shell of 2 dc, ch 2 and 2 dc. Join. **10th rnd:** Sl st in next dc and in next sp, ch 3 and complete a shell as before (shell over shell), * ch 1, shell in sp of each of next 2 shells. Repeat from * around. Join. **11th rnd:** Sl st in next dc and in next sp, ch 3 and complete shell as before, * ch 1, shell over next shell. Repeat from * around. Join. **12th rnd:** Make shell over shell, increasing 1 ch in every other ch bar between shells. Join. **13th rnd:** Make shell over shell, increasing 1 ch in all remaining ch bars (where no increases were made on previous rnd). Repeat 12th and 13th rnds alternately until 30th rnd is completed (there are 22 ch-11 bars and 22 ch-10 bars between shells on 30th rnd). **31st rnd:** Sl st in next dc and in next sp, ch 3, dc in same sp, ch 5, 2 dc in same sp, * ch 11, shell over next shell, ch 11, in sp of next shell make 2 dc, ch 5 and 2 dc. Repeat from * around. Join.

32nd rnd: Sl st in next dc and in next sp, ch 4, 14 tr in same sp; * ch 7, shell over shell, ch 7, 15 tr in sp of next shell. Repeat from * around. Join. **33rd rnd:** Ch 5, * (tr in next tr, ch 1) 13 times; tr in next tr, ch 5, shell over shell, ch 5, tr in next tr, ch 1. Repeat from * around. Join to 4th st of ch-5. **34th rnd:** Sc in sp, * (ch 3, sc in next sp) 13 times; ch 5, shell over shell, ch 5, sc in next ch-1 sp. Repeat from * around. Join last ch-5 to 1st sc made. **35th rnd:** Sl st in next ch, sc in loop, * (ch 3, sc in next loop) 12 times; ch 5, shell over shell, ch 5, sc in next ch-3 loop. Repeat from * around. Join. **36th rnd:** Sl st in next ch, sc in loop, * (ch 3, sc in next loop) 11 times; ch 5, in sp of next shell make (2 dc, ch 2) twice and 2 dc; ch 5, sc in next ch-3 loop. Repeat from * around. Join. **37th rnd:** * (Ch 3, sc in next loop) 10 times; ch 5, shell in 1st ch-2 sp, ch 3, shell in next ch-2 sp, ch 5, sc in next ch-3 loop. Repeat from * around. Join. **38th rnd:** * (Ch 3, sc in next loop) 9 times; ch 5, shell over shell, ch 1, shell in ch-3 sp (this starts stem of 2nd rnd of pineapples); ch 1, shell over shell, ch 5, sc in next ch-3 loop. Repeat from * around. Join. **39th rnd:** * (Ch 3, sc in next loop) 8 times; ch 5, shell over shell, (ch 2, shell over shell) twice; ch 5, sc in next loop. Repeat from * around. Join.

40th rnd: * (Ch 3, sc in next loop) 7 times; ch 5, shell over next shell, (ch 4, shell over next shell) twice; ch 5, sc in next loop. Repeat from * around. Join. **41st rnd:** * (Ch 3, sc in next loop) 6 times; ch 5, shell over shell, ch 6, in sp of next shell make 2 dc, ch 5 and 2 dc; ch 6, shell over shell, ch 5, sc in the next loop. Repeat from * around. Join. **42nd rnd:** * (Ch 3, sc in next loop) 5 times; ch 5, shell over shell, ch 5, 15 tr in sp of next shell, ch 5, shell in next shell, ch 5, sc in next loop. Repeat from * around. Join. **43rd rnd:** * (Ch 3, sc in next loop) 4 times; ch 5, shell over shell, ch 5, (tr in next tr, ch 1) 14 times; tr in next tr, ch 5, shell over shell, ch 5, sc in next loop. Repeat from * around. Join. **44th rnd:** * (Ch 3, sc in next loop) 3 times; ch 5, shell over shell, ch 5, sc in 1st ch-1 sp, (ch 4, sc in next sp) 13 times; ch 5, shell over shell; ch 5, sc in next loop. Repeat from * around. Join. **45th rnd:** * (Ch 3, sc in next loop) twice; ch 5, shell over shell, ch 5, sc in next loop, make 12 ch-4 loops, ch 5, shell over shell, ch 5, sc in next loop. Repeat from * around. Join. **46th rnd:** Sc in next loop, * ch 3, sc in next loop, ch 5, shell over shell, ch 5, sc in next ch-4 loop, (ch 4, sc in next loop) 11 times; ch 5, shell over shell, ch 5, sc in next loop. Repeat from * around. Join.

Any extra fullness will be taken care of in 5th rnd of pineapples and in the blocking of completed cloth.

47th rnd: Sl st in next ch, sc in loop, * ch 5, shell over shell, ch 5, sc in next ch-4 loop,

7592-M

make 10 ch-4 loops—**hereafter all loops on pineapples will be ch-4 loops;** ch 5, shell over shell, ch 5, sc in next loop. Repeat from * around. Join. **48th rnd:** Ch 5, * shell over shell, ch 5, work ch-4 loops across pineapple, ch 5, shell over shell, ch 1, tr in next sc, ch 1. Repeat from * around. Join last ch-1 to 4th st of ch-5. **49th rnd:** Ch 3, in same place as sl st make dc, ch 2 and 2 dc (shell made)—this starts stem of 3rd rnd of pineapples; ch 2, * shell over shell, work across pineapple as before, shell over shell, ch 2, shell in tr, ch 2. Repeat from * around. Join. **50th rnd:** Sl st in next dc and in next sp, ch 3 and complete shell as before, ch 3, shell over shell, * work across pineapple, shell over shell, (ch 3, shell over shell) twice. Repeat from * around. Join. **51st rnd:** Shell over shell, ch 5, shell over shell and continue in pattern around. Join. **52nd rnd:** Sl st to sp, ch 3, dc in same sp, ch 5, 2 dc in same sp, ch 7, shell over shell and continue in pattern around. Join. **53rd rnd:** Sl st to sp, ch 4, 17 tr in same sp (this is base of 3rd rnd of pineapples); * ch 5, shell over shell, work across pineapples, shell over shell, ch 5, 18 tr in loop of next shell. Repeat from * around. Join.

Work in pattern as established, making stem for 4th rnd of pineapples exactly as stem for 3rd rnd of pineapples was made and until 3rd rnd of stem is completed. **Next rnd:** Work across pineapple, shell over shell, (ch 7, shell over shell) twice; and continue in pattern around. **Following rnd:** Work across pineapple, shell over shell, ch 9, in sp of next shell make 2 dc, ch 5 and 2 dc; ch 9, shell over shell and continue in pattern around. **Next rnd:** Work across pineapples, shell over shell, ch 5, 21 tr in ch-5 loop of next shell, ch 5 and continue in pattern around.

Continue in pattern as before until 4th rnd of stem of next (5th) rnd of pineapples is com-

185

pleted. **Next rnd:** Same as previous rnd but working ch 9 on each side of stem shell. **Following rnd:** Sl st to sp, ch 4, tr in same sp, ch 7, 2 tr in same sp, * ch 7, shell over shell, work across pineapple, shell over shell, in sp of next shell make 2 tr, ch 7 and 2 tr. Repeat from * around. Join. **Next rnd:** Sl st to sp, ch 5, 23 d tr in same sp, ch 5, shell over shell and continue in pattern around, making 24 d tr for each pineapple of 5th rnd. Join. **Following rnd:** Ch 6, make (d tr in next d tr, ch 1) 22 times; d tr in last d tr, ch 5 and continue in pattern around. Join to 5th st of ch-6.

Continue in pattern, working 6th rnd of pineapples exactly the same as 5th rnd of pineapples until 2nd rnd of d tr's (of 6th rnd of pineapples) is completed. Now continue to work ch-4 loops as before on 5th pineapple but work ch-5 loops on 6th pineapple until 5th pineapple is completed (there are 14 loops on each pineapple of 6th rnd).

To Make Points: Sl st to sp of next shell. **1st row:** Ch 3 and complete shell as before, ch 5, work across pineapple, ch 5, shell over shell, ch 5, turn. **2nd row:** Shell over shell, ch 5, work across pineapple, ch 5, shell over shell, ch 5, turn. Repeat the 2nd row until 1 loop remains on pineapple. Ch 5, turn. **Next row:** Shell over shell, ch 4, sc in loop, ch 4, 2 dc in next shell, ch 1, sl st back in ch-2 of last shell, ch 1, 2 dc where last 2 dc were made. Break off. Attach thread to sp of shell on next pineapple; complete point in same manner. Continue thus until all points have been completed.

EDGING . . . 1st rnd: Attach thread to tip of one point where shells were joined, ch 3, at base of ch-3 make dc, ch 2 and 2 dc. * (Ch 3, shell in next turning chain between 2 rows) 7 times; ch 2, then holding back on hook the last loop of each dc, make dc in sp of shell (preceding ch 5 on last complete rnd of tablecloth) and dc in sp of next shell (where thread was attached to work next point); thread over and draw through all loops on hook, (ch 3, shell in turning chain between 2 rows) 7 times; ch 3, shell at tip of next point where shells were joined. Repeat from * around. Join last ch-3 to top of starting chain. **2nd rnd:** Sl st in next dc and in next sp, ch 8, sc in 5th ch from hook (picot made). Dc in same place as sl st, * ch 3, sc under next ch-3, ch 3, in next shell make dc, p and dc. Repeat from * 6 more

times; ch 3, sc in tip of joined dc's, ch 3, in next shell make dc, p and dc, ch 3, sc under next ch-3. Continue thus around. Break off.

7592-M . . . Materials: KNIT-CRO-SHEEN, *16 balls . . . Steel Crochet Hook No. 3.*

Tablecloth measures 72 inches in diameter.

Work exactly as for Tablecloth 7592.

7570 . . . Materials: BEST SIX CORD MERCERIZED CROCHET, *Size 30: 3 balls . . . Steel Crochet Hook No. 10.*

Large Doily measures 14 x 19 inches; Small Doily 10 x 13½ inches.

LARGE DOILY—First Motif . . . Starting at center, ch 10. Join. **1st rnd:** Ch 4, 27 tr in ring. Sl st in 4th st of ch-4. **2nd rnd:** Sc in same place as sl st, * ch 5, skip 1 tr, sc in next tr. Repeat from * around, ending with ch 1, tr in 1st sc made. **3rd rnd:** Sl st in loop formed by ch-1 and tr, ch 4, holding back on hook the last loop of each tr make 3 tr in same loop, thread over and draw through all loops on hook—a 3-tr cluster made—(ch 7, 4 tr-cluster in next loop) 13 times, ch 7. Join. Break off.

Second Motif . . . Repeat first 2 rnds of First Motif. **3rd rnd:** Sl st in last loop made, ch 4 and make 4 tr-cluster in same loop, (ch 3, sc in loop of First Motif, ch 3, cluster in next loop of Second Motif) twice. Complete as for First Motif (no more joinings). Break off.

Third Motif . . . Work exactly as Second Motif, joining to Second Motif as Second Motif was joined to First Motif, having 5 free loops between joinings.

Large Pineapple . . . Attach thread to 6th free loop on Third Motif counting from joining. Sc in same loop, ch 15, sc in next loop. Ch 4, turn. **1st row:** 29 tr in ch-15 loop. Ch 5, turn. **2nd row:** (Tr in next tr, ch 1) 28 times; tr in top of turning chain. Ch 6, turn. **3rd row:** (Tr in next tr, ch 2) 28 times; skip 1 ch, tr in next ch. Ch 10, turn. **4th row:** (Sc in next sp, ch 5) 27 times; sc in last sp. Ch 10, turn. **5th row:** * Sc in next loop, ch 5. Repeat from * across (do not make an sc in ch-10 loop). Ch 10, turn. Repeat 5th row until 1 loop remains. Ch 10, turn and make sc in last loop. Break off. At-

tach thread to 6th free loop on First Motif and make another Large Pineapple as before.

Medium Pineapple . . . 1st row: Attach thread to center free loop on center motif, ch 4, 24 tr in same loop. Ch 5, turn. **2nd row:** (Tr in next tr, ch 1) 23 times; tr in top of turning chain. Ch 6, turn. **3rd row:** (Tr in next tr, ch 2) 23 times; skip 1, ch, tr in next ch. Ch 5, sl st in free loop (next to joining) on end motif. Ch 5, turn. **4th row:** (Sc in next sp, ch 5) 22 times; sc in last sp. Ch 5, sl st in free loop (next to joining) on end motif. Ch 5, turn. **5th row:** * Sc in next loop, ch 5. Repeat from * across. Ch 10, turn. Complete this Pineapple as other Pineapples were completed. Break off. Make another Medium Pineapple directly opposite this one.

EDGING . . . 1st rnd: Attach thread to ch-10 loop at right of tip of Large Pineapple, ch 5, then, holding back on hook the last loop of each d tr make 2 d tr in same loop, thread over

and draw through all loops on hook (cluster made); ch 7, make a 3-d tr cluster in same loop, ch 7, in next ch-10 loop make cluster, ch 7 and cluster, * ch 7, cluster in next ch-10 loop. Repeat from * to last ch-10 loop on this pineapple, ch 10, sc in last ch-10 loop, ch 3, 3-tr cluster in 3rd loop of end motif, ch 3, sc in first ch-10 loop of Small Pineapple, ch 5, sl st in last ch-10 loop made on Large Pineapple, ch 5, make a d tr-cluster in next ch-10 loop on Small Pineapple, ** ch 7, cluster in next ch-10 loop. Repeat from ** around, making the tip of each pineapple to correspond with the first pineapple and working between pineapples as before. Join. **2nd rnd:** Sl st in next 3 ch, sc in sp, (ch 10, sc in next sp) 14 times; ch 3, sc in 1st free ch-7 loop on next pineapple, ch 5, sl st in last ch-10 loop made, ch 5, sc in next ch-7 loop on Small Pineapple, ch 10, sc in next ch-7 loop and continue thus around. Join. **3rd rnd:** Sl st in next 5 ch, sc in

187

loop, (ch 13, sc in next loop) 12 times; ch 13, sc in next free ch-10 loop (on Small Pineapple), ch 13, sc in next loop and continue thus around. Join. **4th rnd:** Sl st in next 6 ch, sc in loop, (ch 15, sc in next loop) 11 times; ch 7, sc in next sp (between pineapples), ch 7, sc in next loop (on Small Pineapple), ch 15, sc in next loop and continue thus around. Join. **5th rnd:** Sl st in next 7 ch, sc in loop, (ch 15, sc in next loop) 10 times; ch 5 and complete a d tr cluster in last sc made, make another 3-d tr cluster in center st of next ch-15 loop (on Small Pineapple), ch 5, and complete a cluster in tip of clusters, sl st in center of last ch-15 loop made on Large Pineapple, (ch 15, cluster in same place as last cluster) twice; d tr in same place as 2nd cluster, ch 7, sc in next ch-15 loop on Small Pineapple, ch 15, sc in next loop and continue thus around. Join and break off.

SMALL DOILY (Make 2) . . . Make one motif as for Large Doily. Then make 2 pineapples same as Medium Pineapples of Large Doily on each side of motif, having 6 free loops between pineapples.

Small Pineapple . . . Skip 2 loops on motif, at-tach thread to next loop, ch 7, sc in next loop. Ch 4, turn. **1st row:** 11 tr in loop. Ch 5, turn. Complete pineapple as before, joining the first ch-10 loop on each side to 2nd row of Medium Pineapple. Make another Small Pineapple motif directly opposite previous one. Join.

EDGING . . . **1st rnd:** Work as for 1st rnd of Large Doily to within last free ch-10 loop of Medium Pineapple, ch 10, sc in next loop, sc in first ch-10 loop of Small Pineapple, ch 5, sl st in last ch-10 loop made on Medium Pineapple, ch 5, cluster in next ch-10 loop on Small Pineapple, ch 7 and continue thus around, making the tip of each pineapple to correspond with the first pineapple and working between pineapples as before. Join. **2nd rnd:** Sl st in next 3 ch, sc in sp, (ch 10, sc in next sp) 11 times; ch 10, sc in 1st free ch-7 loop on Small Pineapple and continue thus around. Join. **3rd rnd:** Sl st in next 5 ch, sc in loop and make ch-13 loops around. Join. **4th and 5th rnds:** Sl st in each ch to center of loop, sc in loop, (ch 15, sc in next loop) 10 times; sc in next loop, ch 15 and continue thus around. Join. Break off at end of 5th rnd. Starch and press.

CHAPTER THIRTEEN

Filet

IF YOU want your home to reflect a gracious personality, you will appreciate the exquisite delicacy of filet. There is an elegance about filet that makes it a four-star favorite with women who prize the luxurious. There is nothing more suitable for grand occasions, nothing with a more dressed-for-dinner look than a filet tablecloth in a lovely formal pattern. What a flattering background it makes for your best china and silver, for the glow of candlelight, and yet how eloquently it speaks of a home presided over by a woman of taste and discernment.

Beautiful enough for the most festive occasions, the square-a-day cloth on page 200 is guaranteed to make a holiday bird more impressive, an anniversary gathering more memorable. There's a luncheon set, a rose runner, a rarely beautiful ivy leaf doily, a bread tray doily among some household accessories we've gathered for lovers of fine filet.

7598

7598 . . . **Materials:** Best Six Cord Mercerized Crochet, *Size 30: 7 balls* . . . *Steel Crochet Hook No. 10 or 11.*

Centerpiece measures about 14½ inches square; place doily 12½ inches square; bread and butter doily 8 inches square and glass doily 6 inches square.

GAUGE: 5 sps make 1 inch; 5 rows make 1 inch.

CENTERPIECE . . . Starting at bottom of chart, make a chain 18 inches long (16 ch sts to 1 inch). **1st row:** Dc in 8th ch from hook, * ch 2, skip 2 ch, dc in next ch. Repeat from * across until there are 72 sps. Cut off remaining chain. Ch 5, turn. **2nd row:** Dc in next dc (sp over sp made); (ch 2, dc in next dc) 25 times; 2 dc in next sp, dc in next dc (bl over sp made); make 5 more bls, 8 sps, 6 bls, 25 sps, ch 2, skip 2 sts of turning chain, dc in next ch. Ch 5, turn. **3rd row:** Make 25 sps, 1 bl, dc in 18 dc (6 bls over 6 bls made); make 1 more

PLACE DOILY

START HERE

There are 10 spaces between heavy lines

GLASS DOILY

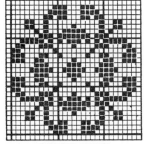

START HERE

BREAD AND BUTTER DOILY

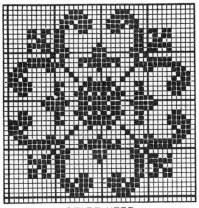

START HERE

CENTERPIECE

START HERE

7131

bl, 6 sps, 8 bls, 25 sps. Ch 5, turn. **4th row:** 24 sps, 10 bls, 4 sps, 10 bls, 24 sps. Ch 5, turn. **5th row:** 23 sps, 5 bls, (ch 2, skip 2 dc, dc in next dc) twice (2 sps over 2 bls made); 4 bls, 4 sps, 4 bls, 2 sps, 5 bls, 23 sps. Ch 5, turn. Starting with 6th row, follow chart to top. Do not break off, but work sc all around, keeping work flat. Break off.

PLACE DOILY (Make 4) . . . Starting at bottom of chart, make a chain 15 inches long. **1st row:** Work as for 1st row of Centerpiece until there are 62 sps. Cut off remaining chain. Ch 5, turn. Starting with 2nd row, follow chart to top. Do not break off but work sc all around, keeping work flat. Break off.

BREAD and BUTTER DOILY (Make 4) . . . Starting at bottom of chart, make a chain 10 inches long. **1st row:** Work as for 1st row of Centerpiece until there are 41 sps. Cut off remaining chain. Ch 5, turn. Starting with 2nd row, follow chart to top. Do not break off but work sc around, keeping work flat. Break off.

GLASS DOILY (Make 4) . . . Starting at bottom of chart, make a chain 8 inches long. **1st**

row: Work as for 1st row of Centerpiece until there are 29 sps. Cut off remaining chain. Ch 5, turn. Starting with 2nd row, follow chart to top. Do not break off but work sc around, keeping work flat. Break off.

7131 . . . **Materials:** THREE CORD MERCERIZED CROCHET, *Size 50: 1 ball . . . Steel Crochet Hook No. 12.*

Bread tray doily measures about 6½ x 11½ inches.

GAUGE: 7 sps make 1 inch; 7 rows make 1 inch.

Starting at short side, ch 56 (to measure about 2¾ inches). **1st row:** Dc in 8th ch from hook, * ch 2, skip 2 ch, dc in next ch. Repeat from * across (17 sps). Ch 5, turn. **2nd row:** * Dc in next dc, ch 2. Repeat from * across, ending with ch 2, skip 2 sts of turning chain, dc in next ch (17 sps over 17 sps). Ch 5, turn. **3rd row:** Make 4 sps, 2 dc in next sp, dc in next dc (bl over sp), 7 sps, 1 bl, 4 sps. Ch 5, turn. **4th row:** Make 4 sps, dc in next 3 dc (bl over bl), make 8 more bls, 4 sps. Ch 5, turn.

5th row: Make 4 sps, 1 bl, ch 2, skip 2 dc, dc in next dc (sp over bl), make 2 more sps, 1 bl, 3 sps, 1 bl, 4 sps. Ch 5, turn. Hereafter follow chart to top row, then work 2 rows of sps.

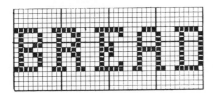

Now work as follows: Sl st across 1st sp, ch 3, 2 dc in next sp, dc in next dc, make sp over sp to within 2 sps from end, 1 bl, turn (2 sps are decreased). Repeat last row until 3 sps remain, then sl st across to last dc of 1st bl, ch 3, * 2 dc in sp, dc in next dc. Repeat from * 2 more times. Break off. Attach thread at opposite short side and work to correspond. Attach thread to dc of bl of 1st decrease row and make 3 dc, ch 2 and 3 dc in corner sp, * dc in next dc, 2 dc in sp. Repeat from * across to 1st decrease row at opposite end and make 3 dc, ch 2 and 3 dc in corner sp, sl st to next dc. Break off. Work other side to correspond, but do not break off.

Now work as follows: **1st rnd:** Ch 5, * sc at tip of ch-3 or dc (as the case may be) of 1st bl on next row, ch 5. Repeat from * 5 more times, ch 5, sc in center dc of 3 bls, ch 5, sc in last dc of same 3 bls. Then make six ch-5 loops as before along next side, ch 5, sc in ch-2 loop, ** ch 5, skip 4 sc, sc in next sc. Repeat from ** across to next ch-2 loop; then work other half of rnd to correspond with first half. Join with sl st. **2nd rnd:** Sl st in each of next 2 ch, ch 5, dc in same loop, * ch 2, 5 sc in next loop, ch 2; in next loop make dc, ch 2 and dc. Repeat from * around, ending rnd with 5 sc in last loop, ch 2. Join with sl st to 3rd st of ch-5 first made. **3rd rnd:** Sl st in ch-2 sp, ch 5, dc in same sp, ch 3, * skip 1 sc, sc in each of next 4 sc, ch 3; in next ch-2 sp make dc, ch 2 and dc; ch 3. Repeat from * around. Join last ch-3 with sl st to 3rd st of ch-5 first made. **4th, 5th, and 6th rnds:** Work as for 3rd rnd, making 1 sc less in each sc-group and 1 ch more in each ch-loop in each rnd, but always making ch-2 between 2 dc in each rnd. Join. **7th rnd:** Sl st in ch-2 sp, ch 5, dc in same sp, * ch 7, sc in sc, ch 7, in next ch-2 sp make dc, ch 2 and dc. Repeat from * around. **8th rnd:** Same as 7th

rnd, but make ch-8 instead of ch-7. **9th rnd:** Sl st in ch-2 sp, ch 3, 2 dc in same place, ch 2, 3 dc in same place, ch 8, * sc in next sc, ch 8; in next ch-2 sp make 3 dc, ch 2 and 3 dc; ch 8. Repeat from * around. Join and break off.

7599 . . . Materials: BEST SIX CORD MER-CERIZED CROCHET, *Size 20: 5 balls of White or Ecru . . . Steel Crochet Hook No. 8 or 9.*

Runner measures about 21 x 46 inches.

GAUGE: 9 sps make 2 inches; 9 rows make 2 inches.

Starting at bottom of chart, ch 42. **1st row:** Dc in 4th ch from hook and in each ch across (40 dc, counting the turning chain as 1 dc).

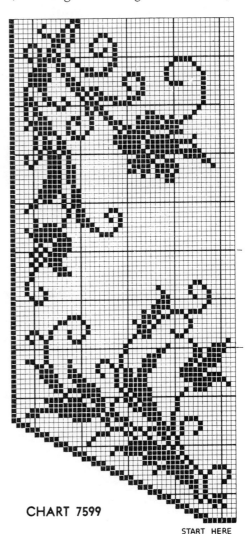

CHART 7599

START HERE

7599

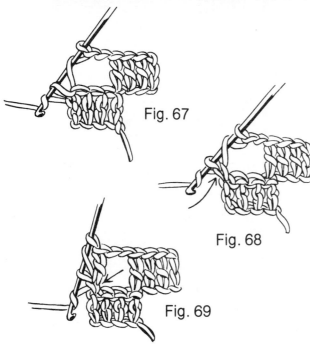

Fig. 67

Fig. 68

Fig. 69

Ch 8, turn. **2nd row:** Dc in 4th ch from hook and in next 4 ch, dc in next dc (2 bls increased at beginning of row), dc in next 3 dc (bl made over bl), ch 2, skip 2 dc, dc in next dc (sp made over bl). Make 10 more sps, then work dc in next 2 dc, make a foundation dc in top of turning chain as follows: Thread over, insert hook in ch and pull loop through, Fig. 67; thread over and draw through 1 loop on hook —*ch st made to be used as a foundation st for next dc*, Fig. 68; (thread over and draw through 2 loops) twice—*foundation dc completed*. * Thread over, insert hook in specified ch st, Fig. 69, and complete another foundation dc as before. Repeat from * 4 more times; then thread over, insert hook in ch at base of last foundation dc and make 1 dc in usual way (2 bls increased at end of row). Ch 8, turn. **3rd row:** Dc in 4th ch from hook and in next 4 ch, dc in next 4 dc, work 15 sps, dc in next 2 dc, work 6 foundation dc

194

and 1 dc in usual way (2 bls increased at each end of row as before). Ch 8, turn. **4th row:** Inc 2 bls, then work 1 bl, 5 sps, 2 dc in next sp, dc in next dc (bl made over sp), 1 sp, 1 bl, 3 sps, 1 bl, 1 sp, 1 bl, 5 sps, 1 bl, inc 2 bls. Ch 8, turn. Starting with 5th row, follow chart to 21st row incl. Chart shows one quarter of design. To make second half of each row, do not repeat center sp or bl, as the case may be, but work back. Ch 5 to turn at end of 21st row. **22nd row:** Dc in 4th ch from hook and in next ch (1 bl increased), then follow chart across, increasing only 1 bl at end of row. Ch 3, turn. **23rd row:** Dc in next 3 dc and follow chart across (no increases). Ch 3, turn. Starting with 24th row, follow chart to top. This completes one half of runner. Do not repeat top row, but reverse chart and work back to the 1st row. Break off.

7630 . . . Materials: THREE CORD MERCERIZED CROCHET, *Size 50: 2 balls of White or Ecru . . . Steel Crochet Hook No. 12.*

GAUGE: 9 sps make 2 inches; 9 rows make 2 inches.

Doily measures about 18 inches in diameter.

LEFT SCALLOP . . . Starting at bottom, ch

28. **1st row:** Tr in 5th ch from hook, tr in next 23 ch. Ch 11, turn. **2nd row:** Tr in 5th ch from hook, tr in next 6 ch (2 bls increased), tr in next 5 tr (bl over bl made), (ch 3, skip 3 tr, tr in next tr) 4 times (4 sps over 4 bls made); tr in next 3 tr, then make a foundation tr as follows: Thread over hook twice, insert hook in top st of turning chain and pull loop through, see Fig. 67; thread over and draw through 1 loop—*1 ch st made to be used as a foundation st for next tr*, see Fig. 68—complete tr in usual manner. Make 7 more foundation tr, see Fig. 69, and 1 tr in usual way (2 bls increased). Ch 11, turn. **3rd row:** Inc 2 bls as on last row, make 1 bl, 2 sps, (ch 3, tr in next tr) 4 times (4 sps made over 4 sps); make 2 more sps, 1 bl, inc 2 bls as on last row. Break off.

CENTER SCALLOP . . . Starting at bottom, ch 24. **1st row:** Tr in 5th ch from hook, tr in next 19 ch. Ch 15, turn. **2nd row:** Inc 3 bls, make 1 bl, 3 sps, 1 bl, inc 3 bls. Ch 11, turn. **3rd row:** Inc 2 bls, make 1 bl, 9 sps, 1 bl, inc 2 bls. Ch 11, turn. **4th row:** Inc 2 bls, make 1 bl, 6 sps, ch 1, skip 1 ch, tr in next ch, ch 1, tr in next tr (shadow sp over sp made, Fig. 70); make 1 more shadow sp, 5 sps, 1 bl, inc 2

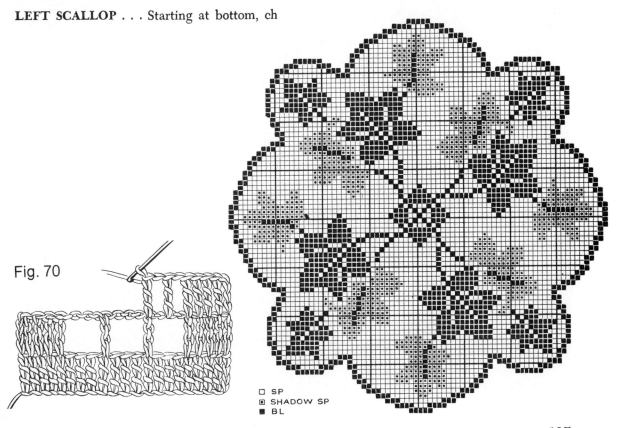

Fig. 70

☐ SP
▣ SHADOW SP
■ BL

195

7630

bls. Ch 11, turn. **5th row:** Inc 2 bls, make 1 bl, 6 sps, 1 shadow sp, (ch 1, tr in next tr) 4 times (2 shadow sps over 2 shadow sps made); make 1 more shadow sp, 7 sps, 1 bl, inc 2 bls. Ch 7, turn. **6th and 7th rows:** Follow chart. Ch 7, turn. **8th row:** Inc 1 bl, make 1 bl, 7 sps, 6 shadow sps, (tr in next ch-1, tr in next tr) twice (bl over shadow sp made); make 4 shadow sps, 7 sps, 1 bl, inc 1 bl. Ch 4, turn. **9th row:** Follow chart. Ch 7, turn. **10th row:** Inc 1 bl, make 1 bl, 10 sps, 4 shadow sps, 1 bl, 3 shadow sps, ch 3, skip 1 tr, tr in next tr (sp over shadow sp made); make 8 more sps, 1 bl, inc 1 bl. Ch 4, turn. **11th row:** Follow chart across. Ch 3, join with sl st in top st of turning chain on 3rd row of Left Scallop. Break off.

RIGHT SCALLOP . . . Work same as Left Scallop but do not break off at end of 3rd row. Ch 3, join with sl st in top st of turning chain on 11th row of Center Scallop. Break off.

To continue, attach thread in last tr on 3rd row of Left Scallop, ch 4, turn. **12th row:** Make 1 bl, 7 sps, 3 tr in next sp, tr in next tr (bl over sp made); make 4 sps, 1 bl, tr in each of the 3 sts of joining ch; make 1 bl, 12 sps, 3 shadow sps, 1 bl, 5 shadow sps, 8 sps, 1 bl, tr in each of the 3 sts of joining ch; make 1 bl, 12 sps, 1 bl. Ch 7, turn. **13th row:** Follow chart. Ch 4, turn. **14th row:** 1 bl, 2 sps, 7 bls, 16 sps, 6 shadow sps, (ch 1, skip 1 tr, tr in next tr) twice (shadow sp over bl made); make 1 bl, 1 shadow sp, 18 sps, 2 bls, 1 sp, 4 bls, 2 sps, 1 bl. Ch 7, turn. Now follow chart until 20th row is complete. Turn. **21st row:** Sl st in 4 tr, ch 4 and follow chart across (1 bl decreased at both ends). Now follow chart until 70th row is complete. Ch 4, turn and work Right Scallop as follows: **71st row:** 3 bls, 8 sps, 3 bls. Turn. **72nd row:** Sl st in 8 tr, ch 4 and complete row. Turn. **73rd row:** Sl st in 8 tr, ch 4 and complete row. Break off.

CENTER SCALLOP . . . Skip 3 tr, attach thread in next tr, ch 4, and finish scallop, following chart. Break off.

LEFT SCALLOP . . . Skip 3 tr, attach thread in next tr, ch 4, and finish scallop, following chart. Break off.

7616 . . . **Materials:** BEST SIX CORD MERCERIZED CROCHET, *Size 30: 14 balls* . . . *Steel Crochet Hook No. 9 or 10.*

GAUGE: 4 bls (16 tr) or 4 shadow sps make 1 inch; 4 rows make 1 inch.

Cloth measures 55 inches square.

Make a chain about 2 yards long (14 ch sts to 1 inch). **1st row:** Tr in 5th ch from hook, tr in next 15 ch (4 bls made), * (ch 1, skip 1 ch, tr in next ch) 8 times (4 shadow sps made); tr in next 16 tr (4 bls made). Repeat from * 26 more times. Cut off remaining chain. Ch 4, turn. **2nd, 3rd, and 4th rows:** Tr in next tr, tr in 15 tr (4 bls over 4 bls made); * (ch 1, tr in next tr) 8 times (4 shadow sps over 4 shadow sps made); tr in next 16 tr. Repeat from * across, making last tr of each row in top st of turning chain. Ch 4, turn. At end of 4th row, ch 5 and turn. **5th row:** (Skip 1 tr, tr in next tr, ch 1) 7 times; skip next tr, tr in next tr (4 shadow sps over 4 bls); * (ch 3, skip next tr, tr in next tr) 4 times (4 sps made over 4 shadow sps); (ch 1, skip next tr, tr in next tr) 8 times. Repeat from * across ending with ch 1, skip last tr, tr in top st of turning chain. Ch 5, turn. **6th, 7th, and 8th rows:** 4 shadow sps over 4 shadow sps, * (ch 3, tr in next tr) 4 times (4 sps over 4 sps); 4 shadow sps over 4 shadow sps. Repeat from * across. Ch 5, turn. At end of 8th row, ch 4 and turn. **9th row:** (Tr in next sp, tr in next tr) 8 times (4 bls over 4 shadow sps made); * (ch 1, skip 1 ch, tr in next ch, ch 1, tr in next tr) 4 times (4 shadow sps over 4 sps); (tr in next sp, tr in next tr) 8 times. Repeat from * across. Ch 4, turn. Repeat 3rd to 9th rows incl until 55 rows in all have been made. Break off.

FRINGE . . . Cut five 8-inch strands of thread. Double these strands forming a loop. Insert hook in a shadow sp at edge of cloth (starting chain edge) and pull loop through; then draw loose ends through loop and pull tight. Make a fringe in both holes of each shadow sp along this edge and opposite edge. Make 2 fringes in each shadow sp along remaining 2 edges (over the tr's or turning chains as the case may be). Trim fringe to length desired.

7616

7590

7590 . . . Materials: THREE CORD MERCER-IZED CROCHET, *Size 10: 35 balls* . . . *Steel Crochet Hook No. 5.*

GAUGE: 2 sps make 1 inch; 2 rows make 1 inch (when blocked). Each square measures about 19½ inches before blocking and about 20½ inches after blocking. Tablecloth measures about 64 x 85 inches.

SQUARE . . . Starting at center, ch 11, join with sl st. **1st rnd:** Ch 4 (to count as tr), 4 tr in ring, (ch 7, 5 tr in ring) 3 times; ch 7, join with sl st to 4th st of ch-4. **2nd rnd:** Ch 4, tr in 4 tr, * ch 3, skip 3 ch, in next ch make tr, ch 7 and tr, ch 3, tr in next 5 tr. Repeat from * 2 more times; ch 3, skip 3 ch, in next ch make tr, ch 7 and tr, ch 3, join to 4th st of first ch-4. **3rd rnd:** Ch 7, skip 3 tr, tr in next tr, * 3 tr in next sp, tr in next tr, in corner sp make 4 tr, ch 7 and 4 tr; tr in next tr, 3 tr in next sp, tr in next tr, ch 3, skip 3 tr, tr in next tr. Repeat from * around. Join. **4th rnd:** Ch 7, * dc in 9 tr, in corner sp make 4 tr, ch 7 and 4 tr; tr in 9 tr, ch 3. Repeat from * around. Join. **5th to 20th rnds incl:** Continue in this manner following chart, making ch-3 for sps and ch-7 for each corner sp, joining each rnd with sl st. The heavy line on chart shows where each rnd begins. At end of 20th rnd, join and break off. Make 3 x 4 squares and sew together on wrong side with over-and-over sts.

EDGING . . . **1st rnd:** Attach thread to a tr, ch 4 and work tr in each tr; in the sps make 2 tr and 3 tr alternately. Work corners same as corners of last rnd of square. Join. **2nd and 3rd rnds:** Ch 4, tr in each tr around, making corners as before. Break off.

CHAPTER FOURTEEN

Irish Crochet

WAY BACK in 1743, Irish crochet was winning handwork prizes. Today, connoisseurs still consider it one of the loveliest designs in the crochet family.

As a decorative accessory, Irish crochet is extraordinarily versatile. Even a small amount used as a trimming—either as an edging or insertion—can transform a counterpane into a notable beauty, give an everyday tablecloth party manners. Curtains, pillow shams, dressing-table skirts—any number of household items—acquire new personalities when treated to an Irish edging.

Nowadays it is a fashion favorite as well. You'll find Irish crochet insertions featured on dresses that sell for fabulous prices. It is used on blouses, on nightgowns, on children's clothes, lending always a note of distinctive beauty to whatever it touches.

8337

8268

8337 . . . **Materials:** THREE CORD MERCERIZED CROCHET, *Size 50* . . . *Steel Crochet Hook No. 12.*

EDGING—First Motif . . . Starting at center, ch 6. Join with sl st, Fig. 71. **1st rnd:** Ch 1, 12 sc in ring, sl st in 1st sc, Fig. 72. **2nd rnd:** Ch 1, sc in same place as sl st, * ch 5, skip next sc, sc in next sc. Repeat from * around, joining last ch-5 with sl st in 1st sc. **3rd rnd:** In each loop make sc, half dc, 3 dc, half dc and sc, Fig. 73. Join. **4th rnd:** Ch 1, sc in same place as sl st, * ch 5, sc between next 2 sc. Repeat from * around. Join. **5th rnd:** In each loop make sc, half dc, 5 dc, half dc and sc. Join. **6th rnd:** Ch 1, sc in same place as sl st, * (ch 5, sc in 3rd ch from hook) twice; ch 2 (p-loop made), sc between next 2 sc. Repeat from * around. Join. **7th rnd:** Ch 1, sc in same place as sl st, * make a p-loop, sc between p's of next p-loop, make a p-loop, sc in next sc between petals, (ch 5, sc between p's of next loop, ch 5, sc in next sc between petals) twice. Repeat from * once more. Join and break off.

Second Motif . . . Work same as First Motif until 6th rnd is complete. **7th rnd:** Ch 5, sc in 3rd ch from hook, ch 1, sc between p's of corresponding p-loop on First Motif, ch 4, sc in 3rd ch from hook, ch 2, sc between p's of next p-loop on Second Motif, ch 5, sc in 3rd ch from hook, ch 1, sc between p's of next p-loop on First Motif, ch 4, sc in 3rd ch from hook, ch 2, sc in sc between petals on Second Motif, ch 5, sc between p's of next p-loop on Second Motif and complete rnd as on First Motif. Break off.

Make necessary number of motifs, joining them as Second Motif was joined to First Motif.

HEADING . . . Attach thread after 2nd p of 2nd p-loop at end of piece and work along one long edge as follows: **1st row:** Ch 10, dc in next ch-5 loop, * (ch 3, sc in next loop) twice; ch 3, dc in next loop, ch 6, d tr before 1st p of next p-loop, d tr after p of next p-loop on next motif, ch 6, dc in next ch-5 loop. Repeat from * across, ending with d tr before 1st p of p-loop on last motif. Ch 5, sc in 3rd ch from hook. Ch 2, turn. **2nd row:** Sc in ch-6 loop, * ch 5, sc in 3rd ch from hook, ch 2, sc in dc, (ch 5, sc in 3rd ch from hook, ch 2, sc in next sc)

Fig. 71

Fig. 72

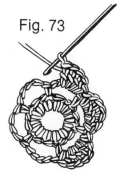
Fig. 73

203

twice; ch 5, sc in 3rd ch from hook, ch 2, sc in next dc, (ch 5, sc in 3rd ch from hook, ch 2, sc in next ch-6 loop) twice. Repeat from * across. Break off.

INSERTION . . . Work same as Edging, making Heading along both long edges (see illustration).

8268 . . . Materials: THREE CORD MERCERIZED CROCHET, *Size 50* . . . *Steel Crochet Hook No. 12.*

EDGING—First Section . . . Starting at center of rosette, ch 10. Join with sl st. **1st rnd:** Ch 1, 20 sc in ring. Sl st in 1st sc. **2nd rnd:** (Right side of rosette) * Ch 3 (to count as 1 dc), dc in next sc, 2 dc in next sc, dc in next 2 sc, ch 3, turn; dc in next 4 dc, 2 dc in top st of turning chain, ch 3, turn; dc in 1st dc, dc in 5 dc, dc in top st of turning chain. Working along side of this petal make ch 3, sl st in same place as last dc, ch 2, sl st in base of ch-3 below, ch 2, sl st in base of dc (petal completed). Repeat from * 3 more times; ch 3, dc in next sc, 2 dc in next sc, dc in next sc, dc in same place as sl st of last rnd, ch 3, turn; dc in next 4 dc, 2 dc in top st of turning chain, ch 3, turn; dc in 1st dc, dc in 5 dc, 2 dc in top st of turning chain (5 petals). **3rd rnd:** * (Ch 5, sc in 3rd ch from hook) twice; ch 2 (p-loop made); sc in 3rd st of turning chain at tip of next petal, make a p-loop, sc in center dc of same petal, make a p-loop, sc at tip of same petal. Repeat from * around, joining last p-loop with sl st in base of 1st p-loop. Now work in rows as follows: **1st row:** Sl st across to the 1st ch st between the p's of next p-loop, ch 1, sc between same p's, * make a p-loop, sc between p's of next p-loop. Repeat from * 2 more times. Turn. **2nd row:** Ch 5, sc in 3rd ch from hook, * make a p-loop, sc between p's of next loop. Repeat from * 2 more times. Turn. **3rd and 4th rows:** Repeat 2nd row. **5th row:** (Ch 5, sc in 3rd ch from hook) 3 times; ch 2, sc between p's of 1st loop, ch 7, sc between p's of next loop, turn; 7 sc in ch-7 loop, turn; ch 5 (to count as dc and ch 2), dc in next sc, (ch 2, dc in next sc) 5 times (a fan made); ch 5, sc in 3rd ch from hook, ch 2, sc between p's of last p-loop. Turn. **6th row:** (Ch 5, sc in 3rd ch from hook) 3 times; ch 2, (sc in next ch-2 sp of fan, ch 3, sc in same sp) 6 times; ch 5, sc in 3rd ch from

hook, ch 2, sc between p's of next p-loop. Turn. **7th row:** (Ch 5, sc in 3rd ch from hook) 3 times; ch 2, sc in next ch-3 loop of fan, make a p-loop, skip three ch-3 loops, sc in next ch-3 loop, a p-loop, sc between p's of next loop. Turn. **8th and 9th rows:** Repeat 2nd row. Break off.

Second Section . . . Work same as First Section until 8th row is complete. Turn. **9th row:** (Ch 5, sc in 3rd ch from hook) twice; ch 1, skip 4 free p-loops on right side of rosette of First Section, sc between p's of next p-loop on First Section, * ch 4, sc in 3rd ch from hook, ch 2, sc between p's of next p-loop on Second Section, ch 5, sc in 3rd ch from hook, ch 1, sc between p's of next p-loop on First Section. Repeat from * once more, ch 4, sc in 3rd ch from hook, ch 2, sc between p's of next p-loop on Second Section. There are 4 free p-loops on each side of rosette. Break off. Make necessary number of sections, joining them as Second Section was joined to First Section.

HEADING . . . With wrong side facing, attach thread between p's of 4th free p-loop to the right of joining on end rosette. **1st row:** Ch 10, * (sc between p's of next loop, ch 7) twice; dc between p's of next loop, ch 7, skip 2 p's, tr before next p, (ch 7, tr between p's of next loop) 4 times; ch 7, dc between p's of free p-loop on next rosette, ch 7. Repeat from * across. Ch 1, turn. **2nd row:** Work 9 sc in each sp across. Break off.

SCALLOPED EDGE . . . Attach thread to 4th free p-loop of 1st rosette. **1st row:** * Ch 9, sc between p's of next loop. Repeat from * across. Ch 1, turn. **2nd row:** Sl st in 4 ch, ch 1, sc in loop, * ch 9, sc in next loop, ch 3, turn; make 14 dc in loop, ch 3, turn; dc in 13 dc, dc in top st of turning chain, turn; (ch 5, skip next dc, sc in next dc) 6 times; ch 5, sc in top st of turning chain, turn; (ch 5, sc in next loop) 7 times; sc in next loop on 1st row, ch 9, sc in next loop. Repeat from * across, ending with 7 ch-5 loops, sc in next loop on 1st row. Turn. **3rd row:** Sl st in 2 ch, ch 1, sc in loop, * (ch 5, sc in next ch-5 loop) 6 times; ch 5, sc in next ch-9 loop, ch 5, sc in next ch-5 loop. Repeat from * across. Break off.

INSERTION . . . Work same as Edging omitting Scalloped Edge and making Heading along both long edges.

7557 . . . Materials: THREE CORD MERCERIZED CROCHET, *Size 50: 7 balls* . . . *Steel Crochet Hook No. 12.*

Centerpiece measures about 14 inches in diameter; place doily 11 inches in diameter; bread and butter doily 7½ inches in diameter, and glass doily 5 inches in diameter.

CENTERPIECE . . . Ch 10, join with sl st. **1st rnd:** Ch 4, 29 tr in ring, sl st in 4th st of ch-4. **2nd rnd:** Ch 4, tr in same place as sl st, 2 tr in each tr around. Join. **3rd rnd:** Ch 4, tr in each tr around. Join. **4th rnd:** Ch 5, * tr in next tr, ch 1. Repeat from * around. Join. **5th rnd:** Ch 6, * tr in next tr, ch 2. Repeat from * around. Join. **6th rnd:** Ch 1, sc in first ch-2 sp, ch 6, sc in 4th ch from hook (p), ch 3, p, * ch 2, skip 2 sps, sc in next sp, ch 2, p, ch 3, p. Repeat from * around, ending with ch 2, skip 2 sps, join with sl st in 1st sc. **7th rnd:** Sl st in first 3 sts of next loop, sl st in loop, ch 4, 2 tr in same loop, * ch 3, 3 tr in same loop, ch 3, 6 tr in center of next loop, ch 3, 3 tr in next loop. Repeat from * around, ending with ch 3. Join. **8th rnd:** Sl st in next 2 tr, sl st in ch-3 sp, ch 4, 2 tr in same sp, * ch 3, 3 tr in same sp (shell over shell made), ch 4, tr in 6 tr, ch 4, skip 1 sp, 3 tr in next sp. Repeat from * around, ending with ch 4. Join. **9th rnd:** Sl st in next 2 tr, sl st in ch-3 sp, ch 4, 2 tr in same sp, ch 3, 3 tr in same place (shell over shell made—*1st shell at beginning of the following rnds is made in the same manner*), * ch 4 (tr in next tr, ch 1) 5 times; tr in next tr, ch 4, in next ch-3 sp make 3 tr, ch 3 and 3 tr (another shell made). Repeat from * around, ending with ch 4. Join. **10th rnd:** * Shell over shell, ch 5, (tr in next tr, ch 1) 5 times; tr in next tr, ch 5. Repeat from * around. Join. **11th rnd:** * Shell over shell, ch 5, (tr in next ch-1 sp, ch 4) 4 times; tr in next ch-1 sp, ch 5. Repeat from * around. Join. **12th rnd:** * Shell over shell, ch 6, (tr in next ch-4 loop, ch 5) 3 times; tr in next loop, ch 6. Repeat from * around. Join. **13th rnd:** * Shell over shell, ch 7, (tr in next ch-5 loop, ch 6) twice; tr in next loop, ch 7. Repeat from * around. Join. **14th rnd:** * Shell over shell, ch 11, tr in ch-6 loop, ch 6, tr in next loop, ch 11. Repeat from * around. Join. **15th rnd:** Sl st in next 2 tr, sl st in next ch, ch 1, sc in sp, * (ch 2, make a ch-4 p) twice; ch 1 (p-loop made), sc in ch-11 loop, make another p-loop, sc in same loop;

make another p-loop, sc in next sp. Repeat from * around. Break off.

16th rnd: Petals are made individually as follows: **First Petal: 1st row:** Starting at center, ch 10, sc in 3rd ch from hook and in each of next 6 ch, 3 sc in last ch, then, working along opposite side of starting chain, make sc in next 7 ch, sc in turning chain, ch 2, turn. **Hereafter pick up only the back loop of each sc throughout. 2nd to 5th rows incl:** Skip 1 sc, sc in each sc to center of 3-sc group, 3 sc in center sc, sc in each sc across, sc in turning chain. Ch 2, turn. **6th row:** Skip 1 sc, sc in each sc to center sc at base of petal, sc in center of p-loop on 15th rnd, sc in same place as last sc on petal, sc in each sc across, sc in turning chain. Break off.

Second Petal: 1st to 5th rows incl: Repeat 1st to 5th rows of First Petal, ending with ch 1. **6th row:** Sl st in last sc of First Petal, ch 1, skip 1 sc, and complete as for First Petal, joining base of petal to 2nd loop following the one where First Petal was joined. Continue in this manner around, joining petals to previous one and to loops on 15th rnd, always skipping a loop between petals. Join last petal to First Petal made. Do not break off at end of rnd.

17th rnd: Ch 1, sc between two petals, * make a p-loop, skip 3 rows of petal, sc in next row, make another p-loop, skip 4 rows of petal, sc in next row, make another p-loop, sc in sp between petals. Repeat from * around. Join. **18th and 19th rnds:** Sl st to center of loop, * make a p-loop, sc in center of next p-loop. Repeat from * around. Break off at end of 19th rnd. **20th rnd:** Work as for 16th rnd, only having 8 rows of sc on each petal (instead of 6 rows) and skipping 2 p-loops (instead of 1 p-loop) when joining to previous rnd. **21st rnd:** Sc between 2 petals, * make a p-loop, skip 3 rows of petal, sc in next row, make a p-loop, skip 4 rows of petal, sc in starting chain of petal, make a p-loop, skip 4 rows of petal, sc in next row, make a p-loop, skip 3 rows of petal, sc between petals. Repeat from * around. **22nd to 26th rnds incl:** Repeat 18th rnd, ending last rnd with sl st in center of 1st p-loop. Break off.

PLACE DOILY (Make 4) . . . Work as for Centerpiece until 19th rnd is complete. Then repeat 18th and 19th rnds once more. Break off.

7557

BREAD AND BUTTER DOILY (Make 4) . . . Work as for Centerpiece until 10th rnd is complete. **11th rnd:** Sl st to sp, * ch 2, p, ch 3, p, ch 2, sc in next sp, ch 2, p, ch 3, p, ch 2, skip 1 dc, sc in next dc, ch 2, p, ch 3, p, ch 2, skip 2 dc, sc in next dc, ch 2, p, ch 3, p, ch 2, sc in next sp, ch 2, p, ch 3, p, ch 2, sc in sp of next shell. Repeat from * around. Now repeat 16th to 19th rnds incl of Centerpiece. Break off.

GLASS DOILY (Make 4) . . . Work as for Centerpiece until 6th rnd is complete, skipping 3 (instead of 2) sps under each loop on the 6th rnd. **7th rnd:** Work petals as for 16th rnd of Centerpiece, joining a petal to center of each loop. **8th, 9th and 10th rnds:** Repeat 17th, 18th and 19th rnds of Centerpiece. Break off.

7486 . . . Materials: BEST SIX CORD MERCERIZED CROCHET, *Size 30: 51 balls* . . . *Steel Crochet Hook No. 10 or 11.*

Motif measures 4 inches square and 5½ inches diagonally. Tablecloth measures about 72 x 110 inches.

FIRST MOTIF . . . Ch 8. Join with sl st. **1st rnd:** Ch 1, 18 sc in ring. Sl st in 1st sc. **2nd rnd:** Ch 1, sc in same place as sl st, * ch 5, skip 2 sc, sc in next sc. Repeat from * around. Join (6 loops). **3rd rnd:** Sl st in 1st loop, in each loop around make sc, half dc, 5 dc, half dc and sc (6 petals). **4th rnd:** * Ch 7, insert hook in next loop (from back of work) and in following loop (from front of work), thread over and draw loop through, thread over and draw through both loops on hook. Repeat from * around (6 loops). **5th rnd:** Sl st in 1st loop, in each loop around make sc, half dc, dc, 7 tr, dc, half dc and sc. **6th rnd:** Sl st in first 4 sts of next petal, ch 1, sc in same place as last sl st, * ch 5, sc in 4th ch from hook (p made), ch 2, p, ch 1, skip 5 tr, sc in next tr, ch 1, p, ch 2, p, ch 1, sc in 1st tr of next petal. Repeat from * around (12 loops). **7th rnd:** Sl st to center of next loop (between p's), ch 4, tr in same place as last sl st, ch 1, p, ch 2, p, ch 1, then, holding back on hook the last loop of each tr, make 2 tr in same place where last tr was made, thread over and draw through all loops on hook (2-tr cluster made); * ch 1, p, ch 2, p, ch 1, sc between p's of next

loop, ch 9, sc between p's of next loop, ch 1, p, ch 2, p, ch 1, skip p of next loop and the following ch, make 2-tr cluster in next ch, ch 1, p, ch 2, p, ch 1, 2-tr cluster in same place as last cluster. Repeat from * around. Join to top of 1st tr made.

8th rnd: Sl st to center of next loop, ch 4, tr in same place as last sl st, ch 1, p, ch 2, p, ch 1, 2-tr cluster in same place as last tr, * ch 1, p, ch 2, p, ch 1, sc in next loop, ch 3, in ch-9 loop make (a 3-tr cluster, p) 3 times and a 3-tr cluster; ch 3, sc in next loop, ch 1, p, ch 2, p, ch 1, skip the p of next loop and the following ch, make a 2-tr cluster in next ch, ch 1, p, ch 2, p, ch 1, 2-tr cluster in same place as last cluster. Repeat from * around. Join. **9th rnd:** Sl st to center of next loop, ch 5, p, ch 1, tr in same loop, ch 1, p, ch 1, tr in same loop, * ch 1, p, ch 1, tr between p's of next loop, ch 1, p, ch 1, tr in next ch-3 sp, ch 1, p, ch 1, skip next cluster, dc in top of each of next 2 clusters; ch 1, p, ch 1, skip next cluster, tr in next ch-3 sp, ch 1, p, ch 1, tr between p's of next loop, ch 1, p, ch 1, in next loop (between p's) make 5 tr with ch 1, p and ch 1 between each tr. Repeat from * around. Join with sl st to 4th st of ch-5 first made. **10th rnd:** Ch 17, tr in same place as sl st, * (ch 1, p, ch 1, tr in next tr) 4 times; ch 1, p, ch 1, skip 1 dc, tr in next dc, (ch 1, p, ch 1, tr in next tr) 4 times; ch 1, p,

207

7486

ch 1, in next tr make tr, ch 13 and tr. Repeat from * around. Join and break off.

SECOND MOTIF ... Work as for First Motif until 9th rnd is complete. **10th rnd:** Ch 10 (to count as tr and ch 6), sl st in center ch of corner loop on First Motif, ch 6, tr in same place as sl st on Second Motif, (ch 3, sl st in corresponding p on First Motif, ch 2, sc in 2nd ch of last ch-3, thus joining p's, ch 1, tr in next tr on Second Motif) 4 times; ch 3, sl st in next p on First Motif, ch 2, sc in 2nd ch of last ch-3, ch 1, skip 1 dc, tr in next dc on Second Motif, (ch 3, sl st in next p on First Motif, ch 2, sc in 2nd ch of last ch-3, ch 1, tr in next tr on Second Motif) 5 times; ch 6, sl st in center ch of corner loop on First Motif, ch 6, tr in

same place as last tr on Second Motif. Complete rnd same as for First Motif (no more joinings). Break off.

Make 488 motifs, joining adjacent sides as Second Motif was joined to First Motif (where 4 corners meet, join 3rd and 4th corners to joining of previous 2 corners). Join motifs in the following order: **1st row:** 1 motif. **2nd row:** 3 motifs (1 motif extending on each side of previous row). **3rd row:** 5 motifs. **4th row:** 7 motifs. Continue thus, having 2 more motifs on each row until there are 25 motifs on row. Make 7 more rows of 25 motifs each, having 1 motif extend beyond left edge and having 1 motif less on right edge. Now make 2 motifs less on each row (1 motif less on each side) until last row has 1 motif.

7577

7577 . . . Materials: BEST SIX CORD MERCERIZED CROCHET, *Size 30: 4 balls* . . . *Steel Crochet Hook No. 10 or 11.*

Motif measures about 2¾ inches in diameter. Runner measures about 14 x 31 inches.

FIRST MOTIF . . . Ch 10. Join with sl st. **1st rnd:** Ch 1, (sc in ring, ch 5) 6 times. Sl st in 1st sc made (6 sps). **2nd rnd:** In each loop make sc, half dc, 5 dc, half dc and sc (6 petals). **3rd rnd:** * Ch 5, insert hook in next loop (from back of work) and in following loop (from front of work), thread over and draw loop through, thread over and draw through both loops on hook. Repeat from * around (6 loops). **4th rnd:** Work petals as before, making 7 dc (instead of 5) in each petal. **5th rnd:** Sl st in first 3 sts of next petal, sc in next st, * ch 5, sc in 3rd ch from hook (p made), ch 3, p, ch 2, skip 3 sts, sc in next st, ch 2, p, ch 3, p, ch 2, skip 3 sts of next petal, sc in next st. Repeat from * around. Sl st in 1st sc made. **6th rnd:** Sl st across to the ch following next p, sl st in loop, ch 4, holding back on hook the last loop of each tr, make 3 tr in same loop, thread over and draw through all loops on hook (cluster made), ch 3, p, ch 5, p, ch 3, make a 4-tr cluster in same loop. In each loop around make cluster,

ch 3, p, ch 5, p, ch 3 and a cluster. Join last cluster to top of 1st cluster. Break off.

SECOND MOTIF . . . Work as for First Motif until 5th rnd is complete. **6th rnd:** Complete 1st cluster, (ch 3, p, ch 2, sc in corresponding loop on First Motif, ch 2, p, ch 3, cluster in same place as last cluster on Second Motif; make a cluster in next loop) twice. Complete rnd with no more joinings. Break off.

Make 5 x 11 motifs, joining motifs as Second Motif was joined to First Motif, leaving one loop free on each motif between joinings.

FILL-IN-LACE . . . Ch 10. Join with sl st. **1st rnd:** Ch 1, 16 sc in ring. Join. **2nd rnd:** * Ch 2, p, ch 2, sl st in free loop between joinings, ch 2, p, ch 2, skip 3 sc on ring, sc in next sc, ch 10, sl st in joining, ch 10, sc in same place in last sc. Repeat from * around. Join and break off. Fill in all sps between motifs in this way.

EDGING . . . **1st rnd:** Attach thread to a joining on outer edge, * ch 12, sc between p's of next loop. Repeat from * to next joining, ch 12, sc in joining, ch 12, sc in next loop and continue thus around, ending with sl st in same place where thread was attached. **2nd rnd:** In each loop around, make 2 sc, 2 half dc, 2 dc, 9 tr, 2 dc, 2 half dc and 2 sc. Join with sl st to 1st sc made. Break off.

CHAPTER FIFTEEN

Baby Clothes

Sᴏᴍᴇᴏɴᴇ ᴇxᴛʀᴀ been added to your family? Or the family of one of your friends? As one of the welcoming committee, it behooves you to be ready with a suitable token of affection and esteem.

What's it to be? A baby bunting, deliciously warm for a certain small party to cuddle in, or a woolly blanket, soft as a cloud in shell pink or heavenly blue? An enchanting miniature cardigan? Mittens, bootees, an elfin cap? You can be practical and make a soaker or the trio of little feeders, or you can crochet the beautiful sacque—doubles as a bathrobe—and matching bootees that are sure to bring out the Kodak in every parent. Everything a baby would love for every baby you love!

5302

5302 . . . Materials for Infant Size: BABY YARN *(1-ounce skeins), 3 skeins for Sacque; 4 skeins for Kimono; 1 skein for Bootees . . . Crochet Hook D-3.*

GAUGE: 1 shell and 1 dc make 1 inch; 2 rows make 1 inch.

SACQUE OR KIMONO

Starting at lower edge, ch 147 to measure 25 inches. **1st row:** In 6th ch from hook make 2 dc, ch 1 and 2 dc (shell made), * skip 2 ch, dc in next ch, skip 2 ch, in next ch make 2 dc, ch 1 and 2 dc (another shell made). Repeat from * across, ending with skip 2 ch, dc in last ch (24 shells with dc between). Ch 3, turn. **2nd row:** * Shell in ch-1 sp of next shell, dc in next dc. Repeat from * across, ending with dc in top st of turning chain. Ch 3, turn. Repeat 2nd row until piece measures 7 inches for Sacque, or 14 inches for Kimono.

For Right Front, work across until there are 6 shells, dc in next dc. Ch 3, turn. Work in pattern across this set of sts only until piece measures 9 inches for Sacque, or 16 inches for Kimono, ending at inner edge. Ch 3, turn. **Next row:** Work across until there are 3 shells, dc in next dc. Ch 3, turn. Work in pattern across this set of sts only until piece measures 11 inches in all for Sacque, or 18 inches for Kimono. Break off.

For Back, skip next shell, attach yarn in next dc, ch 3 and continue across until there are 10 shells, dc in next dc. Ch 3, turn and work over these sts only until piece measures same as Right Front. Break off.

For Left Front, skip next shell, attach yarn in next dc, ch 3 and work across remaining 6 shells, dc in top st of turning chain. Ch 3, turn and work to correspond with Right Front. Break off. Sew shoulder seams. With right side facing, attach yarn at neck edge of Right Front, ch 4, * skip 1/4 inch of neck edge, dc in edge. Repeat from * along neck edge. Do not break off but work edging along entire outer edge as follows: Sc in side of last dc, ** skip 1/4 inch on edge, 5 dc in edge, skip 1/4 inch, sc in edge. Repeat from ** around entire edge, excluding neck edge. Break off.

SLEEVES . . . **Wrist band:** Ch 9. **1st row:** Sc in 2nd ch from hook, sc in each ch across. Ch 1, turn. **2nd row:** Sc in back loop of each sc across. Ch 1, turn. Repeat 2nd row until piece measures 4 inches. Ch 1 and work 33 sc along edge of Wrist band. Ch 3, turn. **Next row:** * Skip 1 sc, shell in next sc, skip 1 sc, dc in next sc. Repeat from * across. Ch 3, turn and continue in pattern until piece measures 8 inches in all. Break off. Sew sleeve seams and sew sleeves in. Run 1 yard of ribbon through beading at neck.

BOOTEES

TOE PIECE . . . Ch 10. **1st row:** Sc in 2nd ch from hook and in each ch across. Ch 3, turn. **2nd row:** Dc in 2nd sc and in each sc across. Ch 1, turn. **3rd row:** Sc in each dc and in top st of turning chain. Ch 3, turn. Repeat 2nd, 3rd and 2nd rows. Do not ch 1 at end of last row. Ch 35 for ankle, sl st in first st at beginning of last row. Break off.

FOOT . . . Attach yarn in center st of ch-35 (center back). **1st rnd:** Ch 1, sc in same place where yarn was attached, sc in next 17 ch, work 8 sc along side of Toe Piece, sc in each st across end of Toe Piece, 8 sc along side of Toe Piece, sc in remaining 17 ch (60 sc). Join with sl st in 1st sc. **2nd rnd:** Ch 3 (to count as 1 dc), dc in each sc around. Join with sl st in top st of starting chain (60 dc). **3rd rnd:** Ch 1, sc in same place as sl st, sc in each dc around (60 sc). Join. Repeat 2nd, 3rd and 2nd rnds. **Next rnd:** Ch 1, sc in each dc around, decreasing 5 sc evenly across toe and 3 sc evenly across heel—*to dec, work off 2 sc as 1 sc. See Figs. 25 and 26, page 18.* Join. **Following rnd:** Repeat 2nd rnd of Foot. Repeat last 2 rnds once more. Break off. Sew edges together for sole.

TOP . . . Attach yarn at center back of ankle and work 48 sc around opening. Join. **1st rnd:** Ch 3, * skip 2 sc, shell in next sc, skip 2 sc, dc in next sc. Repeat from * around, joining last shell with sl st in 3rd st of starting chain. Ch 3, turn. **2nd rnd:** * Shell in ch-1 sp of next shell, dc in next dc. Repeat from * around. Join. Repeat 2nd rnd 2 more times. Ch 1, turn. **Next rnd:** Sc in same place as sl st, * 5 dc in next shell, sc in next dc. Repeat from * around. Join and break off.

Run 1/2 yard of ribbon in and out around ankle. Tie in bow at front. Make other bootee in the same way.

4046

4046 . . . Materials: BABY YARN *(1-ounce skeins), 2 skeins for each size . . . Crochet Hook B-1.*

Sizes	Small	Medium	Large

Starting at toe, ch 5. **1st rnd:** In 5th ch from hook make 18 tr — 20 tr — 22 tr.

Join with sl st to 1st tr. **2nd rnd:** Ch 1, 2 sc in each st around. Join with sl st. There are on rnd 36 sts — 40 sts — 44 sts

3rd rnd: Ch 1, turn. Hereafter **work in the back loop only of each sc.** * Sc in next sc, 2 sc in next sc. Repeat from * around. Join. There are on rnd 54 sts — 60 sts — 66 sts

4th rnd: Ch 1, turn. Sc in each st around. Join. Repeat the 4th rnd until piece measures in all 4½" — 5" — 5½"
Ch 1 to turn at end of last rnd.

Work is now done in rows instead of rnds. 1st row: Sc in each sc across. Do not join. Ch 1, turn. Repeat 1st row until piece measures in all 8" — 9" — 10"

Break off. Fold last row evenly and sew edges together (back seam).

CUFF . . . Attach yarn to top of back seam and work as follows: **1st rnd:** Sc in end st of each row around. Sl st in 1st sc. **2nd rnd:** Ch 1, sc in same place as sl st, * ch 1, skip 1 sc, sc in next sc. Repeat from * around, ending with ch 1. Join. **3rd rnd:** Ch 1, 2 sc in each ch-1 sp around. Join. Turn. **4th to 8th rnds incl:** Ch 1, sc in back loop of each st around. Join and turn. **9th rnd:** Same as previous rnd but do not turn. **10th rnd:** Sc in same place as sl st, * skip 2 sc, 7 dc in next sc, skip 2 sc, sc in next sc. Repeat from * around, ending with 7 dc. Join. Break off.

Run 1 yard of ribbon through ch-1 sps of Cuff. Tie in a bow.

5300

5300 . . . Materials for Infant Size: BABY
YARN *(1-ounce skeins), 2 skeins . . . Crochet
Hook D-3.*

GAUGE: 2 puff sts and 2 sc make 1¼ inches.

CAP

Starting at center of back, ch 2. **1st rnd:** 6 sc
in 2nd ch from hook. **2nd rnd:** 2 sc in each sc
around (12 sc). **3rd rnd:** * Sc in next sc, 2 sc

in next sc. Repeat from * around (18 sc). **4th
rnd:** * Sc in next 2 sc, 2 sc in next sc. Repeat
from * around (24 sc). See Fig. 22, page 9.
Continue thus, increasing 6 sc evenly on each
rnd until there are 90 sc on the rnd and piece
measures about 4¼ inches in diameter. Work
1 rnd without increasing. Now work front as
follows: **1st row:** Working in **back loop only**
of sc's, make * sc in next sc, ch 1, skip next sc.

yarn over, insert hook in next sc and pull loop through, (yarn over, insert hook in same sc and pull loop through) twice; yarn over and draw through all loops on hook (puff st made, Fig. 74). Repeat from * until there are 26 puff sts, sc in next sc after last puff st. Remaining 11 sc are for back of neck. Ch 1, turn. **2nd row:** Sc in 1st sc, * sc in 2 top loops of puff st, sc in ch-1 sp, sc in next sc. Repeat from * across (79 sc). Ch 1, turn. **3rd row:** Working in **both** loops of sc's, work same as 1st row. Repeat 2nd and 3rd rows alternately until piece measures 4 inches from last rnd of back, ending with 2nd row. Ch 1, turn.

EDGING . . . 1st row: Sc in 1st sc, * skip next sc, 5 dc in next sc (shell made), skip next sc, sc in next sc. Repeat from * across. Ch 1, turn. **2nd row:** Sl st in each st across. Break off.

Work a row of shells (same as Edging) in remaining free loops of sc's of last rnd of back. Continue shells across back of neck, joining last shell with sl st in 1st sc. Ch 1, turn and work sl st in each st around. Break off.

Using 1 yard of narrow ribbon for each rosette, make 2 rosettes and sew in place. Use ½ yard of 1-inch ribbon for each tie.

MITTENS

Starting at wrist, ch 33 to measure 5½ inches. Join with sl st to form ring. **1st rnd:** Ch 1, sc in same place as sl st, sc in each ch around (33 sc). **2nd rnd:** Sc in each sc around. Repeat 2nd rnd until piece measures 2½ inches. **Next rnd:** Sc in each sc around, decreasing 4 sts evenly around—*to dec 1 sc, work off 2 sc as 1 sc.* See Figs. 25 and 26, page 10. Following **rnd:** Sc in each sc around. Repeat last 2 rnds alternately (being careful decreases do not fall directly over each other) until 21 sc remain. **Next rnd:** Work off 2 sc as 1 sc all around (11 sc). Break off, leaving an 8-inch length. Thread a needle with this length and run

through remaining sts. Pull tight and darn in end on wrong side.

CUFF . . . 1st rnd: With wrong side facing, attach yarn at wrist edge and work sc in base of each sc around (33 sc). Sl st in 1st sc. Ch 1, turn. **2nd rnd:** Sc in same place as sl st, * ch 1, skip next sc, puff st in next sc, sc in next sc. Repeat from * around, ending with puff st in last sc, sl st in 1st sc. Ch 1, turn. **3rd rnd:** Sc in same place as sl st, * sc in the 2 top loops of puff st, sc in ch-1 sp, sc in next sc. Repeat from * around (33 sc). Sl st in 1st sc. Ch 1, turn. Repeat 2nd and 3rd rnds alternately until Cuff measures 1½ inches, ending with 3rd rnd. Ch 1, turn and work 2 rnds same as 1st and 2nd rows of Edging on Cap. Break off.

Run ½ yard of narrow ribbon in and out around wrist. Make other mitten same as this.

5297 . . . Materials: Baby Yarn (*1-ounce skeins*), 9 skeins . . . *Crochet Hook E-4.*

GAUGE: 6 dc make 1 inch; 3 rows make 1 inch.

BUNTING . . . Starting at lower edge, ch 219 to measure 37 inches. **1st row:** Dc in 4th ch from hook, dc in each ch across (217 dc, counting turning ch-3 as 1 dc). Ch 3, turn. **2nd row:** Yarn over, insert hook between first 2 dc, bring it out between next and following dc, * pull loop through, (yarn over and draw through 2 loops) twice; yarn over, insert hook between same 2 dc where hook was brought out, bring it out between next 2 dc, pull loop through, yarn over and complete as for a dc, Fig. 75, dc in next dc, yarn over, insert hook between this and next dc, bring it out between that and following dc. Repeat from * across, making last dc in top st of turning chain. Ch 3, turn. **3rd row:** * Dc in next 2 dc, yarn over, insert hook between last and next dc, bring it out between that and following

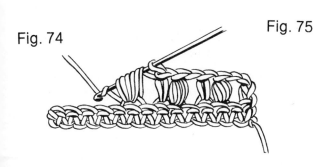

Fig. 74

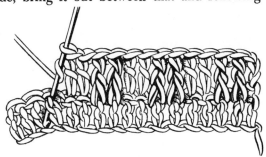

Fig. 75

5297

dc, draw loop through and complete as for a dc. Repeat from * across, ending with dc in last 2 dc, dc in top st of turning chain. Ch 3, turn. Repeat 2nd and 3rd rows alternately until piece measures 20 inches, ending with 3rd row. Ch 3, turn.

LEFT FRONT . . . 1st row: Work in pattern across 54 sts. Ch 3, turn. **2nd row:** (Inner edge) Dec 1 dc—*to dec a dc, work off 2 dc as 1 dc. See Figs. 44–47, pages 16 and 17.* Dec. 1 more dc, then continue in pattern across remaining sts of Left Front. Ch 3, turn. **3rd row:** Work in pattern across to last 2 dc and turning chain, work off the 2 dc as before, do not work in the turning chain (2 dc decreased). Ch 3, turn. Repeat 2nd and 3rd rows alternately (2 dc decreased at inner edge on each row) until 36 sts remain. Break off.

BACK . . . Attach yarn in next dc, ch 3 and work in pattern across next 108 sts (109 sts, counting starting chain). Dec 2 dc at both ends of each row until 73 sts remain. Break off.

216

RIGHT FRONT . . . Attach yarn in next dc, ch 3 and work in pattern across remaining 53 sts (54 sts, counting starting chain). Dec 2 dc at inner edge on each row until 36 sts remain. Break off.

HOOD . . . **Back Piece:** Starting at top edge, ch 27 to measure 4½ inches. Work 1st, 2nd, and 3rd rows same as Bunting. Then dec 1 dc at both ends of each row until 1 dc remains. Break off.

FRONT PIECE . . . Starting at front edge, ch 87 to measure 14½ inches. Work in pattern same as Bunting until piece measures 6 inches. Break off.

Sew back edge of front piece of hood along entire outer edge of back piece. Starting at inner edges and working toward center, sew curved edges of bunting together, leaving 2½ inches free on each side of front and 5 inches free at back of neck (neck opening). Sew lower edge of hood to neck opening. Bind front edges of bunting and hood with ribbon 1½ inches wide. Sew lower edges of bunting together. Sew ribbon-bound edges together for 9 inches, starting at bottom of bunting. Close remainder of opening with hooks and eyes sewed on wrong side.

5296 . . . Materials: KNITTING WORSTED (4-ounce skeins) 4 skeins . . . Crochet Hook G-6.

Blanket measures approximately 27 x 32 inches.

GAUGE: 2 patterns (2 shells and 2 sc) measure 2¾ inches.

Starting at narrow end, ch 110 loosely to measure 26 inches. **1st row:** Sc in 2nd ch from hook, * skip 2 ch, 7 dc in next ch (shell made), skip 2 ch, sc in next ch. Repeat from * across. Ch 2, turn. **2nd row:** Insert hook in front loop of next sc and pull loop through, insert hook in front loop of each of next 3 dc and pull loops through, yarn over and draw through all loops on hook, ch 1 to fasten (half group st made); * sc in front loop of next dc, pull a loop through the front loop of each of next 3 dc, next sc and next 3 dc, yarn over and draw through all loops on hook, ch 1 to fasten (group st made). Repeat from * across, ending with sc in front loop of next dc, pull a loop through front loops of last 3 dc and last sc,

yarn over and draw through all loops on hook, ch 1 to fasten (half group st made). Ch 3, turn. **3rd row:** 3 dc in fastening ch of half group st below (half shell made), * sc in next sc, shell in fastening ch of next group st. Repeat from * across, ending with 4 dc in top st of turning chain. Ch 1, turn. **4th row:** Working in front loop of each st, make sc in 1st dc, * work a group st over next 7 sts, sc in next dc. Repeat from * across, ending with sc in top st of turning chain. Ch 1, turn. **5th row:** Sc in 1st sc, * shell in fastening ch of next group st, sc in next sc. Repeat from * across, ending with sc in last sc. Ch 2, turn.

Repeat 2nd to 5th rows incl until piece measures 30 inches, ending with either the 2nd or the 4th row. Break off.

EDGING . . . With right side of shells facing, attach yarn in end of starting chain. Ch 1, sc in same place where yarn was attached, * 7 dc in base of next shell, sc in base of next sc. Repeat from * across, ending with sc in last sc. Then, working along ends of rows, make ** shell in the joining of next 2 rows, sc in the joining of next 2 rows. Repeat from ** across, ending with sc in corner. Complete remaining 2 edges to correspond. Break off.

5293 . . . Materials for Infant Size: BABY YARN (1-ounce skeins), 2 skeins . . . Crochet Hook D-3.

GAUGE: 6 half dc make 1 inch; 3½ rows make 1 inch.

Starting at waistband, ch 9. **1st row:** Sc in 2nd ch from hook, sc in each ch across (8 sc). Ch 1, turn. **2nd row:** Working in back loop of each sc, make sc in each sc across. Ch 1, turn. Repeat 2nd row until piece measures 19 inches. Then, working along long edge of waistband, make 132 sc across to other end. Ch 2, turn. **Next row:** Half dc in each sc across. Ch 2, turn. **Following row:** Skip 1st half dc, work off next 2 half dc as 1 half dc, see Figs. 34 and 35, page 21 (2 half dc decreased), half dc in each half dc across to last 2 half dc, work off last 2 half dc as 1 half dc (1 more half dc decreased). Ch 2, turn. Repeat last row until 39 half dc remain. Now dec 1 half dc at both ends of each row until 3 half dc remain. Break off. Sew ends of waistband

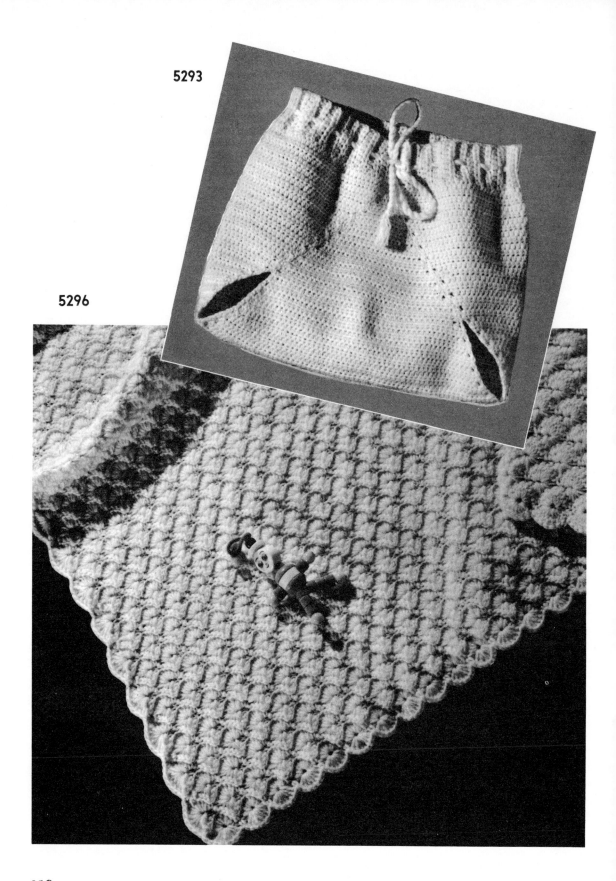

5293

5296

together. Turn point up to bottom of waist-band and sew edges together for 5 inches.

Cut four 2½-yard strands of yarn. Make a twisted cord—see Figs. 49, 50, and 51, page 17. Tie a knot 1 inch in from each end of cord. Trim ends. Run cord in and out through center of waistband.

5310 . . . Materials for Infant Sizes 2 and 3: BABY YARN (*1-ounce skeins*), *3 skeins for Infant Size 2, 4 skeins for Infant Size 3 . . . Crochet Hook D-3.*

GAUGE: 7 sts make 1 inch; 6 rows make 1 inch.

Sizes	2	3

WAISTBAND . . . Starting at narrow end, ch 11. **1st row:** Sc in 2nd ch from hook, sc in each ch across (10 sc). Ch 1, turn. **2nd row:** Sc in back loop of each sc across. Ch 1, turn. Repeat 2nd row until piece measures

	18″	20″

Ch 1, turn and work across long edge making

	136 sc	148 sc

Ch 1, turn and work in pattern as follows: **1st row:** * Sc in back loop of next sc, sc in front loop of next sc. Repeat from * across. Ch 1, turn. Repeat last row until piece measures in all

	7½″	8″

RIGHT FRONT . . . Work in pattern across

	34 sts	37 sts

Ch 1, turn.

Work over this last set of sts only, decreasing 1 st at both ends of next

	4 rows	5 rows

—*to dec, work off 2 sc as 1 sc.* See Figs. 25 and 26, page 10.

Work inner (armhole) edge straight but continue decreases on front edge as before until there remain for shoulder

	15 sts	16 sts

Work straight until piece measures in all

	11″	12″

Break off.

5310

BACK . . . Attach yarn and work across next

	68 sts	74 sts

decreasing 1 st at both ends of each row until there remain

	60 sts	64 sts

Work straight until piece measures same as Right Front. Break off.

LEFT FRONT . . . Attach yarn and work across remaining

	34 sts	37 sts

to correspond with Right Front. Break off.

SLEEVES . . . **Wrist band:** Work same as Waistband for

	4″	4½″

Ch 1, turn and work across long edge making

	52 sc	56 sc

Ch 1, turn and work in pattern until piece measures in all

	7½″	8″

To Shape Top: Dec 1 st at both ends of each of the next

	4 rows	5 rows

Break off.

Sew shoulder seams. Sew sleeve seams and sew sleeves in.

With right side facing, work sc evenly up right front edge, along neck edge, holding it in to fit, then down left front edge. Ch 1, turn. **2nd row:** Sc in back loop of each sc. Ch 1, turn. **3rd row:** Place 6 pins, evenly spaced, on right front edge, * work sc in back loop of each sc to pin, ch 2, skip 2 sc, sc in back loop of next sc. Repeat from * until 6 buttonloops have been made, sc in back loop of each remaining sc. Ch 1, turn. **4th row:** Sc in back loop of each sc and 2 sc in each ch-2 loop. Ch 1, turn. **5th row:** Sl st in each sc. Break off.

Sew on buttons.

5208 . . . Materials: KNIT-CRO-SHEEN, 2 *balls each of 3 colors referred to in directions as 1st, 2nd, and 3rd colors . . . Steel Crochet Hook No. 7.*

5208

GAUGE: 9 sts make 1 inch; 7 rows make 2 inches. Each square on chart is equivalent to 3 dc.

To Change Color: Before drawing through last 2 loops of last dc of one color group, drop this color, pick up other color, thread over and draw through the 2 loops on hook. Continue with other color, carrying the dropped color along top of previous row and working over it to conceal it.

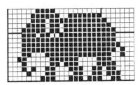

ELEPHANT BIB . . . With 1st color ch 83 to measure 9½ inches. **1st row:** Dc in 4th ch from hook and in each ch across (81 dc, counting turning chain as 1 dc). Ch 3, turn. **2nd to 9th rows incl:** Dc in each dc, dc in top st of turning chain. Ch 3, turn. **10th row:** Holding 2nd color along top of previous row, with 1st color make dc in 8 dc (thus concealing 2nd color), changing color in last dc. With 2nd color make dc in 6 dc, carrying 1st color concealed in dc's and changing color in last dc. With 1st color make dc in 6 dc, carrying 2nd color concealed in dc's and changing color in last dc. Conceal 1st color in next 9 dc, changing color in last dc. Conceal 2nd color in next 3 dc, changing color in last dc. Conceal 1st color in next 9 dc, changing color as before. Conceal 2nd color in next 9 dc, changing color as before. Conceal 1st color in next 9 dc, changing color. Conceal 2nd color in next 21 dc. With 1st color ch 3, turn. **11th row:** Carrying unused color and changing color as before, make 11 dc of 1st color, 3 of 2nd color, 9 of 1st color, 6 of 2nd color, 12 of 1st color, 6 of 2nd color, 6 of 1st color, 6 of 2nd color, 3 of 1st color, 9 of 2nd color, 9 of 1st color. With 1st color ch 3, turn. Starting with 3rd row, follow Elephant chart to top. Break off 2nd color. Work 9 rows straight with 1st color. Ch 3, turn.

For Neck Shaping . . . 1st row: Dc in 36 dc, half dc in next dc sc in next dc, sl st in next dc. Turn. **2nd row:** Sl st in sc, half dc and dc, sc in next dc, half dc in next dc, dc in remaining sts. Ch 3, turn. **3rd row:** Dc in 30 dc, half dc in next dc, sc in next dc, sl st in next dc.

Turn. **4th row:** Repeat 2nd row. **5th row:** Dc in 24 dc, half dc in next dc, sc in next dc, sl st in next dc. Turn. Neck shaping is complete. **6th row:** Sl st in sc, half dc and dc, ch 3, dc in 20 dc; half dc in next 2 dc, sc in next dc, sl st in top st of turning chain. Turn. **7th row:** Sl st in sc, 2 half dc and dc, sc in next dc, half dc in next 2 dc, dc in remaining sts. Ch 3, turn. **8th row:** Dc in 12 dc, half dc in next 2 dc, sc in next dc, sc in next dc, sl st in next dc. Turn. **9th row:** Repeat 7th row. **10th row:** Dc in 4 dc, half dc in next 2 dc, sc in next dc, sc in next dc, sl st in next dc. Turn. **11th row:** Sl st in sc, 2 half dc and dc, sc in next dc, half dc in next 2 dc, dc in top st of turning chain. Break off. Skip 1 st, attach thread in next st, sc in next st, half dc in next st, and continue thus, working other side to correspond. Break off. Bind outer edge with bias tape. Bind neck edge, allowing 12 inches of tape at each end for ties. Machine stitch the edges of each tie to prevent raveling.

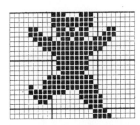

BEAR BIB . . . With 3rd color ch 83 to measure 9½ inches. Work 1st to 5th rows incl same as on Elephant Bib. **6th row:** Carrying unused color and changing color as described in Elephant Bib, make 14 dc of 3rd color, 12 dc of 1st color, 54 dc of 3rd color. With 3rd color, ch 3, turn. Starting with 2nd row follow Bear chart to top. Break off 1st color. Work 6 rows straight with 3rd color. Ch 3, turn. Shape neck and remainder of bib same as for Elephant Bib. Finish outer and neck edges with bias tape.

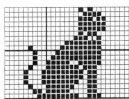

CAT BIB . . . With 2nd color ch 83 to measure 9½ inches. Work 1st to 7th rows incl same as on Elephant Bib. **8th row:** Carrying unused color and changing color as described in Elephant Bib, make 17 dc of 2nd color, 9 dc of 3rd color, 6 of 2nd color, 27 of 3rd color, 21 of 2nd color. With 2nd color, ch 3, turn. Starting with 2nd row, follow Cat chart to top. Break off 3rd color. Work 7 rows straight with 2nd color. Ch 3, turn. Shape neck and remainder of bib same as for Elephant Bib. Finish outer and neck edges with bias tape.

5227 . . . Materials: Baby Yarn (*1-ounce skeins*), 18 skeins . . . *Crochet Hook Size G.*

Blanket measures approximately 36 x 50 inches.

GAUGE: 3 star sts make 1 inch; 2 rows make 1 inch.

Starting at side edge, make a loose chain about 60 inches long. **1st row:** Insert hook in 2nd ch from hook and pull loop through, (insert hook in next ch and pull loop through) 3 times; yarn over and draw through all 5 loops on hook, ch 1 to fasten (star st). See Fig. 62, page 39. * Insert hook in fastening ch of star st just made and pull loop through, insert hook in last loop of same star st and pull loop through, insert hook in ch where last loop of previous star st was pulled through and pull loop through, skip 1 ch, insert hook in next ch and pull loop through; yarn over and draw through all 5 loops on hook, ch 1 to fasten (another star st). See Fig. 62, page 39. Repeat from * across until row measures 50 inches. Cut off remaining chain. Ch 3, turn. **2nd row:** Insert hook in 2nd ch from hook and pull loop through, insert hook in next ch and pull loop through, insert hook in fastening ch of 1st star st and pull loop through, insert hook in fastening ch of next star st and pull loop through; yarn over and draw through all loops on hook, ch 1. * Insert hook in fastening ch just made and pull loop through, insert hook in last loop

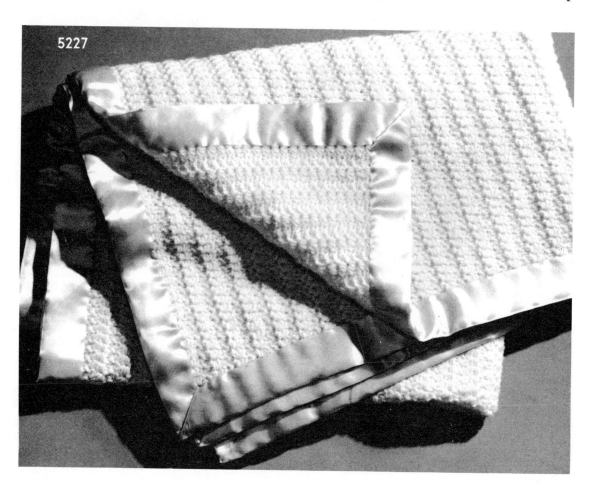

5227

of previous star st and pull loop through, insert hook in same fastening ch where last loop of previous star st was pulled through and pull loop through, insert hook in next fastening ch and pull loop through; yarn over and draw through all loops on hook, ch 1. Repeat from * across, pulling last loop of last star st through at top of turning chain of previous row. Ch 3, turn. Repeat 2nd row for 36 inches. Break off. Sew blanket binding all around.

5241 . . . Materials: BABY YARN (*1-ounce skeins*), *2 skeins* . . . *Crochet Hook Size G.*

GAUGE: 6 sts make 1 inch; 8 rows make 1 inch.

Starting at front edge, ch 36 to measure 6 inches. **1st row:** Sc in 4th ch from hook, * ch 1, skip 1 ch, sc in next ch. Repeat from * across (17 sc). Ch 2, turn. **2nd row:** * Sc in next skipped ch on starting chain, ch 1. Repeat from * across, ending with sc in the turning chain (17 sc). Ch 2, turn. **3rd row:** Sc in 1st sc of row before last, * ch 1, sc in next sc of same row. Repeat from * across (17 sc). Ch 2, turn. Repeat 3rd row until piece measures 2¾ inches. Ch 2, turn. **Next row:** Sc in same place as last sc of previous row, ch 1, sc in 1st sc of row before last, ch 1 and continue in pattern across (18 sc). Ch 2, turn. Repeat the 3rd row 3 more times (18 sc). Ch 2, turn. Repeat the last 4 rows, thus increasing 1 sc at top edge on every 4th row until piece measures 5¾ inches from beginning. Break off (back edge). Make another piece same as this.

Sew back and top seams. Attach yarn and work in pattern across bottom edge, holding edge in to measure 7½ inches and making band ½ inch wide. Break off.

CORD . . . Using 3 strands of yarn make a chain 30 inches long. Run cord through crocheted fabric, ½ inch in from front edge. Make 5 yarn bows. Sew three on hood as in illustration and one at each end of cord.

5241

4037
COASTER

4036
JACKET

CHAPTER SIXTEEN

Gifts and Toys

Iт's FUN TO GIVE people presents. It's a way of saying you think of them, are fond of them, remember them. It's the most fun to give children presents, see the stars grow in their eyes as they undo the wrappings, watch the glow of pleasure that lights their faces when they discover their newest treasure. Neither the size nor importance of a gift matters as much as the sentiment behind it, and that's where the gift you make yourself always has the advantage. It says far better than anything you buy that thought and love have gone into it, and such a gift is always doubly welcomed, doubly cherished.

Needless to say, anything in this book would make an exciting and memorable gift—one of the luncheon sets for a bride-to-be, a pretty sweater for a favorite niece, one of the rare, lovely, lacy tablecloths for a friend's anniversary. But here we've assembled a group of useful and attractive smaller gifts, bright little ideas that you can make in an evening or two . . . a pretty pincushion, an unusual apron, a set of coasters and jackets, a knitting bag in a good-looking checkered design. There's a cozy pair of bedroom slippers to promote friendly understanding, a doll with pigtails that will spell bliss to some wide-eyed miss . . . more than a dozen engaging ways of remembering your favorite people.

4037 . . . Materials: Pearl Cotton, *Size 5, 2 balls each of White and Blue* . . . *Steel Crochet Hook No. 6.*

BOTTOM . . . **1st rnd:** Starting at center with White, ch 4, 11 dc in 4th ch from hook. Sl st in top st of starting chain. **2nd rnd:** Drop White, attach Blue, ch 1, sc in same place as sl st, * 2 sc in next st, sc in next st. Repeat from * around (18 sts). Join. **3rd rnd:** Drop Blue, pick up White, ch 3, dc in each st around, increasing 12 dc evenly around (see Fig. 43 on page 16)—*to inc a dc, make 2 dc in 1 st.* **4th rnd:** Drop White, pick up Blue, ch 1, sc in each st around, increasing 6 sc evenly around (see Fig. 22, page 9). **5th and 6th rnds:** Repeat 3rd and 4th rnds. **7th rnd:** Repeat 3rd rnd, increasing 14 dc (68 dc on rnd).

TOP EDGING . . . **1st rnd:** Drop White, pick up Blue, ch 1, turn and make sc in back loop of each st around. Join. **2nd rnd:** Drop Blue, pick up White, ch 1, sc in same place as sl st, * ch 5, 3 dc where last sc was made, skip 3 sc, sc in next sc. Repeat from * around. Join. Break off White. **3rd rnd:** Pick up Blue, * 5 sc in ch-5 loop, sc in next 3 dc. Repeat from * around. Join and break off.

BOTTOM EDGING . . . Attach Blue and work in remaining free loops of last dc-rnd of Bottom. **1st rnd:** Sc in each st around, increasing 7 sc evenly around (75 sts). Join. **2nd rnd:** Repeat 2nd rnd of Top Edging, only skipping 2 (instead of 3) sts. Join and break off. Complete as for Top Edging. Make 4 more coasters same as this.

4036 . . . Materials: Pearl Cotton, *Size 5, 4 balls of White, 3 balls of Steel Blue* . . . *Steel Crochet Hook No. 6.*

BOTTOM . . . Starting at center of bottom, with White, ch 4. **1st rnd:** 11 dc in 4th ch from hook. Join with sl st in top of starting chain. **2nd rnd:** Ch 3, dc in same place as sl st, 2 dc in each st around. Join (24 sts). **3rd rnd:** Ch 3, * 2 dc in next dc, dc in next dc. Repeat from *

around. Join (36 sts). **4th rnd:** Ch 3, dc in each dc around, increasing 12 dc evenly around (see Fig. 43, page 16)—*to inc a dc, make 2 dc in 1 dc.* Join. Repeat the 4th rnd until piece measures same as bottom of glass.

SIDE . . . **1st rnd:** Drop White, attach Blue, ch 1, sc in back loop of each st around. Join. Drop Blue, pick up White. **2nd and 3rd rnds:** Ch 1, sc in each st around. Join. **4th rnd:** Drop White, pick up Blue, ch 1, sc in same place as sl st, * sc in next st on previous Blue rnd (long sc made); sc in next st on last rnd. Repeat from * around. Join. Drop Blue, pick up White. Repeat 2nd, 3rd, and 4th rnds until Side measures 3 inches, ending with the 4th rnd. Break off.

Attach Blue to a free loop on last rnd of Bottom and make sc in each st. Join and break off. Make 5 more jackets same as this.

9407 . . . Materials: Knit-Cro-Sheen, *2 balls each of light and dark colors* . . . *Steel Crochet Hook No. 4.*

GAUGE: 1 shell makes 1 inch; 3 rows make 1 inch.

SIDE . . . Starting at lower edge with Dark, make a chain 20 inches long (9 ch sts to 1 inch). **1st row:** Sc in 2nd ch from hook, * skip 3 ch, in next ch make 3 tr, ch 1 and 3 tr (shell made), skip 3 ch, sc in next ch. Repeat from * across until there are 18 shells, ending with an sc. Cut off remaining chain. Break off Dark, attach Light, ch 4, turn. **2nd row:** 3 tr in 1st sc (half shell), * sc in ch-1 sp of next shell, shell in next sc. Repeat from * across ending with 4 tr in last sc. Break off Light, attach Dark, ch 1, turn. **3rd row:** Sc in 1st tr, * shell in next sc, sc in ch-1 sp of next shell. Repeat from * across, ending with sc in top st of turning chain. Break off Dark, attach Light, ch 4, turn. Repeat 2nd and 3rd rows alternately until piece measures 13 inches. Break off. Make another piece same as this. Sew lower edges together. Starting at lower edge, sew side edges together for 8 inches. Line bag and sew top edges to bag handles.

9407

X-127 . . . Materials: RUG YARN *(70-yard skeins)*, *4 skeins of main color for Body (Yellow, Cream, or Ecru); 1 skein of Brown for Hair* . . . SIX STRAND EMBROIDERY FLOSS, *1 skein Red, Blue, and Brown* . . . *Crochet Hook Size G* . . . *Steel Crochet Hook No. 7.*

GAUGE: 3 sts make 1 inch; 3 rnds make 1 inch.

HEAD . . . Starting at top with main color and G hook, ch 22. **1st rnd:** Sc in 2nd ch from hook and in each ch across. Then, working along opposite side of starting chain, make sc in each ch across (42 sts around). Work sc in each st around until piece measures 7 inches. Break off.

BODY . . . Starting at bottom with main color, ch 29. Work as for Head (56 sts around) until piece measures 11 inches. Break off.

ARM (Make 2) . . . With main color, ch 9 and work as for Head (16 sts around) until piece measures 9 inches. Break off.

LEG (Make 2) . . . Work as for Arms for 10 inches. Break off.

Stuff Head and Body with cotton batting. Run a drawstring around opening of Head and draw in slightly for neck. Sew Head to open end of Body, having Body extend beyond Head on both sides for shoulders. Stuff Arms and Legs and sew in place on Body.

EYE (Make 2) . . . With Blue Six Strand and No. 7 hook, ch 2. **1st rnd:** 7 sc in 2nd ch from hook. **2nd rnd:** 2 sc in each sc around (14 sts). **3rd rnd:** * Sc in next sc, 2 sc in next sc. Repeat from * around (21 sts). Break off.

LOWER LIP . . . With Red ch 8; sc in 2nd ch from hook, half dc in next, dc in next, tr in next, dc in next, half dc in next, sc in next. Break off.

UPPER LIP . . . With Red, ch 10, sc in 2nd ch from hook, half dc in next, dc in next, (tr in next) twice; dc in next, half dc in next, sc in next. Break off.

BANGS . . . Wind Brown Rug Yarn flatly over width of a piece of paper 1 inch wide and 6 inches long. Machine stitch 2 or 3 times along one edge. Tear out paper. Then cut one thickness of Rug Yarn close to stitching thus making Bangs 2 inches long. Sew in place across top of Head.

HAIR . . . Cut remainder of Brown Rug Yarn into 1-yard lengths. Lay them side by side to cover a 6 x 36-inch area. Machine stitch them together down middle (stitching should measure 6 inches), having 18-inch strands on each side of stitching. Place Hair on Head, one end of machine stitching in center of Bangs, remainder of stitching down back of Head. Sew securely to Head. Drape Hair over back of Head and across top of Bangs. Fasten strands close to Head at ends of Bangs. Make 2 braids and tie ends with ribbon. Tack braids in place. Sew Eyes and Mouth in place. Embroider eyelashes with Brown Six Strand. Dress as desired.

X-127

4026

4031

4026 . . . Materials: Baby Yarn *(1-ounce skein)*, *3 skeins* . . . Six Strand Embroidery Floss, *1 skein of Black* . . . *Crochet Hook F-5.*

Use yarn double throughout.

BODY . . . Starting at bottom, ch 2. **1st rnd:** 6 sc in 2nd ch from hook. **2nd rnd:** 2 sc in each sc around (12 sc). **3rd rnd:** * 2 sc in next sc, sc in next sc. Repeat from * around (18 sc). **4th rnd:** * 2 sc in next sc, sc in next 2 sc. Repeat from * around (24 sc). **5th rnd:** * 2 sc in next sc, sc in next 3 sc. Repeat from * around (30 sc). Sl st in next sc. Turn and work loop st

pattern as follows: **1st rnd:** * Insert hook in next st, holding hook between thumb and forefinger of left hand, with right hand place yarn over hook and over left forefinger, then place yarn over hook **only**, transfer yarn to left hand and draw the last 2 yarn overs on hook through the st where hook was inserted, yarn over hook and draw through all loops on hook (a loop st made, Fig. 76). Remove finger from loop. Repeat from * around. **2nd rnd:** Make a loop st in each loop st around. Repeat 2nd rnd until piece measures 3 inches from 1st rnd of loops. **Next 2 rnds:** Work as before but dec 3 sts evenly on each rnd—*to dec 1 st, skip 1 st.* **Last rnd:** Loop st in each st around. Break off.

HEAD . . . Ch 2. **1st rnd:** Make 6 loop sts in 2nd ch from hook. Work in loop st pattern, increasing 6 loop sts evenly apart on 2nd and 3rd rnds and 7 loop sts on the 4th rnd—*to inc a loop st, make 2 loop sts in 1 st* (25 loop sts on 4th rnd). Now work as before without increasing until piece measures 3 inches from starting ch-2. Break off.

LEG (Make 4) . . . Starting at tip of paw, ch 2. **1st rnd:** 5 sc in 2nd ch from hook. **2nd rnd:** 2 sc in each sc around. **3rd rnd:** Sc in each sc around. **4th to 7th rnds incl:** Work a loop st in each st around. Break off.

TAIL . . . Starting at tip, ch 2. **1st rnd:** 6 loop sts in 2nd ch from hook. **2nd rnd:** 2 loop sts in each st around. **3rd to 8th rnds incl:** Make a loop st in each st around. Break off.

EAR (Make 2) . . . Ch 10. **1st row:** Sc in 2nd ch from hook and in each ch across. Ch 1, turn. **2nd row:** Make a loop st in each sc across. Ch 1, turn. **3rd row:** Sc in each st across. Ch 1, turn. Repeat the 2nd and 3rd rows alternately until there are 7 loop st rows. Break off.

NOSE . . . Starting at tip, ch 2. **1st rnd:** 6 sc in 2nd ch from hook. **2nd to 5th rnds incl:** Sc in each sc around. Break off at end of 5th rnd.

Stuff body, head, nose, legs and tail firmly with cotton batting. Sew head to body. Sew nose, legs and tail in place. Turn under both long edges of each ear for ¼ inch and sew. Sew ears in place. Sew buttons in place for eyes.

With Six Strand, ch 2. **1st rnd:** 5 sc in 2nd ch from hook. **2nd rnd:** 2 sc in each sc around. Break off. Sew this piece to tip of nose. Tie ribbon in a bow around neck.

4031 . . . **Materials:** Knitting Worsted, *scraps of Red, White, and Blue* . . . *Crochet Hook F-5.*

With White, ch 4. **1st rnd:** 9 dc in 4th ch from hook. Insert hook in top st of starting chain, drop White and draw through a loop of Red. **2nd rnd:** With Red, ch 1, sc in same place as sl st, * 2 sc in next dc (an inc), sc in next dc. Repeat from * around (15 sc). Sl st in 1st sc, dropping Red and drawing through a loop of White. **3rd rnd:** With White, sc in each st around, increasing 5 sc evenly around (20 sc). Join as before, drawing through a loop of Blue. **4th rnd:** Sc in each sc around (20 sc). Join, drawing through a loop of White. **5th rnd:** Ch 3, * 2 dc in next sc (an inc), dc in next sc. Repeat from * around (30 dc). Join, drawing through Red. **6th rnd:** Sc in each dc around (30 sc). **7th rnd:** Sc in each sc around, increasing 10 sc evenly around (40 sc). Join, drawing through Blue. **8th rnd:** Sc in each sc around (40 sc). Join, drawing through White. Break off Blue. **9th rnd:** Ch 3, dc in each sc around (40 dc). Join, drawing through Red. Break off White. **10th rnd:** Sc in same place as sl st and in each dc around (40 sc). Join and break off.

This is half of ball. Work other half in same manner, using Blue where Red was used and Red where Blue was used. With double strand of White, sew the 2 halves together with over-and-over sts, stuffing firmly with cotton batting before opening is closed.

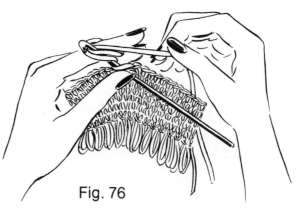

Fig. 76

9411

9411 . . . Materials: Knit-Cro-Sheen, *1 ball each of Light and Dark colors* . . . *Steel Crochet Hook No. 5 or 6.*

Starting at bottom with Light, make a chain about 2 inches longer than hanger. **1st row:** Sc in 2nd ch from hook, * ch 1, skip 1 ch, sc in next ch. Repeat from * across until row measures same as hanger. Cut off remaining chain. Ch 2, turn. **2nd row:** Sc in 1st sp, * ch 1, sc in next sp. Repeat from * across. Ch 2, turn. Drop Light, attach Dark. Repeat 2nd row, working 2 rows of Dark, then 2 rows of Light alternately until piece is wide enough to cover hanger, ending with Dark. Break off. Draw hook of hanger through center of crocheted piece and sew edges together, thus covering hanger. Make 3 more hangers same as this.

3991 . . . Materials: Knitting Worsted *(4-ounce skein), 1 skein of Nile Green for style A; 1 skein of light pink for style B . . . Crochet Hook Size H . . .* For Each Pillow: 9-inch round foam pillow; 1½ yards of 1-inch lace; 15 inches narrow ribbon.

BOTTOM . . . Starting at center with Nile Green for Style A and Lt. Pink for Style B, ch. 5. Join with sl st to form ring. **1st rnd:** Ch 1, 10 sc in ring. Join with a sl st to first sc. **2nd rnd:** Ch 5, yarn over, draw up a 1-inch loop in joining and complete a dc—**long dc made**; make 2 long dc in each remaining st around. Join to top of ch-5—20 long dc, counting ch-5 as 1 long dc. **3rd and 4th rnds:** Repeat 2nd rnd—80 long dc. Break off and fasten.

3991

TOP . . . Starting at center with same color as Bottom, ch 5. Join with a sl st to form a ring. **1st rnd:** Ch 1, 8 sc in ring. Join to first sc. **2nd rnd:** Ch 4, pulling first loop of each long dc up to measure ¾ inch, make 2 long dc in joining, 3 long dc in each of remaining 7 sc. Join to top of ch-4—24 long dc. **3rd rnd:** Ch 1, in joining make sc, ch 3 and 3 long dc as for last rnd—shell made; * skip 2 dc, shell in next dc. Repeat from * around, ending with skip last 2 dc. Join to first sc—8 shells. **4th rnd:** Ch 1, sc in joining, * ch 5, skip 3 dc, sc in next sc. Repeat from * around, ending with ch 5, skip 3 dc. Join to first sc. **5th rnd:** Ch 1, shell in joining, * shell in center ch of ch-5, shell in next sc. Repeat from * around. Join. **6th rnd:** Repeat 4th rnd. **7th rnd:** Ch 4, long dc in

joining, * 2 long dc in next ch, (skip a ch, 2 long dc in next ch) twice; 2 long dc in sc. Repeat from * around. Join to top of ch-4—128 long dc. **8th rnd: Ruffle:** Ch 6, pulling first loop of each long dc up to measure 1 inch, make a long dc in next dc, * ch 1, long dc in next dc. Repeat from * around, ending with ch 1. Join to 5th ch of ch-6. Break off and fasten. Gather lace to fit around base of ruffle and sew in place.

Using a 5-inch piece of ribbon for each bow, make 3 bows and tack in place as shown. With right side of pieces out, place pillow between top and bottom, sew outer edge of bottom to edge of 7th rnd of top, allowing ruffle to extend free.

232

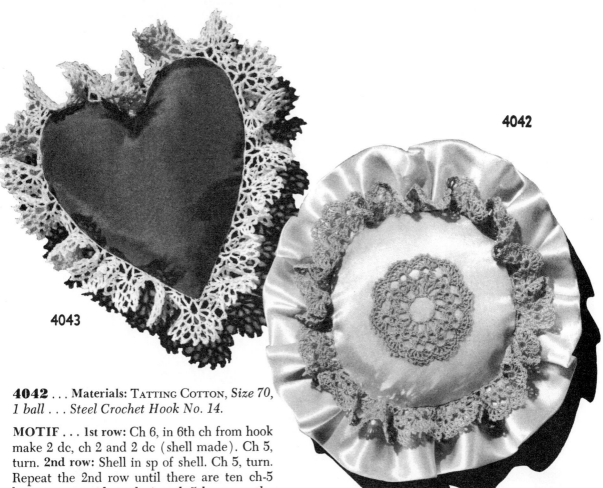

4042

4043

4042 . . . Materials: TATTING COTTON, *Size 70, 1 ball . . . Steel Crochet Hook No. 14.*

MOTIF . . . 1st row: Ch 6, in 6th ch from hook make 2 dc, ch 2 and 2 dc (shell made). Ch 5, turn. **2nd row:** Shell in sp of shell. Ch 5, turn. Repeat the 2nd row until there are ten ch-5 loops on one side and nine ch-5 loops on the other side. Ch 5, turn. **Next row:** 2 dc in sp of shell, ch 1, sl st in st where 1st shell was made, thus joining strip to form ring; ch 1, 2 dc in same place where last 2 dc were made. **Following rnd:** * Ch 2, sc in next loop on inner side of ring. Repeat from * around, ending with ch 2, sl st in 1st sc. Break off.

Now work along outer edge of ring as follows: **1st rnd:** Attach thread to a ch-5 loop, ch 4, in same loop make (dc, ch 1) 5 times and dc; * in next ch-5 loop make (dc, ch 1) 6 times and dc. Repeat from * around, ending with sl st in 3rd st of ch-4. **2nd rnd:** * Sc in next ch-1 sp, (ch 3, sc in next sp) 5 times. Repeat from * around. Sl st in 1st sc. Break off.

EDGING . . . Repeat 1st and 2nd rows of Motif until one edge fits around cushion at base of ruffle. Join inner loops same as for Motif. Then work 1st and 2nd rnds of outer edge of Motif. Break off. Sew motif and edging to cushion.

4043 . . . Materials: TATTING COTTON, *Size 70, 1 ball . . . Steel Crochet Hook No. 14.*

Make a chain to measure slightly longer than outer edge of cushion. **1st row:** Sc in 2nd ch from hook, ch 3, skip 1 ch, sc in next ch. * ch 3, skip 2 ch, in next ch make dc, ch 5 and dc; ch 3, skip 2 ch, sc in next ch, ch 3, skip 1 ch, sc in next ch. Repeat from * across. Ch 3, turn. **2nd row:** 3 dc in ch-3 loop, * in ch-5 sp (between dc's) make (dc, ch 2) 6 times and dc; skip next ch-3, 3 dc in next ch-3 loop. Repeat from * across. Ch 1, turn. **3rd row:** Sc in 2nd dc, * (ch 3, in next ch-2 sp make sc, ch 3 and sc) 6 times; ch 3, sc in center dc of 3-dc group. Repeat from * across. Ch 1, turn. **4th row:** * Sc in next loop, ch 4, sc in 3rd ch from hook (p made), ch 1. Repeat from * across. Break off.

Sew edging to cushion and sew narrow ends together.

233

6064

CHAPTER SEVENTEEN

Afghans

Afghans come under the heading of luxurious necessities—necessities because they're so infinitely useful, luxurious because they're so lovely to look at. Nothing's cozier on a rainy afternoon when you're tired or out of sorts than to curl up on the sofa and cover yourself with a soft woolly afghan. Warmly regarded as a draft evader, an afghan makes a fine extra blanket on frosty winter nights. And on brisk fall days you'll find it a smart and colorful antifreeze companion at football games.

Here's a chance to have a fling at color. Somehow afghans call for color and plenty of it—cheerful eye-filling colors—warm russets, rich crimsons, glowing burgundies. . . . Suit your pattern to your room. The flower motifs are lovely for a bedroom, the plaid afghan is perfect for a den. There's a matching rug and afghan set that would be handsomely at home in a modern setting, a deer design for an inviting bookfilled pine or maple room, a tassel beauty, cozy as a log fire. Make one for your home and see if it doesn't come to be one of your most warmly cherished possessions.

6064 . . . **Materials:** KNITTING WORSTED *(1-ounce skeins), 50 skeins of A; 6 skeins of B; 2 skeins of C; 4 skeins of D; 6 skeins of E; 4 skeins of F; 2 skeins of G; 2 skeins of H . . . Afghan Hook H (5 mm size).*

Afghan measures 62 x 71 inches.

GAUGE: 5 sts make 1 inch; 4 rows make 1 inch.

NARROW STRIP . . . Starting at short end, with A, ch 45. **1st row:** Insert hook in 2nd ch and draw up a loop, retaining all loops on hook, draw up a loop in each ch across, Fig. 77 (45 loops). This is half of row; work other half as follows: Yarn over and draw through 1 loop, * yarn over and draw through 2 loops, Fig.78. Repeat from * across. The loop which remains on hook always counts as first st of next row. **2nd row:** Retaining all loops on hook, * insert hook in vertical bar of next st and draw loop through, Fig. 79. Repeat from * across to within last bar; insert hook through double vertical bar and draw a loop through (thus giving a firm edge to this side—45 loops on hook). Work other half of row as before, Fig. 80. Repeat 2nd row until piece measures about 70 inches in all (281 rows). Work an sc in each vertical bar across. Break off. With F, work a row of sc along right side of one long edge, keeping work flat. Break off. With B, work sc in back loop of each F sc. Break off. Finish other long edge in same way. Make another strip exactly the same as this.

WIDE STRIP . . . Starting at short end, with A, ch 64. Work as for Narrow Strip (having 64 sts on each row instead of 45), until piece measures about 70 inches in all (281 rows). Work an sc in each vertical bar across. Break off. Finish long edges with F and B, same as on Narrow Strip. Break off.

Embroidery . . . With basting thread, mark off center 46 vertical bars of wide strip. These 46 bars correspond to the 46 spaces of chart. Start embroidering on 2nd row from one narrow end of strip. Each symbol on chart indicates one cross stitch (see cross stitch detail, Fig. 81). Work in cross stitch, following chart to top. Repeat entire chart 2 more times. Now

work from 1st to 21st rows incl. Make 2 more strips same as this.

Place the 2 Narrow Strips between the 3 Wide Strips (have design on center strip reversed), and join by sewing together one loop of B sc on each strip. Work F and B sc's along top and bottom edges. Break off.

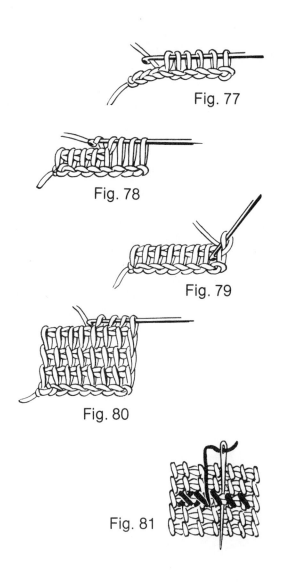

Fig. 77

Fig. 78

Fig. 79

Fig. 80

Fig. 81

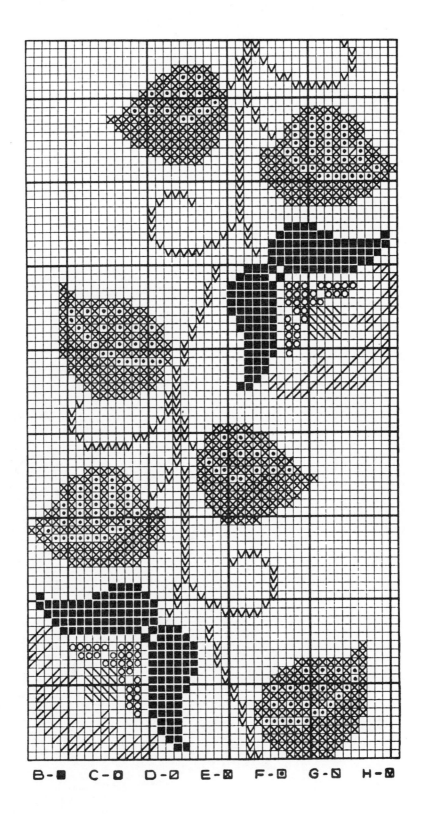

B-■ C-◨ D-◩ E-▨ F-◪ G-◧ H-▧

664 . . . Materials: KNITTING WORSTED (*1-ounce skeins*), *8 skeins of A; 22 skeins of B; 7 skeins of C and 17 skeins of D* . . . *Crochet Hook Size H-8.*

Afghan measures 50 x 70 inches.

Each square measures about 3 inches along each side; about 4 inches diagonally across from corner to corner.

SQUARE . . . Starting at center with C, ch 6, join with sl st. **1st rnd:** Ch 1, * sc in ring, ch 3, tr in ring, ch 3, tr in ring, ch 3. Repeat from * 3 more times, ending with sl st in 1st sc made (4 petals). Break off. **2nd rnd:** Attach D to a tr following the ch-3 at center of a petal, ch 1, sc in same tr, * sc in top st of next ch-3, 2 dc in sc between petals, sc in top st of next ch-3, sc in next tr, sc in next ch, ch 3, skip 1 ch, sc in next ch, sc in next tr. Repeat from * around,

ending with ch 3, sc in ch preceding 1st sc made, sl st in 1st sc. **3rd rnd:** Ch 3 (to count as dc), dc in each st to corner ch-3; in corner ch-3 make dc, ch 3 and dc. Continue thus around. Join with sl st in 3rd st of ch-3 first made. Break off. This completes one square.

Make 176 squares in all like this one. Make 204 squares using A for center and B for outside. Place squares as on diagram and sew together on wrong side with neat over-and-over sts, picking up only the back loop of each st.

□ A & B   □ C & D

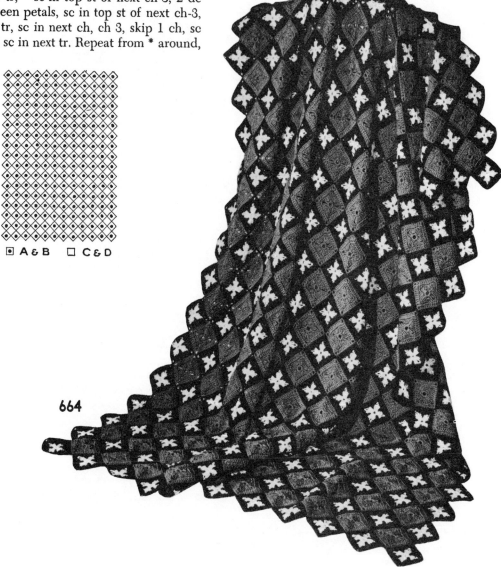

664

6087 . . . Materials: BABY YARN (*1-ounce skeins*), *41 skeins of White* . . . *Steel Crochet Hook No. 2/0 (double zero).*

GAUGE (Background): 4 sps make 1 inch before loops are made; 3 sps make 1 inch after loops are made.

Afghan measures 48 x 66 inches.

Starting at narrow end, make a chain 55 inches long (about 7 ch sts to 1 inch). **1st row:** Dc in 6th ch from hook, * ch 1, skip 1 ch, dc in next ch. Repeat from * until there are 144 sps. Cut off remaining chain. Ch 4, turn. **2nd row:** * Dc in next dc, ch 1. Repeat from * across, ending with skip 1 st of turning chain, dc in next ch. Ch 4, turn. Repeat 2nd row until piece measures 66 inches. Break off.

LOOPS . . . **Leave one row of spaces open around entire piece.** Attach yarn at edge on narrow end, and **in each ch-1 sp** make (sc, draw loop on hook out to measure 1 inch) 4 times. Break off. Attach yarn at same edge as before and work loops across next row of ch-1 sps. Break off. Continue thus until 2 rows of sps remain; do not break off but work last row of loops across in the opposite direction. Break off.

Bind entire edge (sps left free) with satin ribbon, mitering corners.

6087 . . . Materials: KNITTING WORSTED (*4-ounce skeins*), *36 skeins of White* . . . *Crochet Hook Size H.*

GAUGE (Background): 5 sps make 2 inches before loops are made; 2 sps make 1 inch after loops are made.

Rug measures 28 x 40 inches.

Starting at narrow end, make a chain 30 inches long (about 5 ch sts to 1 inch). **1st row:** Dc in 6th ch from hook, * ch 1, skip 1 ch, dc in next ch. Repeat from * until there are 56 sps. Cut off remaining chain. Ch 4, turn. Work exactly as for Afghan until piece measures 40 inches. Break off.

LOOPS . . . Work exactly as for Loops on Afghan. Machine stitch upholsterer's tape on right side along sps left free on all edges. Fold over tape and whip down on wrong side.

6072 . . . Materials: KNITTING WORSTED (*1-ounce skeins*), *6 skeins of A; 19 skeins of B; 34 skeins of C* . . . *Crochet Hook Size H.*

Motif measures about 4¼ inches from side to side across center; about 4¾ inches from point to opposite point.

MOTIF . . . Starting at center with A, ch 4. Join with sl st. **1st rnd:** Ch 3, yarn over hook, insert hook in ring and draw loop out to length of ch-3, yarn over hook and draw through all 3 loops on hook (a long half dc made); make 16 more long half dc in ring. Join with sl st to top of ch-3. Break off. **2nd rnd:** Attach B, ch 1 and, working through the 2 back loops only of each long half dc, make 2 sc in each st around, thus forming a ridge on right side (36 sc in rnd). Join by inserting hook in 1st sc made and drawing through a loop of C. Do not break off B. **3rd rnd:** Working over B with C, make ch 4, 3 tr in base of ch, * drop C (do not work over it) and, with B, yarn over hook twice and, holding back on hook the last loop of each tr, make tr in same place as C tr's and in each of next 6 sts, drop B and, with C, yarn over hook and draw through all 8 loops on hook (a cluster made). Working over B, make 7 C tr in same place as last B tr of cluster. Repeat from * around, ending with C, 3 tr in same place as last tr of cluster, sl st in top of ch-4. Break off B. **4th rnd:** Ch 3, dc in same place as sl st, ch 2, 2 dc in same place, * dc in next 7 sts, in next st make 2 dc, ch 2 and 2 dc. Repeat from * around. Join with sl st to top of ch-3. Break off. This completes one Motif.

Make 201 motifs in all and sew together as in diagram with neat over-and-over sts on wrong side, picking up only the back loop of each st.

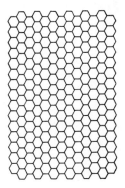

6087

6072

6068 . . . Materials: AFGHAN WOOL (*1-ounce skeins*), 10 skeins each of A, B, C, and D . . . *Crochet Hook Size G.*

Afghan measures 47 x 65 inches.

GAUGE: 1 shell makes 1¼ inches; 3 rows make 2¼ inches.

Starting at bottom with A, make a chain to measure about 60 inches (5 ch sts to 1 inch). **1st row:** Make 4 tr in 4th ch from hook, * skip 5 ch, sc in next ch, ch 2, 4 tr in same place where last sc was made. Repeat from * across until row measures 47 inches. Cut off remaining chain. Break off. **2nd row:** Turn, attach B in first ch-2, sc in same place, * ch 2, 4 tr in same ch-2, sc under next ch-2. Repeat from * across, ending with 4 tr in last ch-2. Break off. **3rd and 4th rows:** Repeat 2nd row, using C for 3rd row and D for 4th row. Continue in this manner, using colors in established order, until piece measures 65 inches, ending with A, to correspond with the beginning.

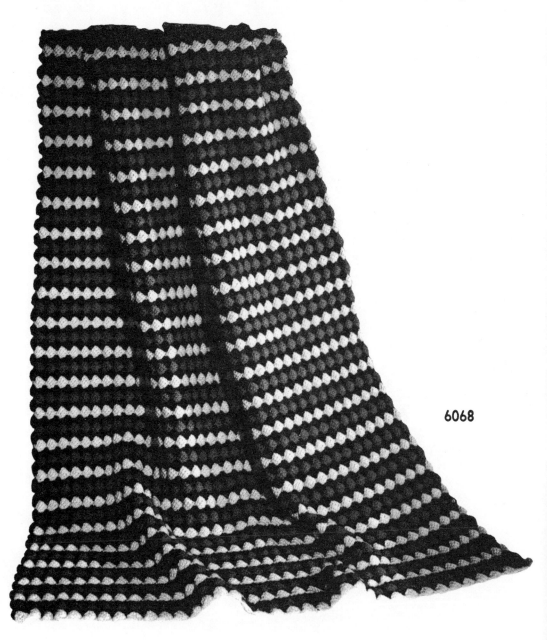

6068

6075 . . . Materials: KNITTING WORSTED (1-ounce skeins), 17 skeins of A; 16 skeins of B; 18 skeins of C; 16 skeins of D; 9 skeins of E . . . Crochet Hook Size H.

Afghan measures 50 x 65 inches.

Each motif measures about 4 inches square and 5¼ inches diagonally from point to point.

MOTIF . . . Starting at center with any color, ch 2. **1st rnd:** 12 sc in 2nd ch from hook. Join with sl st in 1st sc made. **2nd rnd:** Draw loop out to measure 1¾ inches, * yarn over, insert hook in same place as sl st, yarn over and draw loop through to measure 1¾ inches. Repeat from * 6 more times, yarn over and draw through all loops on hook, ch 1 to fasten (a long cluster made). ** Yarn over, insert hook in next sc and complete a long cluster as before. Repeat from ** around. Join with sl st to top of 1st cluster made. **3rd rnd:** Ch 1, 2 sc in same place as sl st, * 2 sc between clusters, 2 sc in next cluster. Repeat from * around (48 sc). Join. **4th rnd:** Ch 3, dc in next st, * half dc in next 2 sts, sc in next 3 sts, half dc in next 2 sts, dc in next 2 sts, 3 tr in next st (corner), dc in next 2 sts. Repeat from * around, ending with 3 tr in last st, sl st in 3rd st of ch-3. Break off. This completes one Motif. Make 36 motifs with A, 48 motifs with B, 54 motifs with C, 48 motifs with D, and 27 motifs with E. Sew together as on diagram with over-and-over sts, picking up only the back loop of each st, thus forming ridges on right side.

TASSEL . . . Make 40 tassels with A. Cut a piece of cardboard 5 inches wide. Place a dou-ble strand of yarn across cardboard; then wind single strand 26 times around 5-inch width of cardboard over double strand. Slip off cardboard and tie the ends of the double strand tightly for top of tassel. Wind a single strand 6 times tightly around tassel about ¾ inch down from top and fasten securely. Cut loops at bottom.

Fasten tassels around Afghan between motifs. Trim tassels to same length as points of motifs.

6067 . . . Materials: KNITTING WORSTED (1-ounce skeins), 28 skeins of A; 2 skeins of B; 13 skeins of C; 4 skeins of D; 7 skeins of E . . . Afghan Hook H (5 mm size).

Afghan measures 50 x 71 inches.

GAUGE: 5 sts make 1 inch; 4 rows make 1 inch.

SIDE STRIP (Make 2) . . . Starting at short end, with A, ch 50 to measure 10 inches. **1st row:** Insert hook in 2nd ch and draw up a loop, retaining all loops on hook, draw up a loop in each ch across (50 loops on hook). This is half of row, work other half as follows: Yarn over and draw through 1 loop, * yarn over and draw through next 2 loops on hook. Repeat from * across. The loop which remains on hook always counts as the first st of next row. **2nd row:** Retaining all loops on hook, * insert hook in vertical bar of next st and draw loop through. Repeat from * across to last bar; insert hook through double vertical bar of last st and draw a loop through (thus giving a firm edge to this side—50 loops on hook). Work other half of row as before. Continue in this manner until piece measures 68 inches. Work an sc in each vertical bar across. Break off.

Embroidery . . . With basting thread, mark off the center 36 vertical bars at one end of strip. These 36 bars correspond to the 36 spaces of Deer Chart. Start embroidering Deer on 5th row from one end of strip. Each symbol on chart indicates one cross stitch (see cross stitch detail on page 247). Work in cross stitch, following chart for color, until all sts on chart are completed. Reverse strip and, starting on 5th row from other end of strip, reverse design

A- ◆ B- ◇ C- ⊗
D- ◈ E- ◆

6075

244

6067

so that Deer faces left instead of right, and embroider. Mark center of length of strip and starting at center of Snowflake Chart, embroider Snowflake at exact center of strip. Now embroider Snowflake twice more, halfway between Deer and center Snowflake.

CENTER STRIP . . . Work crochet same as for Side Strips.

Embroidery . . . Starting on 5th row from end of strip, embroider Snowflake at both ends of strip. Embroider 3rd Snowflake at exact center of strip, then embroider Heart and "X" detail of Deer Chart at even intervals between Snowflakes.

PATTERN STRIP (Make 2) . . . Each pattern strip consists of 5 narrow strips, made as follows: Starting at narrow end, with D, ch 7 and work as for Side Strip for 6 complete rows. **7th row:** Draw up 2 loops as before (3 loops on hook, including the loop left on hook at end of previous row), yarn over, skip the last loop made, insert hook under vertical bar directly below the previous loop on the 3rd row down, draw up a loop, yarn over and draw through 1 loop, yarn over and draw through 2 loops. Yarn over, insert hook under next vertical bar on 4th row down (this will be directly under the last loop picked up on 7th row), draw up a loop, yarn over and draw through 1 loop, yarn over and draw through 2 loops. Yarn over twice, insert hook under next vertical bar on 5th row down, draw up a loop, (yarn over and draw through 2 loops)

twice. Yarn over, insert hook under next vertical bar on 4th row down and complete as before. Yarn over, insert hook under next vertical bar on 3rd row down and complete as before. Yarn over and draw through the last 5 loops on hook; then ch 1 (thus completing a fan). Skip the next vertical bar on the 7th row (directly behind center of fan), draw up a loop in each of next 3 bars. Work other half of row as before. This completes a pattern row. Work in this manner, making 6 plain rows and then a pattern row, until strip measures 68 inches, ending with 1 plain row. Sc in each vertical bar across. Break off. This completes one narrow strip. Make 2 narrow strips with C and sew them to each long side of the D strip; then make 2 narrow strips with E and sew them to outer edges of C strips. This completes 1 Pattern Strip. Place Pattern Strips between Embroidered Strips, as in illustration, and sew together neatly.

EDGING . . . Attach C to one narrow end of Afghan. **1st row:** Work across width of Afghan as follows: Sc in 1st st, * ch 3, (yarn over hook, draw up a loop in same place as sc) 5 times; yarn over and draw through all loops on hook, skip 3 sts, sc in next st. Repeat from * around, skipping 2 rows on both long sides of Afghan instead of 3. Join and break off. **2nd row:** Attach A and work * 2 sc in ch 3 sp, sc in st on Afghan preceding C sc (long sc made between clusters). Repeat from * around, making sc, ch 3 and sc at corners. Join and break off.

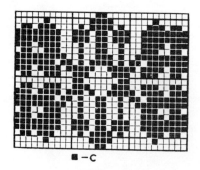

■ —C

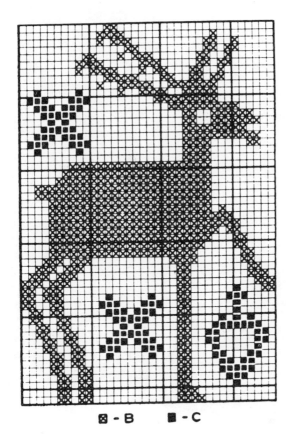

There are 10 spaces between heavy lines

▨ - B   ▧ - C

9139

9140

248

CHAPTER EIGHTEEN

Rugs

IT'S TRUE the floor can make or break a room, but that's no reason to feel sorry for yourself because the exchequer can't accommodate wall-to-wall carpeting or an expensive new rug. There are two schools of thought on the subject of floor covering. One believes in lots of carpet and the other believes in waxed, shining floors and small scatter rugs.

You'll find a handsome selection of scatter rugs in this chapter in a gamut of colors and designs. Choose a red for a stunning effect—ruby, cardinal, crimson, rose, strawberry, wine. Or try a rug in daffodil yellow, or a checkerboard design in pink and black. To add a dramatic touch to a modern room, use a soft beige with a black or crimson stripe.

9139 . . . Materials: RUG YARN *(70-yard skeins), 7 skeins of Red, 4 skeins of Tan, 3 skeins of White, and 2 skeins of Brown . . . Crochet Hook Size G or H.*

GAUGE: 2 sps make 1 inch; 2 rows make 1 inch.

Rug measures 30 x 50 inches, including Fringe.

Starting at short end, with Red ch 124 (4 ch sts to 1 inch). **1st row:** Dc in 6th ch from hook, * ch 1, skip 1 ch, dc in next ch. Repeat from * across (60 sps). Ch 4, turn. **2nd row:** Skip 1st dc, * dc in next dc, ch 1. Repeat from * across, ending with ch 1, skip 1 ch, dc in next ch. Ch 4, turn. Repeat 2nd row, changing colors as follows: ** 4 rows Red, 2 rows Tan, 2 White, 4 Red, 2 Tan, 2 Brown. Repeat from ** 4 more times. Then repeat 1st to 12th rows incl once more. Break off. Block to measure 30 x 46 inches.

WEAVING . . . Cut 4 strands of Tan, each 66 inches long. Starting at short end, weave these 4 strands in and out each sp lengthwise, leaving center ridge of each color-stripe on top, taking care not to draw strands too tight in order to keep blocked measurements (leave extra length of strands free at each end, for fringe). Fill in all other spaces in same manner, using colors as follows: another row of Tan, 2 Brown, 4 Red, 2 White, 2 Tan, 4 Red, 2 White, 2 Brown, 4 Red, 2 White, 2 Tan, 4 Red, 2 Brown, 2 White, 4 Red, 2 Tan, 2 White, 4 Red, 2 Brown, 2 White, 4 Red, 2 White, 2 Tan.

FRINGE . . . Pick up 4 strands left free at one end of 1st row of weaving and make a knot close to rug. * Knot together 4 strands each of next 2 rows. Repeat from * across, knotting last 4 strands. Trim ends evenly. Now make fringe on other end of rug.

9140 . . . Materials: Rug Yarn (70-yard skeins), 6 skeins of dark color and 3 skeins of light color . . . Crochet Hook Size G or H.

GAUGE: 3 dc make 1 inch; 3 rows make 2 inches (each individual square on chart indicates 3 dc).

Rug measures 28 x 42 inches, excluding Tassels.

To Change Color: Before drawing through last 2 loops of last dc of one color-group, drop this color, pick up 2nd color, yarn over, and draw through last 2 loops with 2nd color. Continue with 2nd color according to chart.

With Dark, make a chain about 50 inches long (7 ch sts to 2 inches). **1st row:** Dc in 4th ch from hook and in each ch across until there are 126 dc, counting turning chain as 1 dc (row should measure about 42 inches). Cut off remaining chain. Ch 3, turn. **2nd and 3rd rows:** Dc in each dc across, dc in top st of turning chain. Ch 3, turn.

4th row: Dc in next 25 dc, yarn over, insert hook in next st and draw loop through, yarn over and draw through 2 loops. Drop Dark, attach Light and draw Light through last 2 loops on hook. With Light make dc in next 14 dc, attach a new ball of Dark and change from Light to Dark in the next dc. Drop Light, make 17 Dark dc, attach a 2nd ball of Light and change from Dark to Light in the next dc. Drop Dark, make 14 Light dc, attach 3rd ball of Dark, change color as before, drop Light, make 17 Dark dc. Attach 3rd ball of Light, change color as before. Drop Dark and make 23 Light dc. Attach 4th ball of Dark, change

color as before and make 9 Dark dc. Ch 3, turn.

Now starting at "X," follow chart, working back and forth and changing colors as before. When the distance between colors is only 3 dc (represented on chart by 1 square), work over unused color in order to conceal it. Break off unnecessary balls or join in new ones as occasions arise. Block to measure 28 x 42 inches.

TASSEL (Make 65 of Dark color) . . . Cut a piece of cardboard 2½ inches wide and 4 inches long. Place a 7-inch strand across length of cardboard. Now wind one strand 18 times around width of cardboard. Tie strands together at one end. Cut free ends and remove cardboard. Wind a single strand 3 times around strands, about ¾ inch down from top, and tie securely. Trim tassel to measure 2¼ inches in all. With a strong thread of same color, sew tassels along outer edges of rug, spacing them evenly.

9152 . . . Materials: Rug Yarn (70-yard skeins), 14 skeins . . . Crochet Hook Size G or H.

Rug measures 36 inches in diameter, excluding Tassels.

Starting at center, ch 6. Join with sl st to form ring. **1st rnd:** Ch 3 (to count as dc), 15 dc in ring. Join with sl st to top st of ch-3. **2nd rnd:** Ch 1, * sc behind post of next dc—*to make an sc behind post of dc, insert hook between next 2 sts from back to front of work, pass hook over next dc and insert hook between sts from front to back, yarn over, draw loop through and finish as for an sc (sc will be behind post of dc).* Repeat from * around. Join with sl st to 1st sc made (16 sts). **3rd rnd:** Ch 3 (to count as dc), dc in same place as sl st, * 2 dc in next sc. Repeat from * around; join (32 sts). **4th rnd:** Repeat 2nd rnd (32 sts). **5th rnd:** Ch 3, 2 dc in next sc (an increase), * dc in next sc, 2 dc in next sc (an increase). Repeat from * around; join (48 sts). **6th rnd:** Repeat 2nd rnd (48 sts). Continue thus, increasing 16 sts on each odd rnd (being careful increases do not fall above one another), and repeating the 2nd rnd on each even rnd until piece measures 33 inches in diameter, ending with the 2nd rnd.

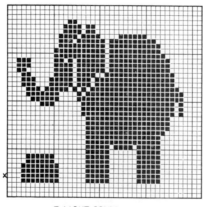

■ LIGHT COLOR
□ DARK COLOR

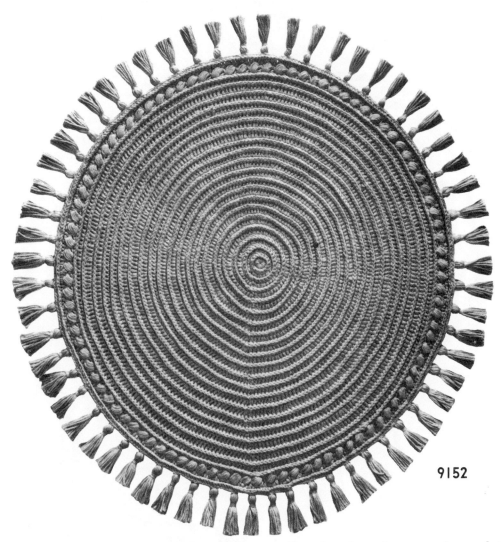

9152

Do not break off but work next rnd as follows: Ch 3, * insert hook in same place as sl st and pull loop out to measure 1 inch, yarn over. Repeat from * 5 more times, draw loop through all loops on hook, ch 1 to fasten (a loop-cluster made). ** Skip 2 sc, sc in next sc, ch 2 and complete a loop-cluster in same place where last sc was made. Repeat from ** around; join. Ch 3, work a rnd of dc into clusters, increasing 32 sts evenly around; join. Now repeat 2nd rnd of pattern stitch once. Break off.

TASSEL (Make 61) . . . Cut a cardboard 3½ inches wide and 5 inches long. Place a 10-inch strand of yarn across length of cardboard. Wind 1 strand of yarn 20 times around width of cardboard. Break off. Pick up both ends of 10-inch strand and tie securely (top). Remove cardboard and cut loops at other end. Wind a strand of yarn tightly 3 times around, about ¾ inch from top, and fasten securely. Sew tassels around on outer sc-rnd, spacing them evenly apart.

9135-A . . . Materials: Rug Yarn (*70-yard skeins*), *5 skeins of main color and 1 skein of contrasting color* . . . Crochet Hook Size G or H.

GAUGE: 2 star sts make 1 inch; 2 rnds make 1¼ inches.

Small Oval Rug measures 22 x 33 inches.

Starting at center, with main color ch 33 to measure about 12 inches. **1st rnd:** Insert hook in 2nd ch from hook and pull loop through, (insert hook in next ch and pull loop through) 3 times: yarn over and draw through all loops

251

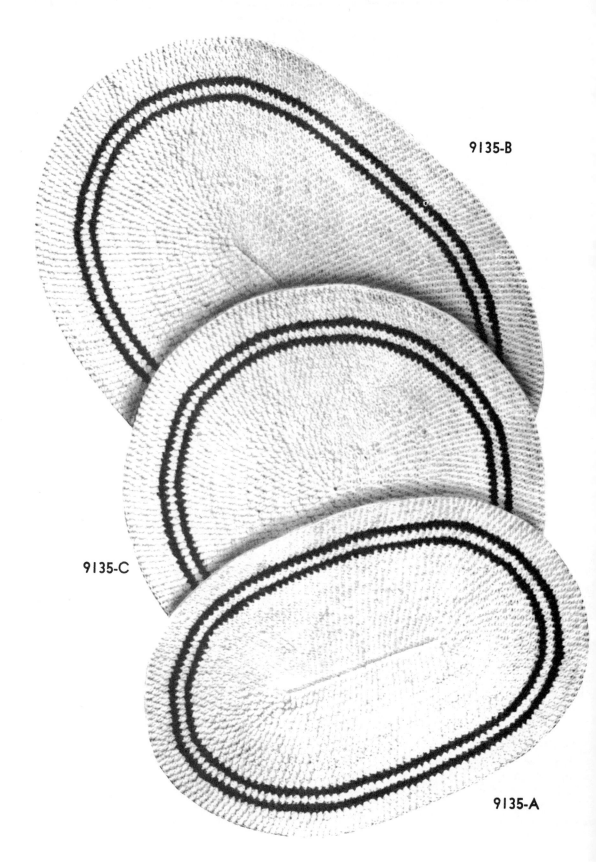

9135-B

9135-C

9135-A

on hook, ch 1 to fasten (a star st made—Fig. 62, page 39). * Insert hook in fastening ch just made and pull loop through, insert hook in last loop of previous star st and pull loop through, insert hook in st where last loop of previous star st was pulled through and pull loop through, insert hook in next ch and pull loop through, yarn over and draw through all loops on hook, ch 1 to fasten (another star st). Repeat from * across; then work along opposite side of starting chain to correspond. **2nd rnd:** Pull up first 3 loops of next star st as before (4 loops on hook), pull up next loop in 1st ch preceding 1st star st made and complete star st as before. (Make another star st, pulling up last loop of star st in next st of same chain) twice. * Now make a star st pulling up last loop in fastening ch of next star st below. Repeat from * to opposite end of oval, then inc as necessary to keep work flat—*to inc, work directly into the top of star st as well as into the fastening ch.* Continue thus around, increasing at ends of oval to keep work flat, until piece measures 15 x 26 inches. Make a sl st in fastening ch of next star st. Break off.

Attach contrasting color where sl st was made, ch 2, insert hook in 2nd ch from hook and pull loop through, insert hook in fastening loop (of contrasting color) and pull loop through, insert hook in same place where sl st was made and pull loop through, insert hook in fastening ch of next star st and pull loop through, complete star st as before. Work 1 rnd of contrasting star st as before. Join with sl st to 2nd ch of ch-2 first made. Break off. Attach main color and work 1 rnd. Break off. Work 1 rnd of contrasting color. Break off. Now work with main color until rug measures approximately 22 x 33 inches. Break off.

9135-B . . . Materials: RUG YARN (70-yard skeins), 9 skeins of main color and 1 skein of contrasting color . . . Crochet Hook Size G or H.

Large Oval Rug measures 28 x 40 inches.

Work in main color as for Rug 9135-A until piece measures 20 x 32 inches. Break off. Now work 1 rnd of contrasting color, 1 rnd of main color and 1 rnd of contrasting color as for Rug 9135-A. Attach main color and work in pattern until rug measures 28 x 40 inches. Break off.

9135-C . . . Materials: RUG YARN (70-yard skeins), 6 skeins of main color and 1 skein of contrasting color . . . Crochet Hook Size G or H.

Round Rug measures 31 inches in diameter.

Starting at center, with main color ch 8. Join with sl st. **1st rnd:** Ch 4, insert hook in 2nd ch from hook and pull loop through, insert hook in the next ch and pull loop through, insert hook in next ch and pull loop through, insert hook in same place as sl st and pull loop through, yarn over and draw through all loops on hook, ch 1 to fasten (a star st made—Fig. 62, page 39). * Insert hook in fastening ch just made and pull loop through, insert hook in last loop of previous star st and pull loop through, insert hook in st where last loop of previous star st was pulled through and pull loop through, insert hook in next st and pull loop through, yarn over and draw through all loops on hook, ch 1 to fasten (another star st). Repeat from * around (8 star sts in rnd). **2nd rnd:** * Draw up first 3 loops of next star st as before, draw up last loop in top of next star st—**not in the fastening ch;** complete star st as before (an inc made). Make another star st, drawing up last loop through fastening ch (star st made over star st). Repeat from * around (8 increases made—16 star sts in rnd). Continue to work in rnds, making star st over star st and increasing as necessary to keep work flat, until piece measures 22 inches in diameter—**when not increasing, work into the fastening ch's only; when increasing, work into the top of the star sts as well as into fastening ch's.** Sl st in fastening ch of next star st of last rnd. Break off.

Attach contrasting color where sl st was made, ch 2, insert hook in 2nd ch from hook and pull loop through, insert hook in fastening ch of contrasting color and pull loop through, insert hook in same place where sl st was made and pull loop through, insert hook in fastening ch of next star st and pull loop through; complete star st as before. Work a rnd of star sts, increasing as necessary to keep work flat. Join with sl st to 2nd ch of ch-2 first made. Break off. Attach main color and work 1 rnd as before. Break off. Attach contrasting color and work 1 rnd as before. Break off. Now work with main color until rug measures 31 inches in diameter, ending with sl st in fastening ch of next star st. Break off.

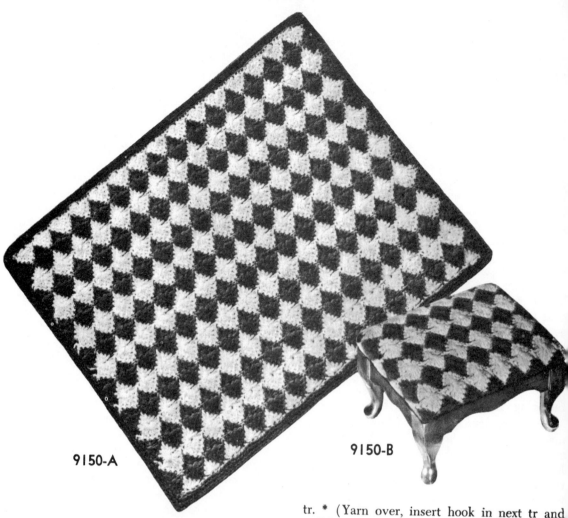

9150-A

9150-B

9150-A . . . **Materials:** Rug Yarn *(70-yard skeins)*, 4 *skeins each of light and dark colors* . . . *Crochet Hook Size G or H.*

GAUGE: 2 diamonds (measuring across center) make 3¼ inches; 4 rows make 2¾ inches.

Rug measures 24 x 30 inches.

Starting at long side, with Light make a chain about 40 inches long (7 ch sts make 2 inches). **1st row:** Make 7 tr in 4th ch from hook, * skip 3 ch, sl st in next ch, skip 3 ch, 7 tr in next ch. Repeat from * across until row measures 28½ inches, ending with skip 3 ch, sl st in next ch (15 half diamonds). Cut off remaining chain. Drop Light, turn, attach Dark. **2nd row:** Ch 3, (yarn over, insert hook in next tr and pull loop through; yarn over and draw through 2 loops) 3 times; yarn over and draw through all 4 loops on hook; ch 4, sl st in next

tr. * (Yarn over, insert hook in next tr and pull loop through; yarn over and draw through 2 loops) 3 times; yarn over twice, insert hook in sl st and pull loop through. (Yarn over and draw through 2 loops) twice; (yarn over, insert hook in next tr and pull loop through; yarn over and draw through 2 loops) 3 times; yarn over and draw through all 8 loops on hook; ch 4, sl st in next tr. Repeat from * across, ending with (yarn over, insert hook in next tr and pull loop through; yarn over and draw through 2 loops) 3 times; yarn over and draw through all loops on hook. Ch 5, turn.

3rd row: 3 tr in 5th ch from hook, * sl st in next sl st, skip 3 ch, 7 tr in next ch. Repeat from * across, ending with skip 3 ch, 3 tr in next ch, tr in top of turning chain. Drop Dark color, pick up Light and draw through last loop, turn. **4th row:** * (Yarn over, insert hook in next tr and pull loop through; yarn over and draw through 2 loops) 3 times. Yarn over twice, insert hook in sl st and pull loop hrough; (yarn over, draw through 2 loops) twice. (Yarn over, insert hook in next tr and pull loop through; yarn over and draw through 2 loops) 3 times; yarn over, draw through all loops on hook, ch 4, sl st in next tr. Repeat from * across, ending with ch 4, sl st in turning chain. Ch 1, turn. **5th row:** * Skip 3 ch, 7 tr in next ch, sl st in next sl st. Repeat from * across, ending with sl st in turning chain. Drop light color, pick up dark color and draw through last loop, turn. The last 4 rows (2nd to 5th rows incl) constitute the pattern. Work in pattern until piece measures 22½ inches, ending with 1 row of light color. Break off. Attach dark color and work 3 rnds of sc around edge, making 3 sc in each corner to keep work flat.

9150-B . . . Materials: RUG YARN (70-yard skeins), 2 skeins each of light and dark colors . . . Crochet Hook Size G or H.

Make starting chain about 5 inches longer than long edge of footstool. Work as for Rug 9150-A, having 1st row of diamond pattern measure at least 2 inches longer than long edge of footstool. Continue in pattern until piece covers top of stool, plus enough to turn under. Break off.

9137 . . . Materials: RUG YARN (70-yard skeins), 7 skeins of main color, 2 skeins of color A and 1 skein of color B . . . Crochet Hook Size G or H.

GAUGE: 3 star sts make 1⅛ inches; 2 rows (1 star st row and 1 sc row) make ⅞ inch.

Rug measures 24 x 36 inches, including Fringe.

Starting at narrow end, with main color make a chain about 30 inches long (3 ch sts to 1 inch). **1st row:** Sc in 2nd ch from hook, sc in each ch across until row measures 24 inches. Cut off remaining chain. Ch 3, turn. **2nd row:** Insert hook in 2nd ch from hook and pull loop through, insert hook in next ch and pull loop through, insert hook in 1st sc and pull loop through, insert hook in next sc and pull loop through; yarn over and draw through all loops on hook, ch 1 to fasten (a star st made—Fig. 74, page 51). * Insert hook in fastening ch just made and pull loop through, insert hook in last loop of previous star st and pull loop through, insert hook in st where last loop of previous star st was pulled through and pull loop through, insert hook in next sc and pull loop through;

9137

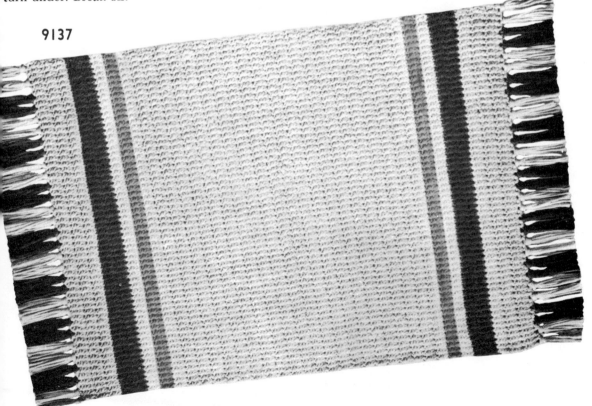

255

yarn over and draw through all loops on hook, ch 1 to fasten (another star st made). Repeat from * across. Ch 1, turn. **3rd row:** Sc in fastening ch of 1st star st and in fastening ch of each star st across; sc in top st of turning chain. Ch 3, turn. The 2nd and 3rd rows constitute the pattern. Repeat these 2 rows 2 more times, omitting the turning chain at end of last row. Break off. Attach color A, ch 3 and work 2 patterns (4 rows) as before. Break off. Now work 1 pattern (2 rows) of main color and 1 pattern of color B, breaking off after each color. This completes border. Attach main color and work 18 more inches in pattern. Then work border to correspond with opposite end. Break off.

FRINGE . . . For each fringe, cut five 9-inch strands. Double these strands to form a loop. Insert hook into a stitch at narrow end of rug and draw loop through. Then draw loose ends of strands through this loop; pull tight. Knot a fringe into every other stitch at both narrow ends, alternating 2 main color fringes with 2 color A fringes. Trim evenly.

9337 . . . Materials: RUG YARN, *odds and ends of different colors . . . Crochet Hook Size G or H.*

Rug measures 24 x 36 inches.

For center 4 rnds and last 2 rnds of rug, use the darkest color (preferably Black). Introduce other colors as desired.

Starting at center with darkest color, make a chain 12 inches long (3 ch sts to 1 inch). **1st rnd:** Sc in 2nd ch from hook and in each ch across to last ch, 3 sc in last ch. Now working along opposite side of starting chain, make sc in each st across to last st, 2 sc in last st. Join with sl st to 1st sc made. **2nd rnd:** Ch 2, yarn over hook, insert hook in same place as sl st and pull loop through, yarn over, insert hook in next sc and pull loop through, yarn over and draw through all loops on hook (an sc-cluster made), * ch 1, yarn over, insert hook in same place as last leg of previous cluster, and pull loop through, yarn over, insert hook in next sc and pull loop through, yarn over and draw through all loops on hook (another sc-cluster made). Repeat from * around, making last leg of last cluster in same place where 1st leg of

9337

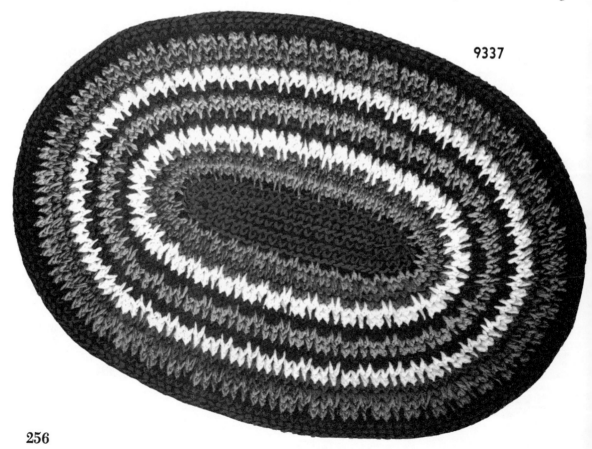

256

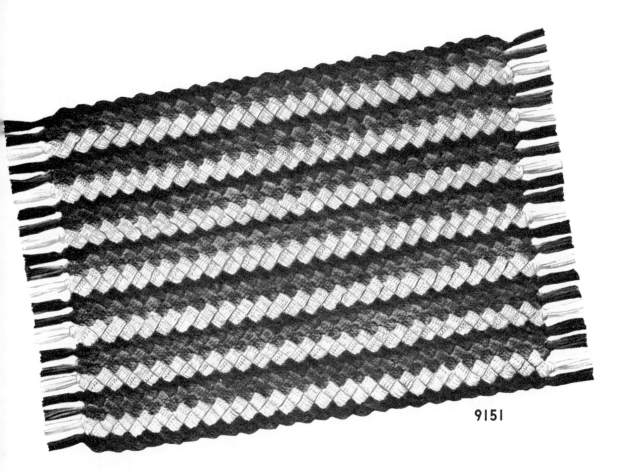

9151

1st cluster was made, ch 1, sl st in tip of 1st cluster made. **3rd and 4th rnds:** Ch 2, yarn over, insert hook in ch-1 sp (between clusters) and pull loop through, yarn over, insert hook in ch-1 sp between next 2 clusters and complete cluster as before; * ch 1, yarn over, insert hook in same place as last leg of previous cluster and pull loop through, yarn over, insert hook in next sp and pull loop through and complete cluster as before. Repeat from * around, making necessary increases at ends of oval to keep work flat—*to inc, make both legs of cluster in same place*—and ending rnd in same way as 2nd rnd. Break off. Hereafter attach new colors as desired. **5th rnd:** Ch 2, and complete 2 clusters as before, * yarn over, insert hook in next sp 2 rnds down (directly below sp where last leg of previous cluster was made), yarn over, insert hook in next sp 2 rnds down and complete cluster as before (this cluster will be referred to as a long cluster). Make 2 more clusters as before. Repeat from * around, making necessary increases at ends of oval to keep work flat. **6th rnd:** Repeat 3rd

rnd. Repeat the 5th and 3rd rnds alternately until rug measures 24 inches x 36 inches, introducing new colors as desired, and ending with 2 rnds of darkest color. Be careful to keep continuity of pattern by making long clusters directly above long clusters. Introduce new long clusters at ends of oval in a manner that will not disturb established pattern.

9151 . . . **Materials:** Rug Yarn (*70-yard skeins*), *3 skeins each of light, medium, and dark colors* . . . Steel Crochet Hook No. 2/0 (*double zero*).

GAUGE: 1 shell makes 1 inch diagonally.

Rug measures 24 x 36 inches, including Fringe.

With Dark, make a 45-inch chain (4 ch sts to 1 inch). Work loosely throughout. **1st row:** In 5th ch from hook make 3 dc, * dc in next ch, skip 3 ch, sc in next ch (a shell made). Ch 3, 3 dc in same place as last sc. Repeat from * until row measures 32 inches, ending with an sc. Cut off remaining chain. Ch 4, turn. **2nd row:** 3 dc in 1st sc, * dc in next st, sc in next ch-3, ch 3, 3 dc in same place as sc.

Repeat from * across, ending with sc in last ch-4 (there should be the same number of shells on each row). Break off.

Attach Light, ch 4, turn and repeat 2nd row twice. Break off. Attach Medium, ch 4, turn and repeat 2nd row twice. Break off. Continue thus, repeating colors in established order until rug measures approximately 24 inches, ending with a Dark stripe. Fasten all ends securely.

FRINGE . . . For each fringe, cut five 9-inch strands of color to correspond with stripe. Double these strands to form a loop. Insert hook into end of stripe and draw loop through. Then draw loose ends of strands through this loop. When all fringe has been made along ends, trim evenly.

9136 . . . Materials: RUG YARN (*70-yard skeins*), *10 skeins each of a light and a dark color . . . Crochet Hook Size G or H.*

GAUGE: 3 V clusters make 1⅝ inches; 2 rows make 1¼ inches.

Rug measures 31 x 54 inches.

Starting at narrow end with Light, make a chain about 40 inches long (3 ch sts to 1 inch).

1st row: Holding Dark along starting chain and working over it in order to conceal it, yarn over, insert hook in 4th ch from hook and pull loop through loosely; yarn over, insert hook in same ch and pull loop through, yarn over, * skip 1 ch, insert hook in next ch and pull loop through; yarn over and draw through all 7 loops on hook, ch 1 (a V cluster made). (Yarn over, insert hook where last loop was pulled through and pull loop through loosely) twice; yarn over and repeat from * once more, skip next ch, insert hook in next ch and pull loop through, yarn over and draw through all loops on hook. Drop Light, pick up Dark and draw loop through to replace fastening ch-1 (a group of 3 V clusters completed).

Now make a group of 3 V clusters of Dark and a group of 3 V clusters of Light alternately across (always working over unused color to conceal it), until there are 19 groups in all—**always pick up new color to form last ch-1 of group as before.** Row should measure 31 inches. Cut off remaining chain. Ch 3, turn. **2nd row:** Yarn over, insert hook in 4th ch from hook (fastening ch of 1st V cluster st) and pull loop through loosely, yarn over, insert hook in same ch and pull loop through, yarn over, insert hook in next ch-1 and pull loop through, yarn over and draw through all 7 loops on hook, ch 1. (Yarn over, insert hook in

9136

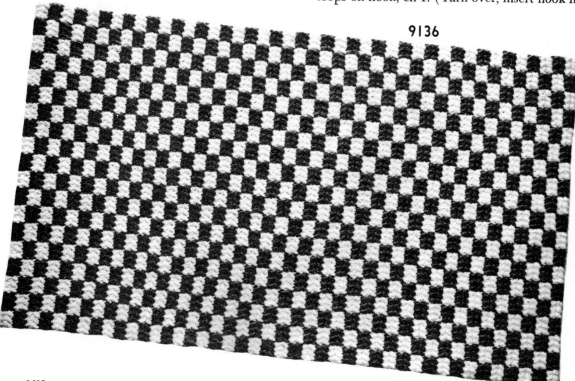

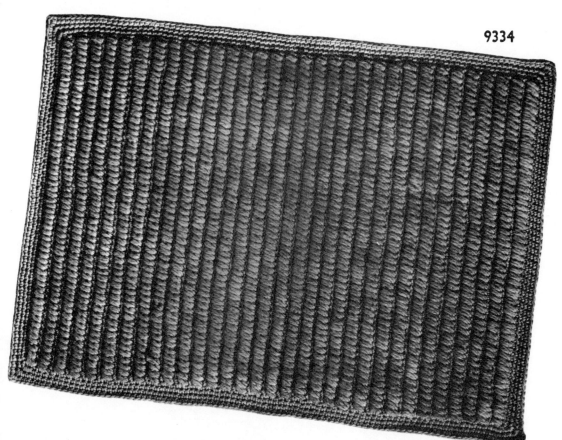

same ch-1 where last loop was pulled through and pull loop through) twice. Yarn over, insert hook in next ch-1 and pull loop through, yarn over and draw through all loops on hook, ch 1. Continue thus across, having colors correspond with previous row and pulling up last loop of last V cluster in top of turning chain. These 2 rows complete 1 row of blocks. Make turning ch-3 with carried color and work 2 more rows in pattern stitch, reversing colors to form checkerboard design. Continue to alternate colors to form checkerboard design as before until 43 rows of blocks in all are made. Break off.

9334 . . . Materials: RUG YARN *(70-yard skeins), 10 skeins . . . Crochet Hook Size G or H.*

GAUGE: 3 group sts make 1 inch; 1 group-st row and 1 sc-row make 1 inch.

Rug measures 20 x 32 inches.

Starting at narrow end, make a chain about 25 inches long. **1st row:** Sc in 2nd ch from hook and in each ch across, until row measures 18 inches. Cut off remaining chain. Ch 3, turn. **2nd row:** (Yarn over, insert hook in 1st sc and pull loop out to height of turning chain) twice; yarn over, insert hook in next sc and pull loop out as before, yarn over and draw through all loops on hook (a group st made); * (yarn over, insert hook in same place where last loop was pulled through and pull loop through) twice; yarn over, insert hook in next sc and pull loop through as before, yarn over and draw through all loops on hook (another group st made). Repeat from * across. Ch 2, turn. **3rd row:** Sc in each group st across, sc in top st of turning chain. Ch 3, turn. Repeat the 2nd and 3rd rows alternately until piece measures 30 inches, ending with the 3rd row. Do not break off, but work sc along long side of rug. Join to end of 1st row. Break off. Attach yarn to opposite end of 1st row and work sc evenly along the other long edge of rug. Join to end of last row. Do not break off, but work 4 rnds of sc all around, joining each rnd and making 3 sc at each corner. Break off.

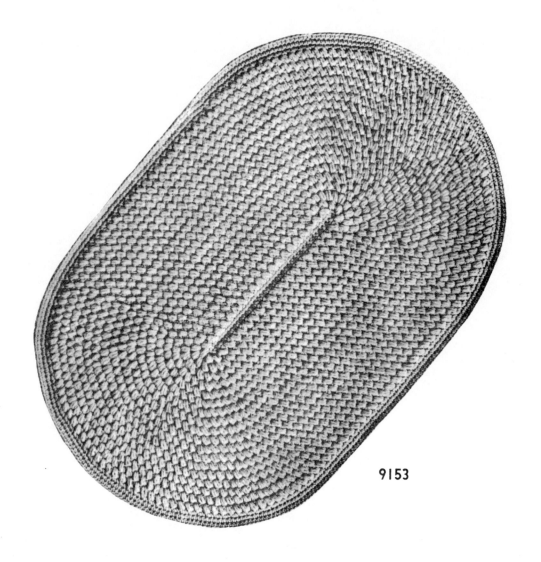

9153

9153 . . . Materials: RUG YARN *(70-yard skeins), 9 skeins . . . Crochet Hook Size G or H.*

Rug measures 24 x 36 inches.

Starting at center, make a 13-inch chain (about 3 ch sts to 1 inch). **1st rnd:** Sc in 2nd ch from hook, sc in each ch across, making 3 sc in last ch. Sc along other side of starting chain, making 2 sc in same ch as 1st sc made. Sl st in 1st sc. **2nd rnd:** Ch 1, (yarn over hook, insert hook in same place as sl st and pull loop through) twice; yarn over, skip 1 sc, insert hook in next sc and pull loop through, yarn over and draw through all loops on hook, ch 1

tightly (a pattern st made). * (Yarn over, insert hook in same sc where last loop was pulled through and pull loop through) twice, yarn over, skip 1 sc, insert hook in next sc and pull loop through; yarn over and draw through all loops on hook, ch 1 tightly (another pattern st made). Repeat from * to other end. Make pattern sts as before, but do not skip any sc's in middle of pattern sts, thus increasing to keep work flat. Continue in pattern to opposite end, increasing to correspond. Do not join at end of rnd. **3rd rnd:** Yarn over, insert hook in ch-1 preceding first pattern st made, pull loop through, yarn over, insert hook in same place and pull loop through, yarn over, insert hook in top of pattern st (not in the sp) and pull loop through. Yarn over and draw through all loops; ch 1 tightly. (Yarn over, insert hook in top of same pattern st and pull loop through) twice; yarn over, insert hook in st directly above sp and draw loop through, yarn over and draw through all loops, ch 1 tightly. (Note: By working into the top of the pattern st and into the st above sp, you have been increasing at the curve.) Make another pattern st, working into the same st above sp twice, and into top of next pattern st once. Now work in pattern across to curve, skipping all sts directly above sps. Increase at curve as before; then continue around in pattern, working over opposite curve to correspond.

Now continue in rnds, increasing at both curved ends to keep work flat, until piece measures approximately 22 x 34 inches. Next rnd: Work 2 sc at top of each pattern st, increasing if necessary to keep work flat—to inc, make 2 sc in each st. Work 2 more rnds of sc, increasing if necessary to keep work flat; then sl st in next 2 sts and break off.

CHAPTER NINETEEN

General Information

FINISHING

Finishing is just as important as any other part of your work. Expert needleworkers pride themselves that the reverse side of each article looks as neat as the front. When you break off the thread or yarn, leave a piece from 4 to 8 inches long beyond the last loop. Thread a needle with this length and darn through the solid part of the crochet until securely fastened. Cut off the remainder close to work. Starting threads should be sufficiently long to finish in the same manner. When sewing pieces together, instead of knotting the thread, catch in the loose end with several small over-and-over-stitches, or darn the thread through the solid portion for a small distance.

HOW TO LAUNDER LACES

Make a lather of soapy suds and hot water, taking care to have all soap particles well dissolved before immersing the lace. Squeeze the lace gently, forcing the suds in and out, until it is thoroughly cleansed. Rinse in lukewarm water several times until all traces of soap have been removed. Rinse once in cold water and roll up in a bath towel to absorb excess moisture.

HOW TO BLOCK LACES

Before blocking, launder lace, if necessary, and starch. Pin the damp article face down with rust-proof pins to a padded ironing board, gently stretching and shaping it to the measurements specified in the directions. Pins should be spaced about ½ inch apart. Press through a cloth. If the lace does not require laundering or starching, pin it dry in the same way and use a damp cloth for pressing. Raised patterns should be placed face down over heavy toweling.

HOW TO LAUNDER WOOLENS

Launder with fine-fabric cold-water detergent according to directions on the container.

HOW TO LAUNDER SYNTHETICS (such as WINTUK, SAYELLE)

Follow instructions on wrapper of skein.

HOW TO BLOCK WOOLENS AND SYNTHETICS

See Blocking Directions on page 19.

HOW TO PAD POT HOLDERS

If pot holder consists of two pieces, one for each side, cut flannel, muslin, or any soft material slightly smaller than crocheted pieces. Tack to wrong side of one piece. Complete according to directions. If pot holder consists of only one piece, cut a lining, allowing ½ inch all around for seams, turn back seam allowance, and sew neatly in place on wrong side.

HOW TO JOIN HEXAGON MOTIFS

Place motifs together exactly as in diagram. Each set of directions specifies the exact number of motifs on each row.

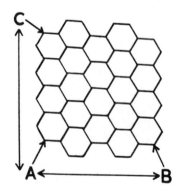

Index

Unless otherwise stated, entries refer to directions for crocheting the articles named; e.g., "afghans, 234–248" means that directions for crocheting afghans appear on pages 234 through 248.